Jesus Ou

Teacher's Manual

Jesus Our Life

Teacher's Manual

Faith and Life Series
Revised Edition
BOOK TWO

Ignatius Press, San Francisco
Catholics United for the Faith, Steubenville

Director of First Edition: The late Rev. Msgr. Eugene Kevane, Ph.D.
Assistant Director and General Editor of First Edition: Patricia I. Puccetti, M.A.
First Edition Writer: Sister Theresa Wynne, I.H.M.

Revision Writer: Colette Ellis, M.A.
Director and General Editor of Revision: Christopher A. Bess

Catholics United for the Faith, Inc. and Ignatius Press gratefully acknowledge the guidance and assistance of the late Reverend Monsignor Eugene Kevane, former Director of the Pontifical Catechetical Institute, Diocese of Arlington, Virginia, in the production of the First Edition of this series. The First Edition intended to implement the authentic approach in Catholic catechesis given to the Church through documents of the Holy See and in particular the conference of Joseph Cardinal Ratzinger on "Sources and Transmission of Faith." The Revised Edition continues this commitment by drawing upon the *Catechism of the Catholic Church* (Libreria Editrice Vaticana, 1994, 1997).

ISBN 0-89870-978-4
Printed in Hong Kong

Contents

Introduction to the *Faith and Life* Revised Edition

The *Faith and Life* series, which includes a student text, Teacher's Manual, and *Activity Book* for grades 1-8, has been used in schools and parishes across the country since its original publication in 1987. This revision of the original series continues our commitment to the faithful transmission of the teachings of the Roman Catholic Church by emphasizing the importance of Scripture and the *Catechism of the Catholic Church*.

The Student Textbook:

The *Faith and Life* student texts have undergone minimal revision. The beautiful and inspiring religious artwork has been maintained, for faith has inspired art for centuries, and religious art has, in turn, inspired our faith. Art is a valuable educational tool, especially in the teaching of religious truths to children, for it offers a visual image in addition to the oral and written word. Art can also be a source of meditation for students and teachers as they investigate the paintings, discuss the religious imagery, and come to understand the beautiful symbols and the artistic expressions they communicate.

In the primary grades, the *Faith and Life* student texts are written at an advanced reading level. In these early years a child's oral comprehension far surpasses his reading ability (e.g., children can understand a religious video though they would have a difficult time reading the script). Doctrine is presented in a way that both challenges the student's intellect and avoids the boredom that is often fatal in catechetical efforts.

New vocabulary in all the grades is now indicated by bold type. New words have been added to enhance each lesson in the revised text, and each definition can now be found both within the chapter and in the glossary.

The questions provided for memorization in each chapter have been expanded and carefully revised for age-appropriateness; the relevant reference to the *Catechism of the Catholic Church* is indicated next to every question. Each chapter in the revised text opens with an appropriate Scripture passage, with relevant Bible verses quoted throughout. These changes demonstrate Biblical backing for the faith as well as the significance of the new *Catechism* to the Church as a fruit of Vatican II. Additional common Catholic prayers have been inserted in the revised text, with an expansive list of prayers at the back of the student textbook.

The Teacher's Manual

The *Faith and Life* Teacher's Manuals are the most heavily updated and expanded aspects of this extensive revision process. Useful information previously provided in the supplemental Resource Binders of the original series has been fully incorporated into the new Teacher's Manuals, thus eliminating the need for individual binders.

Each chapter of the Teacher's Manuals begins with a list of important references to the *Catechism of the Catholic Church*, and Scripture passages that support the chapter's lessons. This is followed by a clear and succinct summary of the doctrine discussed in the preceeding four lessons; this summary may be used as a guide for once-a-week catechism or CCD classes.

The revised Teacher's Manual provides a full week of detailed lesson plans for each chapter, including four days of teaching and one day of review and assessment. Each color-coded lesson clearly indicates the teaching aims and materials necessary for that day. Optional craft materials, songs, appendix pages, and additional video and book resources are also included. The lesson plans themselves are designed to be guides in teaching even the most complex truths of the faith with age-appropriate examples.

Comprehensive chapter quizzes and optional unit tests can be found in Appendix A. In the primary grades, these quizzes may be completed together in class; an asterisk beside a question indicates that the topic is not in the student text but is included in the lesson plans. Appendix B contains additional activities such as stories, games, crafts, and skits.

One entirely new addition to the revision is the "Catholic Culture and Tradition" box found on the second page of each lesson. These boxes include supplemental materials for the teacher, lives of the saints, explanations of terms, descriptions of Church traditions and rituals, relevant citations, suggestions for activities, additional resources, and prayers.

To assist Parish and CCD Programs, "once-a-week lesson plans" can be formulated by using the summary boxes for doctrinal content from the chapter introductory page, then using the italicized sections throughout the four lessons. A recommended format would be: read the entire chapter, use a lesson plan consisting of the italicized sections which cover the material and doctrines necessary with sufficient development, then spend time reinforcing with memorization of questions, vocabulary and prayers. The quizzes can then be sent home for family reinforcement and review. The unit quizzes can still be administered in class once a month to assist the teacher with monitoring the students' progress.

The Activity Book:

The *Faith and Life* Activity Books have been significantly expanded to include one activity for each lesson, that is, four activities per chapter. The goal was to offer the teacher a wide variety of reinforcement tools in a separate text, without losing the interest of the students. In the primary grades the activities focus upon drawing, coloring, and simple puzzles and exercises, while in the later years reading comprehension and memorization are emphasized.

The *Faith and Life* series, revised edition, aspires to aid teachers and parents (the primary educators) in transmitting the truths, doctrines, wealth of traditions, and richness of culture found in the Roman Catholic Church.

For Teachers and Catechists

Text and Grade Level

The second grade text, *Jesus Our Life*, is a simple introduction to Bible stories and teachings of the faith. The second grader has an active imagination and is more easily convinced by his emotions rather than by his reason. The teacher should, therefore, make use of creative presentations reinforced through repetition, such as those included in this Manual, in addition to the catechist's personal good example.

Catechesis: Nature and Purpose

Catechesis is the systematic instruction of children, young people, and adults in the faith of the Church through the teachings of Christian doctrine with the goal of making them into Christ's disciples (cf. CCC 5). It is the handing-on of Christ's message to His people. The *General Catechetical Directory* describes catechesis as a form of ministry of God's Word, "which is intended to make men's faith living, conscious, and active, through the light of instruction" (GCD 17; 1971).

The Catechist: God's Instrument

To be a catechist is to be God's instrument. Every catechist has a responsibility to teach the fullness of the truth faithfully, while witnessing to those entrusted to his care. A fervent sacramental life and regular prayer life are the catechist's best personal preparation. Any instructor can use textbooks and teaching tools, learn various methods for effective classroom participation, and develop lesson plans to facilitate an academic environment. But nothing is as important as witnessing through your words and deeds and petitioning God for the on-going formation and spiritual growth of the students. No matter how much knowledge you impart to your students, you should recognize that you merely plant the seeds of faith that God Himself must cultivate in their souls.

John Paul II states in *Catechesi Tradendae*: "at the heart of catechesis we find . . . the Person of Jesus of Nazareth . . . in catechesis it is Christ . . . who is taught . . . and it is Christ alone who teaches . . ." (CT 5,6). Religious education must always be centered on the Triune God, and on Christ Himself. God chose to reveal Himself throughout salvation history, through His creation, the prophets, the Scriptures, and most perfectly in the Person of Jesus Christ. This revelation, preserved faithfully through sacred Scripture and Tradition, has been entrusted to the Church that every catechist is called to serve.

Catechesis in today's ministry is often coupled with evangelization—a first hearing of the Good News of Salvation. Through catechesis, you should guide your students to seek, accept, and profoundly investigate the Gospel so that they in turn may become witnesses to Christ. The new *Catechism of the Catholic Church*, together with sacred Scripture, provides catechists with the tools necessary to achieve this.

The Role of Parents: The First Catechists

The family provides the first and most important introduction to Christian faith and practice for any child, since parents are the primary educators of their children. Instruction in the faith, which begins at an early age, should include not only the parent's good Christian example, but also a formation in prayer and an explanation and review of what students have learned from religious instruction and attending liturgical events.

Parental cooperation is very important to a teacher's success as a catechist. You should try to involve parents in their children's instruction. Discuss with them the program and methods you are using, consult them about better ways to teach their children, and ask for assistance if problems arise. Let parents know that you are there to help them fulfill their duties in forming and educating their children in Christ (cf. GCD 78, 79).

Methodologies

The *General Catechetical Directory* provides an overview of various successful methodologies you may find useful. Knowledge can be transmitted through prayer and liturgy, through words and deeds, or through texts and activities, but the students learn it primarily from you, the catechist.

Induction and Deduction: Inductive methods serve well in the presentation of facts and in considering and examining those facts in order to recognize their Christian meaning. Induction is the process of reasoning from a part to a whole, from particular to general principles. It is not independent of deductive methods, which reason from the general to the particular and include interpretation and determining cause and effect. These two methods, taken together, aid in the students' understanding of the unity of the faith, the inter-relation of topics, and, most importantly, their practical applications.

Formulas: Expressing throughts or ideas succinctly and accurately in a memorable form allows for ease of memorization and better understanding of a topic. In the early stages of education, memorization should be utilized more frequently since children first need language to communicate meaning. In theology, semantics are very important, for Christians have died for their faith and schisms have occured because of word use (e.g., the *Filioque* in the Nicene Creed still distinguishes Roman Catholics from the Eastern Orthodox). Such formulas also provide a uniform method of speaking among the faithful.

Experience: Personal experience is reflective and practical, and it transforms abstract theories into applicable and memorable concepts. Catechists should use concrete examples in class and encourage their students to judge personal experience with Christian values.

Creativity: Creative activities enable students to meditate upon and express, in their own words, the messages they have learned.

Groups: In catechesis the importance of group instruction is becoming more apparent. Groups aid the social and ecclesial formation of students, and they foster a sense of Christian co-responsibility and solidarity.

The Catechism of the Catholic Church: An Important Tool

Today's classrooms are filled with children who have various needs and backgrounds. Complicated by an atmosphere of religious indifference, religious hostility, and an apparent absence of Catholic culture, knowledge, and meaningful practice, your catechetical work becomes especially valuable. One important tool that belongs to all the faithful is the *Catechism of the Catholic Church*, which is divided into four sections: the Creed, Sacraments, Moral Life, and Prayer.

The Creed: The Creed is a summary of the faith and the Church's baptismal promises. As a public profession of faith, Catholics find in it their identity as members of Christ's Mystical Body. This is the faith handed down from Christ to the Apostles and to the entire Church.

Sacraments: The seven sacraments are outward signs instituted by Christ to confer grace. Active participation in the sacramental life of the Church, such as attending Mass prayerfully and faithfully, should be encouraged from a young age.

The Moral Life: The moral life does not limit; instead it provides the boundries that define the Catholic indentity and allow for proper love of God and neighbor. A right moral life is man's gift to God, a response to His unconditional love, and a pathway to true freedom. Every Catholic should be an example to others.

Prayer: Prayer unites a person with God (through words, actions, silence, and presence), and should be encouraged and put into practice from early childhood. There are many forms of prayer, but each brings the soul closer to God.

The *Faith and Life* Teacher's Manual provides much of what you will need to be an effective catechist, but it will only be as fruitful as you make it when you teach and minister the Word of God to your students. Take your responsibilities as a catechist very seriously. Call upon Christ frequently, as His witness and disciple, to help you spread His message. Persevere and draw near to God, bringing your students with you.

Additional material, resources, crafts, and information may be found on the Catechetical Resource website: www.CatecheticalResources.com and at www.Domestic-Church.com

CHAPTER ONE
OUR HEAVENLY FATHER

Catechism of the Catholic Church References

Attributes of God Shown in and through Creation: 268–78, 293, 315, 341
Dignity of Man: 1700–1712
Equality and Differences among Men: 1934–38, 1944–46
God Adopts Us as His Children: 2782–85
God as Creator of Heaven and Earth: 279–81, 295–300, 325–27
God Creates out of Wisdom and Love: 295, 315
God Inspires Scripture: 105–6
God is Love: 218–21, 231
God Transcends Creation: 300–301, 320
God's Omnipotence: 268–78
Heaven: 1023–29, 1053
Holiness of God: 2809
Man as Body and Soul: 362–68, 382
New Testament: 124–27, 139, 515
Old Testament: 121–23
Providence: 302–14
Scripture in the Life of the Church: 131–33, 141
Speaking about God: 39–43, 48
Ways of Knowing God: 31–38, 46–48, 286

Scripture References

Creation of Man: Gen 2:7–25; Ps 36:7; Mt 6:9–13

Background Reading: *The Fundamentals of Catholicism* by Fr. Kenneth Baker, S.J.

Volume 2:
"God Created the Heavens and the Earth," pp. 121–24
"Why Did God Create the World?" pp. 124–27

Summary of Lesson Content

Lesson 1

God is our Father in Heaven.

God is all good and holy.

God loves each person.

God created each person and gave each one unique qualities.

Lesson 2

Each person has a soul, which gives him life.

The human soul is rational.

People can freely choose to do good or bad.

The soul lives forever and it has eternal life.

Lesson 3

God is in Heaven and He is everywhere.

God watches over mankind; this is His providence.

God is all knowing.

God is the Father; people are His Children.

Lesson 4

The Bible reveals much about God to us that we could not otherwise know.

God is the author of the Bible. He inspired the writers.

The Bible has two parts: the Old Testament and the New Testament. They reveal salvation history.

At Mass we hear readings from the Bible.

LESSON ONE: GOD, OUR HEAVENLY FATHER

Aims

The students will learn that God is their Father, Who loves them very much.

They will learn that God is in Heaven, that He is all good and holy, and that He created each of them with many gifts.

Materials

- Pictures of God the Father (see student text p. 6)
- Pictures of children with their fathers
- *Activity Book*, p. 1

Optional:
- A mirror
- "Holy God, we praise thy name!" *Adoremus Hymnal*, #461

Begin

Have a picture (or many pictures) of God the Father on display and begin the class by asking the children: Who is in the picture? Look at various artists' depictions, and point out what is common among them. Though God has no body, He is represented as powerful, usually old, radiant, in Heaven, or on a throne. Sometimes God is depicted with people or creating the world. From these pictures, ask the children to tell you what they already know about God the Father. He is the Creator of Heaven and earth. He is our Father, and loves us all.

Develop

1. Have a discussion with the students about the role of fathers and children. You may foster this discussion with pictures: fathers working with, playing with, or watching over their children. Ask the children what their fathers do for them, and how they are examples of God's love. Help them understand that God, their Father, loves and cares for them.

2. Read aloud paragraphs 1 and 2 of the text with the children. Ask the class, "Who made you?" They should answer that God made them. Ask the children what it means for God to be their Father. Their answers will vary. They should understand that they are children of God, Who is in Heaven, and that fathers love their children very much.

3. Ask the children how they know their own fathers. They spend time together and talk. They do things together. Ask the children how they can know God their Father better. They can pray to Him, listen to Him, learn about Him through religion class, learn about Him at Mass. They can spend time with Him in prayer, and do works of charity.

4. Ask the children how they resemble their earthly fathers. They may have the same eye color or smile, the same sense of humor or same likes/dislikes. Help the children to see that they are all different, but have similarities with their fathers. If appropriate for the class, pass a mirror around, and ask each student to choose something in himself that resembles his father, or makes him unique (e.g., his nose is different).

5. Explain that just as they resemble their earthly fathers, they are all different, and their differences are a gift from God. They, too, have something the same as their Heavenly Father. They will learn about this in the next lesson.

Name:__________________

"How precious is thy steadfast love, O God!" Psalm 36:7

I am a child of God!

Draw a picture of yourself and God the Father.

Faith and Life Series • Grade 2 • Chapter 1 • Lesson 1 1

Reinforce

1. Ask the students to name the ways God shows them that He loves them.

2. Have them complete *Activity Book*, p. 1. They are to draw a picture of themselves with God. They may want to include in the picture God showing them His love for them. (e.g., God giving the child a special gift.)

3. Have them begin to memorize Questions 1 and 2, p. 8 of the text.

Conclude

1. Lead the children in thanking God for the many gifts He gives them and for being His children. Then lead them in praying the Our Father.

Note: If they have not yet memorized this prayer, prepare flash cards for them to take home. They may work on this in spare class time too. They should have this prayer memorized by the end of the week.

2. Teach and sing the song: "Holy God, we praise thy name!" *Adoremus Hymnal,* #461.

Preview

We will learn about the soul and that our souls live forever.

A NOTE ABOUT FATHERS

Jesus teaches us to call God "Father" with the prayer the Our Father: Mt 6:9–13.

It is important to be sensitive to the specific needs of the children when teaching about fathers; some children may not have a father at home, or may not have strong relationships with their fathers. You may ask them what fathers should do, or what they think a fictional father (or father on television) should do, as opposed to what their fathers do. Be prepared for whatever answers they give, and remind the children that their heavenly Father is perfect.

NOTES

LESSON TWO: OUR RATIONAL SOUL LIVES FOREVER

Aims

The students will discover that God gave each of them a special gift called a soul, the invisible part of them that lives forever.

They will learn that their souls give them life and allow them to think and to choose freely to do good or bad.

Materials

- Balloons
- Staircase of Creation (Appendix, p. B-2)
- *Activity Book*, p. 2
- Children's Bible

Optional:

- "Holy God, we Praise thy name!" *Adoremus Hymnal*, #461

Begin

Read from the children's Bible the creation of man (Gen 2:7–25). Explain to the children that man and woman were both created by God. Make special note that God breathed the breath of life into man's nostrils. It is the soul that gives us life. It cannot be seen, and it will live forever (like God)! Everyone has a soul. Explain to the children that today they will learn more about their souls.

1 Our Heavenly Father

How precious is thy steadfast love, O God!
The children of men take refuge in the shadow of thy wings.

Psalm 36:7

Do you know Who God is? He is our Father in **Heaven**. He is great and holy. He loves you more than anyone else loves you.

God always wanted there to be someone just like you. So He made you. He gave you your hands and feet, your eyes and ears. God made you different from everyone else, because you are very special to Him.

God has also given you a **soul**. You cannot see your soul, but your soul is what gives you life. If you did not have a soul, you could not think. You could not laugh. You could not talk. Your soul is what makes you do these things. Your soul gives you the power to do what is right and good. The soul is the part of you that never dies. It lives forever.

God our Father does not live only in Heaven. He is everywhere. He always sees you and watches over

7

Develop

1. Pass out balloons to the children and have the students inflate them. Explain that the air that fills the balloons is invisible, but very real. Without the air, the balloons are not the same. It is the air that makes the balloons so much better.

2. Explain that as the balloons are made big by invisible air, our bodies have souls that cannot be seen, but are very real. The soul gives the body life. Without the soul, the body is dead. This is what happens when someone dies, the soul leaves the body.

3. The human soul is very special. It is like God because it is rational. This means that we can think and we can choose to do good instead of bad. The soul is what makes us able to laugh or cry. Without the soul we could not do all the fun things with our bodies like run and play, jump and skip. Our soul is needed for our bodies to do what they do. Read paragraph 3 in the textbook together. Can the students think of other things that our souls do?

4. Our soul allows us to love. It allows us to choose to love God, other people, and all of God's creation. We are all made to be in relationships—that is why we are born into families and baptized into God's family—so we can love, just as God loves us.

5. The soul will never die. It will live forever. If we are good and stay close to God, when we die, our soul will go to Heaven to be with God forever! This is the greatest gift He could give us. Heaven is a wonderful place—the most wonderful place.

Name:____________________

Look up these words in the back of your book and write their meanings.

Heaven: The place of reward for those who were good and asked God to forgive their sins. In Heaven we see God and are happy with Him forever

Soul: The part of us that thinks, loves, and wishes good or evil. The soul lives forever.

Can you answer these questions?

1. Who made you?
God

2. Who is God?
Our Father in Heaven

3. Where is God?
God is not only in Heaven. He is everywhere

4. Does God know everything?
Yes

2 *Faith and Life Series • Grade 2 • Chapter 1 • Lesson 2*

Reinforce

1. Have the students list the ways that their souls are different from animals, plants, and angels. They may draw a picture depicting these differences.

2. Ask them to explain their pictures to one another.

3. Discuss ways they can take care of their souls (e.g., prayer, sacraments, rest, worship, good friendships, avoiding sin).

4. Assign *Activity Book*, p. 2.

5. Have them work on memorizing Questions 1 and 2, p. 8 of their text.

Conclude

1. Sing with the children: "Holy God, we praise thy name!" *Adoremus Hymnal*, #461.

2. Lead them in praying the Our Father. You may have them say it individually to see how well their memorization is coming along.

Preview

In the next lesson, we will learn about God's attributes.

QUESTIONS ABOUT DEATH

When discussing the soul, children may ask questions about death. Explain that, at death, the body dies and the soul lives forever. If we live good lives that are pleasing to God, we will be with Him forever in Heaven. You may want to add that at the end of time, our bodies will rejoin our souls, and they will be glorious. In Heaven, we will be happy forever with God, the angels, and the saints.

NOTES

LESSON THREE: GOD'S ATTRIBUTES

Aims

The students will learn that God is in Heaven, and everywhere.

They will discover that God is all knowing and that He watches over mankind.

They will see that God is the Father and people are His children.

Materials

- A picture of God in Heaven
- Pictures of various places where God is (nature, among the poor, in churches)
- *Activity Book*, p. 3

Optional:
- "Holy God, we praise thy name!" *Adoremus Hymnal*, #461

Begin

Have a picture of God the Father in Heaven (preferably one used in Lesson 1. You may use the one on p. 6 of the textbook.) Begin the class discussing the picture, asking the children, "Where is God in this picture?" God is in Heaven. How do they know it is Heaven? Ask the children if God is only in Heaven. Where is God?

you. He always knows what you are doing and what you are thinking about. If you are ever alone or afraid, you should remember that God is with you and that He is your friend.

God wants you to be His child and to live someday with Him in Heaven.

Q. 1 *Who made you?*
God made me (CCC 355, 371–73).

Q. 2 *Who is God?*
God is the all-perfect Being, Creator of Heaven and earth (CCC 41, 290–91).

Q. 3 *Where is God?*
God is in Heaven, in the Church, on earth and everywhere (CCC 294, 303, 326, 773).

Q. 4 *Does God know everything?*
Yes, God knows everything, even our thoughts (CCC 299, 303–5).

8

Develop

1. Read paragraphs 4 and 5 from the textbook together as a class. Student volunteers may read them aloud.

2. Gather the children and lay on the floor many pictures of where they may find God. Ask them each to pick a picture and then take turns explaining how they see God in this picture.

3. Ask the children if God is anywhere else. They may have numerous suggestions.

4. Ask the children if they are ever alone. No. God is always with them. Ask them how many persons are in the room now. Did they count God too? Reinforce that God is always present.

5. Play a memory game: "God is everywhere, He is ______," and have each child repeat all the places where God is and then add his own idea.

6. *What else did we learn about God from the readings? You may need to reread paragraphs 4 and 5 from the text:*

- *God watches over us. This is called His providence. This means He lovingly cares for each and every one of us.*
- *God knows what you are doing and what you are thinking. He is all good. God is all that is great and pleasing.*
- *Earlier in the chapter we learned that God is holy.*
- *God is our friend. Friends are faithful, love us for who we are, and want for us what is good.*
- *God is our Father. This means He created us and loves us as His children.*

Name:________________

God Is Everywhere

List some places where God is.

1. Answers will vary
2. ________________
3. ________________

Draw a picture of one of these places.

Faith and Life Series • Grade 2 • Chapter 1 • Lesson 3 3

Reinforce

1. Have the students complete *Activity Book*, p. 3. They may show each other their pictures and explain them.

2. Have them begin memorizing Questions 3 and 4, p. 8 of their text.

Conclude

1. As a class, sing "Holy God, we praise thy name!" *Adoremus Hymnal*, #461.

2. Together, pray the Our Father.

Preview

In the next lesson, we will learn about the Bible, God's way of teaching us about Him.

SAINT THÉRÈSE OF LISIEUX

Also known as the "Little Flower," Saint Thérèse was born in France in 1873. She became a Carmelite nun at age fifteen with special permission from the Pope. She died of tuberculosis in 1897 and was canonized in 1925. She is the patron saint of missions. Her feast day is October 1.

SAINT THÉRÈSE OF LISIEUX

As a very young girl, Saint Thérèse understood the beauty of Heaven and the joy of being with God forever. She loved her parents and God so much that she wanted her Mom and Dad to be happy with Him forever. She knew that they could only be happy with God if they died. Because of this, she was not afraid for her parents to die.

NOTES

LESSON FOUR: THE BIBLE, GOD'S WORD

Aims

The students will learn that the Bible is God's word, telling us much about God, which we could not otherwise know.

They will know that the Bible has two parts: the Old Testament and the New Testament.

Materials

- A map of your local area
- Bible (the biggest one you have)
- Missalettes
- *Activity Book*, p. 4

Optional:

- "Holy God, we praise thy name!" *Adoremus Hymnal*, #461

Begin

Open a street map on the floor and gather the children for a close look. Point out their current location. Ask the children to help you find your way (on the map) to a different location. You may need to help the children read the map. Explain to them that the map was drawn to help people to know how to get where they want to go. God gave us a map to Heaven: it is the Bible. If we read it, we will know how to get to Heaven.

Note: Find in your Bible the Sunday Mass readings.

One of God's great gifts to us is the **Bible**. The Bible is a big book. It tells us many things about God that we could not find out in any other way. God did not write the Bible. But He told the men who wrote it what to say. That is why we call the Bible the Word of God.

The Bible has two parts. The Old Testament tells how God made Heaven and Earth. It tells the story of the first sin. It tells us what people did for many years as they waited for the Savior.

The New Testament tells the story of Jesus: His birth, His life and teachings, and how He saved us from sin. It tells how the Church began.

At Mass on Sunday we hear three readings from the Bible.

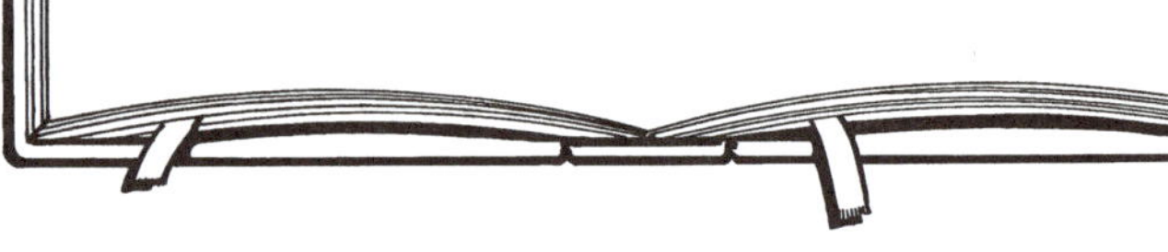

Words to Know:

Heaven soul Bible

9

Develop

1. As a class, read p. 9 of the textbook.

2. Show the students your Bible. Open the Bible and let the children see the maps, pictures, and the writing.

3. Show them the two parts of the Bible: the Old Testament and the New Testament. Have them notice how big the Old Testament is in comparison to the New Testament. Ask them to find in their text what is in the Old Testament and what is in the New Testament.

4. Ask the children why we have the Bible. God wanted us to know about Him and how we can be with Him forever in Heaven. The Bible is God's word. He is the author and told men what to write. They wrote only what God wanted, no more and no less.

5. Ask a child to read the last paragraph from the text: "At Mass on Sunday, we hear three readings from the Bible." Hand out missalettes to the children and have them find the Sunday readings in the missalettes.

6. Using your Bible, point out to the children the Sunday readings. Show the students that the first reading is from the Old Testament (or depending on the time of year, from the New Testament), the Psalm is from the Book of Psalms, the second reading is from the New Testament. Then, the Gospel is taken from the New Testament. The first four books of the New Testament are called the Gospels. The books of the Gospels are called: Matthew, Mark, Luke, and John. (You may want to write important words on the board as you explain all of this to the children.)

7. Remind the children that because the Bible is the word of God, it is the best book—it tells us what God wants us to know!

We Pray:

"I give thee thanks, O LORD,
with my whole heart."

Psalm 138

"I will not forget you. Behold, I have graven you on the palms of my hands."

Isaiah 49:15–16

10

Reinforce

1. Have the students answer questions about the Bible on *Activity Book*, p. 4.

2. Be sure they have memorized Questions 1–4, p. 8 of their text.

3. If time permits, quiz them individually on the Memorization Questions.

Conclude

1. As a class, sing "Holy God, we praise thy name!" *Adoremus Hymnal*, #461.

2. Read the Bible verse, p. 10 of the text, as a closing prayer and lead them in saying the Our Father.

Preview

In the next lesson, we will review the material covered in this chapter.

SAINT THÉRÈSE AND THE LITTLE WAY

Saint Thérèse of Lisieux is a good example of someone who was very aware of the difficult journey to Heaven. Her spiritual path, called the "Little Way," has become popular in modern times. Thérèse wanted to be a saint, but she felt that she could not become a great one, so she comforted herself by making small daily sacrifices. This was what she called her "little way to Heaven," short and direct. By remaining child-like she asked Jesus to carry her in His arms to the Father. She felt she was too little to attain Heaven like the saints before her, so she found her own pathway. See p. 7 of the Teacher's Manual for a short biography.

NOTES

CHAPTER ONE:
REVIEW AND ASSESSMENT

Aims

The students' understanding of the material covered this week will be reviewed and assessed.

Materials

- Quiz 1 (Appendix, p. A-1)
- "Holy God, we praise thy name!" *Adoremus Hymnal*, #461

Review

1. Review with the students that God is their Father in Heaven, Who loves them very much.

2. Ask the children what gifts God gave them in creating them. Be sure they know about the special gift of their souls.

3. The children should understand that their souls are what give them life and that the soul lives forever. God wants the students to go to Heaven to be happy with God forever. (The students should also understand that, while God is in Heaven, He is everywhere else, too.)

4. The children should know that God gave man the Bible to teach us about Himself and how people can be with Him forever in Heaven. The Bible has two parts: the Old Testament and the New Testament. At Mass, readings are taken from the Bible. The Bible is the word of God.

Name:

Our Heavenly Father **Quiz 1**

Matching

God	The part of the Bible that tells us about Jesus and the Church.
Bible	The Creator of Heaven and earth, our Father.
Soul	The part of the Bible that tells us how people prepared for Jesus.
Heaven	The part of you that makes you live – it will live forever.
Old Testament	The Word of God.
New Testament	A place of perfect happiness where we will someday be with God.

Fill in the blanks *Use the words below to help you.*

Heaven	special	Father	forever	soul
Bible	New	Old	Sunday	Mass

1. God is our Father. He watches over us and takes care of all our needs. He wants you to be with Him forever in Heaven.

2. God made you different from everyone else, because you are special.

3. God's special gift to you is a soul. It allows you to live, to think, and to live forever.

4. God wanted us to know about Him and how to get to be with Him in Heaven. He gave us His Word in the Bible, which has two parts: the Old Testament and the New Testament.

5. At Mass we hear readings from the Bible. On Sunday we hear three readings.

Faith and Life • Grade 2 • Appendix A *A - 1*

Assess

1. Distribute Quiz 1 and answer their questions. As they turn them in, quiz them on the Our Father, the questions on p. 8 of the text, and the Words to Know.

2. When the students have handed in the quizzes, you may want to review the correct answers.

Conclude

End with singing "Holy God, we praise thy name!" and pray together the Our Father.

CHAPTER TWO
THE BLESSED TRINITY

Catechism of the Catholic Church References

Belief in One God: 199–202, 228
Consequences of Faith in One God: 222–29
Creation as the Work of the Trinity: 290–92, 316
Divine Economy and Common Works: 257–60
Divine Person: 252
- Consubstantial: 242, 253
- Distinction: 254, 267
- Unity: 685, 689

Dogma: 253–56
Holy Trinity in the Doctrine of the Faith: 249–56, 266
In the Name of the Father and of the Son and of the Holy Spirit: 232–36, 265
Mystery of Faith: 42, 50, 158, 206, 230, 232, 234, 237, 261, 266, 1066
Revelation of God as Trinity: 238–48, 261–64
Sign of the Cross: 2157, 2166

Scripture References

Creation: Gen 1–3; Mt 28:19

Background Reading: *The Fundamentals of Catholicism* by Fr. Kenneth Baker, S.J.

Volume 2:
"The Most Holy Trinity," pp. 77–79
"God Is Both One and Three," pp. 80–83

Summary of Lesson Content

Lesson 1

God is eternal. He has no beginning and no end.

Before creation God was neither unhappy nor alone.

God created freely.

Lesson 2

There is only one God. There are three Persons in one God: God the Father, God the Son, and God the Holy Spirit.

The three Persons are equal and eternal. They are all wise, all powerful, and all holy.

The mystery of one God in three Persons is called the Trinity.

Lesson 3

With the Son and the Spirit, God the Father created Heaven and earth. He is the First Person of the Trinity.

God the Son is the Second Person of the Trinity. He came down from Heaven to become our Savior Jesus Christ. He taught us about God, died for our sins, and rose from the dead.

The Holy Spirit is the Third Person of the Trinity. He helps us to pray, be good, and love God.

Lesson 4

The Blessed Trinity is a mystery revealed to us by God.

The Sign of the Cross reminds us of our faith in the Trinity (and the saving love of Jesus).

LESSON ONE: GOD IS ETERNAL

Aims

The students will learn that God is eternal. He has always existed, even before Creation.

They will know that God was not lonely or unhappy before Creation.

They will see that God created of His own free will.

Materials

- Clock
- Children's Bible
- *Activity Book*, p. 5

Optional:
- "God Father, praise and glory," *Adoremus Hymnal*, #464

Begin

Begin by asking a student what time it is and what he is currently doing. He will give you the time and tell you that he is sitting in your class. Ask him what he did one hour ago, one day ago, a month ago, a year ago? What about 20 years ago—he didn't exist yet! But his parents did. What about 200 years ago? Maybe his great-great-grandparents were alive. What about 2000 years ago—Jesus was born! What about millions of years ago—maybe dinosaurs? What existed before then? Before the earth was made? Nothing existed but God. He always existed.

2 The Blessed Trinity

Go therefore and make disciples of all nations, baptizing them in the name of the Father and of the Son and of the Holy Spirit.

Matthew 28:19

God has always existed, even before there was a world, a sky, people, or animals. There was nothing but God.

You may wonder, was God unhappy to be all alone? God did not need other things to make Him happy. And He was not really alone.

There is only one God, but in God there are three Persons. Their names are God the Father, God the Son, and God the Holy Spirit. The Father did not make the Son and the Spirit. The three Persons are equal and always were. All three are God. They are all wise, all powerful, and all holy. We call the three Persons in one God the Blessed **Trinity**.

With the Son and the Spirit, God the Father created Heaven and earth. He made us and He

11

Develop

1. Ask the children to tell you what they learned about God in the last chapter:

- God watches over us. This guiding and governing quality of God is called His Providence, demonstrating that He lovingly cares for each and every one of us.
- God knows what you are doing and what you are thinking. He is all good. God is all that is great, and pleasing, and holy.
- God is our friend. Friends are faithful, loving us for who we are and wanting for us what is good.
- God is our Father. This means He created us and loves us as His children.

2. Explain to the children that as the Creator, God made everything out of nothing. He existed before everything else. He created the world, the sun and moon, the seas and land. He created all the creatures of the world.

3. Read the account of Creation from a children's Bible (Gen 1—3).

4. Ask how we tell time. From the rotation of the earth around the sun. Because God made both of them, we can say He is outside of time. He existed before time existed! He has always existed.

5. Ask if they know what it was like before Creation. Together, read paragraphs 1 and 2 in the textbook. Before Creation, God was alone (and He is one). He was not unhappy or lonely. Do the children know what the text means when it says: "And He was not really alone"? They will learn more about this in the next lesson.

Name:____________________

Draw a picture of yourself with God in your heart.

Faith and Life Series • Grade 2 • Chapter 2 • Lesson 1 5

Reinforce

1. Have the students draw themselves with God in their hearts on *Activity Book*, p. 5.

2. Ask them to learn Question 5, p. 14 of the text.

3. Teach and sing the hymn "God Father, praise and glory," *Adoremus Hymnal*, #464.

Conclude

1. Have the students learn, pray, and memorize the Sign of the Cross and the Glory Be.

Note: They should memorize these prayers by the end of the week.

Preview

In the next lesson, we will learn about the three Persons in one God.

SAINT THOMAS AQUINAS

While his Five Proofs are far too complicated for second graders, they provide useful background for teachers (please see below).

THOMAS AQUINAS' FIVE PROOFS

Following are brief summaries of Aquinas' Proofs:
First Proof: everything that exists has a mover that puts it in motion; therefore, there must be a first mover.

Second Proof: everything that exists has a cause; therefore, there must be an uncaused first cause.

Third Proof: every being finds its necessity in another being; therefore, there must be a being with its own necessity, not receiving necessity from another.

Fourth Proof: everything that exists is a species of a genus, or maximum; therefore, there must be "a maximum cause of being, goodness, and every perfection in all being."

Fifth Proof: natural things function properly; therefore, there must be an intelligent being who directs natural things to their proper end.

NOTES

____

____

____

____

____

____

____

____

____

____

LESSON TWO: ONE GOD, THREE PERSONS

Aims

The students will learn that the one God is God the Father, God the Son, and God the Holy Spirit: three equal and eternal Persons in one God.

They will know that the mystery of three Persons in one God is called the Blessed Trinity.

Materials

- Three candles matches
- *Activity Book*, p. 6

Optional:
- "God Father, praise and glory," *Adoremus Hymnal*, #464
- "Patrick: Brave Shepherd of the Emerald Isle," CCC of America, video, available through Ignatius Press

Begin

Begin the class by gathering the students for a candle/flame presentation. Light one candle, from the one candle, light all three—they are all of the same fire. Explain that the three flames are all separate, but equal. Bring the three flames together into one flame and explain that though they are separate they are the same. Ask the students how this exercise reminds them of the Trinity.

Develop

1. Read together the third paragraph in the textbook.

2. On the chalk board, write the names of the three Persons. Emphasize that each Person is God.

The Blessed Trinity

Three Persons	*One God*
The Father is the First Person	*The Father is God.*
The Son is the Second Person	*The Son is God.*
The Holy Spirit is the Third Person	*The Holy Spirit is God.*

3. To emphasize the three Persons, distinct but unified, use the sun-heat-light analogy. Ask the children what two things come from the sun (heat and light). Point out that we cannot have a sun without having heat and light at the same time. No one can say which came first. Although they are together; they are different from one another. The sun is not just heat and the heat is not light. This analogy is the one way to explain the mystery of the Trinity. Explain that in the Trinity the Persons are different, but one did not come before the others. Each Person has always existed.

4. Draw the Chalk Talk at right on the chalkboard. Have the children draw this for themselves on notepaper. They may use colors to better depict this diagram.

5. Ask the children questions based on this diagram: Is the Father the Son? Is the Son the Holy Spirit? Is the Holy Spirit the Father? Is the Father God? Is the Son God? Is the Holy Spirit God? Are there three Gods? How many Persons are there?

Name:__________________

The Trinity

One God in three Persons

Color the circle with "The Father" red, "The Son" blue, and "The Holy Spirit" yellow. Then color the sections with the word "is" orange, and the sections with "is not" black.

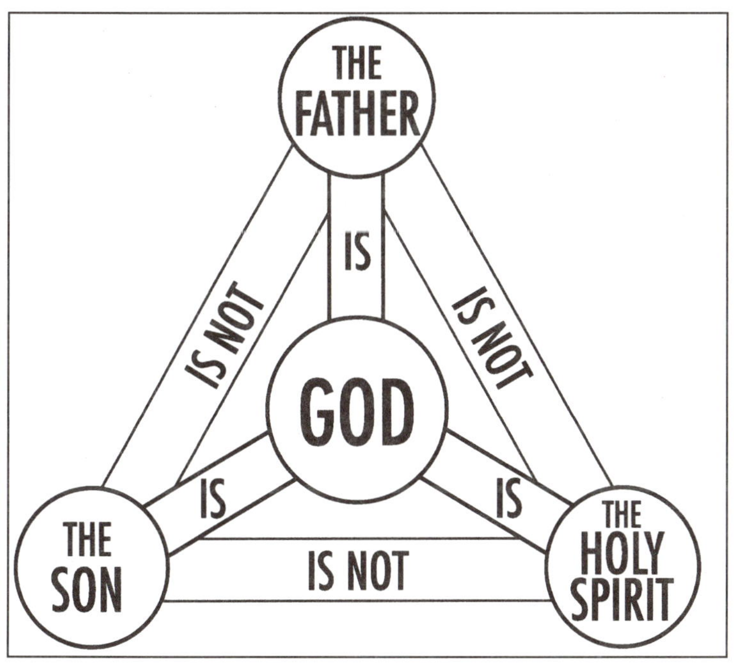

6 *Faith and Life Series • Grade 2 • Chapter 2• Lesson 2*

CHALK TALK: THE TRINITY

Reinforce

1. Have the students complete *Activity Book*, p. 6.

2. You may review the answers to the questions in the *Activity Book* as a class.

3. If time permits, show the video, "Patrick: Brave Shepherd of the Emerald Isle" from CCC of America, available through Ignatius Press, 30 minutes.

Conclude

1. Sing "God Father, praise and glory," *Adoremus Hymnal*, #464.

2. Lead them in praying the Sign of the Cross and the Glory Be.

Preview

In the next lesson, we will learn more about the Persons of the Trinity.

Saint Patrick used the shamrock to explain to the Irish people about the mystery of the Trinity. The shamrocks have 3 different leaves, but all are united as one leaf of clover

NOTES

LESSON THREE: THE PERSONS OF THE TRINITY

Aims

The students will learn that the Father is the First Person of the Trinity, the Creator of Heaven and earth.

They will learn that God the Son is the Second Person of the Trinity. He came down from Heaven to become our Savior Jesus Christ.

They will learn that the Holy Spirit is the Third Person of the Trinity. He helps us to pray, be good, and love God.

Materials

- *Activity Book*, p. 7

Optional:
- "God Father, praise and glory," *Adoremus Hymnal*, #464

Begin

Begin by asking your class who you are. They should call you by your title and last name. Ask the children what you do. They will say that you are a teacher. Ask the children if they would come to you on the street and say "Hello, Teacher!" No, they would call you by name, though they would know what it is that you do. Knowing what you do is one way to know you better. Today, the students will learn about the works of the different Persons of the Trinity and will know them better.

made all things for us. He is the First Person of the Blessed Trinity.

God the Son is the Second Person of the Blessed Trinity. He came down from Heaven to be our Savior, Jesus Christ. He taught us all about God and showed us how to love Him. Jesus died for us and rose from the dead.

The Third Person of the Blessed Trinity is God the Holy Spirit. He helps us to pray, to be good, and to love God. The Holy Spirit comes to live in our souls when we are baptized.

It is hard to understand how God can be both three and one at the same time. Even very smart people don't understand it. So we say that the Blessed Trinity is a mystery. A **mystery** is something God wants us to know about, even if it is hard to understand. And if we love God, we want to know about Him, too!

Whenever we begin our prayers we make the Sign of the Cross. Every time we make the Sign of the Cross we are showing that we believe in the Trinity and the saving love of Jesus.

13

Develop

1. With the children, read paragraphs 4–6. You may have volunteer students take turns reading the paragraphs aloud.

2. Ask the children about God the Father:
   - What work did the Father do?
   - What is the name of this Person?
   - Is the Father God?
   - Did the Father create Heaven and earth alone?
   - Is the Father the First, Second, or Third Person of the Trinity?

3. Ask the children about God the Son:
   - What work did the Son do?
   - What is the name of this Person?
   - Is the Son God?
   - Did the Son create Heaven and earth?
   - Does the Son live in Heaven with the Father?
   - What is special about Jesus Christ?
   - Is Jesus God?
   - What did God the Son do as Jesus the Savior?
   - What did the Son teach us about the Father?
   - Is the Son the First, Second, or Third Person of the Trinity?

4. Ask the children about God the Holy Spirit:
   - What work does the Holy Spirit do?
   - What is the name of this Person?
   - Is the Holy Spirit God?
   - Did the Holy Spirit create the world? Did the Holy Spirit die for our sins?
   - How does the Holy Spirit come to live in us?
   - Is the Holy Spirit the First, Second, or Third Person of the Trinity?

5. Ask the students how the Trinity is like a family. They are Persons, they have different works to do, they are united by love.

Name:___________________

The Blessed Trinity

Use the following words to help you fill in the blanks.

One	Father	always	died
God	Son	Jesus	rose
three	Holy Spirit	Heaven	cowboy
Person	earth	Savior	four

There is only One God, but in God there are three Persons. The three Persons are equal and always were. The Father is the First Person. He created Heaven and Heaven. The Son is the Second Person. His name is Jesus. He came down from Heaven to be our Savior. Jesus died for us and rose from the dead. The Holy Spirit is the Third Person of the Blessed Trinity.

Faith and Life Series • Grade 2 • Chapter 2 • Lesson 3 7

Reinforce

1. Have the students complete *Activity Book*, p. 7.

2. Have them memorize Questions 5–7, p. 14, and the Words to Know, p. 15 by referring to the glossary.

3. You may wish to review the fill-in-the-blanks, *Activity Book*, p. 7, when everyone has completed the work.

Conclude

1. Sing "God Father, praise and glory," *Adoremus Hymnal*, #464.

2. Lead them in praying the Sign of the Cross and the Glory Be.

Preview

In the next lesson, we will learn about the concept of a mystery of faith.

Reminder of Baptism

Jesus instituted the Sacrament of Baptism, Mt 28:19. Remind the students that it is through Baptism that the Holy Spirit comes to live in us.

"DOING" VS. "BEING"

Note that some people refer to the Persons of God as the Creator, Redeemer and Sanctifier. This is referring to God by His works, not by His persons/names. This formula places "doing" before "Being". It is important that the children understand the difference between these ideas.

NOTES

LESSON FOUR: THE MYSTERY OF THE TRINITY

Aims

The students will learn that the Blessed Trinity is a mystery, revealed to us by God; it is not a puzzle for us to solve.

They will learn that the Sign of the Cross reminds us of our faith in the Trinity (and the saving love of Jesus).

"In the Name of the Father and of the Son and of the Holy Spirit. *Amen.*"

Q. 5 *Is there only one God?*
Yes, there is only one God (CCC 233).

Q. 6 *How many Persons are there in God?*
In God there are three Persons: the Father, the Son and the Holy Spirit (CCC 253).

Q. 7 *What do we call the three Persons in one God?*
We call the three Persons in one God the mystery of the Blessed Trinity (CCC 234).

14

Materials

- Simple 20 piece puzzle
- *Activity Book*, p. 8

Optional:
- "God Father, praise and glory," *Adoremus Hymnal*, #464

Begin

Begin this class with the prayers the students have been working on this week: The Sign of the Cross and the Glory Be. Tell the students that today they will learn more about what these prayers mean.

Develop

1. As a class, read the last two paragraphs of the chapter. These two paragraphs cover "mystery" and the Sign of the Cross.

2. Bring out a simple puzzle and ask a volunteer to assemble it. This should not take too long. Explain that a puzzle can be solved. It is simply a matter of putting all the pieces together.

3. Give the students a simple math problem to solve. Explain that a problem can be solved. We might need to find out some information, but it can be solved with effort.

4. Explain to them that a mystery is not a puzzle or a problem. It is not something to be solved. Even the smartest people do not fully understand a mystery.

5. Reread the textbook definition of the word "mystery": A mystery is something God wants us to know about, even if it is hard to understand. Tell them that Jesus taught us about the mystery of the Trinity. He called God "His Father" and Himself the "Son of God." He also said that He and the Father would send the Holy Spirit. He also taught the Apostles to baptize all people in the Name of the Father and of the Son and of the Holy Spirit—but only one Name! Jesus revealed much about the different persons of the Trinity and so we accept this mystery by faith.

6. Reread the last paragraph. The Sign of the Cross is a simple prayer that reminds us of our belief in the mystery of the Trinity. It also reminds us that Jesus died on a cross to save us from our sins.

7. Recite the Glory Be together. Explain that this prayer reminds us of the Trinity and that God always was, is, and always will be—all three Persons in one God.

We Pray:

Glory be to the Father, and to the Son, and to the Holy Spirit, as it was in the beginning, is now, and ever shall be, world without end. *Amen.*

Words to Know:

Trinity mystery

Praise God, from Whom all blessings flow;
Praise Him, all creatures here below;
Praise Him above, you heavenly host:
Praise Father, Son, and Holy Ghost.

15

Reinforce

1. You may perform an overall review of the material covered in this chapter.

2. Have the students complete the word search found on *Activity Book*, p. 8. If they have time, they may make sentences using the words found in the puzzle. Have them read their sentences or correct their word searches with one another.

Conclude

1. Sing "God Father, praise and glory," *Adoremus Hymnal*, #464.

2. Orally review the definitions of the Words to Know and the answers to Questions 5–7.

3. Pray the Sign of the Cross and the Glory Be.

Preview

In the next lesson, we will review the material covered in this chapter.

THE SIGN OF THE CROSS: TRINITY AND CALVARY

Remind the class that the Sign of the Cross expresses two wonderful beliefs: that God is a Trinity and that the gates of Heaven were opened again when Jesus died on the Cross. Because He died, everyone may someday enter Heaven and live with God in His home forever.

NOTES

CHAPTER TWO:
REVIEW AND ASSESSMENT

Aims

The students' understanding of the material covered this week will be reviewed and assessed.

Materials

- Quiz 2 (Appendix, p. A-2)
- "God Father, praise and glory," *Adoremus Hymnal*, #464

Review

1. Ask the students what existed before the world was made: only God. How long has God existed? God has always existed.

2. Ask them who the three Persons of the Trinity are: Father, Son, and Holy Spirit. They should know that the Father is the First Person, the Son is the Second Person, and the Holy Spirit is the Third Person of the one God.

3. They should know the primary works of each Person of the Trinity:
Father: Creator of Heaven and earth.
Son: Savior of mankind.
Holy Spirit: Helper to make us holy and loving.

4. Ask them how God can be three and one. This is a mystery. What is this mystery called? The Blessed Trinity. Is a mystery a puzzle or a problem? No, a mystery can never be fully understood.

5. What two prayers did the students learn that remind them of the Trinity? The Sign of the Cross and the Glory Be.

Name:

The Blessed Trinity **Quiz 2**

For each question, write the Person of the Trinity which best suits the description: Father, Son or Holy Spirit.

1. Son — Died for our sins on a Cross and rose from the dead.
2. Father — Created the whole world out of nothing.
3. Holy Spirit — Helps us to pray.
4. Son — Came down from heaven and became man.
5. Holy Spirit — Comes to live in you at Baptism.
6. Son — Jesus Christ.
7. Father — Is the first Person.
8. Son — Is the second Person.
9. Holy Spirit — Is the third Person.
10. Holy Spirit — Is not the Father or the Son.
11. Father — Is not the Son or the Holy Spirit.
12. Son — Is God and Man.

Part Two:

Draw your own picture of the Trinity. (You may use the back of this quiz if you need more space.)

Answers will vary

A - 2 *Faith and Life • Grade 2 • Appendix A*

Assess

Distribute Quiz 2 and answer any questions they may have. As they turn in their quizzes, individually quiz them on Questions 5–7, the Words to Know, and their prayers. When all have turned in their quizzes, review the correct answers.

Conclude

Conclude with singing "God Father, praise and glory," *Adoremus Hymnal*, #464, and pray the Sign of the Cross and the Glory Be.

CHAPTER THREE
GOD THE CREATOR

Catechism of the Catholic Church References

Attributes of God Shown in and through Creation: 293–95, 315, 341
Catechesis on Creation: 282–89
Conservation of Creation: 2415–18, 2456
Creatures:
- Goodness: 339
- Hierarchy: 342
- Interdependence: 340
- Man as Summit: 343, 353, 355
- Order of Creation: 346

God as Creator of Heaven and Earth: 279–81, 286, 325–27,
God Continues to Care for His Creation: 302–14, 321–24
God Creates an Ordered and Good World: 299
God Creates out of Nothing: 296–98, 317–18
God Creates out of Wisdom and Love: 295, 315
God's Omnipotence: 268–78
Heaven: 1023–29, 1053
Purpose of Creation: 356, 38
Ways of Knowing God: 31–38, 46–48, 286
World as Created for the Glory of God: 293–94, 319

Scripture References

Genesis 1:1—2:24

Rev 4:11

Background Reading: *The Fundamentals of Catholicism* by Fr. Kenneth Baker, S.J.

Volume 2:
"The Best Possible World?" pp. 127–30

"The Beginning of the World," pp. 130–33

Summary of Lesson Content

Lesson 1

God created to reveal His love for others.

All of creation is a reflection of the glory of God.

Through creation, man can have knowledge of the existence and beauty of God.

Lesson 2

Through the order of the world, man can know about the wisdom and providence of God.

Lesson 3

God created all things for the enjoyment of His creatures.

Man's response to God for His creation should be to give God praise and glory.

Man has been entrusted with the stewardship of creation.

Lesson 4

Through man's rational soul, he can express his love and praise for God through words, song and poetry (as well as actions and gestures).

All creation gives God praise through its very nature. Man must choose to give God praise.

LESSON ONE: GOD IS THE CREATOR

Aims

The students will learn that God created to reveal His love.

They will see that all creation is a reflection of the glory of God.

They will understand that, through creation, man can have knowledge of the existence and beauty of God.

Materials

- Pictures of God-created vs. man-made things, poster board, glue
- *Activity Book*, p. 9

Optional:
- "All creatures of our God and King," *Adoremus Hymnal*, #600

Begin

Begin the class by having the students distinguish between those things that are God-created and those things that are man-made. God created, out of nothing, things that man could never make. Man-made things are things that have been made using God's creation to make something else. Give the children examples, like God created wheat and water, which man can use to make bread. Have the children tear out pictures and glue them, under the proper categories, onto a poster board divided into two columns: God-created vs. man-made.

Develop 

1. Have the students read the first three paragraphs of the chapter. Volunteers may take turns reading aloud.

2. Ask the children why God created. Because He wanted others to be happy. What are some of the wonderful things God has created? The children may list many things. Ask the children what some of their favorite things are that God created.

3. Discuss the qualities of God's creation and how they reflect God's all-perfect qualities. Flowers are beautiful, so God is all beautiful. Rivers are powerful, so God is all powerful. Men are wise, God is all wise. Seasons are good, God is all good.

4. Write "Creator"on the board vertically. Ask them to think of something that is created that starts with the letter C, then R, etc. Write each created item next to the letter on the board for example:

C at
R iver
E arth
A ngel
T iger
O tter
R ain

5. Ask them to think of ways they may recognize the glory of God in nature.

Name:__________________

The Order of Creation

God created many things that do not have life in them. In the box above, draw something God created that does not have life.

God created plant life. It is the lowest form of life. Draw an example of plant life.

God created animal life. It is above plant life, but below human life. Animals can move and grow. They can also be trained. Draw an example of animal life.

Human life is the highest form of life. We can grow and move like the animals, but we can also think and act freely. Draw a picture of yourself.

Faith and Life Series • Grade 2 • Chapter 3 • Lesson 1 9

Reinforce

1. Have the students complete *Activity Book*, p. 9

2. Teach and lead the children in singing: "All creatures of our God and King," *Adoremus Hymnal*, #600.

Conclude

1. Lead the students in thanking God for creation and specifically for many the things in creation.

2. Lead them in praying the Glory Be, and read from Daniel 3, p. 20 of the textbook.

Preview

In the next lesson, we will learn about God's Providence.

CHALK TALK: GOD CAN BE SEEN IN HIS CREATURES

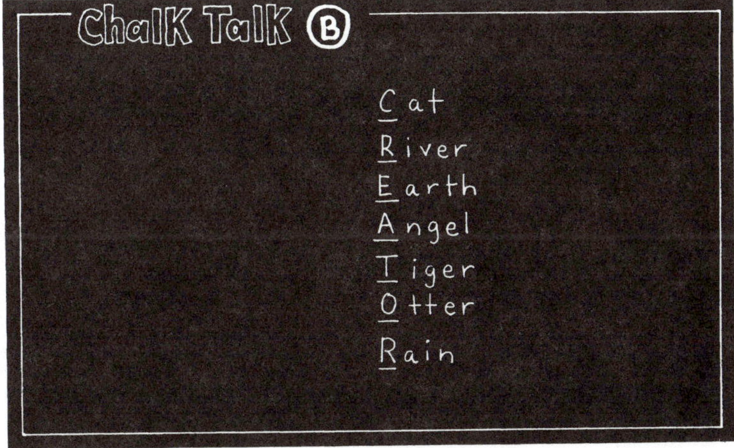

NOTES

LESSON TWO: GOD'S PROVIDENCE

Aims

The students will learn that, from the world around us, they can know about the wisdom of God.

They will understand that God continues to care for the world because of His love for creation.

Materials

- Potted plant, seeds, cups, dirt, spoons, water and direct sun light
- *Activity Book*, p. 10

Optional:
- "All creatures of our God and King," *Adoremus Hymnal*, #600

Begin

Begin the class by showing the students a potted plant. Ask the children how a plant grows. It needs sunlight and water. God provides these things for plants so that they can live. What things do plants need to live? What is their purpose? Animals eat them, and some even use shrubs and trees as homes! Everything has a purpose. Your class will learn more about plants and help God in his plan by planting!

Plant seeds in cups of dirt, place them in the sunlight and water them regularly.

3 God the Creator

"Worthy art thou, our Lord and God, to receive glory and honor and power, for thou didst create all things, and by thy will they existed and were created."

Revelation 4:11

God was happy all by Himself, but He wanted others to be happy, too. So God made the world. Then God made people to enjoy all the wonderful things He made.

God the **Creator** made the world and everything in it. If we look at the sky, the ocean, or a mountain, we can learn how great God is. They are very big and powerful. Because God made them, we know He is even more powerful.

God made many beautiful things, too, like flowers, birds, sunsets, and rainbows. The beauty of these things comes from God.

We see that God is wise when we learn how He makes things grow and work together. He made great big trees come from tiny seeds. And each tree

17

Develop

1. Have the students read paragraph 4 in the textbook. Ask them to think of other ways that God takes care of things. You may start their thinking with an example from the textbook of trees drawing from seed, giving homes to animals, which give food to people.

2. Review the qualities of God that can be known through creation by giving the Chalk Talk. Ask them to open their texts to p. 17. Ask them to find the words that tell us what God is like (wise, powerful, takes care of us, great). On the board, write "all wise," "all good," "all powerful," and "all beautiful" horizontally. Explain what each of these words, which tell us about God, means. Tell them that we know that God possesses these qualities because we find them in His creatures. Find examples in creation that reflect these qualities in God. (See Chalk Talk).

3. Focus on the attribute of "all wise." What other creatures have an intellect: angels and men, because they have rational souls. Discuss the dignity of the rational soul. We can choose to do good, we can think and laugh. We can love.

4. We can also use God's creation to make things and to reflect God's wisdom. Just as God takes care of all creation, so too, man can take care of creation by helping God, e.g., we take care of our pets.

5. Angels reflect God's wisdom, as they take care of us (guardian angels).

6. Discuss other ways we see God's wisdom through creation: food chains, seasonal changes, geographical differences.

Name:______________

God Is the Creator!

1. Why did God make Heaven and earth?

He wanted us to be happy and he knew that we would like them

2. How did God make things?

He made things beautiful

3. By looking at the sky, the ocean, or a mountain, we see that they are mighty and powerful. What can they teach us about God?

That He is great and powerful

4. How can we praise and thank God for His gifts?

By singing a hymn or reciting a poem

5. Does God take care of all His creation?

Yes

6. Does God take care of you?

Yes

10 *Faith and Life Series • Grade 2 • Chapter 3 • Lesson 2*

Reinforce

1. Have the students complete *Activity Book*, p. 10.

2. Have them begin memorizing Questions 8 and 9, p. 19 of the textbook.

Conclude

1. Lead the students in singing "All creatures of our God and King," *Adoremus Hymnal*, #600.

2. Have them pray Daniel 3 and add their own verses, too.

3. End by praying the Glory Be.

Preview

In the next lesson, we will learn how the proper use of these gifts of creation gives praise to God.

VISUALIZING ANGELS

Remind the children that angels do not have bodies or wings but that people imagine them that way. Though angels sometimes communicate with mankind, most angels are invisible.

CHALK TALK: THE CREATOR

Chalk Talk Ⓐ

"If a (creature) is (quality), then God must be all (quality)."

Wise	Good	Beautiful	Powerful
man	man	peacocks	mountains
angels	angels	sunsets	oceans
	seasons	flowers	sun

God is all wise, all good, all beautiful, and all powerful.

NOTES

LESSON THREE: THE PURPOSE OF CREATION

Aims

The students will learn that God created all things out of love for man and that man should respond by giving thanks, praise, and glory to God.

They will learn that man has been entrusted with the stewardship of creation.

Materials

- Children's Bible (Genesis 1)
- *Activity Book*, p. 11

Optional:

- "All creatures of our God and King," *Adoremus Hymnal*, #600

Begin

Have the students perform a skit, using Daniel 3. Each child should portray a different creature, from Daniel 3, p. 20. Write a simple script with the way in which each creature blesses the Lord. (e.g., Sun: I am the Sun and I bless the Lord with my heat and light. I help people grow food, I keep the earth warm, and I help people to see God's beautiful world.)

Then after each child presents, have all the children say thanks to God for that creature. (e.g., Thank you God for the Sun!).

is a home for animals, birds, and bugs. God's plan takes care of everything He made.

God made all these things because He knew that we would like them. He made food that is good to eat and stars that are nice to look at. He even made things that make us laugh, like monkeys and puppies. God made them all because He loves us.

We can praise and thank God for His gifts by using them the right way. We should not waste our food. We should be kind to animals. We should keep the parks and forests clean when we visit them.

We can give God praise and thanks by singing a hymn, like the one below:

All things bright and beautiful,
All creatures great and small,
All things wise and wonderful,
The Lord God made them all.

Or by saying a poem:

Each little flower that opens, each little bird that sings,
He made their glowing colors, He made their tiny
wings.

The purple-headed mountain, the river running by,
The sunset, and the morning that brightens up the sky.

18

Develop

1. Together read paragraphs 5 and 6.

2. Ask the students what things God created to make us laugh. What did God create to make us feel small? What did God create to make us feel big? What did God create to make us happy or sad? What did God create that is your favorite thing? What did God create to show his love for you? What did God create that helps us to be thankful to God? What did God create to help us praise God? What did God create that shows His glory?

3. Remind them that God created the world out of love for us and gave man stewardship over His creation (this means we are to help God take care of it). Read from a children's Bible the story of Creation from Genesis 1.

4. Ask the students to name ways that they can help God as stewards of the earth:

- *Recycling*
- *Cleaning up parks/forests when we visit them*
- *Not wasting food*
- *Not polluting*
- *Using things for which they are intended*
- *Being kind to animals*

5. Ask the students how they may give God thanks, praise, and glory through His creation:

- Prayer
- Art
- Songs/poetry

Name:__________________

Write a letter to God thanking Him for His gift of Creation.

Dear God,

Answers will vary

____

____

____

____

Love,

____

Faith and Life Series • Grade 2 • Chapter 3 • Lesson 3 11

Reinforce

1. Have the students complete *Activity Book*, p. 11. Collect these pages when finished, as you will use them again in Lesson 4.

2. They may work on costumes for their skit, "Blessing the Lord," so they may perform in them on the day of review.

3. Be sure to water the planted seeds regularly.

Conclude

1. Sing "All creatures of our God and King," *Adoremus Hymnal*, #600.

2. As a class, pray the Glory Be.

Preview

In the next lesson, we will learn different ways to respond to God for His gift of creation.

GOD AND THE PROBLEM OF EVIL

"Can God do bad or evil things?" If this comes up, explain to the children that God cannot do bad things. This is not because He does not have the power to do them, but because they are things that should not be done, and He is all good.

LITANY OF GRATITUDE

God gave us parents,
Thank You God our Father!

God gave us friends,
Thank You God our Father!

God gave us trees and plants,
Thank You God our Father!

God gave us animals,
Thank you God our Father!

God gave us His love,
Thank you God our Father!

NOTES

LESSON FOUR: GIVING THANKS, PRAISE, AND GLORY TO GOD

Aims

The students will learn that because God gave them the gift of a rational soul, they can express thanks, love, and praise for God through words, song, poetry, actions, and gestures.

They will learn that all creation gives God praise. Man, however, chooses to praise God.

Materials

- *Activity Book*, p. 11

Optional:
- "All creatures of our God and King," *Adoremus Hymnal*, #600

Begin

Take the class outside for a nature walk. Ask the children to take turns pointing out things that God created. Ask the students how they give glory to God. Then ask the children if these things can choose to give glory to God, or if they must because God made them that way. (All creatures without a rational soul cannot choose to give glory to God.)

The cold wind in the winter, the pleasant summer sun,
The ripe fruits in the garden, He made them every one.

He gave us eyes to see them, and lips that we might tell
How great is God Almighty, Who has made all things
well.

Cecil Frances Alexander

Q. 8 *Why is God called "the Creator of Heaven and earth"?*
God is called "the Creator of Heaven and earth" because He made Heaven and earth out of nothing (CCC 279, 296).

Q. 9 *Does God take care of all things?*
Yes, God takes care of all things because of His love (CCC 301).

Words to Know:

Creator

19

Develop

1. Ask the students what was common among all of creation seen on the nature walk: nature could not choose to give thanks, praise, or glory to God.

2. Ask how they (as persons) are different from rocks, plants, and animals? They can choose to give God thanks, praise, and glory. They can love God.

3. Ask them ways they can give thanks to God:
- *Prayer*
- *Take care of the gifts He gives us*
- *Use His gifts properly*
- *Share these gifts with others*
- *Appreciate nature*

4. Ask the students to name ways by which they can give praise or glory to God:
- Take time to appreciate nature
- Take time to think about How nature reflects God
- Tell God how much you appreciate nature
- Stop to see the beauty, wisdom, goodness, and power in nature

5. As a class, read the rest of the chapter. Explain to the children that these are examples of giving God thanks and praise. Look at the adjectives used: bright, beautiful, great, small, wise, wonderful. Also look at the attention given to the creatures in the Cecil Frances Alexander poem. We are friends and should appreciate nature and giving praise to God.

6. You may also look at the words of "All creatures of our God and King," *Adoremus Hymnal*, #600, which your class has been singing all week, and explain that by reading/singing, you are giving God praise and glory.

We Pray:

Bless the Lord, sun and moon
Bless the Lord, stars of heaven
Bless the Lord, all rain and dew
Bless the Lord, all winds
Bless the Lord, lightnings and clouds
Let the earth bless the Lord
Bless the Lord, mountains and hills
Bless the Lord all things that grow on the earth
Bless the Lord, you springs
Bless the Lord, seas and rivers,
Bless the Lord, you whales and all
creatures that move in the waters
Bless the Lord, all birds of the air
Bless the Lord, all beasts and cattle
praise to him and exalt him for ever.

Daniel 3:40–43, 51–59

"And God saw everything that he had made, and behold, it was very good."

Genesis 1:31

20

Reinforce

1. Pass out the student's letters (*Activity Book*, p. 11.) They may take turns reading their letters/prayers of thanksgiving for creation. Be sure to praise each student for his work.

(You may use the example of the "Canticle of Creation" by St. Francis—bottom of the page—to give the children ideas about what to write)

Conclude

1. Sing "All creatures of our God and King," *Adoremus Hymnal*, #600.

2. End by praying the Glory Be.

Preview

In the next lesson, we will review the material covered in this chapter.

CANTICLE OF CREATION BY SAINT FRANCIS

Most high, all powerful, good Lord,
to You be praise, glory, and honor and all blessing.
To You alone, Most High,
do they belong, and there is no man worthy
to name You.
Praise be to You, my Lord, with all Your creatures.
Chief of all is Sir Brother Sun,
who is our day; through whom You give light.
Beautiful is he, radiant, with great splendor.
He is a true revealer of You, Most High.
Praise be to You, my Lord,
for Sister Moon and for the stars.
In heaven You have formed them,
bright, precious, and fair.

NOTES

CHAPTER THREE:
REVIEW AND ASSESSMENT

Aims

The students' understanding of the material covered this week will be reviewed and assessed.

Materials

- Quiz 3 (Appendix, p. A-3.)
- "All creatures of our God and King," *Adoremus Hymnal*, #600

Name:

God Made Us **Quiz 3**

Please answer in complete sentences.

1. Why did God create the world and people?
To show His love for us

2. How can we help God take care of His creation?
By using things the right way

3. How can we give thanks and praise to God?
By singing a hymn or reciting a poem

Multiple Choice *Circle the correct answer.*

1. We know God is wise because:
(a.) All creation works together.
b. Rocks cannot think.
c. Plants do not talk to us.

2. We know God is powerful because:
a. Flowers are delicate.
(b.) He made mountains, rivers, and the stars.
c. Monkeys make us laugh.

3. We know God is good because:
a. Some animals bite.
b. We sometimes make mistakes.
(c.) God gives us all we need.

4. We know God is beautiful because:
a. Rocks are very hard.
(b.) We can see beauty in creation.
c. We cannot see beauty in creation.

Faith and Life • Grade 2 • Appendix A *A - 3*

Review

1. The students should remember that God created all things out of nothing because He loves us.

2. They should be able to discuss the qualities of God and how they are reflected in nature.

3. They should be able to discuss ways God takes care of the created world and all people.

4. They should understand that man is called to care for God's creation.

5. They should be able to relate that man can choose to give God thanks and praise, but other creatures (other than angels) cannot choose to do this. Man should choose to praise God as a loving response to His loving generosity.

Assess

1. Distribute Quiz 3 and answer any questions the children may have. As the students hand in their quizzes, quiz them individually on Questions 8 and 9, and the Words to Know.

2. When all have handed in their quizzes, review the correct answers.

Conclude

1. Sing, "All creatures of our God and King," *Adoremus Hymnal*, #600.

2. Perform the skit from Daniel 3.

3. Pray the Glory Be.

CHAPTER FOUR
GOD MADE US

Catechism of the Catholic Church References

Angels: 328–36, 350–52
Creation of Man: 343, 353, 355–56, 374, 381
Equality and Difference between Man and Woman in Creation: 369–73, 383
Equality and Differences among People: 1934–38, 1944–46
Grace: 1996–2005, 2021–24
As Charism: 2003
As Gift of the Holy Spirit: 2003
As God's Help: 1996, 2021
Guardian Angels: 336
Heaven:
Place of God: 326

Scripture References

Creation of Man: Gen 1:27, 2; 2 Cor 6:18

Background Reading: *The Fundamentals of Catholicism* by Fr. Kenneth Baker, S.J.

Volume 2:
"The Origin of Man," pp. 139–42
"Angels by the Millions," pp. 174–77

Summary of Lesson Content

Lesson 1

God is the Creator of Heaven and earth.

God made man, who lived in the Garden of Eden.

He made Eve to be the helpmate of Adam.

Adam and Eve are the first man and woman.

Lesson 2

Adam and Eve were created happy in the Garden of Eden. They had original justice which included:

- Adam and Eve were never sick or hurt; they would not die.
- They did not have temptation to sin.
- They knew everything they needed to know to live.
- They had all the food they needed.
- They lived in harmony with the animals and with one another.
- They were in the presence of God.
- They had grace, which is a share in God's life.

Lesson 3

God made all other people in the world, too.

All people are unique.

All people are made in the image and likeness of God.

All people are created to know, love, and serve God, and to be happy with Him forever in Heaven.

Lesson 4

God has given each of us a guardian angel to guide and protect us.

Angels are pure spirits, messengers of God.

LESSON ONE: GOD MADE MAN AND WOMAN

Aims

The students will learn that God is the Creator of Heaven and earth.

They will know that God made Adam, the first man, who lived in the Garden of Eden.

They will know that He made Eve, the first woman, to be the helpmate of Adam.

Materials

- Children's Bible
- Modeling clay
- *Activity Book*, p. 12

Optional:
- "All people that on earth do dwell," *Adoremus Hymnal*, #622

Begin

Gather the students and read from the children's Bible the Creation of Man and Woman (Gen 2). Ask the children to recount the story in their own words. You may ask them questions about the story, such as:

- Who made Man, and how?
- Who made Woman, and how? Did the man help?
- Why did God make Woman?
- Were Man and Woman happy together?
- Is it good for Man and Woman to be together?

4 God Made Us

So God created man in his own image, in the image of God he created him; male and female he created them.

Genesis 1:27

God wanted to share the wonderful world He made, so He made the first man.

God gave him the name Adam. Adam lived in a beautiful place called the Garden of Eden. He was friends with all the animals, and he gave them their names. But soon God saw that Adam needed more than just the animals. God gave Adam someone who would love and help him. He made a good and beautiful woman. Her name was Eve.

Adam and Eve were very happy in the garden. They were safe with the animals in the garden, which was their home. They were never sick or hurt. They never felt like doing anything bad. They did not have to go to school, because God told them what they had to know. All the food they wanted was growing on the trees in the garden. Best of all, God would come to the garden to talk to them.

21

Develop

1. Read the first two paragraphs of this chapter. Ask the children review questions such as: What is the man's name? Where did the man live? What did the man do? Why did God create the woman?

2. The students may take turns asking each other the questions. If a child answers a question correctly, he may ask the next question.

3. Have them make something out of clay (a person or an animal) and pay great attention to detail—even if they make snakes, there are scales, eyes, tongue, nostrils, etc. Give them plenty of time for this activity.

4. Have the students present their creations to each other.

5. Ask thems if their creations can live. Do they have all the details (every hair of fur? every scale? every tooth? every organ?)? Certainly not. They are great, but they are not perfect. Ask the students if they put a lot of care into making their creatures (yes). So too, God took great care in making us! For example, our noses are not upside down. If they were, we might drown when it rains! Our knees don't bend backwards or we would have a hard time sitting in chairs! God considered all of His creatures well and made them with great care. God took special care when making the man and woman because they were made to help each other. They have souls, and they would love the world God created for them so they needed eyes, ears, noses, mouths, the sense of touch, too!

6. Ask the children to name some ways they can use their senses to appreciate the world God made for them. Then take time to thank God for the senses. Thank God for taking great care in making man the way He did. Thank Him for all our gifts.

Name:____________________

Word Search

Can you find these words in the puzzle?
Look carefully! The words go across and down.

EVE	ANIMALS	NEIGHBOR
CHILDREN	GOD	GARDEN OF EDEN
GUARDIAN	FATHER	GRACE
HEAVEN	LOVE	KNOW
LIFE	PRAYER	NAMES
PEOPLE	ANGEL	SERVE

```
L X C H I L D R E N X E
X E V E H J A N G E L A
G A R D E N O F E D E N
O D L X L S G R A C E I
D A O X P U X X P R A M
A M V X X P R A Y E R A
C P E O P L E X X F X L
H X H E A V E N S A X S
X E N A M E S N E T L R
K N O W T L E S R H I E
N E I G H B O R V E F X
G U A R D I A N E R E X
```

12 *Faith and Life Series • Grade 2 • Chapter 4 • Lesson 1*

VALUE IN EVERY HUMAN LIFE

God took great care in creating each person, including those with physical and mental disabilities. Many great figures in history were given special challenges by their bodies. For example, tradition holds that the greatest poet of Greece, Homer, was blind. The great German composer Beethoven became completely deaf, yet he continued to write beautiful music. In the Church, there have been numerous saints with physical disabilities. Saint Colette, for instance, was very small and weak, but her faith in God was great enough and strong enough to influence others. Blessed Herman the Cripple was so terribly deformed that he could barely move on his own, yet he had a brilliant mind and is still famous today for the hymns Salve Regina and Alma Redemptoris Mater, which he composed (see box above right).

Reinforce

1. Have the students complete *Activity Book*, p. 12.

2. Teach and lead the children in "All people that on earth do dwell," *Adoremus Hymnal*, #622.

Conclude

Lead the students in praying the Our Father.

Preview

In the next lesson, we will learn about original justice.

BL. HERMAN THE CRIPPLE

Also known as Herman Contractus, Herman the Cripple was one of the most brilliant minds of the Middle Ages. Though he could barely move as a result of his physical deformity, he lived a saintly life in a Swiss monastery while composing hymns, mathematical treatises, and poetry. His feast day is September 25.
(See box below.)

NOTES

____
____
____
____
____
____
____
____
____
____

LESSON TWO: ORIGINAL JUSTICE

Aims

The students will learn that Adam and Eve were given the gift of original justice:

- Adam and Eve were never sick or hurt; they would not die.
- They knew everything they needed to know to live and they had all the food they needed.
- They lived in harmony with the animals and one another.
- They were in the presence of God and had grace, which is a share in God's life.

Materials

- Permanent markers
- *Activity Book*, p. 13

Optional:

- "All people that on earth do dwell," *Adoremus Hymnal*, #622

Begin

Tell the students a story along this line:
As a gift for my ______ (child, nephew, etc.), I gave him beautiful markers. I told him that they would be great for writing and making crafts. As he used them for writing and drawing, it made me very happy. As he used them well, he showed respect for the gift and for me, who gave him the gift.

Note: You may use some markers to demonstrate this story.

Develop

1. Explain to the children that this present was like God's grace. He had given grace to Adam and Eve. Grace was not theirs to begin with; it was to be used properly. Its proper care would show a gift to God.

2. Explain to the students that God gave Adam and Eve a special gift called grace. Grace is a share in God's life. It made them able to live forever. His grace made them very happy and allowed them to live in justice (everyone getting and giving what is his due). This is called "original justice" because it was how things were at the beginning of the world.

3. Read paragraphs 3 and 4 (pp. 21 and 23 of the text) with the children, and review with them the gifts of God. With grace, Adam and Eve were happy. They were safe in the garden with the animals. They did not fight even among themselves. They did not get sick or hurt—they would never die! They did not want to do anything bad. They did not have to go to school. They already knew everything they needed to know. They had all the food they needed growing in the garden. The greatest gift was that God Himself would come to the garden to talk to them.

4. Explain to the children that today, God offers us the same gift of grace—His life in us. Although we do not live in the Garden of Eden, we can have God live in union with us when we have grace. We receive grace when we are baptized. (This should be review from last year.) Remind the students that at Baptism, the priest pours water over them three times saying "I baptize you in the Name of the Father and of the Son and of the Holy Spirit." When the priest does this, God comes to live inside us and brings us His life. This is a gift from Him, a gift that we did not earn, or even deserve; it is simply a gift that God wants us to Have. We must, however, care for God's life in our soul.

Name:____________________

God's Children

As God's Children, we are called to know, love, and serve God. How can we know God? Unscramble the words below to find out.

1. DARE HET LIBBE: Read the Bible
2. RPAY: Pray
3. ERLNA YROU GELRINOI: Learn your religion
4. OG TO SASM: Go to Mass
5. LAKT OT ROUY RAPETNS Talk to your parents

pray	Commandments	learn
neighbor	everyone	worship

We are to love God. How can we do this? Fill in the blanks with the words above to find out.

6. To love God, I can keep His Commandments. I can pray to Him and tell Him I love Him. I can love my neighbor, who is everyone. I can learn about God and worship Him.

Faith and Life Series • Grade 2 • Chapter 4 • Lesson 2 13

Reinforce

1. Have the students complete *Activity Book*, p. 13.

2. Have them begin to memorize Questions 10 and 11 from textbook p. 25, and look up the words "grace" and "Adam and Eve" in the glossary.

Conclude

1. Lead the students in singing "All people that on earth do dwell," *Adoremus Hymnal*, #622.

2. Lead them in prayer, thanking God for the gift of grace that we received at Baptism, and then pray the Our Father. You may remind them that at Baptism, they became Children of God, so it is right to call Him "Father."

Preview

In the next lesson, we will learn what it means to be made in the image of God.

SAINT AUGUSTINE OF HIPPO

Augustine was so fond of drinking and parties before his conversion that he is now the patron saint of brewers.

SAINT AUGUSTINE AND GRACE

Sometimes a life without grace and filled with sin is dramatically altered by God. In the history of the Church, one of the most striking stories of God's grace and redemption can be found in the person of Saint Augustine. Born into privilege in the twilight years of the Western Roman Empire, Augustine lived a life that was focused upon pleasure, greed, and pagan philosophy. Throughout his youth and young adulthood, he had nothing but contempt for the Christian Church. He thought the Gospels and Letters of Paul to be nothing but badly written rhetoric, undeserving of his attention. Augustine's way of living made his mother very sad, for she knew God had other plans for her son. Soon Augustine, became frustrated with his life and prayed for guidance. (Continued on p. 37)

NOTES

LESSON THREE: WE ARE MADE IN GOD'S IMAGE

Aims

The students will learn that God made all people in the world and that He made each of us unique and special.

They will come to understand that all people are made in the image of God.

They will learn that they are made to know, love, and serve God, and be happy with Him forever in Heaven.

Materials

- Pictures of different people (races, colors, ages)
- *Activity Book*, p. 14

Optional:
- "All people that on earth do dwell," *Adoremus Hymnal*, #622

Begin

Have many pictures of different people and groups of people. You may want to include the children's pictures. Ask the students what is similar between the people. The answer is that they are all made in the image of God.

You may want to ask the children what God looks like. Is this what we mean by image? Today the class will learn more about what it means to be made in the image of God.

God loved Adam and Eve very much. He gave them a special gift called grace. **Grace** is a share in God's own life. With grace in their souls, Adam and Eve became God's children. Because of grace, Adam and Eve would someday be able to live with God in Heaven.

Later on, God made all the other people in the world; He made you. No two people look the same. Some of us are tall, others are short. Some of us have dark skin, others are light. There are boys and there are girls. We are all special. God made all of us in His image. He loves each of us very much.

God wants us to know Him, to love Him, and to **serve** Him. He wants us to be His children and be happy with Him in Heaven.

Words to Know:

Adam and Eve grace
serve guardian angel

"I will be a Father to you, and you shall be my sons and daughters, says the Lord Almighty."

2 Corinthians 6:18

23

Develop

1. Remind the students that they are made up of two parts: body and soul. Ask them if all the people in the pictures look the same? No. Their bodies are different. Ask the children if their souls are the same? No. We all think differently, have different interests, and intellectual gifts. We all, however, have bodies and souls.

2. Ask the students how we are like God (the Father). Does He have a body? No. He is a spiritual being. Our souls are spiritual, too! God is all wise, all knowing, all good, all powerful; man can reflect these qualities. He has a rational soul. God made us out of love; man can love God in return. It is because of our rational souls that we are in the image of God. We are like God in some ways. When we have grace, we have God's very life within us.

3. Read p. 23 of the text together. Because we are men and God created us in His image, we desire union with Him. In fact, God made us so that we will be happiest when we know Him, love Him, and serve Him. The more we know him now, the better prepared we will be to live with Him forever in Heaven.

4. Ask the students to think of ways they can know God:
- Study religion
- Pray
- Go to Mass

5. Ask the students to think of ways they can love God:
- Keep the Commandments
- Receive the sacraments
- Make sacrifices

6. Ask the children to think of ways they can serve God:
- Help their neighbors, do good works
- Share their love for God with others

Name:___________________

Angel of God, my guardian dear,
To whom God's love commits me here,
Ever this day, be at my side,
To light and guard, to rule and guide.
Amen.

This week, before getting dressed, pray the Guardian Angel Prayer. Put a check in the box each day you pray to your Guardian Angel.

Monday	Tuesday	Wednesday	Thursday	Friday	Saturday	Sunday

14 *Faith and Life Series • Grade 2 • Chapter 4 • Lesson 3*

Reinforce

1. Have the students complete *Activity Book,* p. 14.

2. Have the students each think of one way they can know, love, or serve God, and have them complete this assignment before the next class. Be sure to follow-up the next day.

Conclude

1. Lead the students in singing "All people that on earth do dwell," *Adoremus Hymnal*, #622.

2. End with the Our Father.

Preview

In the next lesson, we will lean about other spiritual creatures: angels. Specifically, we will learn about our guardian angels.

QUOTATIONS FROM SAINT AUGUSTINE

"My soul will not rest until it rests in thee . . ."

"Man was made for union with God—it is the longing of his heart."

AUGUSTINE AND GRACE

(Continued from p. 35) Augustine, fed up with his life of sin, threw himself to the earth and begged for God's help. Just then, he heard a child singing "Take up and read." Taking the child's song as a sign from God, Augustine began reading the Scriptures. He decided to follow Paul's admonition to live as Christ lived. To his mother's great joy, Augustine was baptized and began a life of dedication to Jesus. Not only was his once sin-filled life now filled with God's own life, but he was so dedicated that he became a bishop, a defender of the Church against heresy, and a saint. Augustine wrote of his conversion in his autobiographical masterpiece, the *Confessions*.

NOTES

LESSON FOUR: GUARDIAN ANGELS

Aims

The students will learn that God has given each of us a guardian angel to guide and protect us.

They will understand that angels are pure spirits, messengers of God.

Materials

- *Activity Book*, p. 15
- Appendix, p. B-8

Optional:
- "All people that on earth do dwell," *Adoremus Hymnal*, #622

Begin

Begin the class by asking the students if they had a hard time completing their assignments. Have the students share what they did to know, love, or serve God since the last class. Be sure to praise the children for what they have done. If they have forgotten to do this assignment, have them think of ways they knew, loved, or served God when they may not have been aware that they were, e.g., did they complete their religion homework? Did you help your sister? Did you say your prayers before bed?

God has given each of us a **guardian angel**. Our angels protect us and help us to be good. You cannot see your angel, but he is always there. He follows you everywhere. You are never without your heavenly friend.

We Pray:

Learn this prayer to your guardian angel. Say it each day. Say it any time you feel lonely or afraid.

GUARDIAN ANGEL PRAYER

Angel of God, my guardian dear,
To whom God's love commits me here,
Ever this day be at my side,
To light and guard, to rule and guide. *Amen.*

24

Develop

1. Ask the students if they had a hard time completing their assignments. Did they forget or did they remember late at night? Tell the students that God gives them a special helper so we can better know, love, and serve Him, and so prepare for Heaven.

2. Have the students read p. 24 of their text. Discuss the content of this reading. You may ask the students the following questions:
- Does each person have a guardian angel?
- What does a guardian angel do?
- Does your guardian angel ever leave you?

3. For activity fun, make guardian angel light-catchers (See Appendix, p. B-8, for the pattern). Copy the image onto transparencies, and have the students color them with markers, then hang them in a window for a brilliant display.

4. *If time permits, you may wish to teach the children about angels. Angels are creatures. Angels are pure spirits. "Angel" is not a specific type of creature, but a specific office. An angel is a messenger between God and man. Angels have rational souls and are free. They do not have a gender. Every person has a guardian angel, but there are other types of angels. Each angel is its own species. The angels are present with us. At Mass they gather around the altar to worship God.*

5. Briefly mention the names of the nine choirs of angels (see box at right).

Q. 10 *Why did God make you?*
God made me to show His goodness and to be happy with Him forever in Heaven (CCC 293–94).

Q. 11 *Who were the first man and the first woman?*
The first man was Adam and the first woman was Eve (CCC 369, 375).

25

Reinforce

1. Have the students complete *Activity Book*, p. 15.

2. Have them work on memorizing Questions 10 and 11.

3. Have them look up all the Words to Know in the glossary and memorize them.

4. Have the students begin to memorize the Guardian Angel Prayer.

Conclude

1. Sing "All people that on earth do dwell," *Adoremus Hymnal*, #622.

2. Learn and pray the Guardian Angel Prayer.

Preview

In the next lesson, we will review the material covered in this chapter.

NINE CHOIRS OF ANGELS

In order from greatest to least:

- Seraphim
- Cherubim
- Thrones
- Dominions
- Virtues
- Powers
- Principalities
- Archangels
- Guardian Angels

You may want to show "My Secret Friend: A Guardian Angel Story," CCC of America, available through Ignatius Press; 30 minutes.

NOTES

CHAPTER FOUR:
REVIEW AND ASSESSMENT

Aims

The students' understanding of the material covered this week will be reviewed and assessed.

Materials

- Quiz 4 (Appendix, p. A-4.)
- Unit 1 Test (Appendix, pp. A-5 and A-6.)
- "All people that on earth do dwell," *Adoremus Hymnal*, #622

Review

1. Have the students recount the story of the Creation of Adam and Eve, remembering:
   - God created out of love.
   - The first man is Adam, the first woman is Eve.
   - God created Adam first and Eve from the rib of Adam.
   - Adam and Eve were happy together, helped each other, and loved each other.

2. They should be able to recount the gifts Adam and Eve shared in the beginning:
   - They were happy
   - They were not afraid of the animals
   - They did not get sick or hurt
   - They would not die
   - They did not want to do anything bad
   - They did not need to go to school
   - They had all the food they needed
   - God walked and talked with them
   - Adam and Eve shared God's life, called grace

3. They should know that God made all people in His own image. All people have rational souls and are made to know, love, and serve God, so that they can live forever with Him in Heaven.

4. God gave all of us a guardian angel to help us to know, love, and serve Him and to help us prepare for Heaven. Angels are pure spirits.

Name:

God Made Us **Quiz 4**

Fill in the blanks *You may find clues by unscrambling the words in the word bank..*

GUARDIAN ANGEL	GRACE	IMAGE OF GOD	GARDEN OF EDEN

1. God made Adam and Eve, and they lived in the Garden of Eden.
2. Adam and Eve had a gift called grace.
3. We are all made in the image of God.
4. God gave us a special friend to help us to know, love and serve God. This friend is our guardian angel.

Write three ways you can know God.

1. Answers will vary
2.
3.

Write three ways you can love God.

1.
2.
3.

Write three ways you can serve God.

1.
2.
3.

A - 4 *Faith and Life • Grade 2 • Appendix A*

Assess

Distribute Quiz 4 and read through it with the students, answering any questions that they may have. As they turn in their quizzes, test them on this chapter's Memorization Questions, Words to Know, and Guardian Angel Prayer. After all the students have handed in their quizzes and their tests, you may wish to review the correct answers.

Conclude

1. End the class with the children singing "All people that on earth do dwell," *Adoremus Hymnal*, #622.

2. Pray the Guardian Angel prayer.

CHAPTER FIVE
GOD IS OFFENDED

Catechism of the Catholic Church References

Angels: 328–36, 350–52
Intelligent and Free: 331
In Heaven: 326, 1023
Consequences of Original Sin: 55–58, 399–409, 416–19
Differences of Mortal and Venial Sin: 1854
Fall of Man: 385–90, 413
Fall of the Angels: 391–95, 414
Grace: 1996–2005, 2021–24
Heaven: 1023–29, 1053
Hell: 1033–37, 1056–57
Justification through Jesus' Death: 421, 615, 1708
Man in Paradise: 374–79, 384
Man's Freedom: 1730–48
Mortal Sin: 1855–59, 1860, 1874
Original Sin: 388–90, 396–401, 415
Consequences: 405, 953, 1008, 1505, 1865
Promise of a Redeemer: 410–12, 420–21
Reality of Sin: 386–87, 413
Teaching of Original Sin: 387
Transmission of Original Sin to All Men: 404
Venial Sin: 1855, 1875, 1863

Scripture References

The Test: Gen 2:16–17; Ps 91:10–12

The Fall: Gen 3; Rev 12:7–10

Background Reading: *The Fundamentals of Catholicism* by Fr. Kenneth Baker, S.J.

Volume 2:
"The Angels Were Tested Too," pp. 181–84
"The Sin of Our First Parents," pp. 159–62

Summary of Lesson Content

Lesson 1

Angels are created pure spirits.

Angels are intelligent and free.

The fallen angels are called "devils." Fallen angels chose to not serve God and were sent to hell.

The good angels that serve God are with God and minister to His work on earth.

Lesson 2

God tested Adam and Eve.

Their test was to not eat of the fruit of the Tree of Knowledge of Good and Evil.

Lesson 3

In the beginning, Adam and Eve were obedient to God.

Eve was tempted by the devil, who was disguised as a serpent. She was tempted to disobey God by eating the forbidden fruit.

Eve gave the fruit to Adam, and he ate the fruit, too.

Lesson 4

Making the choice to disobey God is a sin.

Adam and Eve's sin caused the loss of original justice and grace for all mankind. Without grace, man cannot go to Heaven.

Though Adam and Eve sinned, God stilled loved them and promised to send a Savior Who would still make it possible for man to go to Heaven to live with God.

LESSON ONE: GOD CREATED ANGELS

Aims

The students will learn that God created angels: intelligent, free, pure spirits.

They will learn of the fall of the angels.

They will know that the good angels that serve God are with God and minister to His work on earth.

Materials

- Image of Saint Michael (text, holy cards or medals)
- *Activity Book*, p. 15

Optional:
- "Come, thou long expected Jesus," *Adoremus Hymnal*, #310

Begin

Begin the class by gathering the students and asking them to name things that we know exist, though we cannot see or touch them. You may need to give them examples, such as air, sunlight, types of gas, heat, cold, or smells, such as the scent of a flower. Ask the children if these things are real. Yes. Can they see them? No. Can they be touched? No.

Tell the children that God also created angels, who are real, but cannot be seen or touched. We will learn about them today.

Develop

1. Open to the picture on p. 26 in the textbook. Ask the children if they know who this is. Some may know about Saint Michael already. Ask them what is happening in this picture. You may guide them with these questions:
   - Who is the main figure in this picture? Why does he have wings? (Saint Michael, he is an angel.)
   - Who or what is he stepping on? (The devil) How do we know? (He is ugly, his wings are like a bat, he looks bad).
   - What are they doing? Dancing? (No. They are fighting).
   - Why are they fighting? (We don't know, but we will learn a bit about this today).
   - One last question, can we see the angels and devils? (No. They do not have bodies).

2. Read the first three paragraphs from the text. Question the children on the content. Be sure they understand that angels are creatures. They are pure spirits without bodies. They are intelligent and free creatures. They are often depicted like humans with wings because they are smart and because they are messengers that can move quickly.

3. Discuss the test and fall of the angels. Be sure that the children understand that devils are bad angels. The devils were sent to hell, and angels serve God faithfully in Heaven. Let the students know that we, too, can choose to be bad or good and that we should choose to be good like the angels. You may have them think of examples of choosing to be bad or good.

4. Teach the students about Saint Michael. You may read from Rev 12:7–10. Teach them the Saint Michael the Archangel prayer and explain that Saint Michael can help us to choose to serve God and protect us from those who want us to not serve God. You may give the students prayer cards or medals if you have them. If possible, have a priest come in and bless them.

Name:____________________

Saint Michael, the Archangel, defend us in the battle; be our protection against the wickedness and snares of the devil; may God rebuke him, we humbly pray, and do thou, O Prince of the Heavenly host, by the power of God, cast into hell Satan and all the evil spirits who wander about the world seeking the ruin of souls. *Amen.*

This week, before bed, pray the Saint Michael Prayer. Put a check in the box each day you pray.

Monday	Tuesday	Wednesday	Thursday	Friday	Saturday	Sunday

Faith and Life Series • Grade 2 • Chapter 5 • Lesson 1 15

Reinforce

1. Have the students color *Activity Book*, p. 15 and work on memorizing the prayer.

2. They should start memorizing Question 12, p. 29, as well as the Words to Know: angels, devils, obey.

3. You may begin teaching the students the song for this chapter: "Come, thou long expected Jesus," *Adoremus Hymnal*, #310.

Conclude

1. Time permitting, have the students act out the fall of the angels.

2. Lead them in praying the Saint Michael prayer, with the Sign of the Cross (our powerful weapon).

Preview

In the next lesson, the students will learn about the test of Adam and Eve.

POPE LEO XIII AND THE SAINT MICHAEL PRAYER

Pope Leo XIII realized the extent of the bad angels' influence in the modern world, as well as the power of the good angels to battle against them. So he wrote a prayer to the greatest of angels, Saint Michael, who threw Lucifer and his angels into Hell:

Saint Michael the Archangel, defend us in battle, be our protection against the wickedness and snares of the devil; may God rebuke him, we humbly pray; and do thou, O Prince of the Heavenly host, by the power of God, cast into hell Satan and all the evil spirits who wander about the world seeking the ruin of souls. *Amen.*

NOTES

____

____

____

____

____

____

____

____

____

____

LESSON TWO: THE TEST

Aims

The students will learn that God tested Adam and Eve.

They will learn that Adam and Eve's test was to not eat of the fruit of the Tree of Knowledge of Good and Evil.

Materials

- Treats (food) for every student in the class
- Children's Bible (Gen 2:16–18)
- *Activity Book*, p. 16

Optional:
- "Come, thou long expected Jesus," *Adoremus Hymnal*, #310

Begin

Tell the students that you will give them some treats but that you want them to obey you. Tell them that they are not to eat the treats. Be sure these treats are not individually wrapped, so it may be tempting to taste them, nibble them, or eat them when no one is looking. Distribute the treat.

5 God Is Offended

> Then the LORD God said to the woman, "What is this that you have done?" The woman said, "The serpent beguiled me, and I ate."
>
> Genesis 3:13

God created the **angels**. Angels do not have bodies like us. They are spirits. Angels are much smarter and stronger than we are. We draw angels to look like people because they can think like us. We draw them with wings because angels can go anywhere as quickly as they wish to.

God made the angels to be happy with Him in Heaven and to be His helpers. But first He tested them to see if they loved Him. Some of the angels did not love God. They did not obey Him. They became **devils**. They were sent to Hell.

The good angels went to Heaven to praise God and to do His work on earth.

God also wanted to see if Adam and Eve loved Him. He gave them a test, too. He told Adam and

27

Develop

1. Begin by reading from the text, paragraph 4. Reinforce the exact command of God by reading it from the children's Bible: Gen 2:16–18.

2. Ask the students why God wanted to test Adam and Eve?
   - To see if they would obey Him
   - To see if they would be faithful
   - To see if they loved Him
   - To see whom they would serve: God or themselves
   - To make Adam and Eve stronger

3. Why did God forbid Adam and Eve from eating from the Tree of Knowledge of Good and Evil? This was their test. What was special about the fruit?

4. Was it unfair of God to tell Adam and Eve that they could not eat from this tree? No, He gave them every other tree from which to eat. It was only this one from which they could not eat. Also, God is the Lord, the Creator; He makes the rules for our own good and safety. Ask the students if their parents have household rules for their own good and safety (e.g., don't play with matches, don't talk to strangers, don't tell people on the telephone that you're alone, etc.).

5. Explain to the students that very often we are tested, too. We can say "yes" or "no" to God by what we say, do, or don't do. Ask the students to think of examples when they can say yes or no to God. They may remember the Ten Commandments, they may think of very practical examples. You may discuss why their actions may say yes or no to God. Have every student think of at least one example.

6. If the children have eaten their treats, remind them how hard it was to not eat them and obey your command. Tell the students the game is over, and they may eat them.

Name:_______________

We can say Yes or No to God through words, actions, and even through things we don't do at all.

Circle your answers to these questions.

1. You ask your mother if you may go out and play with a friend. She says No. Do you go and ask your Father? YES NO
2. Your two best friends are fighting. Do you stay out of it and hope they will make peace without your help? YES NO
3. Someone in your class forgot his lunch. Do you share yours? YES NO
4. Your brother or sister has been bothering you all week. You receive two cookies. Do you share them with him or her? YES NO
5. You break a rule at home. Do you lie about it? YES NO
6. A friend has hurt your feelings. Do you call him a bad name? YES NO

16 *Faith and Life Series • Grade 2 • Chapter 5 • Lesson 2*

PRAYER TO MY GUARDIAN ANGEL

Angel of God, my guardian dear,
To whom God's love commits me here,
Ever this day be at my side,
To light and guard, to rule and guide.
Amen.

Reinforce

1. Have the students complete *Activity Book*, p. 16.

2. Review the answers, and discuss why there are ways of saying "yes" or "no" to God. If there are ways of saying "no" have them come up with ways to say "yes" to God.

Conclude

1. Lead the students in singing "Come, thou long expected Jesus," *Adoremus Hymnal*, #310.

2. Together, pray the Saint Michael and Guardian Angel prayers.

Preview

In the next lesson, the students will learn about the fall of Adam and Eve.

PSALM 91:10–12

". . . No evil shall befall you, no scourge come near your tent. For he will give his angels charge of you to guard you in all your ways. On their hands they will bear you up, lest you dash your foot against a stone."

NOTES

LESSON THREE: THE FALL

Aims

The students will learn about the fall of Adam and Eve.

Materials

- Children's Bible: Gen 3:1–6
- *Activity Book*, p. 18
- Appendix, p. B-9

Optional:
- "Come, thou long expected Jesus," *Adoremus Hymnal*, #310

Begin

Review with the children by asking the following questions: "Why did God make Adam and Eve?" "What special gifts did they have?" "What was the most important gift that God gave them?" "What did this do for them?"

You may itemize Adam and Eve's gifts before Original Sin on the board:
- No death, sickness or suffering
- No work or school
- They all got along, even with the animals
- Grace and Heaven

Eve not to eat the fruit from one of the trees in the garden. It was called the tree of knowledge of good and evil. They could have all they wanted from the other trees. God also said that if they ate from that one tree, they would die.

At first, Adam and Eve **obeyed** God. Then, one day Eve was alone in the garden. She met a snake. She did not know it, but it was really the devil.

"Eve," said the snake, "why don't you and Adam eat the fruit from this one tree?"

"God said not to," said Eve. "He said we would die if we ate of its fruit, or even touched it."

"That is not true," said the snake. "If you eat this fruit you will be like God. You will know all things."

Eve should have known better than to think that God would lie to her. But she listened to the devil and ate the fruit. Then she told Adam, and he ate it too.

Because they disobeyed God, Adam and Eve had to leave the Garden of Eden. They had to work hard to get food to eat. The animals were now afraid of them.

Adam and Eve **offended** God. They sinned. Their **sin** took away the special gift of grace that God gave them. Without God's life in their souls, Adam and Eve could not please God. They could not go to Heaven.

28

Develop

1. Together, read from the textbook, paragraphs 5–9 (stop before: "Because they disobeyed God . . .").

2. You may reinforce this reading by reading/acting out the same story from the children's Bible (Gen 3:1–6). The children may make a puppet-show for the story of the fall, using Appendix, p. B-9.

3. Remind them how hard it was to not eat their treats during the previous lesson. Adam and Eve felt the same temptation. The snake, who was really the devil, made them think it was okay to eat the forbidden fruit, even though it was not.

4. Ask them why it was wrong to eat the fruit. Because they would disobey God. Ask the students why Adam and Eve might have eaten the fruit. Were they hungry? Was it because they wanted to be mean to God? Were they tricked? Was it an accident? Do they have any ideas why? Adam and Eve were proud.

5. Ask the children if disobeying God is something serious. Yes, He is God, and we are His creatures. We owe Him respect and obedience. Ask the students if Adam and Eve knew this was serious. Yes, they were told they would die! Ask the students if Adam and Eve chose to eat the fruit. Yes, the snake/devil did not force them to eat the fruit. (This is important because the students will soon learn the elements of mortal sin.)

6. Ask the students how Adam and Eve were like the angels. They were both put to the test. They both had to decide if they would obey God. Just as some of the angels decided to disobey, so did Adam and Eve decide to disobey God. Be sure the students understand this parallel.

Name:__________________

Can you fill in the blanks? Use your textbook for help.

God loved Adam and Eve very much. He gave them a special gift called grace.

Grace is a share in God's own life. With grace in their souls, Adam and Eve became God's children. Because of grace, Adam and Eve would someday be able to live with God in Heaven. Today, God offers us the same gift He gave Adam and Eve. We receive God's grace in the Sacrament of Baptism. God wants us to be His children and to be happy with Him in Heaven.

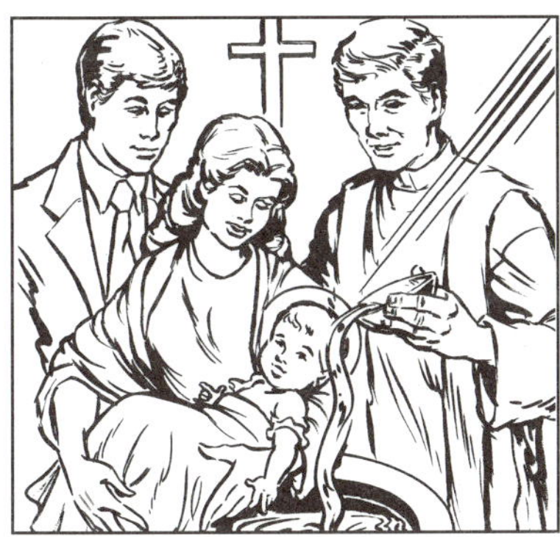

18 *Faith and Life Series • Grade 2 • Chapter 5 • Lesson 3*

VIRTUE OF OBEDIENCE
In the *Catechism of the Catholic Church*

"The duty of obedience requires all to give due honor to authority and to treat those who are charged to exercise it with respect, and, insofar as it is deserved, with gratitude and good-will" (1900).

"To obey (from the Latin *ob-audire*, to "hear or listen to") in faith is to submit freely to the word that has been heard, because its truth is guaranteed by God, who is Truth itself. Abraham is the model of such obedience offered us by Sacred Scripture. The Virgin Mary is its most perfect embodiment" (144).

Reinforce

1. Have the students complete *Activity Book*, p. 18. You may wish to review the answers.

2. Have the students start memorizing Questions 13 and 14, pp. 29 and 30, as well as the Words to Know: sin and offend.

Conclude

1. Lead the children in singing "Come, thou long expected Jesus," *Adoremus Hymnal*, #310.

2. End by praying the Saint Michael and Guardian Angel prayers.

Preview

In the next lesson, the students will learn about the consequences of Adam and Eve's sin.

DEFINITION OF OBEDIENT

To be obedient is to be someone who does what he is told to do by those with legitimate authority over him.

NOTES

LESSON FOUR: THE EFFECTS OF SIN

Aims

The students will learn the definition of sin.

They will learn that sin caused the loss of original justice and grace for all mankind. Without grace, man cannot go to Heaven.

They will understand that even though Adam and Eve sinned, God still loved them and promised to send a Savior.

Materials

- Balloon
- Pin
- Children's Bible: Gen 3:8–24
- *Activity Book*, p. 19

Optional:
- "Come, thou long expected Jesus," *Adoremus Hymnal*, #310

Begin

Gather the students and inflate a balloon. Do not tie it and hold it so it stays inflated. Ask the children to imagine that this balloon is a soul full of grace like what Adam and Eve had when they lived in the Garden of Eden. Next deflate the balloon and poke a hole through the balloon with a pin. Explain that the pin is like sin, it hurts the soul. Then try to reinflate the balloon. Explain that no matter what Adam and Eve did they could not get grace back in their souls. This damage is the effect of Original Sin.

We call this first sin of Adam and Eve **Original Sin.**

God still loved Adam and Eve even though they had sinned. So He promised to send someone who would save them and make it possible for them to go to Heaven someday.

Words to Know:

angels devils obey
offend sin Original Sin

Q. 12 *What are angels?*
Angels are created spirits without bodies. They are servants and messengers for God (CCC 328, 329).

Q. 13 *What is sin?*
Sin is disobedience to God's law (CCC 1849–50).

29

Develop

1. Finish reading the text from this chapter (paragraphs 10–13).

2. Review with the students the gifts Adam and Eve had in the Garden of Eden before the fall. These gifts were reviewed in the Begin section of the previous lesson. Write them on the chalkboard.

3. Ask them to list the effects of Original Sin. Write these on the board beside the list of gifts to make a chart (see Chalk Talk on opposite page).

4. Ask them to review the effects of Original Sin in practical ways to be sure they understand. You may ask: "Before the fall, would Adam catch a cold?" "After the fall, could Adam and Eve go to Heaven?" "Before the fall, could dogs eat cats?" "After the fall, could Adam play with a tiger?", etc.

5. Explain that the first sin of Adam and Eve, Original Sin, is passed on to all people because Adam and Eve are our first parents. We are all born with Original Sin on our souls, and we have no grace. We cannot do anything for ourselves to put grace in our souls (like the balloon from the Begin section).

6. Reread the last paragraph. God promised to send a Savior. Jesus is the Savior. He died on the Cross for our sins, so we can have grace and go to Heaven. Review words to the song "Come, thou long expected Jesus," *Adoremus Hymnal*, #310. Let the children know that Jesus saves us from sin and saves us for Himself in Heaven.

Q. 14 *Who committed the first sin on earth?*
Our first parents, Adam and Eve, committed the first sin on earth (CCC 390).

Q. 15 *What is this first sin in us called?*
This sin in us is called Original Sin (CCC 388–89).

"Now therefore, if you will obey my voice and keep my covenant, you shall be my own possession among all peoples."

Exodus 19:5

30

Reinforce

1. Have the students complete the chart on *Activity Book*, p. 19, and review the answers.

2. Give the children time to memorize Questions 12–15, and all the Words to Know for this chapter.

Conclude

1. Sing "Come, thou long expected Jesus," *Adoremus Hymnal*, #310.

2. End by praying the Saint Michael and Guardian Angel prayers.

Preview

In the next lesson, the students will review the material covered in this chapter.

POPE LEO XIII

Leo XIII, author of the Saint Michael Prayer, was born on March 2, 1810; elected Pope on February 20, 1878; and died in Rome on July 20, 1903.

CHALK TALK: BEFORE AND AFTER ORIGINAL SIN

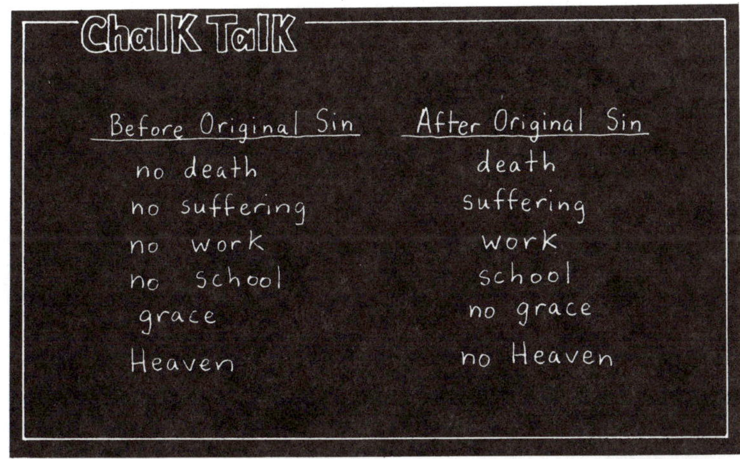

NOTES

CHAPTER FIVE:
REVIEW AND ASSESSMENT

Aims

The students' understanding of the material covered this week will be reviewed and assessed.

Materials

- Quiz 5 (Appendix, p. A-7)
- "Come, thou long expected Jesus," *Adoremus Hymnal*, #310

Review

Review with the children that angels:

- Are creatures of God
- Are pure spirits (no bodies)
- Are intelligent
- Have free will

Review the fall of the angels:

- Good angels serve God in Heaven
- Bad angels (devils) were sent to hell

Review the test of Adam and Eve:

- The forbidden fruit
- The snake (devil in disguise)
- Components of sin: acting wrongly when we know that our actions are wrong

Review the effects of Original Sin:

- Death and suffering
- Work/school
- Man and animals no longer friends
- Loss of grace
- Loss of Heaven

Review that God promised to send a Savior

- This savior would make it possible for man to go to Heaven.

Name:

God Is Offended **Quiz 5**

Matching

Angels	God made him and called him Adam.
Man	Creatures that are pure spirits, which serve God.
Woman	God made her to love and help Adam.
Devils	Creator of Heaven and earth.
God	Creatures that did not obey God and were sent to hell.

Place these events in the right order. Put a 1 beside what happened first, a 2 beside what happened next, and a 3 by what happened last.

3 A snake told Eve to eat the forbidden fruit.
1 Some angels did not obey God and were sent to hell.
2 God told Adam and Eve not to eat of a tree in the garden.

Put a 4 by what happened next, a 5 by what happened next, and a 6 by what happened last.

2 Adam and Eve had to leave the Garden of Eden.
1 Eve ate the fruit and gave it to Adam to eat.
3 God promised to send a Savior.

True or False:

T F Adam and Eve knew it was wrong to disobey God.
T F Adam and Eve knew it was wrong to disobey God.
T F Adam and Eve chose to disobey God.

Faith and Life • Grade 2 • Appendix A A - 7

Assess

1. Distribute Quiz 5 and answer any questions that the students may have. As the children hand in their quizzes, individually quiz them on the Memorization Questions, Words to Know, and the Saint Michael and Guardian Angel prayers.

2. After all the quizzes are handed in, review the correct answers.

Conclude

1. Sing "Come, thou long expected Jesus," *Adoremus Hymnal*, #310.

2. Pray the Saint Michael and Guardian Angel prayers.

CHAPTER SIX
BECOMING A CHILD OF GOD

Catechism of the Catholic Church References

Baptism: 1213–16, 1276
- Administration and Reception: 903, 1246, 1256, 1272, 1284
- Christian Initiation: 1212, 1275, 1425, 1533
- Effects: 167–70, 683, 803, 1272–74, 1279–80
- Indelible Mark on Soul: 698, 1121
- Rite: 189, 1239–40, 1278
- (and) Sin: 405, 977–78, 985, 1263, 2520

Baptism in the Church: 1226–28
Baptism: First Sacrament of Forgiveness of Sins: 977–78
Christian Holiness: 2021–26, 2028–29
Church as a People of God: 781–86, 802–4
Communion of Saints: 946–62
Consequences of Original Sin: 55–58, 399–409, 416–19
Grace: 1996–2005, 2021–24
Grace of Baptism: 265, 1262–74, 1279–80
Heaven: 1023–29, 1053
Indwelling of the Trinity: 257–60
Original Sin: 388–90, 396–401, 415
Sacraments of Christian Initiation: 1212, 1275
Saints as Companions in Prayer: 2683–84, 2692–93
Saints as Patrons: 2156

Scripture References

Baptism: John 3

Background Reading: *The Fundamentals of Catholicism* by Fr. Kenneth Baker, S.J.

Volume 2:
"The Transmission of Original Sin," pp. 162–65

Summary of Lesson Content

Lesson 1

Adam and Eve lost God's life (grace) and the ability to go to Heaven because of Original Sin.

Their Original Sin is passed on to all men, as they are our first parents. We are all born with Original Sin and do not have grace in our souls.

Lesson 2

At Baptism, Original Sin is washed away and grace is infused into the soul.

Baptism makes it possible for us to go to Heaven.

At Baptism, we are born into God's family, the Church.

At Baptism, the Trinity comes to live in our souls; this is the life of God, grace.

Lesson 3

Man must try to keep his soul free from sin and filled with grace.

Grace is necessary to go to Heaven.

Lesson 4

Most Catholics are given a saint's name, a patron saint.

Saints are those honored for serving God faithfully in this life. They are united with God forever in Heaven.

LESSON ONE: OUR NEED FOR BAPTISM

Aims

The children will review that Adam and Eve lost God's life (grace) and the ability to go to Heaven by their sin.

They will learn that, as Adam and Eve are our first parents, Original Sin is passed on to all men. Therefore, we are all born with Original Sin and do not have grace in our souls.

Materials

- *Activity Book*, p. 20
- Paper, pencils, crayons

Optional:
- "Sing praise to our Creator," *Adoremus Hymnal*, #500

Begin

Review with the children the effects of Original Sin:
- Pain and suffering
- Death
- Work/study
- Man and animals wouldn't get along
- Loss of grace
- Man could not go to Heaven

6 Becoming a Child of God

Jesus answered him, "Truly, truly, I say to you, unless one is born of water and the Spirit, he cannot enter the kingdom of God."

John 3:5

When Adam and Eve sinned, they lost the gift of God's life in their souls, called grace. They could not get to Heaven. Their children were born with Original Sin, too. They had no grace in their souls.

We call Adam and Eve our first parents because all people came from them. So do you. We were all born with Original Sin on our souls.

At **Baptism**, Original Sin was washed away, and your soul was filled with God's life of grace. Now you are able to go to Heaven and be with God.

Baptism is like being born again. The first time we were born into the family of our mothers and fathers. At Baptism we are born into God's family, the Church. Then the Blessed Trinity comes to live in us.

31

Develop

1. *Discuss with the students the importance of grace. It is God's life in our souls. Grace is what allows us to live forever with God in Heaven.*

2. Have them read the first two or three paragraphs of the chapter.

3. Ask one student to name his parents, then his grandparents, then his great-grandparents, as far back as he knows. Ask him, if he goes far enough back, who were his first parents: Adam and Eve. You may want to do this with a few students, all of them coming to realize that their first parents were Adam and Eve.

4. Ask them if they have inherited any qualities or features from their parents, e.g., blue eyes, same smile, same humor, same interests, etc. Explain that they also inherited Original Sin from their first parents, Adam and Eve. We all have inherited this trait. We are "damaged goods." Because of their Original Sin, we all can experience the effects of pain and suffering, death, having to work/study, not being able to talk with tigers and elephants, being born without grace and with Original Sin. In these ways, we are like our first parents.

5. Have the students imagine what it would be like if they lived in the Garden of Eden, what they would do if they were tempted by the devil. How would they feel if they ate the forbidden fruit and had to leave the Garden of Eden? They would be sad. They would want God's gifts back. Remind them that God promised a Savior who would open the gates of Heaven.

6. Read from the Bible the account of Jesus' Baptism (John 5). They can dramatize this reading.

Name:__________________

Baptism

grace	first	Adam	Baptism
Original Sin	Eve	washed	
souls	Heaven	God	

Fill in the blanks with the words above.

When Adam and Eve sinned, they lost the gift of God's grace in their souls. They could not get to Heaven. Their children were born with Original Sin, too. They had no grace in their souls.

We call Adam and Eve our first parents because all people came from them. So did you. And we were all born with Original Sin on our souls.

At Baptism, Original Sin was washed away, and your soul was filled with God's life of grace. Now you are able to go to Heaven and be with God.

20 *Faith and Life Series • Grade 2 • Chapter 6 • Lesson 1*

Reinforce

1. Have the students fold a piece of drawing paper in half. On one side, draw a picture of Adam and Eve, and on the other side, have them draw themselves. In the pictures, have them draw the effects of sin.

2. Have the students complete *Activity Book,* p. 20.

3. Teach and lead the students in singing: "Sing praise to our Creator," *Adoremus Hymnal*, #500.

Conclude

Lead the students in praying the Our Father and Glory Be.

Preview

In the next lesson, the students will learn about the gift of Baptism.

THE LAST OLD TESTAMENT PROPHET

Write the letters of the word PROPHET vertically on the chalkboard. After each letter, write the following or similar phrases that explain the job and purpose of a prophet. How was John the Baptist a model of each trait?

P - Prepared people for the Savior
R - Reminded people of God's love for them
O - Obeyed God by telling the people what He told them
P - Proclaimed future events
H - Helped people get ready for the Savior
E - Ended with Saint John the Baptist
T - Told people what God wanted them to do

NOTES

LESSON TWO: EFFECTS OF BAPTISM

Aims

The students will understand that Baptism washes away Original Sin and infuses the soul with grace.

They will know that Baptism makes it possible for us to go to Heaven because we receive grace.

At Baptism, we are born into God's family, the Church.

Materials

- Appendix, pp. B-10–B-15
- White garment, candle, oil (Chrism and Oil of Catechumens), water and something from which to pour it, a basin, doll, rite book
- *Activity Book*, p. 21

Optional:

- "Sing praise to our Creator," *Adoremus Hymnal*, #500
- Invite a priest to demonstrate Baptism

Begin

Gather the children and together read paragraphs 3 and 4 from the textbook. Explain that Baptism is a very important sacrament because it washes away Original Sin, gives us grace, and makes us members of God's Family, the Church. Today the children will learn what happens at a Baptism.

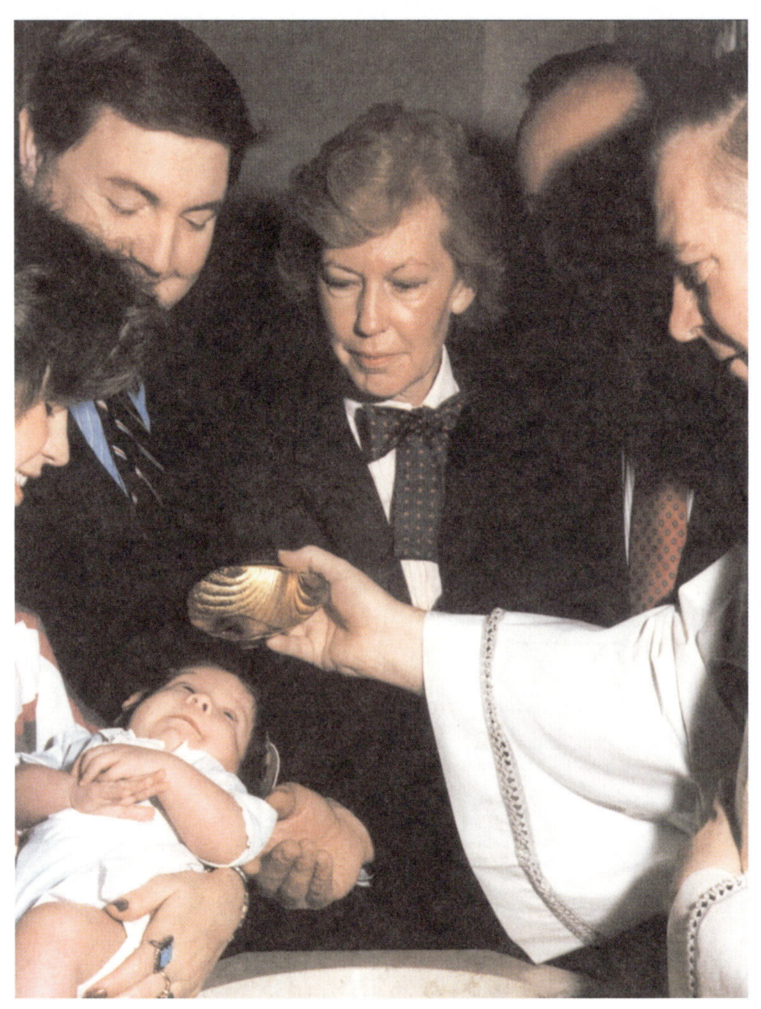

Develop

1. Explain each of the symbols used in Baptism:

- *White garment: a sign of purity, the cleanliness of our souls, and of becoming a new creation in Christ.*
- *Candle: a sign of Christ, Who is the Light of the World. In Baptism, He gives us His grace, which He won for us on the Cross.*
- *Oil: a sign of prophets, priests, and kings. We share in these ministries, which belong to Christ. We are prophets as we speak the truth, priests because we worship God, and kings because we will inherit the kingdom of Heaven. Oil is also a sign of strength and life.*
- *Water: a sign of death and life. In Baptism, we die with Christ on the Cross and share in His life, the Resurrection.*

2. Explain that each sacrament is a sign of Christ working in our lives. Sacraments show us what God is doing to our soul because we cannot see what He is doing to our soul. For example, water is used to show that Original Sin is washed away, and it reminds us that we die and rise with Christ.

3. Explain that each sacrament has matter (the stuff used) and form (the words said). In Baptism, the matter is water being poured or into which the person is immersed in three times. The form is the baptismal formula: "I baptize you in the Name of the Father and of the Son and of the Holy Spirit."

4. Explain that the normal minister is a priest or deacon. However, in case of an emergency, anyone can baptize someone if he has water and says the correct words, intending the Baptism of the other.

5. If possible, have a priest come in for this demonstration and assign the different roles. There is a script provided on Appendix, pp. B-10–B-15. You may make copies of this script so the students can follow along and then play different roles.

Name:__________________

Can you answer these questions?

1. What are angels?
Angels do not have bodies. They are spirits who are much smarter and stronger than we are.

2. What is sin?
Any wrong that we do. Sin takes away God's grace.

3. Who committed the first sin on earth?
Adam and Eve

4. What is this sin called in us?
Original Sin

5. What is Baptism?
It is like being born again. It takes away Original Sin.

6. What did Baptism do for you?
It took away Original Sin and made me a member of God's Church.

Faith and Life Series • Grade 2 • Chapter 6 • Lesson 2 21

Reinforce

1. Upon completion of the Baptismal Rite, review the matter, form, and minister of Baptism. Also review the symbols involved in the rite.

2. Have the students complete *Activity Book*, p. 21.

3. Have the students memorize the Baptismal formula, and start memorizing Questions 16 and 17 and the Words to Know.

Conclude

1. Together, sing "Sing praise to our Creator," *Adoremus Hymnal*, #500.

2. End by praying the Our Father and the Glory Be.

Preview

In the next lesson, the students will learn their responsibilities as baptized children of God.

SAINTS TO INVOKE FOR:

- Diseases of the Throat: Saint Blaise (February 3)
- Diseases of the Tongue: Saint Catherine (November 25)

ORIGINAL SIN AND BAPTISM

The Sacrament of Baptism, which is one of the sacraments of Christian initiation, washes away Original Sin, and any personal sin if a person is baptized after he has reached the age of reason. The Catholic Church recognizes the validity of Protestant baptism because this idea of one baptism for all is found in Scripture.

"Baptism is necessary for salvation for those to whom the Gospel has been proclaimed and who have had the possibility of asking for this sacrament... *God has bound salvation to the sacrament of Baptism, but he himself is not bound by his sacraments," Catechism of the Catholic Church*, #1257.

NOTES

LESSON THREE: BEING A CHILD OF GOD

Aims

The students will understand their responsibilities as baptized children of God.

They will know that they must try to keep their souls free from sin and filled with grace, so they may go to Heaven.

Materials

- *Activity Book*, p. 22

Optional:
- "Sing praise to our Creator," *Adoremus Hymnal*, #500

Begin

Review what they did in the previous lesson with the dramatization of Baptism:
- The matter and form
- The minister
- The symbols of water, candle, oil, garment
- Effects of washing away sin, being filled with grace.

We should try to keep our souls free from sin and filled with grace, like they were on the day of our Baptism. We should ask God to help us so we don't offend Him. If we keep God's life in our souls we will one day live with Him in Heaven.

What are some things we can do to keep our souls holy and pleasing to God?

First, we should pray. Thank God each day for making you His child. Talk to Him about the things that are on your mind. He is your friend.

Second, try to do the things God wants you to do. God wants you to love everyone. He wants you to obey your mother and father, even when you don't like what they tell you. God wants you to tell the truth.

Does that sound hard? Ask God and your guardian angel to help you to be good. Remember this: as long as you do no wrong, God wants you to have fun and enjoy the things He made for you!

"I baptize you in the Name of the Father, and of the Son, and of the Holy Spirit."

Words of Baptism

33

Develop

1. Read aloud paragraphs 5–9.

2. Have the children imagine how difficult it would be to keep a beautiful white outfit clean all the time. Would we be careful when we go to play and when we eat. Would we wash it regularly? We would have to work very hard at keeping it clean. But we would be so happy when people would say how impressivly clean the outfit was!

3. Remember that the white outfit is a sign of our souls, cleansed from sin and filled with grace, at Baptism. We must also work hard at keeping our souls clean from sin. We must be obedient to God, obey our parents, watch what we do and say (and do not do and say). If we sin, we must tell God we are sorry, and soon we will even be able to go to Confession to have our souls washed clean again.

4. Ask the students to name things they can do to keep their souls free from sin:
- *Keep the Ten Commandments*
- *Pray that God will help them to not offend Him*
- *Ask their guardian angels for help*
- *Read the Bible and learn our faith so we can learn what is right and wrong*
- *Love their neighbor and do good works*
- *Make sacrifices so they will not put other things before God*
- *Obey our Church leaders and those God places in authority over us*
- *Receive communion in a state of grace*

Have each student think of at least one way they can work at keeping their soul free from sin, and filled with grace.

Name:____________________

It is very important to try our best to keep our souls as clean as the day we were baptized. What are some things we can do to keep our souls holy and pleasing to God?

Answers will vary

22 *Faith and Life Series • Grade 2 • Chapter 6 • Lesson 3*

JESUS ON BEING BORN ANEW

"Truly, truly I say to you, unless one is born of water and the Spirit, he cannot enter the kingdom of God. That which is born of the flesh is flesh, and that which is born of the Spirit is spirit. Do not marvel that I said to you, 'You must be born anew.' The wind blows where it wills, and you hear the sound of it, but you do not know whence it comes or whither it goes; so it is with every one who is born of the Spirit."

John 3:5–8

Reinforce

1. Allow the students to perform skits showing how a child of God should act in various circumstances. (You may need to do this as charades with words, but have them draw out of a hat the various circumstances and who will play what role, e.g., a mother asks a child to help wash the dishes, or a priest asks a man to visit the sick.)

2. Have them complete *Activity Book*, p. 22.

3. Have them work on memorizing the questions, Words to Know, and the Baptismal formula.

Conclude

1. Sing "Sing praise to our Creator," *Adoremus Hymnal*, #500.

2. Together, pray the Our Father and the Glory Be.

Preview

In the next lesson, the students will learn about their patron saints.

NOTES

LESSON FOUR: PATRON SAINTS HELP US

Aims

The students will learn that most Catholics are given a saint's name, a patron saint.

They will know that saints are those honored for serving God faithfully in this life by being united with Him forever in Heaven.

Materials

- Children's saints books or pre-made fact sheets for your students on their patron saints.
- *Activity Book*, p. 23

Optional:

- Patron saint holy cards
- "Sing praise to our Creator," *Adoremus Hymnal*, #500

Begin

Review with the students the part of the Baptismal Rite in which the parents are asked for the name of the child. This name is the baptismal name. Catholics are usually named after saints. The saints are good examples for us and they pray for us. Today, the students will learn more about their patron saints.

Words to Know:

Baptism

Q. 16 *What is Baptism?*
Baptism is the sacrament that makes us Christians and adopted children of God (CCC 1262–65).

Q. 17 *What did Baptism do for you?*
Baptism washed away Original Sin from my soul and made it rich in the grace of God (CCC 1262–65).

Many Catholic children are given a saint's name. It may be your first name, or it may be your middle name. A saint is someone who lives with God in Heaven. A saint is someone who loved God very much while on earth.

Ask your parents or teacher about the saint whose name you have. Maybe they know a story about him or her. Ask your saint to help *you* to be a saint someday, too!

34

Develop

1. Read aloud the text on p. 34 of the textbook.

2. Explain to the students that all people in Heaven are saints. Some of those saints in Heaven have been recognized by the Church because of their good example, and the works they have done. These are the canonized saints, like Saint Francis or Saint Thérèse.

3. There are many, many patron saints. By "patron," we mean that a saint is given the care of something or someone. For example, Saint Joseph is the Patron of the Church. So, when we pray for the Church, we ask Saint Joseph to pray, too. We know that Saint Joseph has a special interest in the Church because he is its patron. There are many different types of patron saints: Saint Thérèse of missionaries; Saint Michael of the Armed Forces; Saint Blaise of sore throats; Saint Lucy of bad eyes; Saint Joan of Arc of France; and Saint Peregrin of people with cancer.

4. Help each of the students find information on his patron saint. (This may take some preparation.) If possible, give each child a prayer card of his patron saint. The students may present to the class their findings on their patron saint.

Name:____________________

Draw a picture of your patron saint or your favorite saint.

23 *Faith and Life Series • Grade 2 • Chapter 6 • Lesson 4*

Reinforce

1. Have the students complete investigating their patron saints.

2. Assign p. 23 of the *Activity Book*.

Conclude

1. Sing "Sing praise to our Creator," *Adoremus Hymnal*, #500.

2. Pray the Our Father and the Glory Be.

Preview

In the next lesson, we will review the material covered in this chapter.

PATRON SAINT OF MANY

Saint Giles, a noble Greek born in the late seventh century, is the patron of:

- The physically disabled
- Lepers
- Forests

His feast day is September 1.

SOME INTERESTING PATRON SAINTS

- Actors: Saint Vitus, M. (June 15)
- Archers: Saint Sebastian (January 20)
- Architects: Saint Barbara (December 4)
- Bakers: Saint Honorius (September 30)
- Barbers: Saint Cosmas (September 26)
- Boatmen: Saint Julian Hospitallor (January 9)

NOTES

CHAPTER SIX:
REVIEW AND ASSESSMENT

Aims

The students' understanding of the material covered this week will be reviewed and assessed.

Materials

• Quiz 6 (Appendix, p. A-8)

• "Sing praise to our Creator," *Adoremus Hymnal*, #500

Review

1. Review that they inherited Original Sin from their first parents, Adam and Eve.

2. Review the necessity of Baptism to go to Heaven for, in Baptism, Original Sin is washed away and our souls are filled with grace.

3. Review the Sacrament of Baptism:
   - Matter: water poured 3 times or immersion 3 times
   - Form: "I baptize you in the Name of the Father and of the Son and of the Holy Spirit"
   - Minister: usually a priest or deacon, but in an emergency, anyone can baptize
   - Symbols: white garment, oil, candle, water
   - Effects: Original Sin washed away, soul filled with grace
   - Responsibilities: Our souls must be kept free from sin and filled with grace (they should be able to think of practical ways this may be done)

Review who patron saints are. Each child should know his own.

Name:

Becoming a Child of God **Quiz 6**

Fill in the blanks *Use the words below to help you.*

Heaven	grace	sacrament	children	Baptism
family	Original Sin			

At Baptism, we become members of God's family. Baptism is a sacrament. It washes away Original Sin, and fills our soul with grace. It makes us children of God, and allows us to go to Heaven.

List two ways you should try to keep your soul free from sin and filled with grace.

1. pray, try to do the things God wants you to do
2. thank God, talk to Him

Write a little about your patron saint, or another saint.

Answers will vary

A - 8 *Faith and Life • Grade 2 • Appendix A*

Assess

1. Distribute Quiz 6 and read through it with the students, answering any questions that they may have. As they turn in their quizzes, individually quiz them (orally) on Questions 16 and 17, the Words to Know, and the Baptismal formula.

2. After the students have turned in their quizzes, review the correct answers.

Conclude

1. Lead the children in singing "Sing praise to our Creator," *Adoremus Hymnal*, #500.

2. End with praying the Our Father and Glory Be.

CHAPTER SEVEN
OBEYING GOD OUR FATHER

Catechism of the Catholic Church References

Abraham and the Prayer of Faith: 2570–72, 2592
Call of Abraham: 59–61, 72
Covenant with Noah: 56–58, 71
David and the Prayer of the King: 2578–80, 2594
Economy of Salvation: 51–67, 489, 1092, 1095, 1168
Faith of Abraham: 144–46, 165, 1080
God's Promise to Abraham: 705–6, 762
Jesus as Born into the Messianic Line of David: 437, 439, 559
Revelation of God's Plan of Salvation: 51–53, 68
Stages of Revelation: 54–55, 69–70

Scripture References

Noah: Gen 6—9:18
Abraham: Gen 12—22
David: 1 Sam 16—17, 2 Sam 6—7
Jer 17:7

Background Reading: *The Fundamentals of Catholicism* by Fr. Kenneth Baker, S.J.

Volume 2:
"Why Did God Become Man?" pp. 269–72

Summary of Lesson Content

Lesson 1

God promised to send Adam and Eve a Savior.

For many years, the people of God prepared for the coming of the Savior.

Because of Original Sin, many people became very sinful in their actions, forgetting about God's promise.

Lesson 2

Noah was called by God to build an ark in order to save His creation and Noah's family from the great flood.

Noah responded faithfully out of obedience to God.

In the flood, all that was evil was washed from the earth and new life came forth. This event prefigures Baptism.

Lesson 3

Abraham was called by God to be the Father of God's nation. Abraham and Sarah, his wife, were aged when Isaac, their son, was born.

God tested Abraham by asking him to sacrifice his beloved son. God stopped Abraham, who was ready to make this sacrifice, and blessed him for his obedient love.

Lesson 4

David was a simple shepherd called by God to become the king of His nation. David fought a giant named Goliath in order to save God's nation, then David became king.

Mary, Joseph, and Jesus are descendants (from the family) of David.

LESSON ONE: WAITING FOR A SAVIOR

Aims

The students will learn that God promised to send Adam and Eve a Savior. For many years, the people of God prepared for the coming of the Savior.

They will know that many people became very sinful in their actions, forgetting about God's promise.

Materials

- Children's Bible
- *Activity Book*, p. 24

Optional:
- "Savior of the nations, come," *Adoremus Hymnal*, #302
- "Adam and Eve," video; In the Beginning: Stories from the Bible

Begin

Review with the students that God promised Adam and Eve a Savior. However, no one knew when the Savior would come. Ask the students, what is the longest they have had to wait for something. It seems like waiting for Christmas to come takes forever! Sometimes waiting in line takes too long, or waiting for someone takes longer than you thought it would. Can the students imagine waiting their whole lives for something and not living to see it come? What about 5000 years? Wow. Now that is waiting!

7 Obeying God Our Father

"Blessed is the man who trusts in the LORD, whose trust is the LORD."

Jeremiah 17:7

God still loved Adam and Eve, even after they disobeyed Him. He promised to send a Savior to make up for their sin and bring the Sacrament of Baptism. Then Adam, Eve, and all people would have the chance to go to Heaven.

But God did not say when the Savior would come. The people had to wait many years before Jesus came. Many people became tired of being good. They forgot about God. Soon there was only one family that still loved God. It was the family of **Noah**. Do you know the story about Noah and the ark? God asked Noah to build an ark and put every kind of animal, male and female, inside of it. Noah and his family also entered the ark. Because of Noah's trust and obedience, God was able to save the goodness of creation. God washed away all that was bad and sinful from the earth in a flood.

35

Develop

1. Read paragraphs 1 and 2 (up to Noah) with the students.

2. You may read a sample of how people became bad, such as Cain and Abel (Gen 4:1–16) from a children's Bible. Ask the children what Cain did that was so bad. He killed his brother. What else did he do? He was jealous. He harbored anger. He spoke without respect to God. He tricked his brother into going into the field. He was deceitful.

3. Cain went on to have children, and his brother Seth also had children. They filled the earth, and their children became very bad. They did not listen to God and did not obey Him. Some even forgot about God. How ungrateful!

4. Did God still love all the people even though they sinned? How did God show he still loved Cain? He gave him a mark to protect him.

5. *Did God love all other people, too? Yes. Did God ever take away His promise to send a Savior? No. He loved all His people and wanted them to be saved. Does God even love us when we sin? Yes. In fact, He sent His Savior for each and every one of us. He would have sent His Savior even if there was just one of us. That is how much God loves us.*

6. Cain was a bad example of patience. What should he have done? God wants each of us to be saved, and sometimes we must wait to know God's will in our lives. God has a plan for each of us, so we must be patient and wait to know God's plan. We will be learning about some people for whom God had special plans. They helped God's people prepare for the coming of the Savior.

7. *Have the students think of ways in which they may have to wait to know God's plan for them to get to Heaven.*

Name:____________________

Draw Adam and Eve 1	Draw Noah and his Ark 2
Draw Abraham and Isaac 3	Draw David and Goliath 4

24 *Faith and Life Series • Grade 2 • Chapter 7 • Lessons 1–4*

Reinforce

1. Have the students complete the first box on *Activity Book*, p. 24.

2. If time permits, show the video "Adam and Eve," from the series In the Beginning: Stories from the Bible, available through Ignatius Press; 30 minutes.

3. Teach and sing with them, "Savior of the nations, come," *Adoremus Hymnal*, #302.

Conclude

End by praying the Our Father and the Glory Be.

Preview

In the next lesson, we will learn about Noah.

SAINTS TO INVOKE FOR:

- Diseases of the Eye:
  Saint Lucy (December 13)
  Saint Odilia (December 13)

- Sore Eyes:
  Saint Fara (December 7)

PATRON SAINTS FOR MANY

- Children: Saint Nicholas (December 6)
- Dogs: Saint Hubert (November 3)
- Eloquence: Saint Catherine (November 25)
- Fortifications: Saint Barbara (December 4)
- Gardens: Saint Phocas (September 22)
- Girls: Saint Ursula (October 21)
- Horses: Saint Eligius (December 1)

NOTES

LESSON TWO: GOD'S SERVANT, NOAH

Aims

The students will learn that Noah was called by God to build an ark in order to save His creation and Noah's family from the great flood.

They will learn that Noah responded faithfully out of obedience to God.

Materials

- Children's Bible
- *Activity Book*, pp. 24 and 26
- Appendix, pp. B-25–B-28

Optional:

- "Savior of the nations, come," *Adoremus Hymnal*, #302
- "Noah's Ark," video; In the Beginning: Stories from the Bible

Begin

Review with the students that the people of the world became impatient and bad while waiting for the Savior to come.

Ask them how the world could become so bad when God created it so good. God gave us free will, and we can choose to do bad or good. Because it got so bad, God wanted to cleanse all evil from the earth (remind them of the cleansing of the soul in Baptism). However, God saw that His creation was good, so He wanted a way to save it. He asked His servant Noah to help.

Develop

1. Read the story of Noah from the textbook, p. 35.

2. You may give a more detailed account from a children's Bible (Gen 6:1—9:18) or show "Noah's Ark," a video from the series In the Beginning: Stories from the Bible, available through Ignatius Press; 30 minutes.

3. Help the students understand how hard it must have been for Noah to obey God. He lived in a desert land very far from water. He was building a boat about the size of a football field—it was huge! Incredibly, he was telling everyone that God told him to build this ark. People probably thought he was crazy.

4. Have the students begin to make the ark on Appendix, pp. B-25–B-28.

6. Have them imagine what it must have been like on the Ark with all those animals—what noise! What an odor. A lot of work, too. The animals needed to be fed and cleaned. The family would have become tired of living on the ark. Surely it must have been difficult. With all that rain, there were no nice days to go out and play. It was raining every day.

7. Ask the students: Why did God send the flood? Whom did God save from the flood? Why?

8. Ask the students to describe Noah. He was likely a humble man. He was obedient. He loved his family and served God in taking care of them and all the animals. He was faithful. He was patient and persistent, etc. Ask the students how Noah could be a role model for them.

Name:________________

Word Find

ABRAHAM	FAMILY	OBEDIENT
ARK	JOSEPH	TESTED
EVE	DAVID	ANGEL
MARY	ANIMALS	GOD
ADAM	CHILDREN	ISAAC
BAPTISM	HEAVEN	LOVE
		SAVIOR

O	X	A	B	R	A	H	A	M	N	X	E
B	S	R	A	N	N	A	N	G	E	L	V
E	A	K	P	O	G	O	G	H	D	O	E
D	V	L	T	E	S	T	E	D	C	C	S
I	I	G	I	H	U	X	L	P	R	H	J
E	O	O	S	J	O	S	E	P	H	I	O
N	R	D	M	I	S	A	A	C	F	L	S
T	X	H	E	A	V	E	N	D	A	D	E
L	O	V	E	M	A	R	Y	A	D	R	P
F	A	M	I	L	Y	E	S	V	A	E	H
A	N	I	M	A	L	S	R	I	M	N	X
B	A	P	T	I	S	M	N	D	R	E	X

Reinforce

1. Have the students complete the second box on *Activity Book*, p. 24.

2. They may work on *Activity Book*, p. 26.

3. Have them complete Appendix, pp. B-25–B-28.

Conclude

1. Sing with the children "Savior of the nations, come," *Adoremus Hymnal*, #302.

2. End the class by praying the Our Father and the Glory Be.

Preview

In the next lesson, we will learn about Abraham.

SAINTS TO INVOKE FOR:

- Eruptions of Vesuvius: Saint Januarius (September 19)
- Hernia: Saint Gummarus (October 11)
- Fire: Saint Agatha (February 5)

MORE PATRON SAINTS

- Insane People: Saint Dymphna (May 15)
- Invalids: Saint Roch (August 16)
- Penitent Drunkards: Saint Martin of Tours (November 11)
- Penitent Women: Saint Mary Magdalene (July 22)
- Prisoners: Saint Leonard (November 6) and Saint Roch (August 16)
- Schoolboys: Saint Nicholas (December 6)

NOTES

____

____

____

____

____

____

____

____

____

____

____

LESSON THREE: GOD'S SERVANT, ABRAHAM

Aims

The students will learn the story of Abraham and Sarah.

They will learn that God tested Abraham and blessed him for his obedient love.

Materials

- Children's Bible
- *Activity Book*, pp. 24 and 25

Optional:
- "Savior of the nations, come," *Adoremus Hymnal*, #302
- "Abraham's Sacrifice," video; In the Beginning: Stories from the Bible

Begin

Have the students summarize the stories of Adam and Eve, Cain and Abel, and Noah in their own words. Compare these Biblical figures to obedience and trust in God. Ask the children who among these people would be a good example for us and why.

Remind them that even after Noah and the flood, God still did not send the Savior, and again people sinned. God now wanted the service of Abraham.

Years later there was a man named **Abraham** who loved God very much. But Abraham was sad because he didn't have any children. One day, God spoke to Abraham: "Your wife will have a baby soon. And someday you will have grandchildren, and great-grandchildren. Then the family of Abraham will be one of the biggest families of all!" God promised that the family of Abraham would always be very special to Him.

Soon Abraham's wife had a baby. She named him **Isaac**. Abraham loved his little boy more than anything else in the world.

One day, God tested Abraham. He told Abraham to give up his son. This made Abraham afraid and sad, but he wanted to obey God. Abraham trusted God. When he was all ready to do what God had asked, an angel came and said, "Stop! You can keep Isaac with you. God just wanted to see how much you loved Him. God will bless you for being so obedient."

As God promised, the family of Abraham grew very large, and God took care of them all. Many of Abraham's descendants are living today. They are the Jewish people.

37

Develop

1. Have the children read about Abraham from the text or a children's Bible (Gen 12—22).

2. Tell the children that Abraham had to put his faith in God when God told him that he would have a baby. Abraham and Sarah (his wife) were very old (like grandparents) and they normally would never be able to hae a baby. God's gift of a baby was a precious gift to Abraham and Sarah. They loved Isaac very much.

3. Explain that God put Abraham to a test (like Adam and Eve, and the angels; you may want to have the children review these two tests). Review with the children what test God put to Abraham.

4. Abraham's test was to sacrifice his beloved son. He was asked, without a reason, to offer his son back to God. Remember how much Abraham loved Isaac. Abraham was very obedient. He took Isaac to the place God told him and prepared to sacrifice his son, putting all his trust in God. God stopped Abraham's test when he saw that Abraham was faithful and would do what God asked of him. God then blessed him saying that his family would be as numerous as a nation.

5. Have the children describe Abraham and his qualities.
- He was faithful
- He was obedient
- He was trusting
- He was blessed by God
- He was patient
- He was loving

6. Ask the children how Abraham is a good example for them. In what ways can they be like Abraham?

Name:___________________

Can you match the person with the event?

PERSON	EVENT
ADAM	Was his old father's only son.
EVE	Wanted to fight.
NOAH	Named the animals.
ABRAHAM	Built an ark.
ISAAC	Was sad because he did not have children.
GOLIATH	Was tricked by a snake.

Questions from your text.

1. Why were the people waiting? When did they start waiting? They were waiting for the Savior. They started waiting after the Original Sin.
2. What happened when the people were waiting? They got tired of waiting and soon forgot about God.
3. Why did people laugh at Noah? Because he built an ark.
4. Why did Abraham agree to give up his son Isaac? Did he? Because he was obedient and trusted in God. God spared his son.

Faith and Life Series • Grade 2 • Chapter 7 • Lesson 3 25

Reinforce

1. Have the students complete the third box on *Activity Book*, p. 24.

2. Have them complete *Activity Book*, p. 25. When they have finished, review the answers.

3. If time permits, watch the video "Abraham's Sacrifice" from the series In the Beginning: Stories from the Bible, available through Ignatius Press; 30 minutes.

Conclude

1. Lead the students in singing "Savior of the nations, come," *Adoremus Hymnal*, #302.

2. End by praying the Our Father and the Glory Be.

Preview

In the next lesson, we will learn about King David.

ABRAHAM'S SACRIFICE PREFIGURES JESUS' SACRIFICE ON THE CROSS

Just as God called Abraham to offer his only beloved son as a sacrifice of love, God offered His only Beloved Son, Jesus, as a sacrifice for the love of all. Catholics can go in faith and obedience and trust to Mass, where, upon the altar, the Sacrifice of the Cross is made present. The Mass is a sacrifice, a prayer of thanksgiving, and a covenant (remind the children that a covenant is a promise that makes us part of God's family).

NOTES

LESSON FOUR: GOD'S SERVANT, DAVID

Aims

The students will become familiar with the story of David and Goliath, and David's rise to become king of Israel.

They will learn that Mary, Joseph, and Jesus are descendants (from the family) of David.

Materials

- Children's Bible
- *Activity Book*, pp. 24 and 26

Optional:
- "Savior of the nations, come," *Adoremus Hymnal*, #302
- "David and Goliath," video; In the beginning: Stories from the Bible

Begin

Review with the students the stories of Adam and Eve, Noah, and Abraham. Draw on the chalkboard the time-line pictured on the next page.

Add to the time-line David, Jesus, and the current year. Help the children understand how long ago these events happened, and that they are real events, not just stories.

Many years after Abraham, but still long before Jesus came, there was a boy named **David**. David took care of his father's sheep all day. He was strong and good. He loved to sing and play a harp. He made up songs about God and the beautiful world God made.

One day, something happened that made all of David's people very afraid. A giant named Goliath came and said he wanted to fight! "If you can find someone to beat me," he said, "my king will leave you alone. But if I beat you, you must all be the slaves of my king."

Everyone was afraid to fight Goliath. But not David. "I may be small, but God will help me to beat Goliath."

David took some small stones and put them in a slingshot. When he met Goliath in the field, the giant made fun of David. But David was not afraid because of his trust in God. He put a stone in the sling and shot Goliath right between the eyes. Goliath fell dead. David had saved his people.

Later, David became king of the chosen people. It was from his descendants that Mary and Joseph, the parents of Jesus, would come.

38

Develop

1. Read the story of David from the textbook or from the children's Bible (1 Sam 16—17, 2 Sam 6—7).

2. Ask the students to describe David:
   - He was brave
   - He trusted in God
   - He served God faithfully
   - He had a big job as the king

3. Ask the students how David would be a good example for them. How can they be like David?

4. Have the students interview a panel of characters. Have students pretend they are Adam, Eve, Noah, Abraham, Isaac, and David. The other students can interview them. They may write their own questions, such as:
   - Adam, are you happy that Eve came from your rib?
   - Eve, what was life like outside the Garden?
   - Noah, what was life on the Ark like?
   - Abraham, how hard was it to trust God enough to sacrifice your son?
   - Isaac, how did it feel to have your father almost sacrifice you?
   - David, were you scared when you faced Goliath?

Remind the students to stay in character. Reward them for doing a good job.

5. Ask them to think of everyday examples of obedience, trust, faith, patience, and other virtues they have learned about through the examples in the stories in this chapter.

Q. 18 *How did Noah respond to God with obedience?*
Noah obeyed God and built an ark so that the good of creation would be saved during the great flood (CCC 56).

Q. 19 *How did Abraham respond to God with faith?*
Abraham had such faith in God that he was ready to give even his beloved son to God (CCC 59).

Q. 20 *How did David respond to God with trust?*
David so trusted in God's love and care for His people, the Israelites, that he fought a giant named Goliath with a slingshot (CCC 64).

Words to Know:

Noah Abraham Isaac David

39

Reinforce

1. Have the students complete the fourth box on *Activity Book*, p. 24.

2. Have them complete *Activity Book*, p. 26.

3. If time permits, have the students watch "David and Goliath," a video from the series In the Beginning: Stories from the Bible, available through Ignatius Press; 30 minutes.

Conclude

1. Lead the students in singing "Savior of the nations, come," *Adoremus Hymnal*, #302.

2. Conclude by praying the Our Father and the Glory Be.

Preview

In the next lesson, the students will review the material covered in this chapter.

TIMELINE: WAITING FOR THE SAVIOR

Adam and Eve · Noah · Abraham Isaac · David

NOTES

CHAPTER SEVEN:
REVIEW AND ASSESSMENT

Aims

The students' understanding of the material covered this week will be reviewed and assessed.

Materials

- Quiz 7 (Appendix, p. A-9)
- "Savior of the Nations, come," *Adoremus Hymnal*, #302

Review

1. Review the stories of Adam and Eve, Cain and Abel, Noah, Abraham and Isaac, and David and Goliath.

2. For each of the stories, they should be able to tell you:
   - What God asked of the people
   - How the people responded
   - Why people are a good/bad example for us
   - How the people prepared for the coming of the Savior
   - The students should also be able to tell you the order of the stories.

3. They may review the stories by acting them out or by explaining the pictures in a children's Bible.

4. Review the virtues of faith, hope, trust, and obedience.

5. Ask them how they would have prepared for the coming of the Savior.

Name:

Obeying God Our Father **Quiz 7**

Matching *Write the letter for the person next to the sentence that best describes him.*

a. Adam	f He was a shepherd made king.
b. Noah	a He was the first man, and ate the forbidden fruit.
c. Isaac	g A child of God.
d. Eve	d She was the wife of Adam.
e. Abraham	e He was asked to sacrifice his son.
f. David	c The son of really old parents.
g. You	b He was asked to build a big boat.

Circle T for True, and F for False.

(T)	F	Eve gave the forbidden fruit to Adam to eat.
T	(F)	Abel killed Cain.
(T)	F	Noah built an ark.
T	(F)	Abraham sacrificed his son.
(T)	F	David killed Goliath with a slingshot.

Faith and Life • Grade 2 • Appendix A *A - 9*

Assess

1. Distribute Quiz 7 and read through it with the students, answering any questions they may have. As they turn in their quizzes, individually quiz test them on the Words to Know and their prayers.

2. When all the students have turned in their quizzes, review the correct answers.

Conclude

1. Sing "Savior of the nations, come," *Adoremus Hymnal*, #302.

2. End with the Our Father.

CHAPTER EIGHT
GOD GIVES US HIS LAWS

Catechism of the Catholic Church References

Decalogue: 2067, 2080–81
- Conscience: 1962
- God's Revelation: 2059, 2070–71
- God's Will: 2063
- Man's Duties: 2072

God Forms His People, Israel: 62–64, 72, 218, 2077
Jesus and the Law: 574–82, 592, 2052–55
Moses and the Prayer of the Mediator: 2574–77, 2593
Obligation of the Ten Commandments: 2072–73, 2081–82
Old Law: 1961–64, 1975, 1980–82
Ten Commandments: 2084–557
Ten Commandments and the Natural Law: 2070–71, 2080
Ten Commandments as Path to Heaven: 1724
Ten Commandments in Sacred Scripture: 2056–63, 2077
Ten Commandments in Church Tradition: 2064–68, 2078
Unity of the Ten Commandments: 2069, 2079

Scripture References

Joseph: Gen 37:1—45:28

Moses: Ex 3—19:18, 20:1–17; Deut 28:1

Background Reading: *The Fundamentals of Catholicism* by Fr. Kenneth Baker, S.J.

Volume 1:
"Dignity of the Law," pp. 129–32

Summary of Lesson Content

Lesson 1

God's chosen people became slaves in Egypt. Moses was sent by God to deliver these slaves.

Lesson 2

God gave Moses and His people the Ten Commandments as the Old Covenant.

Lesson 3

We will learn about the Ten Commandments.

Lesson 4

The Ten Commandments are our moral guide.

Through Baptism, the Ten Commandments become God's Laws for us, too.

LESSON ONE: DELIVER US FROM EVIL

Aims

The students will learn that Abraham's descendants became as numerous as a nation. They became slaves in Egypt. God chose Moses to deliver them from slavery.

They will learn the story of the Exodus.

Materials

- Children's Bible
- *Activity Book*, p. 27

Optional:
- "Now thank we all our God," *Adoremus Hymnal*, #607
- "Moses the Egyptian," video; In the Beginning: Stories from the Bible

Begin

Review how God promised Abraham that he would be the father of many descendants. God fulfilled this promise so well, you may wish to explain the genealogy: Abraham and Sarah had Isaac. Isaac had Jacob and Esau, Jacob, who became known as Israel, had twelve boys. One of these boys was named Joseph. Through the work of Joseph, the descendants of Israel moved to Egypt. Many years later, though, they became slaves. God loved His people very much, so He chose a man named Moses to bring His people out of slavery.

Develop

1. Read the story of Joseph from a children's Bible (Gen 37:1—45:28).

2. Remind the students that God loved His people very much, and did not like that they were slaves in Egypt. They worked hard and had little food. They were badly treated.

3. God had a very special plan for His people. Being slaves made it very hard for them to love and worship God. The Egyptians had different gods. They worshiped Ra, the sun god, and some animals, such as cats. The Egyptians had all sorts of gods that were not really gods at all. The Egyptians just thought they had power. The people of Israel were not able to go to worship the true God because they were slaves.

4. Together, read paragraphs 1 and 2 from the textbook.

5. Read the story of Moses, from his rescue in the Nile to the Exodus (up to receiving the Ten Commandments) in a children's Bible (Ex 3—19) or watch "Moses the Egyptian," video from the series In the Beginning: Stories from the Bible, available through Ignatius Press; 30 minutes.

Teacher's Note:
If you teach the students the story of Joseph, the story of Moses may have to wait until the next lesson.

Name:____________________

Color the picture

With the help of your text book, fill in these blanks

God gave the chosen people a leader. His name was Moses. With God's help, Moses set the people free. For many years God led the people so they could find a new land to live in. God wanted His chosen people really to know that they were special to Him. He took care of them and showed His love for them by giving them all they needed. God also wanted them to love Him in return. He gave his chosen people rules and told them that if they loved Him they would obey those rules and they would be happy.

Faith and Life Series • Grade 2 • Chapter 8 • Lesson 1 27

Reinforce

1. Have the students complete *Activity Book*, p. 27.

2. Teach and sing with the children "Now thank we all our God," *Adoremus Hymnal*, #607.

Conclude

End by praying for the students' intentions and the Glory Be.

Preview

In the next lesson, we will learn about Moses receiving the Ten Commandments.

SAINTS TO INVOKE FOR:

- Lost Things: Saint Gracian, Saint Anthony of Padua
- Pestilence: Saint Sebastian (January 20)

THE CURÉ OF ARS

A humble servant, who was almost not ordained because of his slowness in studies, was sent to Ars, where there was very little faith left in the community. He was sent to bring them back to pious devotion to God. His bishop told him, "There is not much love of God in that parish, you will put some there." Soon, his reputation for saintliness and an ability to perform miracles drew tens of thousands to his parish each year. People came because they recognized an opportunity to see a model of true godliness and to move closer to God themselves.

NOTES

LESSON TWO: THE OLD COVENANT

Aims

The students will learn the account of God giving Moses and His people the Ten Commandments.

Materials

- Children's Bible (Ex 20:1–17)
- *Activity Book*, p. 28

Optional:
- "Now thank we all our God," *Adoremus Hymnal*, #607
- "The Ten Commandments," video; In the Beginning: Stories from the Bible

Begin

Explain that God brought the Israelites out of Egypt and that they were freed from slavery. His people, however, having lived in Egypt, had become very confused about how they should live in a way that was pleasing to God. They could have spent years making many mistakes trying to figure this out, but God loved them so much, He gave them His Laws so they could be happy with God and each other.

8 God Gives Us His Laws

"And if you obey the voice of the LORD your God, being careful to do all his commandments which I command you this day, the LORD your God will set you high above all the nations of the earth."

Deuteronomy 28:1

As God promised, the chosen people grew to be very many. Years after Abraham died, a bad thing happened to them. They all became slaves in the land of Egypt.

Then God gave them a leader. His name was Moses. With God's help Moses set the people free. For many years God led the people so they could find a new land to live in. God wanted His chosen people really to know that they were special to Him. He took care of them and showed His love for them by giving them all they needed. God also wanted them to love Him in return. He gave His chosen people rules and told them that if they loved Him they would obey those rules and they would be happy.

41

Develop

1. Explain to the children that rules do not hurt us, but help us. Use the example of a VCR. It comes with rules how to use it. They teach us how to play videos, how to program it to tape shows, etc. We can choose to not follow the rules. We could, for example, decide to not put in a video, but a balogna sandwich. (It'll fit.) This not only breaks the rules, but it will break the VCR.

2. God gave us His Laws. We should not break them because it is wrong to disobey God. But, also, if we break God's Laws we will hurt ourselves. God gave us these rules, knowing they would make us happy.

3. Read the story of God giving Moses the Ten Commandments (Ex 20:1–17), or watch "The Ten Commandments," video from the series In the Beginning: Stories from the Bible, available through Ignatius Press; 30 minutes.

4. Review with the children God's Laws. See if they remember them from the story/video. Write them on the chalk board.

5. Tell them that God shows us that if we keep His Commandments, we will be rewarded. Read Ex 19:5–6: "If you will obey my voice and keep my covenant, you shall be my own possession among all peoples; for all the earth is mine, and you shall be to me a kingdom of priests and a holy nation."

6. You may begin quizzing the children in a game format on the Ten Commandments and the Bible stories they have learned thus far.

7. The students may dramatize the Bible Stories in groups. They could prepare to put on a presentation of Old Testament stories for another class or their parents.

Name:________________

Write the Ten Commandments under the Great Commandments into which they fit.

Love the Lord your God with all your heart, with all your soul, with all your strength and all your mind.

1. You shall not have other gods beside Me
2. You shall not use God's name in vain
3. Remember to keep God's day holy

Love your neighbor as yourself.

1. Honor your father and mother
2. You shall not kill
3. You shall not commit adultery
4. You shall not steal
5. You shall not lie
6. You shall not covet your neighbor's wife
7. You shall not covet your neighbor's goods

28 *Faith and Life Series • Grade 2 • Chapter 8 • Lesson 2*

Reinforce

1. Have the students complete *Activity Book*, p. 28.

2. You may orally quiz the children on the Old Testament materials covered in the last two chapters.

Conclude

1. Sing "Now thank we all our God," *Adoremus Hymnal*, #607.

2. Pray for the intentions and the Glory Be.

Preview

In the next lesson, we will learn more about the Ten Commandments.

THE TEN COMMANDMENTS

1. You shall have no other gods before Me
2. You shall not take the name of the Lord, your God in vain
3. Remember the Sabbath day, and keep it holy
4. Honor your father and your mother
5. You shall not kill
6. You shall not commit adultery
7. You shall not steal
8. You shall not bear false witness against your neighbor
9. You shall not covet your neighbor's wife
10. You shall not covet your neighbor's goods

From Exodus 20:1–17, and Deuteronomy 5:6–21

NOTES

LESSON THREE: GOD'S LAWS

Aims

The students will learn more about the Ten Commandments and how they are to be lived.

Materials

- *Activity Book*, p. 29
- Cue-cards
- Marker
- Scissors

Optional:
- "Now thank we all our God," *Adoremus Hymnal*, #607

Begin

Ask the students to recount the story of Moses, from his trip down the Nile, through the Exodus, to his the receiving of the Ten Commandments.

Talk about the virtues that Moses exemplified:
- Obedience
- Trust in God (especially with the plagues)
- Faith
- Hope (in freedom from slavery)
- Piety

Note: the primary objective of today's lesson is to learn/memorize the Ten Commandments.

We call these rules the **Ten Commandments**. They are God's **Law** of love for all His people. Because we become God's children when we are baptized, these Laws are for us, too. Knowing God's Laws helps us to do what is right.

Q. 21 *What are the Ten Commandments?*
The Ten Commandments are God's Laws of love for all His people (CCC 1962).

Q. 22 *Why did God give Moses and His people the Ten Commandments?*
God gave Moses and His people the Ten Commandments so they would know God and serve Him faithfully while they waited for the Savior (CCC 62, 1961).

Words to Know:

Ten Commandments   Law

42

Develop

1. Have the students turn to p. 43 of their text and read through everything in the tablets.

2. Stress that the Ten Commandments are divided into two sections: the first three show our love for God, the last seven show our love for our neighbor.

3. Also, reinforce that disobeying or breaking these Commandments offends God.

4. Have them close their textbooks and play a memorization review game. Break the students into two teams and give them points for being the first to answer questions about the Ten Commandments. They can play Bible Baseball (see Appendix, p. B-1 for rules).

5. Distribute cue cards to the students and have each student write the Ten Commandments on the cards, one per card, as shown in the example at right. Then have them cut the cards into two. They may then mix up their cards and try to solve their own puzzles, or trade with a friend to make it more of a challenge.

6. The students should be memorizing the proper wording of the Commandments and their proper order.

7. The students should be able to explain the Commandments in their own words. This exercise will show that they understand the Commandment and do not just have a rote memory of them.

Name:____________________

COMMANDMENT	Write in your own words what each Commandment says.
1st Commandment:	Answers will vary
2nd Commandment:	
3rd Commandment:	
4th Commandment:	
5th Commandment:	
6th Commandment:	
7th Commandment:	
8th Commandment:	
9th Commandment:	
10th Commandment:	

Faith and Life Series • Grade 2 • Chapter 8 • Lesson 3 and 4 29

COMMANDMENT CUE CARD PUZZLE

You shall not steal.

The cards for the game described on p. 76 should look like this one: one Commandment per card.

Reinforce

1. Have the students complete *Activity Book*, p. 29. For Commandments 1–5, have them write what each Commandment means in their own words.

2. You may wish to quiz each child individually on the Ten Commandments.

Conclude

1. Sing "Now thank we all our God," *Adoremus Hymnal*, #607.

2. Pray for the students' intentions. You may also ask God to help the students to live and keep the Commandments. End by praying the Glory Be.

Preview

In the next lesson, the students will begin to learn the practical applications of the Ten Commandments.

NOTES

LESSON FOUR: WE OBEY GOD'S LAWS

Aims

The students will learn the importance of the Ten Commandments as our moral guide.

They will learn that, through Baptism, the Ten Commandments become God's Laws for us, too.

Materials

- Children's Examination of Conscience for grade 2 (Appendix, pp. B-16– B-17)

Optional:
- "Now thank we all our God," *Adoremus Hymnal*, #607
- *Activity Book*, p. 29

Begin

As a class, read aloud the Ten Commandments which you have written on the chalk board in a column.

Now have children put the Commandments into their own words, explaining what they mean.

Here are the Ten Commandments:

1. You shall not have other gods beside Me.
2. You shall not use God's name in vain.
3. Remember to keep God's day holy.
4. Honor your father and mother.
5. You shall not kill.
6. You shall not commit adultery.
7. You shall not steal.
8. You shall not lie.
9. You shall not covet your neighbor's wife.
10. You shall not covet your neighbor's goods.

The first three Commandments tell us how to love and respect God. The others tell us how to love and respect other people. Sometimes we obey God's Law by doing what is good, other times we obey by not doing what is bad.

43

Develop

1. With the students, go through the chart, p. 44 of the textbook, writing each example beside the Commandment to which it refers. For example: to pray to God should go beside the First and/or Third Commandment.

2. Go through each of the Commandments specifically, explaining what they mean. Have them give everyday examples for each. For example:

- *First Commandment: God is the most important Person/Thing in our life; e.g., we should not put money or a hobby before God*
- *Second: God's name is holy and should be said reverently; e.g., we should not curse or make promises with God's name that we do not intend to keep*
- *Third: We must worship God on Sunday (the day of the Resurrection); e.g., we should spend Sunday going to Mass and being with family*
- *Fourth: We must love our parents and respect their authority; e.g., obey our parents*
- *Fifth: Do not hurt anyone; e.g., do not hit or fight with others*
- *Sixth: Married loved is sacred. The love of a husband and wife is to be saved for marriage and not given to another in thought, word, or deed; e.g., we should guard our thoughts and what we see on television for purity*
- *Seventh: Do not take what does not belong to you; e.g., do not take another's money or lunch*
- *Eighth: Tell the truth; e.g., you should not tell falsehoods*
- *Ninth: Respect the relationships of others; e.g., you should not want the love that is given to another so much that you get in the way of that love*
- *Tenth: Respect the property of others; e.g., you should not want something that belongs to another so much that you do not want that person to have it*

"You are my friends if you do what I command you." *John 14:15*

The Ten Commandments teach us:

It is right . . .	It is wrong . . .
— to pray to God.	— not to pray to God.
— to listen and pray in church.	— to misbehave in church.
— to use God's name with respect.	— to use God's name in the wrong way.
— to go to Mass on Sundays and holy days.	— to miss Mass on Sundays or holy days because of my own fault.
— to listen to and obey my parents and teachers.	— to disobey my parents and teachers.
— to be kind to everyone.	— to hurt others, to fight, or to be unkind.
— to be pure in my thoughts, words, and actions.	— to think and do bad things or say bad words.
— to be honest.	— to steal or cheat.
— to tell the truth.	— to lie.

44

ACT OF CONTRITION

My God, I am sorry for my sins with all my heart, in choosing to do wrong and failing to do good, I have sinned against You, Whom I should love above all things.

You Son, Jesus Christ, suffered and died for us. In His name, my God, have mercy.

Amen.

Reinforce

Have the students complete Commandments 6–10 in *Activity Book*, p. 29. You may wish to have the students share their answers with one another.

Conclude

1. Sing "Now thank we all our God," *Adoremus Hymnal*, #607.

2. End by praying for the student's intentions and the Glory Be.

Preview

In the next lesson, we will review the material covered in this chapter.

NOTES

CHAPTER EIGHT:
REVIEW AND ASSESSMENT

Aims

The students' understanding of the material covered this week will be reviewed and assessed.

Materials

- Quiz 8 (Appendix, p. A-10)
- Unit 2 Test (Appenix, pp. A-11 and A-12)
- "Now thank we all our God," *Adoremus Hymnal*, #607

Review

1. If you covered the story of Joseph, review the details of this story.

2. Review the story of Moses as a child, the Exodus, and God giving Moses the Ten Commandments.

3. Review each of the Ten Commandments and what they mean. Have the students think of practical examples of what each Commandment tells us to do and to not do.

4. They should be able to recount the gifts Adam and Eve shared in the beginning:
   - They were happy
   - They were not afraid of the animals
   - They did not get sick or hurt
   - They would not die
   - They did not want to do anything bad
   - They did not need to go to school
   - They had all the food they needed
   - God walked and talked with them
   - Adam and Eve shared God's life, called grace

Name:

God Gives Us His Laws **Quiz 8**

Please answer in complete sentences.

1. What bad thing happened to the descendants of Abraham?
They became slaves in the land of Egypt

2. Whom did God send to help His people?
Moses

3. What did God give to His people so they could be happy?
The Ten Commandments

Put the Ten Commandments in order:

5 You shall not kill

2 You shall not use God's name in vain.

8 You shall not lie.

3 Remember to keep God's day holy.

4 Honor your father and mother.

1 You shall not have other gods beside Me.

10 You shall not covet your neighbor's goods.

6 You shall not commit adultery.

7 You shall not steal.

9 You shall not covet your neighbor's wife.

A - 10 *Faith and Life • Grade 1 • Appendix A*

Assess

1. Distribute Quiz 8 and read through it with the students, answering any questions that they may have. As they turn in their quizzes, individually test them on the Ten Commandments.

2. Once all the students have turned in their quizzes, review the correct answers.

3. Do the same for the Unit 2 Test. Review all questions and Words to Know for the unit.

Conclude

1. Sing "Now thank we all our God," *Adoremus Hymnal*, #607.

2. End with praying the Glory Be.

CHAPTER NINE
I CHOOSE TO LOVE GOD

Catechism of the Catholic Church References

Bearing Witness to the Truth: 2471–74, 2506
Charity: 1822–29, 1844
Choices Presented to the Conscience: 1786–89, 1799–1800
Command of Love: 1823
Confession of Sins in Sacrament of Penance: 1447–58
Conscience: 1776–82, 1795–97
Consequences of Original Sin: 55–57, 399–409, 416–19
Decalogue Perfected in the New Testament: 2056
Definition of Sin: 1849–51, 1871
Different Kinds of Sin: 1852–53, 1873
Duties of Children toward Parents: 2214–20, 2247–48, 2251
God Forgives Sin: 1441
Gravity of Sin: Mortal and Venial: 1854–64, 1874–75
Holiness of God's Name: 2142–45, 2160–61
Human Freedom: 1730–48
Jesus Died for Our Sins: 601, 654
Living in the Truth: 2465–70, 2505
Man Sins Freely: 1739, 1874
Mercy and Sin: 1846–48
New Law or Law of the Gospel: 1965–74, 1977, 1983–86
Prayer of Intercession: 2634–36, 2647
Reality of Sin: 386–87, 413
Sin, Mortal: 1854–57, 1861, 1874
Sin, Venial: 1854–55, 1863, 1875
Sin as Offense against Love: 1849, 1855
Sin Rejects God, 415, 1487
Sunday as the Fulfillment of the Sabbath: 2175–95
Worship and Prayer: 2096–98, 2135

Scripture References

Good Samaritan: Lk 10:25–37
Great Commandment: Lk 10:27; Mt 22:37–40; Mk 12:30–31

Background Reading: *The Fundamentals of Catholicism* by Fr. Kenneth Baker, S.J.

Volume 1:
"Faith and Morality," pp. 121–23
"Moral Responsibility," pp. 126–29

Summary of Lesson Content

Lesson 1

God gave His people the Ten Commandments.

Jesus summarized the Ten Commandments into the two great Commandments of love of God and love of neighbor.

Lesson 2

Prayer and worship are forms of responding to God with love.

Prayer is talking to God.

Catholics attend Mass on Sundays and worship God from within a community.

Lesson 3

Love of neighbor is expressed in charity.

Virtues that help us to love our neighbors are: kindness, helpfulness, obedience, cheerfulness, sharing, truthfulness and prayer for others.

Lesson 4

Man chooses to do what is right or wrong. He has free will.

Choosing to do something bad on purpose is a sin, which takes away grace from our souls and turns us away from God.

There are two kinds of sin: mortal and venial.

LESSON ONE: GOD'S LAW

Aims

The students will review the Ten Commandments.

They will learn that Jesus summarized the Ten Commandments into the Two Great Commandments of love of God and love of neighbor.

Materials

- Children's Bible
- Construction paper, scissors, pencils, (glue optional)
- Appendix, pp. B-18–B-20
- *Activity Book*, p. 30

Optional:
- "There's a wideness in God's mercy," *Adoremus Hymnal*, #613

Begin

Review the story of Moses, and the Ten Commandments. Play a review game with the children such as Tic Tac Toe (rules on Appendix, p. B-1) to ensure that the students know the Ten Commandments in their proper order. This is a review of the previous chapter's memorization material.

9 I Choose to Love God

"You shall love the Lord your God with all your heart, and with all your soul, and with all your strength, and with all your mind; and your neighbor as yourself."

Luke 10:27

We learned that God the Father gave His people the Ten Commandments. Jesus gave us the Two Great Commandments. He told us that if we obey them, we would be obeying all the other Commandments at the same time.

The Two Great Commandments are:

1. *Love God with all your heart.*
2. *Love your neighbor as yourself.*

How do we love God? We love our Heavenly Father by praying to Him. Prayer means talking to God. We show our love by going to Mass on Sunday. At church we worship God with the other members of God's family. And we should talk about God with respect and love.

How do we love our neighbor? We love our neighbor by being kind and helpful to everyone we

45

Develop

1. Review the students' understanding of the Ten Commandments. As you review the meaning of each one, have different students offer examples of keeping and breaking each of the Commandments:
   - First: There is only one God
   - Second: Use God's name with reverence
   - Third: Go to Mass, rest, and pray on Sunday
   - Fourth: Obey your parents
   - Fifth: Do not kill
   - Sixth: Love your husband or your wife your whole life
   - Seventh: Do not steal
   - Eighth: Do not lie
   - Ninth: Be happy with your own husband or wife
   - Tenth: Do not be envious of things other people have

2. Ask the students which of these Commandments affect our relationship with God (directly) and which affect our relationship with our neighbors (directly). You may at this time make the Ten Commandments Heart Puzzle from Appendix, pp. B-18–B-20.

3. Read the beginning of the chapter up to and including the Two Great Commandments. Read this material from the Bible, too (Mt 22:37–40; Mk 12:30–31; Lk 10:27).

4. Ask them to think of ways they can love God, then the ways they can love their neighbors. Have them list words that are used regularly such as: love, obey, help, be kind, don't fight, pray, etc. Help them to recognize the virtues (about which they will learn more later in this chapter).

5. Quiz the students, giving them one of the Ten Commandments, asking them into which of the Two Great Commandments each of the Ten fits: e.g., the Third Commandment: Honor the Lord's Day fits into Love of God.

Name:____________________

Unscramble the Ten Commandments. Write them properly below the scrambled words. Put them in order by number.

4 HRONO YROU RHAFTE NDA THOMRE
Honor your father and mother

1 UOY LAHSL ONT VAHE HTOER GDOS DESBIES EM.
You shall not have other gods besides me

8 YUO LLASH TNO IEL.
You shall not lie

9 OYU HALSL ONT VETOC OURY EIGHNOBS'R FIWE.
You shall not covet your neighbor's wife

3 BMEMERER OT EEKP GD'SO YDA OLYH.
Remember to keep God's day holy

5 UYO LLSHA TNO LKIL.
You shall not kill

7 OUY LSAHL NTO LTSEA.
You shall not steal

10 OYU LSLHA ONT VCETO UORY EIGHNS'BRO ODOGS.
You shall not covet your neighbor's goods

2 OUY HSLAL TON SEU D'SOG MNAE NI VIAN.
You shall not use God's name in vain

6 UOY LLSHA OTN MIMOCT DYUALTRE.
You shall not commit adultery

30 *Faith and Life Series • Grade 2 • Chapter 9 • Lesson 1*

Reinforce

1. Have the students create the Commandments Heart on Appendix, pp. B-18–B-20.

2. If time permits, the students may complete *Activity Book*, p. 30.

3. Teach and sing with the children "There's a wideness in God's mercy," *Adoremus Hymnal*, #613.

Conclude

1. Lead the children in praying for their specific needs in growing in ways of loving God and neighbor, such as "Dear God, please let me be kind to people on the street, and let me help my brother with his homework."

2. Pray the Act of Charity.

Preview

In the next lesson, we will learn more about ways to love God.

ACT OF CHARITY

O my God, I love you above all things with my whole heart and soul, because You are all good and worthy of all my love. I love my neighbor as myself for love of You. I forgive all who have injured me, and I ask pardon for all whom I have injured. *Amen.*

NOTES

LESSON TWO: LOVE OF GOD

Aims

The students will learn of ways to love God.

They will learn that, as Catholics, we go to Mass on Sundays to worship God.

They will learn that prayer is a way to talk with God, helping us to love Him.

Materials

- Sentence Strips that say: "I love God by ____________ ."
- *Activity Book*, p. 31

Optional:
- "There's a wideness in God's mercy," *Adoremus Hymnal*, #613

Begin

Review the first of the Two Great Commandments: "You shall love the Lord your God with all your heart, with all your soul, with all your strength and all your mind." Ask them to tell you which of the Ten Commandments this includes. Then ask them for practical ways that they may keep this Great Commandment.

Develop

1. Read from the text book, the paragraph beginning with "How do we love God?"

2. Ask the children who God is. Father, Son, and Holy Spirit are all God. Explain to the students that if they love Jesus, they love God, and if they love the Father, they love God. Also explain that if they love Jesus, the Son, they are also loving the Father and the Holy Spirit, etc.

3. Have the children reread the paragraph and list on the board the ways they can love God found in their texts:
- Prayer
- Go to Mass (worship)
- Speak God's name with reverence

4. Explain prayer to the students. Prayer is talking with God. When we have a relationship with someone, we talk with him—both talking to him, and listening to him. We can pray aloud or in our hearts. There are four ways to pray:
- *Adoration: loving God*
- *Thanksgiving: thanking God*
- *Petition: asking God for things we need*
- *Intercession: praying for other people.*

Explain that the Mass is the perfect prayer that uses all four ways of praying.

5. Have the students think of examples of the different ways to pray.

6. Review with the students what it means to honor the Lord's Day. This means to go to Mass and pay attention. It means to rest to get ready for the week and not to work on Sunday. It also means to spend time with family.

7. Review what it means to use God's name with reverence. This reference extends to the names of the saints and holy objects.

Name:____________________

Prayer is our way of talking with God. It keeps us in a relationship with God. It is our way of talking to God and listening to Him. We can pray out loud or in our hearts. There are four ways to pray. We can adore and love God. We can thank God for His gifts. We can ask God for the things we need. We can pray for other people. Can you think of some things to pray to God about?

ADORATION PRAYER—LOVING GOD

For example: I love You God for giving me my family.

Answers will vary

THANKING GOD

For example: I thank You God for giving me a good day.

ASKING GOD FOR THINGS WE NEED

For example: God, I need to learn more about You. Can You help me?

PRAYING FOR OTHER PEOPLE

For example: Lord, my friend is sick. Can You help my friend get better?

Faith and Life Series • Grade 2 • Chapter 9 • Lesson 2 31

Reinforce

1. Have the students complete *Activity Book*, p. 31.

2. They may write letters to God telling Him how much they love Him.

3. The students may draw pictures of themselves loving God.

Conclude

1. Lead the students in singing "There's a wideness in God's mercy," *Adoremus Hymnal*, #613.

2. Pray the Act of Charity.

Preview

In the next lesson, we will learn more about loving our neighbor.

SAINT ANTHONY OF PADUA

Born in Lisbon in 1195, Saint Anthony was baptized Ferdinand; at the age of fifteen he joined the Canons Regular of Saint Augustine. In 1220 he joined the Order of Friars Minor (Franciscans) to preach to the Saracens and perhaps suffer martyrdom for Christ's sake; at this time he took the name Anthony. He soon became a well-known orator and miracle-worker in Italy and was given the name "Hammer of the Heretics." When he died on June 13, 1231, a group of children in Padua ran through the streets crying, "The holy father is dead; Saint Anthony is dead!" He was quickly canonized on Pentecost, May 30, by Gregory IX, who knew him personally. In 1263 it was discovered that his tongue is incorrupt; he is a Doctor of the Church.

NOTES

LESSON THREE: LOVE OF NEIGHBOR

Aims

The students will review the last seven Commandments, summarized in love of neighbor

They should be able to name the virtues that help us to love our neighbors: charity, kindness, helpfulness, obedience, cheerfulness, sharing, truthfulness, and prayer for others.

Materials

- Children's Bible
- *Activity Book*, p. 32

Optional:
- "There's a wideness in God's mercy," *Adoremus Hymnal*, #613

Begin

Review the second of the Two Great Commandments: "Love your neighbor as yourself." Ask the children how they show love for themselves: they would not want to hurt themselves; they take care of their needs and wants; and they want what is good for them. We should love our neighbors as we love our very selves—that much. Review the last seven Commandments and how they help us live the Great Commandment of love.

meet. We should love our parents and obey them cheerfully. We should share things with other children, and always tell the truth. We should pray for people who need God's help: the poor, the sick, people who are unhappy, and people who don't love God.

God gave you the power to choose to love Him. You can choose to do what you know is right or what you know is wrong. When you do wrong, it isn't because you "have to." No one makes you do wrong. Only you can choose. At times it is hard to be good, but that is when you show God that you really love Him.

If we do something bad on purpose, we commit a sin. We do not love God when we sin. Each sin that we commit takes grace away from our souls. With each sin we turn away from God. It is not a sin if we hurt someone by accident. It is not a sin if we forget to do something. But if we are tempted to do something wrong, and we think, "Yes, I will do it, even though I know it's wrong," then we commit a sin, and turn away from God.

There are two kinds of sin. There are **mortal sins** and **venial sins**. Mortal sins are very big, very bad sins. Mortal sin kills the life of God in us. We cannot

47

Develop

1. Read the rest of p. 45 and the first paragraph of p. 47. You may want to reread the entire page as a beginning review.

2. Ask the students to think of examples of how they may love their neighbors. Have them start with the examples in the text, then have them think of their own examples. List the words that indicate "love" on the board such as: helping, being kind, not fighting, loving, obeying, speaking the truth, being cheerful.

3. Ask them to think of who their neighbors are: their friends and family, the poor, the sick, the homeless, those who do not know or love God, etc.

4. Teach the story of the Good Samaritan. First read the story from the children's Bible (Lk 10:25–37), then have the students discuss and act out this story. Explain to the children the different people in the story. The robbers are people who hurt the man from Jerusalem to take his money. The man from Jerusalem was badly hurt and needed help. The priest who did not help the man was likely worried about becoming "unclean", for he could not encounter blood, or else he could not serve as a priest in temple worship. The Levite, too, was set aside by his family name to be a servant of God. He did not help the Jewish man, maybe because he thought he was dead or that it would be too much work to help. The Samaritan was the hero, though his situation was special, as well. Jews and Samaritans did not speak to each other. They were from different regions, and the Jews looked down upon the Samaritans. While Samaritans were treated badly by the Jews, the Samaritan helped the Jewish man and gave of his time and money to help the stranger.

5. Discuss with the students who acted with love for his neighbor. Is a neighbor only a person whom we know or who treats us well? Ask the children what they would do.

Name:_____________________

LIST WAYS WE LOVE GOD	LIST WAYS WE LOVE OUR NEIGHBORS
Answers will vary	

32 *Faith and Life Series • Grade 2 • Chapter 9 • Lesson 3*

Reinforce

1. Have the students complete *Activity Book*, p. 32.

2. Have them draw pictures of themselves helping their neighbors. They may share their pictures with the class.

Conclude

1. Sing with the students "There's a wideness in God's mercy," *Adoremus Hymnal*, #613.

2. Lead the children by praying for our different neighbors and their needs: e.g., Lord please bless the sick people and heal them so they feel better."

3. End by praying the Act of Charity.

Preview

In the next lesson, we will learn about our choice to love God and that we may also choose to sin.

MIRACLES OF SAINT ANTHONY

- A horse, kept fasting for three days, refused oats until he had knelt down and adored the Blessed Sacrament in Saint Anthony's hand.
- The poisoned food offered him by some Italian heretics was rendered harmless by the Sign of the Cross.
- He preached a sermon to the fish on the bank of a river near Padua.
- After telling a young man who kicked his mother in a fit of anger that the foot of one who kicks his mother deserved to be cut off, the man ran home and did so. The saint took the amputated foot and miraculously rejoined it to the leg.

NOTES

LESSON FOUR: CHOOSING TO LOVE GOD

Aims

The students will learn that they have free will and that they can choose to do good or bad.

They will learn that choosing to do something bad on purpose is a sin, which takes away grace from our souls and turns us away from God. They will learn that there are two kinds of sin: mortal and venial.

Materials

- Appendix, pp. B-16–B-17
- *Activity Book*, p. 33

Optional
- "There's a wideness in God's mercy," *Adoremus Hymnal*, #613

Begin

Ask the students if they can show God that they love Him. Yes, they can by loving Him and their neighbors. Ask the children if they can also show God that they do not love Him. Yes. God gave us free will. We can choose to not love God by doing bad, or choosing to do what is wrong. Any time we break one of the Ten Commandments, we are showing God that we do not love Him above all else. God gave us free will; without it we could not love Him. But we must use this gift well, or else we will be like Adam and Eve, and sin.

go to Heaven if there is a mortal sin on our souls. Venial sins are little sins, but they still make God sad. Most sins are venial sins.

It is sad but true that we all sin sometimes. Because of Original Sin we aren't always strong enough to say "No" to sin and "Yes" to God. But God loves us very much and is always ready to forgive us.

"Thou, O Lord, art good and forgiving."

Psalm 86:5

Q. 23 *What is mortal sin?*
Mortal sin is a serious act of disobedience against the Law of God. A mortal sin has three parts, all of which must be present: 1. the sin must be serious; 2. you must know it is wrong and serious; 3. you must freely choose to do it (CCC 1857).

Q. 24 *What is venial sin?*
Venial sin is a little act of disobedience against the Law of God (CCC 1863).

48

Develop

1. Read the second half of p. 47 through p. 48 of the text.

2. Explain sin to the children. When we choose to do something wrong on purpose, this is a sin. Sin is an offense against God. It takes away His grace in our soul.

3. Explain the difference between sinning and having an accident. An accident is a mistake that we do not mean to happen. A sin is something we choose to do on purpose. Using made up situations, help the children to know the difference.

4. Explain that there are two different types of sin: mortal and venial.

- *Mortal sin is when something is seriously wrong, we know it is seriously wrong, and we choose to do it anyway. Mortal sin takes away God's life or grace in our soul. Without grace we cannot go to Heaven.*
- *Venial sin is when something is seriously wrong, but we do not know it or choose it, or when we know and choose to do something that is wrong, but not seriously wrong. Venial sin lessens God's life of grace in our soul.*

5. Even when we sin, God still loves us, just as he still loved Adam and Eve. He respects our free will and allows us to choose to do good and bad (even though doing bad makes Him sad) because He loves us so much. Jesus came to save us from our sins, and even if we commit a mortal sin, our sins can be forgiven. We will learn more about the Sacrament of Penance, or Reconciliation, later in chapters 17–20.

6. Finish reading the chapter. Lead the children in an examination of conscience using Appendix, p. B-16–B-17 as a guide. Be sure to cover the Ten Commandments and the Great Commandments at an age-appropriate level.

Every night think about the day you had. Did you do anything that was wrong? Are there times you did not do what was good? Look at the chart on page 44 to help you remember. Then tell God you are sorry. Ask Him to make you stronger next time. God will be glad to give you the grace to say "No" to sin.

Words to Know:

mortal sin   venial sin

49

Reinforce

1. Have an Examination of Conscience service.

2. The students may complete *Activity Book*, p. 33.

3. Have them memorize Questions 23 and 24 from the textbook.

Conclude

1. Lead the students in singing "There's a wideness in God's mercy," *Adoremus Hymnal*, #613.

2. End the class by praying the Act of Charity.

Preview

In the next lesson, we will review the material covered in this chapter.

MORE MIRACLES OF SAINT ANTHONY

- Preaching one Holy Thursday. he remembered he had to sing a Lesson of the Divine Office. Suddenly he appeared at that moment among the friars in choir to sing his Lesson, after which he continued his sermon.

- While preaching, he miraculously preserved his audience from the rain.

- He predicted during a sermon that the devil would break down the pulpit, but that all should remain safe. The pulpit was overthrown while he was preaching but no one was hurt.

NOTES

CHAPTER NINE:
REVIEW AND ASSESSMENT

Aims

The students' understanding of the material covered this week will be reviewed and assessed.

Materials

- Quiz 9 (Appendix, p. A-13)
- "There's a wideness in God's mercy," *Adoremus Hymnal*, #613

Review

1. Review the Two Great Commandments, and how they summarize the Ten Commandments. Quiz the children by asking them to say each Commandment, e.g., What is the Fifth Commandment? Into which of the Two Great Commandments does it fit?

2. Ask them to think of ways they can love God.

3. Ask them to think of ways they can love their neighbors.

4. Review the story of the Good Samaritan.

5. Review free will and sin. They should be able to tell you the difference between mortal and venial sin:
   - Mortal: serious matter, knowledge, and choosing to do it.
   - Venial: serious matter without knowledge of free choice, or less serious matter.

6. Review the examination of conscience with the children.

Name:

I Choose to Love God **Quiz 9**

Read each example listed below. On the space provided, write an "A" for accident or "S" for sin.

1. A Cathy bumps her elbow and spills her milk.
2. B Paul does not come when his father calls him.
3. B Jessica refuses to share with her little brother.
4. B Andy tells his mother he finished his homework when he really didn't.
5. B Nancy pretends she is sick so she can miss school.
6. A Roger leaves his homework at home by mistake.
7. B Edward uses God's name in a disrespectful way.
8. B Anna hits her sister when she doesn't get what she wants.
9. A Janet doesn't see the vase on the floor and trips on it.
10. A Adam forgets to feed the cat.

Fill in the missing parts of the Great Commandments below:

1. Love God with all your heart

2. Love your neighbor as yourself

Write what these words mean:

Sin: To do something wrong on purpose

Mortal Sin: Very big, very bad sins that kill the life of God in us

Venial Sin: Little sins that still make God sad

Faith and Life • Grade 2 • Appendix A *A - 13*

Assess

1. Distribute the Quiz 9 and answer any questions that the students may have. As they turn in their quizzes, quiz them individually on the Memorization Questions and the Act of Charity.

2. When they all have handed in their quizzes, review the correct answers.

1. Sing "There's a wideness in God's mercy," Adoremus Hymnal, #613.

2. End by praying the Glory Be.

CHAPTER TEN
PREPARING FOR OUR SAVIOR

Catechism of the Catholic Church References

Advent: 524
Birth of Jesus: 437, 525
Christ at the Heart of Catechesis: 426–29
Coming of Jesus: 522–24
God Forms His People, Israel: 62–64, 72, 218, 2077
Immaculate Conception: 490–93, 508
Incarnation: 461–63, 479, 483
Jesus Son of God and Virgin: 724
Liturgical Year: 1168–71, 1194
Mary: 485, 509, 723
Mary's Consent: 494, 511
Mary's Divine Motherhood: 495, 509

Scripture References

The Annunciation: Lk 1:26–38; Is 40:3

Background Reading: *The Fundamentals of Catholicism* by Fr. Kenneth Baker, S.J.

Volume 2
"Jesus Christ—Redeemer and Liberator of Mankind," pp. 273–76

Volume 2
"Mary, Our Sinless Sister," pp. 330–33

Summary of Lesson Content

Lesson 1

In Original Sin, man could not merit Heaven for himself.

God promised to send a Savior, His own Son, Jesus Christ.

God prepared His people for the coming of the Savior, using the help of the prophets.

Lesson 2

God chose Mary to be the mother of His Son, the Savior.

Mary is the Immaculate Conception. She was without sin and is full of grace.

Lesson 3

God sent the Angel Gabriel to ask Mary to be the mother of Jesus. This event was the Annunciation.

Mary consented by giving her *fiat*: "I am the handmaiden of the Lord. Let it be done to me according to Thy word."

Lesson 4

Advent is the time to prepare for and to celebrate the coming of Jesus at Christmas and at the end of time.

The students will review some Advent traditions.

LESSON ONE: OUR NEED FOR A SAVIOR

Aims

The students will learn that man could not go to Heaven because of Original Sin.

They will remember that God promised to send a Savior. They will learn that the Savior is God's own Son, Jesus Christ.

They will learn that God prepared His people for the coming of the Savior, especially with the help of the prophets.

Materials

• *Activity Book*, p. 34

Optional:
•"Savior of the nations, come," *Adoremus Hymnal*, #302

Begin

Review the effects of Original Sin, focusing on the loss of grace and, therefore, not being able to go to Heaven. Explain that the gates of Heaven were closed to man because of Original Sin—nobody could get to Heaven. Man was sinful and could not merit Heaven on his very own. Man needed a Savior, someone who could open the gates of Heaven to him, and give him grace so that he could go to Heaven. This Savior is Jesus Christ, the Son of God.

Develop

1. Have the students read the first two paragraphs from the textbook.

2. Ask the students the following questions:
- Why did God promise to send a Savior?
- Who is the Savior?
- Did the Savior come right away?
- Who are the prophets?
- Who was Moses?
- What did the prophets do and say?

3. *Explain to the students that this time of waiting for the Savior was very long and that many people were unfaithful to God because they had a hard time waiting. They waited many, many years. God wanted everyone to be prepared for the coming of the Savior, so He sent some prophets. The prophets spoke the truth to the people and reminded them to be faithful to God. Sometimes they warned people that if they were unfaithful to God and sinned, bad things would happen to them. Prophets always told people to serve God faithfully.*

4. *Ask them how Moses was a prophet. He spoke the truth and told the people to be faithful to God and keep His Commandments.*

5. Ask them how they can be prophets, too. They should keep the Commandments and speak the truth.

6. Reviewing the stories of the Old Testament that they have learned thus far, help them to recognize how God was preparing His people for the coming of the Savior, Jesus Christ. With Noah, He washed all evil from the earth. With Abraham, He claimed a people as His own. With David, He gave His people a good king. With Moses, He gave them His Laws so they could be faithful until the Savior came.

Name:____________________

The Savior

1. Why did God send a Savior?
To make up for Adam and Eve's sin and all the sins that were ever committed

2. Who was the Savior?
Jesus, God's Son

3. How did God prepare the people for the Savior?
God spoke to His chosen people through holy men called prophets.

4. How do we get ready for the Savior?
Obey the Commandments.

34 *Faith and Life Series • Grade 2 • Chapter 10 • Lesson 1*

Reinforce

1. Have the students complete *Activity Book*, p. 34. You may wish to review the correct answers when they have completed them.

2. Teach the children the song: "Savior of the nations, come," *Adoremus Hymnal*, #302.

Conclude

Begin teaching the students the Hail Mary. Pray this prayer with the children regularly throughout the week.

Preview

In the next lesson, we will learn about the Blessed Virgin Mary, the Immaculate Conception.

AN EXCEPTION TO ORIGINAL SIN

Through the centuries the Church has become ever more aware that the Blessed Virgin Mary, "full of grace" (Lk 1:28), was redeemed from the moment of her conception. The dogma of the Immaculate Conception confesses, as Pope Pius IX proclaimed in 1854:

> The most Blessed Virgin Mary was, from the first moment of her conception, by a singular grace and privilege of almighty God and by virtue of the merits of Jesus Christ, Savior of the human race, preserved immune from all stain of original sin.
> (*Ineffabilis Deus*, 1854:DS 2803)
> —CCC 491

NOTES

____
____
____
____
____
____
____
____
____
____

LESSON TWO: MARY IS CHOSEN

Aims

The students will learn that God chose Mary to be the mother of His Son, the Savior.

They will learn that Mary is the Immaculate Conception: she was without sin, and full of grace from the moment of her conception.

Materials

- *Activity Book*, p. 35

Optional:

- "Savior of the nations, come," *Adoremus Hymnal*, #302

Begin

Review Original Sin. Remind them that all people since Adam and Eve were born with Original Sin—or almost all people. Remind them that because of Original Sin, all people are tempted to sin. We can become attracted to things that seem good, but they are not really good, and therefore, we lose sight of what God wants. For example, we see some food that would be good to help the poor so we take it, but this is stealing. God does not want us to steal. We thought it was good, but it was not. This temptation toward sin is because of Original Sin.

10 Preparing for Our Savior

A voice cries:
"In the wilderness prepare the way of the
LORD,
make straight in the desert a highway for
our God."

Isaiah 40:3

God wanted all of His people to be happy with Him forever. But because of Adam's sin, everyone lost the chance to go to Heaven. God promised Adam and Eve that He would send a Savior to make up for their sin and all the sins that were ever committed. The Savior would be Jesus Christ, God the Son!

It was a long time before the Savior came. All that time, God spoke to His chosen people through holy men called **prophets**. Moses was a prophet. There were many others. They told people to stop sinning and to get ready for the coming of the Savior.

At last it was time for the Savior to come. God chose **Mary** to be His Mother. Mary was born

51

Develop

1. Read the third paragraph beginning on p. 51 with the class.

2. What special grace did the Blesssed Virgin Mary have? She was born without Original Sin; she was full of grace. What sacrament do we need in order to have the gift of grace? Baptism.

3. Explain to the children that Mary has a special title called the Immaculate Conception. Write this on the board. Tell them that Mary was born without Original Sin. God gave Mary this gift from the time before she was even born, so that she could be the best mother for Jesus.

4. Remind the students that one of the effects of Original Sin is that we are tempted (we want) to sin again because we lose sight of what God wants for us. Because Mary was without Original Sin, Mary was able to spend her whole life without ever sinning, not even a little bit. She was always pleasing to God and doing good. She kept all His Commandments and was able to love others, as Jesus wanted.

5. To reinforce this idea, ask the children questions like: Did Mary ever tell a lie? No. Did Mary ever steal? No. Did Mary ever choose to not pray? No. Did Mary ever disobey her parents? No. Mary was always good and pleasing to God. She chose to love Him with all her heart, soul, strength, and mind, and also to love God through her neighbors.

6. Tell them that God had prepared Mary to be the mother of the Savior, but she could say "yes" or "no" and she still had free will. Mary could still choose to sin, and she could refuse to be the mother of Jesus.

7. Remind them that Jesus is God, so we can say that the Blessed Virgin Mary is the Mother of God.

Name:___________________

Answer the questions.

1. Who did God choose to be the mother of the Savior?

Mary

2. Was Mary born with Original Sin?

No

3. What was Mary's soul like?

Her soul was always full of God's life.

4. Was Mary pleasing to God? Why?

Yes. She loved God and always did what He wanted her to do.

5. Who asked Mary to be the Mother of the Savior?

Gabriel

Faith and Life Series • Grade 2 • Chapter 10 • Lesson 2 35

Reinforce

1. Have the students complete *Activity Book*, p. 35. You may wish to review the correct answers when they have finished.

2. You may wish to review Baptism and parallel the gifts of Baptism with the Immaculate Conception.

Conclude

1. Sing "Savior of the nations, come," *Adoremus Hymnal*, #302.

2. Lead the students in praying the Hail Mary. You may have them say it individually to test their memorization of the prayer.

Preview

In the next lesson, we will learn more about the Annunciation.

FEAST OF THE IMMACULATE CONCEPTION

The Feast of the Immaculate Conception is celebrated on December 8, and it is a Holy Day of Obligation.

OUR LADY OF LOURDES AND THE IMMACULATE CONCEPTION

In 1858 Our Lady appeared to fourteen-year-old Bernadette Soubirous in Lourdes, France. As she was crossing the River Gave, Bernadette saw a beautiful lady standing above her in the hollow of a rock. The bishop doubted the heavenly nature of her visions so, on his prompting, she asked the Lady her name and was told, "I am the Immaculate Conception." The dogma of Immaculate Conception had been declared only four years before and Bernadette was a poor girl who had no knowledge of such matters. The bishop, therefore, knew that the apparation was indeed the Queen of Heaven. A miraculous spring appeared that often cures the sick, even today. The feast of Our Lady of Lourdes of February 11.

NOTES

____

____

____

____

____

____

____

____

____

____

____

LESSON THREE: THE ANNUNCIATION

Aims

The students will learn that God sent the Angel Gabriel to ask Mary to be the mother of Jesus.

They will understand that Mary consented by giving her *fiat*: "I am the handmaiden of the Lord. Let it be done to me according to thy word."

Materials

- Annunciation: Lk 1:26–38
- *Activity Book*, p. 36

Optional:
- "Savior of the nations, come," *Adoremus Hymnal*, #302
- "The Announcement to Mary," video; Jesus: A Kingdom Without Frontiers

without Original Sin. God made her that way. Mary's soul was always full of God's life. She was beautiful and good. Mary always did what God wanted her to do. She never said "No" to God and she kept all His Commandments. She loved God very much and everyone else, too. God was very pleased by Mary.

One day God sent the angel **Gabriel** to Mary's house. He asked her to be the Mother of God's Son. She was surprised that God had picked her to be the Mother of the Savior, but she was happy, too. "Oh, yes," Mary said. "Let it be done to me as you say." Mary wanted to do whatever God asked of her.

God's people had to wait and get ready for many years before the Savior came. Each year, before Christmas, we spend time getting ready for Jesus, too. We call this time **Advent**.

One way we prepare to celebrate the coming of Jesus is by making an Advent wreath. It is a wreath of evergreen branches with four candles—three purple candles and one pink one. Each candle stands for one of the four weeks in which we prepare for Christmas. We have Advent wreaths in our churches and in our homes.

52

Begin

Review how God had prepared the people for the coming of the Savior. Review the various people the students have studied: Noah, Abraham, Moses, David. Ask how God had prepared Mary for the coming of the Savior. Why was Mary so special? What special work did God have for Mary?

Explain to the children that today, they will learn more about Mary and her role in the coming of the Savior.

Develop

1. Read the second paragraph on p. 52 of the text.

2. Review with the children that the Blessed Virgin Mary was prepared from before she was born to become the Mother of the Savior. She was preserved from Original Sin and was full of grace.

3. Mary still had free will. She could have said "yes" or "no" to God. She chose to love God and say "yes" to His plans for her.

4. Have them imagine what Mary might have felt like. Would she have been pleased? Honored? Scared? Worried? Excited? Why?

5. Explain to them that the story of the Angel Gabriel announcing to Mary that she would be the mother of the Savior is called the "Annunciation." You may also read this from the children's Bible: Luke 1:26–38. They may want to act out this dramatic event.

6. After the Bible reading, you may ask the students how Mary was able to become the Mother of Jesus. (The Holy Spirit would overshadow her.) Because of this, Jesus is both human (because of Mary) and divine (because He is God and he became a baby by the power of the Holy Spirit).

7. Go through the Hail Mary line by line, explaining what it means and that the first part of this prayer comes from the Annunciation.

8. If time permits, watch "The Announcement to Mary," video from the series Jesus: A Kingdom without Frontiers, available through Ignatius Press; 30 minutes.

Name:___________________

The Annunciation

Color the picture.

36 *Faith and Life Series • Grade 2 • Chapter 10 • Lesson 3*

Reinforce

1. Have the students color *Activity Book*, p. 36.

2. Have the students dramatize the Annunciation.

3. If you have not done so, watch "The Announcement to Mary," video from the series Jesus: A Kingdom Without Frontiers, available through Ignatius Press; 30 minutes.

4. You may discuss the picture on p. 50 of the text.

5. Have the students memorize Questions 25 and 26 and the Words to Know.

Conclude

1. Sing "Savior of the nations, come," *Adoremus Hymnal*, #302.

2. Pray the Hail Mary.

Preview

In the next lesson, we will learn about Advent, a season of preparation for the coming of the Savior, both at Christmas and at the end of time.

THE FIRST HAIL MARY

Much of the prayer we know as the Hail Mary comes directly from the Gospel according to Luke:

"Hail, full of grace, the Lord is with you!" Lk 1:28

"Blessed are you among women and blessed is the fruit of your womb!" Lk 1:42

"The child to be born will be called holy, the Son of God." Lk 1:35

NOTES

____

____

____

____

____

____

____

____

____

____

____

LESSON FOUR: ADVENT

Aims

The students will learn that Advent is the time to prepare for and celebrate the coming of Jesus at Christmas, and also at the end of time.

They will learn about some Advent traditions.

Materials

- Advent wreath
- Manger scene
- Advent calendar (Appendix, p. B-21)
- Advent angels
- Jesse tree
- Christmas tree

Optional:
- "Savior of the nations, come," *Adoremus Hymnal*, #302

Begin

Today, begin the class by finishing the text on p. 52.

Explain to the children that today they will learn about some of the Catholic Advent traditions.

This lesson is designed to be hands-on. If you cannot attain the supplies needed, at least visit the church to see the nativity set and Advent wreath, and use the Advent calendar from the Appendix, p. B-21 for a sample.

"Hail, full of grace, the Lord is with you!"

Luke 1:28

Words to Know:

prophets Mary Gabriel Advent

Q. 25 *Who is the Mother of Jesus?*
The Mother of Jesus is the Blessed Virgin Mary (CCC 495).

Q. 26 *Was anyone ever free from Original Sin?*
The Blessed Virgin Mary was free from Original Sin (CCC 490–91).

53

Develop

1. **Advent wreath**: The advent wreath is a ring without beginning or end (like God Who has no beginning and no end). It is made of evergreen as a sign of eternal life. There are four candles used in this wreath, three purple and one pink. One candle is lit during each week of Advent. You can say prayers when lighting the candles.

2. **Manger scene**: Saint Francis designed the nativity scene to help us meditate upon the coming of the Christ Child. During Advent, we will often put up the scene, but not the baby Jesus, so we can look forward to His coming.

3. **Advent calendar**: There are different types of calendars. Some you open a door, and there is a Bible verse behind them. Others, there are chocolates inside. The one we will do on Appendix, p. B-21 allows us to color a picture each day.

4. **Advent angels**: The students will draw names and become that person's Advent angel. They will do good works for their child secretly, and maybe even buy him a gift. Each child will learn who his angel is on Christmas.

5. **Jesse tree**: Jesus came from the family tree of Jesse. The Jesse tree uses symbols to trace the family lineage from Jesse up to Jesus. Every Jesse tree is different. If you have one available, you may show the students some of the symbols.

6. **Christmas tree**: The Christmas tree is usually an evergreen, a sign of life. It is a symbol of the tree of life in the Garden of Eden and of the Cross. Jesus in the Eucharist is the fruit of the Tree of Life offered up on the Cross. Sometimes people will hang ornaments reminding them of the life of Christ on the tree, as well as a nail to remind them of Jesus' sacrifice.

We Pray:

HAIL MARY

Hail Mary, full of grace!
The Lord is with thee.
Blessed art thou among women,
and blessed is the fruit of thy womb, Jesus.
Holy Mary, Mother of God,
pray for us sinners,
now and at the hour of our death. *Amen.*

54

Reinforce

Have the students work on memorizing Questions 25 and 26 and the Words to Know.

Conclude

1. Sing "Savior of the nations, come," *Adoremus Hymnal*, #302.

2. End by praying the Hail Mary.

Preview

In the next lesson, we will review the material covered in this chapter.

ADVENT: A TIME OF WAITING

Each year the Church has a special time of waiting before Christmas called "Advent" (from the Latin "Advenire" meaning "to come"). As an Advent activity, prepare a classroom manger using pieces of straw. Tell the children that when Advent begins they should try very hard to perform acts of sacrifice, obedience, and love each day. Explain that an act of sacrifice means giving up something they like for the love of Jesus (candy, T.V., etc.). Each time they perform an act of sacrifice, obedience, or love, they may place a piece of straw in the manger for baby Jesus. When Christmas day comes, the students' good deeds will cushion the Savior's bed.

NOTES

CHAPTER TEN:
REVIEW AND ASSESSMENT

Aims

The students' understanding of the material covered this week will be reviewed and assessed.

Materials

- Quiz 10 (Appendix, p. A-14)
- "Savior of the nations, come," *Adoremus Hymnal*, #302

Review

1. Review God's promise to send a Savior. He saves us from our sins and helps us to get to Heaven.

2. They should know that Jesus is the Savior. He is God the Son.

3. They should know that God prepared His people for the coming of the Savior, especially with the help of the prophets, who spoke the truth and told people how to follow God.

4. God prepared Mary in a special way to be the Mother of the Savior. The special way was the Immaculate Conception. She was conceived without Original Sin and was full of grace. The children should also know that Mary never committed a single sin in her entire life.

5. They should be able to relay the events of the Annunciation. They should also know that Mary had free will and chose to say "yes" to God.

6. They should know that Advent is a season of preparing for the coming of the Savior. They should be able to tell about a few different Advent traditions.

Name:

Preparing for Our Saviour **Quiz 10**

Circle the correct answer.

1. God wanted all people to:
   a) make lots of money
   b) go to school
   c) be happy forever with Him in Heaven

2. God promised to send:
   a) a Savior
   b) a ladder to Heaven
   c) a serpent

3. God chose Mary to be:
   a) the sister to the Son
   b) the aunt to the Holy Spirit
   c) the mother of the Son

4. Mary was free from:
   a) original justice
   b) Original Sin
   c) grace

5. Who came to tell Mary the good news?
   a) Joseph
   b) God
   c) Gabriel

A - 14 *Faith and Life • Grade 2 • Appendix A*

Assess

1. Distribute Quiz 10 and answer any questions that the students may have. As the children hand in their quizzes, individually quiz them on the Memorization Questions, and the Hail Mary.

2. After all quizzes have been turned in, review the correct answers.

Conclude

1. Act out the Annunciation.

2. Sing "Savior of the nations, come," *Adoremus Hymnal*, #302.

3. End by praying the Hail Mary.

CHAPTER ELEVEN
THE SAVIOR IS BORN

Catechism of the Catholic Church References

Birth of Jesus: 437, 525
Christmas Mystery: 525–26
God's Promise of a Redeemer: 410–12, 420–21
Holy Trinity in the Doctrine of Faith: 249–56, 266
Incarnation: 461–63, 479, 483
Jesus as True God and True Man: 464–70, 480–83
Jesus' Human Nature: 470–78, 482
Jesus' Mission of Salvation: 456–60
Mysteries of Jesus' Infancy: 527–30, 563

Scripture References

The Birth of Christ; Lk 2:1–20; Mt 1:18—2:15

Background Reading: *The Fundamentals of Catholicism* by Fr. Kenneth Baker, S.J.

Volume 2:
"What is an Angel?" pp. 177–81

Volume 2:
"Joseph and Mary, Husband and Wife," pp. 337–40

Summary of Lesson Content

Lesson 1

Mary and Joseph went, out of obedience, to Bethlehem for the census.

Jesus was born in the poverty of a manger.

Lesson 2

The first people to learn about Jesus were the poor shepherds.

Angels came to proclaim the birth of the Lord to these Jewish people, who were full of faith.

Lesson 3

From far away, three wise men followed a star to the place of Jesus' birth.

The wise men, who were gentiles, brought gifts for Jesus that were fit for a king.

Lesson 4

Joseph took Jesus and Mary and fled to Egypt to escape the evil plans of King Herod. He was jealous of Jesus and wanted to kill Him.

The Holy Family lived in Egypt until Herod was dead.

LESSON ONE: AWAY IN A MANGER

Aims

They will learn that out of obedience, Mary and Joseph went to Bethlehem for the census.

They will understand that Jesus was born in the poverty of a manger.

Materials

- Children's Bible (Luke 2:1–7)
- Paper and pencils
- *Activity Book*, p. 37

Optional:
- "Once in royal David's city," *Adoremus Hymnal*, #328
- "The King Is Born," video; Jesus: A Kingdom Without Frontiers

Begin

Ask the children what kind of arrival God should have for coming into the world.
- Great feast
- Riches and expensive gifts
- Beautiful clothes
- Great style and comfort
- Nice car; palace to stay in

Tell the students that God, when He became man, wanted to come for everybody, especially the poor and lowly, so He came as one that was poor and lowly.

11 The Savior Is Born

"Behold, a virgin shall conceive and bear
a son,
and his name shall be called Emmanuel"
(which means, God with us).

Matthew 1:23

It was almost time for Mary's baby to be born when she and Joseph heard some news. The ruler of their land wanted to count all the people who lived there. Everyone had to travel to certain cities to be counted. Mary and Joseph had to go to a city called **Bethlehem**.

When they got to Bethlehem, Mary and Joseph could not find a place to stay. So they had to stay in a stable with the animals. There, the baby Jesus was born. His bed was a **manger** filled with straw. This was part of God's plan for **Christmas**. He did not want to come to earth as a rich king. He wanted to share the life of the poor.

That is why the first people to learn about the newborn Savior were poor shepherds. An angel came to them as they watched their sheep.

55

Develop

1. Begin by reading the first two paragraphs of the text.

2. You may read the story of Mary and Joseph going to Bethlehem for the census and the birth of Jesus in the manger from a children's Bible: Luke 2:1–7. The children may act out this story.

3. To help them understand the census, break them into pairs and have them count the number of people in neighboring classrooms, number of boys, girls, teachers, class pets, those with different ages, with different talents (i.e., 3 boys play baseball), etc. They should come back to your class able to report some specific information. Explain that they just did a census.

4. Have the children imagine what the trip to Bethlehem was like. Saint Mary would have been very uncomfortable with Jesus inside her. She would have been very concerned about finding a good place to have her baby. She would need to stop frequently for rests. Saint Joseph would likely have been very concerned about Mary's comfort and where they would stay. Did she have enough to eat and drink, would she need a break? It was a very long trip and many people were traveling, so finding a place to stay each night was very worrisome.

5. Have the children imagine what it would have been like in the stable. It would have been dark and dirty. It would smell like animals. Mary and Joseph might have been very sad there, knowing that their baby deserved much better, but they gave Him the best they could. When Jesus was born, you could only imagine all the excitement with a great star and angels in the sky. The innkeeper might have brought out guests to see the new baby. Jesus made a poor and lowly manger into the most holy of places, for there was found the King of Kings—God Himself!

Name:____________________

Review Questions

1. Who is the Mother of Jesus?

The Blessed Virgin Mary.

2. Was anyone ever free from Original Sin?

Yes. Mary was born free from Original Sin.

3. Where was Jesus born?

Bethlehem, in s stable, and placed in a manger.

4. When was Jesus born?

On the first Christmas Day more than two thousand years ago.

5. Who is Jesus Christ?

The Son of God and Our Savior.

6. Why did the Son of God become man?

To make up for all the sins that were ever committed.

Faith and Life Series • Grade 2 • Chapter 11 • Lesson 1 37

Reinforce

1. Have the students complete *Activity Book*, p. 37. When they have finished, review the correct answers.

2. If time permits, watch "The King is Born," video from the series Jesus: A Kingdom Without Frontiers, available through Ignatius Press; 30 minutes. If time does not permit, try to fit it in another day this week.

3. Teach and sing with the children "Once in royal David's city," *Adoremus Hymnal*, #328. Explain the words of the song to the children.

Conclude

End the class by praying the Act of Faith.

Preview

In the next lesson, we will learn how the shepherds came to visit Jesus in Bethlehem.

SAINT NICHOLAS AND SANTA CLAUS

Though one of the most popular saints in the Church, little is known about Saint Nicholas except that he was born in Parara, a city of Lycia in Asia Minor, and that he was the bishop of Myra in the fourth century. His relics are preserved today in the church of San Nicola in Bari, Italy. He is the patron saint of mariners, merchants, bakers, travelers, and children, and his feast day is December 6. Tradition asserts that he became well known during his life for giving generous gifts to many people, including the poor. In the United States he is identified with Santa Claus, the jolly man in a red suit who brings presents to children every Christmas Eve.

NOTES

____

____

____

____

____

____

____

____

____

____

LESSON TWO: SHEPHERDS CAME TO ADORE

Aims

The students will learn that the first people to learn about Jesus were the poor Jewish shepherds.

They will be able to tell how angels came to proclaim the birth of the Lord to these faith-filled shepherds.

Materials

- Children's Bible: Luke 2:8–19
- Nativity Set
- *Activity Book*, p. 38

Optional:
- "Once in royal David's city," *Adoremus Hymnal*, #328

Begin

Gather the children around a nativity set. Have them make a nativity story using the ornaments as you read the Christmas story from a children's Bible, using Luke 2:1–19. They should have Mary and Joseph going to Bethlehem, Baby Jesus, the angels, animals, and then the shepherds coming to visit. They can sing "Once in royal David's city," *Adoremus Hymnal*, #328, to end their story.

Develop

1. Read paragraphs 3 and 4 from the text.

2. Ask the students what a shepherd is. Someone who watches over flocks of sheep. He takes care of them, feeds them, leads them to good fields to eat. Explain that often the Jewish people were shepherds. It was an honest living. Shepherds did not make much money though. Can they think of a famous shepherd from the Old Testament? King David was a shepherd boy. We often refer to Jesus as the Good Shepherd because He leads us to Heaven.

3. Ask them how the shepherds might have felt. What would it have been like out in the field late the first Christmas night when the angels came? What would the angels have looked like? What did the angels say? Ask the children what angels are. They are pure spirits. They were created by God. They have no body. They are intelligent and free. Some angels chose to not serve God and are now called devils. The good angels serve God in Heaven. "Angel" means messenger. They often act as go-betweens for God and men. Why did God send angels? Why did He send them to shepherds? Would the shepherds have known that a Savior was coming? How? (Review Old Testament preparations and prophets).

4. Read Luke 2:10–12. Ask the children what it means. Ask the children what swaddling clothes are? What is the City of David? What is a manger? What would the shepherds have seen when they got to Bethlehem? What do the children think they would have felt?

5. Ask the children: If they were to go and visit the Baby Jesus, what would they do to prepare? What would they bring? (This may be a gift, or a talent, or a prayer, etc.)

Name:____________________

Pretend you are Mary or Joseph. What would you have written in your diary when Jesus was born?

Answers will vary.

38 *Faith and Life Series • Grade 2 • Chapter 11 • Lesson 2*

Reinforce

1. Have the students complete *Activity Book*, p. 38. They may share their work with the class.

2. They may assemble a classroom nativity set while saying their own prayers, describing what they would like to offer to baby Jesus.

3. They may work on a Christmas reenactment.

Conclude

1. Have the students offer their prayers and talents/gifts to Jesus.

2. Sing "Once in royal David's city," *Adoremus Hymnal*, #328.

3. Pray the Hail Mary.

Preview

In the next lesson, we will learn about the visit of the wise men.

DECEMBER SIXTH CUSTOMS

On December 5 every year, Saint Nicholas passes through towns in Germany, Switzerland, and the Netherlands and leaves coins or other small gifts for the children to discover on the morning of December 6, which is his feast day.

In the Netherlands, where Saint Nicholas is called Sinterklaas, there are many songs that children sing to celebrate the generous saint. Here is one of the most popular: "Sinterklaas kapoentje
gooi wat in mijn schoentje,
gooi wat in mijn laarsje
Dank u, Sinterklaasje"

NOTES

LESSON THREE: WISE MEN SEARCH FOR HIM

Aims

The students will learn that three wise men followed a star to the place of Jesus' birth.

They will understand that the wise men, who were gentiles, brought gifts for Jesus that were fit for a king

Materials

- Wrapped box
- Children's Bible (Mt 2:1–11)
- *Activity Book*, p. 39

Optional
- "Once in royal David's city," *Adoremus Hymnal*, #328

Begin

Hold up the wrapped box and ask the children what it is. A present. Why do we give presents at Christmas? We follow the example of the wise men who brought gifts to Baby Jesus. If you have Christmas presents, you may pass them out. Have the children say thank you for the presents you give them. Also ask them if they enjoy receiving gifts. They may open them at the end of class.

"I bring you good news," said the angel. "A Savior has been born to you. You will find Him lying in a manger." The shepherds hurried to find the newborn Savior. They found the baby Jesus with Mary and Joseph just as the angel had told them.

Far away, three wise men saw a big, bright star moving across the sky. They followed the star to see where it would take them. It led them to Jesus. The wise men gave precious gifts to the Savior, gifts for a king: gold, frankincense, and myrrh. They knew that Jesus was a great king, even though He looked like a poor little baby.

A wicked man named Herod ruled over the land where Jesus was born. He met the wise men and heard them talk about a baby who was a king. Herod wanted no one to be king but himself. He was so angry he tried to have Jesus killed. But God warned Joseph to take Jesus and Mary far away so that Herod could not kill Jesus. They went to the land of Egypt, and there they lived until Herod was dead.

"The angel said to them, 'Be not afraid; for behold, I bring you good news of a great joy . . . for to you is born this day in the city of David a Savior who is Christ the Lord.' "

Luke 2:10–11

57

Develop

1. Review the Christmas story they have learned thus far. You may reread p. 55 and the first paragraph on p. 57 of the text book.

2. Read the second paragraph on p. 57. You may also read this from a children's Bible (Mt 2:1–11).

3. The Wise Men came following a star (you may play follow the leader, with the leader holding up a star, leading the children to the nativity set). Gather around the nativity set and add the wise men to the scene.

4. Discuss who the Wise Men were. Some thought they were kings from far away lands. They were not Jewish, so they were called gentiles. This fact is important because Jesus came for all people, not just Jewish people.

5. The Wise Men brought gifts for Jesus that teach us about Him. They were gifts fit for a king:

- **Gold** was used as money. Kings had gold and jewels. The gift of gold teaches us that Jesus is the true King of Heaven and the Church.

- **Frankincence** is a type of perfume, burned as a pleasing scent. It is often used in worship. It is a sign of our prayers going up to Heaven. This gift teaches us that Jesus is not only God, but also a priest, Who acts on our behalf.

- **Myrrh** is an oil used for burying people. It preserves the body and has a nice smell. This gift reminds us that Jesus came into the world to die for our sins.

6. Ask the children if they enjoy receiving gifts. What are their favorites? What do they hope to receive this Christmas? Remind them that Jesus is the greatest gift of all.

Name:____________________

Joy in Receiving Jesus

We receive Jesus at Christmas.

We receive Jesus in Holy Communion.

Faith and Life Series • Grade 2 • Chapter 11 • Lesson 3 39

Reinforce

1. Have the students complete *Activity Book*, p. 39.

2. Have them work in pairs to memorize Questions 27–30 and the Words to Know.

Conclude

1. Sing "Once in royal David's city," *Adoremus Hymnal*, #328.

2. End by praying the Hail Mary.

3. The children may open their presents and celebrate with a Christmas party.

Preview

In the next lesson, we will learn about the Flight into Egypt.

LITTLE CHRISTMAS

The feast of the Epiphany is sometimes called "Little Christmas," for it was on this day that the birth of the Savior was revealed to the entire world, through the Magi, as He had been revealed to the Jewish people, through the shepherds, on Christmas Day.

WISE MEN, NOT KINGS

Although there is a tradition of calling the wise men kings, their proper name is "Magi." Magi were a priestly caste, or order, of ancient Media and Persia whose religion was similar to that of Zoroaster. There is no scriptural evidence to support the wise men's kingship, nor that they were three in number. Some Fathers of the Church speak of three Magi, but they were very likely influenced by the number of gifts.

NOTES

LESSON FOUR: FLIGHT INTO EGYPT

Aims

The students will learn that Joseph took Jesus and Mary and fled to Egypt to escape the evil plans of King Herod who was jealous of Jesus and wanted to kill Him.

They will learn that the Holy Family lived in Egypt until Herod was dead.

Materials

- Children's Bible (Mt 2:11–21)
- *Activity Book*, p. 40
- Blank paper, crayons

Optional
- "Once in royal David's city," *Adoremus Hymnal*, #328

Begin

Ask the students what composes a family. Today's families are made up of many different combinations of people—some have grandparents living at home, others have adopted siblings, etc. Ask the children why God gave us a family. It is not good that we be alone. Families give us love and support, understanding and protection. These are some of the qualities we will learn about today in the story of the flight into Egypt.

You may teach the children that Jesus, Mary, and Joseph are called the Holy Family and that they are a good example for all families.

Words to Know:

Bethlehem manger Christmas

Q. 27 *Where was Jesus born?*
Jesus Christ was born at Bethlehem in a stable, and placed in a manger (CCC 525).

Q. 28 *When was Jesus born?*
Jesus was born on the first Christmas Day more than two thousand years ago (CCC 526).

Q. 29 *Who is Jesus Christ?*
Jesus Christ is the Second Person of the Holy Trinity. He is true God and true man (CCC 470).

Q. 30 *Why did the Son of God become man?*
The Son of God became man to save us from our sins (CCC 461).

58

Develop

1. Read the rest of this chapter, the last paragraph on p. 57. You may also read this story from the children's Bible found in Mt 2:11–21.

2. The students may act out the entire Christmas story as they now know it. They may perform this for another class or for their families.

3. Ask them why Herod was so mean. He was jealous of Jesus because Herod did not want anyone else to be king. How did Jesus escape Herod? God told the Wise Men to not return to Herod and God also warned Saint Joseph to take Saint Mary and Jesus to Egypt for their safety.

4. Was Saint Joseph a good man? Yes, He was obedient. He also loved Jesus and Saint Mary so much. He wanted to protect them, and give them a safe home. His family was his most valuable gift from God.

5. The Holy Family is a good example for all families. Why? Because they loved one another, and gave of themselves to one another. They were faithful to God. Jesus was the center of their lives. They worked and prayed. They always did what was pleasing to God.

6. Ask how the children's families may be more like the Holy Family:
- Pray together and obey God
- Love one another
- Be more understanding, supportive
- Make their homes a safe place for others (pick up toys, do not leave out dangerous things).

7. Explain to the students that at Baptism, they become members of God's Family, the Church. This family, too, needs their love and support and protection from error.

Away in a manger, no crib for His bed,
The little Lord Jesus laid down His sweet head.
The stars in the sky looked down where He lay,
The little Lord Jesus asleep on the hay.

Be near me, Lord Jesus, I ask You to stay
Close by me forever and love me, I pray.
Bless all the dear children in Your tender care,
And fit us for Heaven to live with You there.

Traditional Carol

59

Reinforce

1. Have the students complete *Activity Book*, p. 40.

2. Have the students fold a piece of paper in fourths, and in each of the quarters, draw the Christmas story as it was divided in this chapter:
   - Going to Bethlehem for the Census
   - Shepherds Visiting the Baby Jesus in the Stable
   - Wise Men Following the Star to Jesus
   - The Flight into Egypt

3. Work on Memorizing Questions 27–30 and the Words to Know.

Conclude

1. Sing "Once in royal David's city," *Adoremus Hymnal*, #328.

2. End by praying to God, thanking Him for our families and for making us His children through Baptism. End with the Hail Mary.

Preview

In the next lesson, we will review the material covered in this chapter.

THE LITTLE DRUMMER BOY

According to legend, a little drummer boy was present in Bethlehem when Jesus was born. When he saw the magnificent gifts of the Magi, he was saddened because he was poor and had no gift to bring to the Christ Child. As the Magi left, he stood alone, then softly began to play his drum for the holy Baby. Walking forward and playing more loudly, he saw Jesus smile at him. With a heart full of love, he continued to play. No longer sad, the little drummer boy's heart sang for he knew that his was the greatest gift of all—the gift of love. It is important to remember that Jesus does not want extravagant or expensive gifts, only the best a person has. Using one's God-given talents for God's glory will certainly make the Christ Child smile.

NOTES

CHAPTER ELEVEN:
REVIEW AND ASSESSMENT

Aims

The students' understanding of the material covered this week will be reviewed and assessed.

Materials

- Quiz 11 (Appendix, p. A-15)
- "Once in royal David's city," *Adoremus Hymnal*, #328

Review

1. The students should understand why Mary and Joseph went to Bethlehem and why there was no place for them to stay (because of the Census).

2. Review that Jesus was born in a stable, wrapped in swaddling clothes, and laid in a manger.

3. Review that the first people to learn of Jesus were the shepherds. An angel appeared to them and told them about Jesus. They then went to Bethlehem to see the Divine Baby.

4. Review that the wise men came from far away, following a star to the stable in Bethlehem.

5. Review that King Herod was jealous of Jesus and wanted to be the only king. He told the wise men to tell him where Jesus was, but they did not. Herod tried to have Jesus killed, but God told Joseph to take Mary and Jesus and to go into Egypt for safety. They stayed there until Herod died.

6. Review that Jesus, Mary, and Joseph are called the Holy Family.

Name: ______

The Savior Is Born **Quiz 11**

Write what happened in the Christmas Story, using these words.

Bethlehem	shepherds	star	poor
manger	Joseph	gifts	
angel	Jesus	Herod	

1. Jesus was born in a city called Bethlehem .
2. Jesus was placed in a manger filled with straw.
3. The first people to learn about the newborn Savior were shepherds
4. God did not wish to share His life with the rich first, but with the poor .
5. An angel came to the shepherds to tell about the birth of Jesus.
6. Three wise men followed a big, bright star moving across the sky.
7. The wise men brought gifts of gold, frankincense, and myrrh to Jesus.
8. A wicked man named Herod ruled over the land where Jesus was born.
9. God warned Joseph to take Jesus and Mary away from Bethlehem.

Faith and Life • Grade 2 • Appendix A *A - 15*

Assess

1. Distribute Quiz 11 and answer any questions that the students may have. As the children hand in their quizzes, individually quiz them on the Memorization Questions and the Words to Know.

2. After all quizzes have been handed in, review the correct answers.

Conclude

1. The children may perform their dramatization of the Christmas Story.

2. Sing "Once in royal David's city," Adoremus Hymnal, #328.

CHAPTER TWELVE
THE HOLY FAMILY

Catechism of the Catholic Church References

Family: Duties of Children: 2215–18
Holy Family as Model of the Domestic Church: 1655–58, 1666
Mary as our Mother: 963–70, 973–75
Mysteries of Jesus' Hidden Life: 531–34, 564
Prayer in Union with Mary: 2673–79, 2682
Prayer of Praise: 2639–43, 2649
Prayer of Thanksgiving: 2637–38, 2648
Saints as Guides and Companions in Prayer: 2683–84, 2692–93

Scripture References

Making of the Holy Family: Mt 1:18–25
Presentation in the Temple: Lk 2:21–40
The Child Jesus: Lk 2:41–52; Mt 2:19–20

Background Reading: *The Fundamentals of Catholicism* by Fr. Kenneth Baker, S.J.

Volume 2:
"Mary, the Mother of God," pp. 340–43

Volume 2:
"Joseph and Mary, Husband and Wife," pp. 337–40

Summary of Lesson Content

Lesson 1

When Herod died, the Holy Family returned from Egypt to live in Nazareth.

Joseph is the foster-father of Jesus and the husband of Mary. He was a carpenter and he is a great saint.

Lesson 2

Mary is the mother of Jesus and wife of Joseph.

Mary had an important role in the Holy Family.

Lesson 3

Jesus was the son of Mary and foster-child of Joseph. His real father is God.

Jesus lived obediently with Mary and Joseph whom He loved dearly.

Jesus knew what God His Father wanted of Him, and He was obedient.

Lesson 4

The Holy Family is a model for all Christian families.

Through Baptism, we are members of God's family.

LESSON ONE: JOSEPH, HEAD OF THE HOLY FAMILY

Aims

The students will learn that when Herod died, the Holy Family returned from Egypt to live in Nazareth.

They will know that Saint Joseph is the foster-father of Jesus and the husband of Mary. He was a carpenter. He is a great saint

Materials

- Statue or picture of Saint Joseph (You can use the one on p. 60)
- Pictures of fathers with children
- Children's Bibles (Lk 2:21–40)
- *Activity Book*, p. 41

Optional:

- "Sleep, holy Babe," *Adoremus Hymnal*, #337
- Popsicle sticks, glue, paint

Begin

Show the children a picture of Saint Joseph. Do they know who he is? Tell them his name and that he is the husband of Mary and the foster-father of Jesus. Have the children name some things they do with their fathers (you may use photos of fathers with children to prompt ideas). Joseph did these sorts of things with Jesus. He loved Jesus very much and treated Him as his own son. Ask them what husbands and wives do together. Explain that Joseph did every-day things with Mary, such as ate meals, prayed, etc. This exercise is to help the children understand what role Joseph played in the life of Jesus.

Develop

1. Reading the first two paragraphs on p. 61 of the text.

2. Explain to the children that Saint Joseph was much like our fathers. He loved God. He loved Jesus and Saint Mary very much. He had a job. Do the children know what job he had? He was a carpenter. What does a carpenter do? He uses tools to make things out of wood: tables, chairs, cribs, cabinets, etc.

3. What do the children think Saint Joseph looked like? What color was his hair? What color were his eyes? What would he have worn?

4. What do the children think Saint Joseph was like? Was he friendly? Was he funny? Was he serious? Was he kind? Was he cheerful? How are their fathers like Saint Joseph?

5. What kinds of things do they think Saint Joseph did around the house? Did he help Saint Mary cook and clean? Did he fix things? Did he spend time with Jesus when he came home from work? What would he have done for fun?

6. We know Saint Joseph was a holy man. He took his faith very seriously. He had visions of angels and obeyed God when God told him to marry Saint Mary, to go to Egypt, and when it was safe to return from Egypt. We know that Saint Joseph practiced his faith—Judaism. He and Saint Mary presented Jesus in the Temple according to the Mosaic Law (Lk 2:21–40).

7. Jesus loved Saint Joseph very much. We, too, love our fathers. The class may make popsicle stick tool boxes for their fathers, or frames out of popsicle sticks to hold a picture of them with their fathers.

Name:____________________

St. Joseph

1. Who is Saint Joseph?

The head of the Holy Family

2. What did he do?

He worked hard to take care of Jesus and Mary

3. What are some words that tell us about Saint Joseph?

Carpenter, worker, foster-father, husband, strong, obedient, faithful, pure, just

Faith and Life Series • Grade 2 • Chapter 12 • Lesson 1 41

Reinforce

1. Have the students complete *Activity Book*, p. 41.

2. Have them memorize Question 26.

3. Teach and sing "Sleep, holy Babe," *Adoremus Hymnal*, #337. Tell them to imagine that Saint Joseph is singing this song (especially the 3rd verse).

Conclude

Pray the litany to Saint Joseph on p. 63 of the student text. Have the children think of other titles for Saint Joseph.

Preview

In the next lesson, we will learn more about Mary's role in the Holy Family.

THE PRESENTATION (CANDLEMAS)

On February 2nd, forty days after Christmas, the Church commemorates the day that Joseph and Mary presented Jesus to God in the Temple, along with a sacrifice of a pair of turtle doves. It also reminds us that Mary underwent the Jewish purification rites following childbirth and, like any other woman of her faith, she redeemed her first-born from the Temple. In the Temple, she was met by the holy prophet Simeon and the prophetess Anna. The least known name for this feast refers to a candle procession that the early Christians instituted to counter a pagan Roman holiday. This Roman feast fell in mid-February, forty days after the Eastern rite's celebration of Christmas on January 6th.

NOTES

LESSON TWO: MARY, HEART OF THE HOLY FAMILY

Aims

The students will learn that Mary is the mother of Jesus and the wife of Joseph.

They will learn that Mary had an important role in the Holy Family.

Materials

- Pictures of mothers with children
- Picture/Statue of Mary
- Children's Bible (Lk 2:41–52)
- *Activity Book*, p. 42

Optional:
- "Sleep, holy Babe," *Adoremus Hymnal*, #337
- Tissue paper, pipe cleaners
- "The Boy Jesus in the Temple," video; Jesus: A Kingdom Without Frontiers

Begin

Show the children a picture of the Blessed Virgin Mary. Do they know who she is? Tell them her name and that she is the wife of Joseph and the mother of Jesus. Have the children name some things they do with their mothers (you may use photos of mothers with children to prompt ideas). Mary did these sorts of things with Jesus. She loved Jesus very much and cared for her son. Ask them what husbands and wives do. Explain that Mary did everyday things with Joseph, such as ate meals, prayed, etc. This is to help the children understand who Mary is.

12 The Holy Family

> But when Herod died, behold, an angel of the Lord appeared in a dream to Joseph in Egypt, saying, "Rise, take the child and his mother, and go to the land of Israel, for those who sought the child's life are dead."
>
> Matthew 2:19–20

After Herod died, it was safe for Jesus, Mary, and Joseph to leave Egypt. They went to live in a small town called **Nazareth**.

Joseph was the head of the **Holy Family**. He loved God very much and he loved Jesus and Mary, too. Joseph worked hard all day so he could take care of Jesus and Mary. But he was always cheerful and kind. Joseph was a carpenter. He cut boards from trees and made them into tables and chairs. Jesus loved to watch Joseph at work. He was even happier when Joseph began teaching Him to be a carpenter.

Mary had a big job too. She took the money that Joseph made and went to buy the food the family needed. She baked bread, fixed meals, and made clothes for the three of them. Mary made the house a clean and happy place for Jesus and Joseph. Jesus also

61

Develop

1. Have the children read the third paragraph on p. 61 of their texts.

2. Explain to the children that the Blessed Virgin Mary was a very holy woman. She loved God dearly, and her Son, Who was God, with all her heart. She lived her faith with Saint Joseph and followed the ancient religious practices of her people, such as going to Jerusalem for Pentecost—in fact they took the whole family (aunts, uncles, cousins, etc.). Just like any family on a trip they too, had problems. (See the story of the Finding of the Child Jesus in the Temple: Lk 2:41–52.) Through this story, show Saint Mary's concern for her son and her resignation to God's will in her life.

3. Ask them what Saint Joseph did. He was a carpenter. He was the head of the Holy Family. A head is important to a body, right? So is the heart. The Blessed Virgin Mary is the heart of the Holy Family. She was equal to Saint Joseph, but different. His work was largely out of the home. She cooked and cleaned, did shopping, and read to Jesus. The home would not have been comfortable without her. Her work was essential. It is important to remember that all different kinds of jobs are needed for our world to work the way it does. People who work in grocery stores are every bit as important as lawyers. Lawyers get their food from grocers. In the Holy Family, Saint Mary was not a carpenter, but she worked very hard at home, with very, very important work.

4. Ask the children what the Blessed Virgin Mary might have looked like, or been like. What kind of mother was she? How are their mothers like Saint Mary?

5. The children can make a bouquet of tissue-paper flowers with pipe cleaner stems for their mothers.

Name:___________________

Blessed Mother

1. Who is the Blessed Virgin Mary?

The Mother of Jesus

2. What did Mary do in the Holy Family?

Mary made the house a clean and happy place for Jesus and Joseph

3. What are some words that tell us about Mary?

Mother, wife, pure, faithful, obedient, prayerful

42 *Faith and Life Series • Grade 2 • Chapter 12 • Lesson 2*

Reinforce

1. Have the students complete *Activity Book*, p. 42.

2. Have the students begin to memorize the Words to Know.

3. Watch "The Boy Jesus in the Temple," video from the series Jesus: A Kingdom Without Frontiers, available through Ignatius Press; 30 minutes.

Conclude

1. Lead the children in praying and really understanding the Hail Mary (line by line as necessary).

2. Sing "Sleep, holy Babe," *Adoremus Hymnal*, #337.

Preview

In the next lesson, we will learn that Jesus is the center of the Holy Family and God's family.

SAINT MARTIN DE PORRES: RESPONDING TO GOD IN FAITH AND DEED

Saint Martin de Porres was born in Lima, Peru, in the year 1579. The unwanted son of a Spanish gentleman and a colored freed woman from Panama, he became a lay Dominican brother at the age of fifteen. Unable to travel and earn for himself the crown of martyrdom, he made a martyr out of his body with his many strict penances. As a reward, God granted him the gifts of prophecy, bilocation, and aerial flight. As a barber and farm laborer, Saint Martin showed love for all those around him, including animals and the poor. He died on November 3, 1639, and was canonized in 1962. His feast day is November 3rd; he is the patron saint of public education, social justice, and interracial relations.

NOTES

LESSON THREE: JESUS, CENTER OF THE HOLY FAMILY

Aims

The students will know that Jesus was the son of Mary and foster-child of Joseph. His real father is God.

They will know that Jesus lived obediently with Mary and Joseph whom He loved dearly.

Jesus knew what God His Father wanted of Him, and He was obedient.

Materials

- Picture of the Holy Family (you may use the one on p. 60 of the text)
- *Activity Book*, p. 43

Optional:

- "Sleep, holy Babe," *Adoremus Hymnal*, #337

Begin

Have the students turn to p. 60 of their textbook, or look at another picture of the Holy Family. Discuss the picture with the children. Look at Joseph. What is he doing? Why is he not holding the baby? Does he look strong? Does he look happy? What is Mary doing? Who is she looking at? Who is Joseph looking at? Do they seem to love each other? Look at Baby Jesus. What is He doing? How do you think Jesus feels asleep in His mother's arms? If you imagine yourself as any member of the Holy Family, who would you want to be and why?

spent time helping His Mother around the house. He thought of ways to help her and to make her job easier.

Jesus loved to tell His parents all about the things He did and the games He played. He told them about His friends and liked to bring them home. Mary and Joseph were glad that Jesus shared these things with them.

Jesus knew that His Heavenly Father wanted Him to do what Mary and Joseph told Him. So He always obeyed them, even when He wanted to do something else.

Jesus, Mary, and Joseph prayed together each day. They praised and thanked their Heavenly Father for His goodness.

Did you know that you and your family can belong to the Holy Family, too? Jesus gave Mary to us to be our Mother. We can pray to Saint Joseph as our friend and protector. And Jesus is our brother. Through Baptism He made us His brothers and sisters.

Words to Know:

Nazareth Joseph Holy Family

62

Develop

1. Have the students read paragraphs 4 and 5 together.

2. List on the board things that Jesus did with His family.

- *Jesus told His parents what He did, games He played*
- *Jesus told His parents about His friends*
- *Jesus probably helped Saint Mary set the table or clean the house*
- *Jesus probably helped Saint Joseph in the workshop*
- *Jesus probably ran errands for His parents*

3. Have them write on the board things they can do with their families. Be sure each child writes one thing.

- They can help their parents
- They can show their parents how much they love them
- They can share the stories of their days, what they do at school, what they learned at church, etc.
- They can go to Mass together, pray together

4. Ask the children how they can be more like Jesus. List some of these traits/qualities/actions on the board. You may have them list ways that they can be more like Jesus in their own families or in their parish family.

- They can be more loving
- They can be more patient
- They do more good works, etc.

5. Read paragraph 5 again. Jesus knew what His Heavenly Father wanted of Him. He was to obey Mary and Joseph and Jesus did so. Jesus was always close to His Heavenly Father. We should be, too. It is important for the students to know that Jesus knew what was necessary for His Divine Mission on earth: He knew the Father's Will. He did not just accept whatever came His way. He had knowledge of what was necessary for our salvation.

Name:____________________

The Child Jesus

1. What do we know about Jesus?
Jesus helped his Mother around the house and loved His parents.

2. What did the Holy Family do together?
They prayed together and served God faithfully.

Faith and Life Series • Grade 2 • Chapter 12 • Lesson 3 43

Reinforce

1. Have the students complete *Activity Book*, p. 43. They may share their answers.

2. Have them work on their memorization of Questions 31 and 32, and the Words to Know.

3. They may perform skits of a day in the life of the Holy Family.

Conclude

1. Sing "Sleep, holy Babe," *Adoremus Hymnal*, #337.

2. Have the children pray for each other's intentions and pray the Hail Mary.

Preview

In the next lesson, we will learn about having a devotion to the Holy Family.

TH BLESSED VIRGIN MARY: SPOUSE OF THE HOLY SPIRIT

After accepting the Father's invitation to become the Mother of God, Mary was overshadowed by the Holy Spirit, and the Son was conceived in her womb. By the power of the Holy Spirit and because of her faith, Mary's virginity became uniquely fruitful. Thus, she is often called the spouse of the Holy Spirit.

NOTES

LESSON FOUR: BECOMING LIKE THE HOLY FAMILY

Aims

The students will learn that the Holy Family is a model for all Christian families.

They will review that, through Baptism, we are members of God's family.

Materials

- *Activity Book*, p. 44

Optional:
- "Sleep, holy Babe," *Adoremus Hymnal*, #337

Begin

Read the remainder of chapter 12 aloud to the class. You may choose to reread the first part of the chapter, as well, for review.

Q. 31 *Who is the Holy Family?*
The Holy Family is Jesus, Saint Mary, and Saint Joseph. Together they loved and served God faithfully. They are an example for all families (CCC 533).

Q. 32 *Who is Saint Joseph?*
Saint Joseph is the foster-father of Jesus, and Mary's husband (CCC 532–34).

Joseph most just . . .
Joseph most strong . . .
Joseph most obedient . . .
Joseph most faithful . . .
Head of the Holy Family . . .

Pray for us

We Pray:

God, our Heavenly Father, help our family to be like the Holy Family in Nazareth.

63

Develop

1. Review with the students the members of the Holy Family: Joseph, Mary, and Jesus. Review with them the roles of each person in the Holy Family.

2. Review with the children that they are born into God's family at Baptism. This makes Jesus their brother, God their Father, and Mary their mother. Review the Baptismal Formula: I baptize you in the Name of the Father and of the Son and of the Holy Spirit. *Amen*. It is then that they enter the Church, God's family here on earth.

3. Reread the text inside the box on p. 62. Jesus gave us the Holy Family, too. Mary is our Mother, Jesus gave her to us on the Cross. Saint Joseph is a good and mighty protector. We can ask him to pray for us and help us. Jesus knows what it is like to be their age. Because He is God, Jesus understands everyone and everyone's special strengths, weaknesses, and failings. We can always turn to Him, for He loves us so much.

4. *God really knew how important family is; in fact, every one of us has a family. We have a mother and father (and sometimes sisters and brothers). We have close friends, who are like family. We have our Church and, in Christ, the members of the Church are our family. We have the holy souls in Purgatory and the angels and saints in Heaven. They are our family, too. We have all of these parts of our family because Jesus made us His brothers and sisters in Baptism.*

5. You may take time to discuss how the children's families and Church communities may be more like the Holy Family.

6. The students may write prayers asking for the help of the Holy Family or write a poem about the Holy Family.

Name:____________________

Word Search

ANGEL	CLOTHES	HOLY
ANIMALS	EGYPT	FAMILY
BABY	FATHER	POOR
BETHLEHEM	FOOD	PROTECTS
CARPENTER	FRIENDS	SAVIOR
CHRISTMAS	GAMES	SHEPHERD
CLEAN	HEROD	STAR

S	C	S	H	E	P	H	E	R	D	P	E
X	L	V	C	L	O	T	H	E	S	R	A
B	E	T	H	L	E	H	E	M	I	O	N
A	A	H	R	E	S	O	F	E	S	T	I
K	N	E	I	P	F	L	A	G	E	E	M
E	S	R	S	O	O	Y	M	Y	E	C	A
D	T	O	T	O	O	E	I	P	F	T	L
A	A	D	M	R	D	E	L	T	A	S	S
N	R	G	A	M	E	S	Y	E	T	L	B
G	N	O	S	A	V	I	O	R	H	I	A
E	F	R	I	E	N	D	S	V	E	F	B
L	C	A	R	P	E	N	T	E	R	E	Y

44 *Faith and Life Series • Grade 2 • Chapter 12 • Lesson 4*

THE FEAST OF THE HOLY FAMILY

With origins in the seventeenth century, the Feast of the Holy Family has been celebrated by the Universal Church since 1921, when, under Pope Benedict XV, it was officially established. Celebrated on the first Sunday after Christmas (or on December 30, when Christmas is on Sunday), the Feast of the Holy Family celebrates the perfect family of Jesus, Mary, and Joseph as a model for all Christian families.

Reinforce

1. Have the students complete the puzzle on *Activity Book*, p. 44.

2. Have them perform skits of what life in the Holy Family may have been like. (They may act out the Presentation in the Temple or the Finding of the Child Jesus in the Temple, too.)

Conclude

1. Have the students pray the prayer on the bottom of p. 63 of the text.

2. Sing "Sleep, holy Babe," *Adoremus Hymnal*, #337.

3. The children may make their own litany to the Holy Family, following the example of the one for Saint Joseph on p. 63 of the text.

Preview

In the next lesson, we will review the material covered in this chapter.

NOTES

CHAPTER TWELVE: REVIEW AND ASSESSMENT

Aims

The students' understanding of the material covered this week will be reviewed and assessed.

Materials

- Quiz 12 (Appendix, p. A-16)
- Unit 3 Test (Appendix, pp. A-17 and A-18)
- "Sleep, holy Babe," *Adoremus Hymnal*, #337

Review

1. The students should know that the Holy Family came back to Judea from Egypt after Herod died. They lived in Nazareth.

2. Review that Saint Joseph was a carpenter and he was the husband of Mary and the foster-father of Jesus. He worked hard and loved God. He taught Jesus how to be a carpenter, too. He took care of Mary and Jesus and was obedient to God. He loved Mary and Jesus very much.

3. Review facts about the Blessed Virgin Mary. She was the wife of Saint Joseph and the mother of Jesus (the Mother of God). She kept the home and worked hard for the Holy Family. Jesus gave Mary to us to be our Mother.

4. The students should know the role of Jesus in the Holy Family. Though He is God, He was a child cared for by Mary, His mother, and Joseph, His foster-father. God was Jesus' real Father. Jesus lived His life as a boy in a family, and He was obedient to Mary and Joseph.

5. The students should be able to think of ways to follow Jesus' example within their own families. They should also be able to think of ways that their families can imitate the Holy Family.

Name:

The Holy Family **Quiz 12**

Fill in the blanks *Use the words below to help you.*

Mary	God	Holy Family	sister
Joseph	Nazareth	brother	heavenly
foster-father	obedient	home	carpenter

1. After Herod died, the Holy Family went to live in Nazareth.
2. Joseph was Jesus' foster-father.
3. For a job, Joseph was a carpenter.
4. Mary was the wife of Joseph and mother of Jesus.
5. Mary kept the home for the Holy Family.
6. Jesus was obedient to Mary and Joseph.
7. The Father of Jesus is God.
8. Jesus, Mary and Joseph are the Holy Family.
9. Through Baptism, Jesus is our brother.
10. Jesus always did what was pleasing to His heavenly Father.

Write five ways you can follow Jesus' example in your family.

1. Answers will vary
2. ________
3. ________
4. ________
5. ________

A - 16 *Faith and Life • Grade 2 • Appendix A*

Assess

1. Distribute Quiz 12 and answer any questions that the students may have. As they turn in their quizzes and tests, individually quiz them on the Memorization Questions and the Words to Know.

2. When all quizzes and tests have been turned in, review the correct answers.

Conclude

1. End with singing "Sleep, holy Babe," Adoremus Hymnal, #337.

2. The students may act out a story of the Holy Family and end with a prayer.

CHAPTER THIRTEEN
GOOD NEWS

Catechism of the Catholic Church References

Baptism of Jesus: 535–37, 565
Good News: God Has Sent His Son: 422–29
Jesus' Mission of Salvation: 456–60
Jesus: The Only Son of God: 441–45, 454
John: Forerunner, Prophet, and Baptizer: 523, 717–20
Kingship of Christ: 2105
Proclamation of the Kingdom of God: 543–46
"The Kingdom of God Is at Hand": 541–42, 567
The Twelve Disciples: 551–53

Scripture References

Mustard Seed: Mt 13:31–32; Lk 13:18–19
Buried Treasure: Mt 13:44–46
Twelve Apostles: Mt 10:1–4; Mk 3:10–19; Lk 6:10–18
Baptism of Jesus: Mt 3:4–17; Mk 1:4–13; Lk 3:1–23
Temptation in the Desert: Mt 4:1–11; Mk 1:12; Lk 4:1–13

Background Reading: *The Fundamentals of Catholicism* by Fr. Kenneth Baker, S.J.

Volume 3:
"Baptism into the Body of Christ," pp. 194–97

Summary of Lesson Content

Lesson 1

At the beginning of the public ministry of Christ, Jesus went to the Jordan to be baptized by John the Baptist.

At the Baptism of Jesus, the Holy Spirit descended as a dove, and God the Father said "This is my beloved Son, with Whom I am well pleased."

Jesus went into the desert for 40 days.

Lesson 2

When Jesus came out of the desert, He began to preach to people about the Good News of salvation.

Jesus picked twelve disciples.

Jesus told many stories to teach about the Kingdom of God.

Lesson 3

The parable of the Mustard Seed.

Lesson 4

The parable of the Buried Treasure.

LESSON ONE: THE BAPTISM OF JESUS

Aims

The students will learn that Jesus went to the Jordan to be baptized by John the Baptist.

They will learn that, at the baptism of Christ, the Holy Spirit descended as a dove, and God the Father said "This is my beloved Son, with Whom I am well pleased."

Materials

- Children's Bible (Mt 3:4–17; Mk 1:4–13; Lk 3:1–23)
- Image of Our Lady of Perpetual Help
- *Activity Book*, p. 45

Optional:
- "O Love, who drew from Jesus' side," *Adoremus Hymnal*, #562
- "The Baptism of Jesus," video; Jesus: A Kingdom Without Frontiers

Begin

Review the hidden life of Jesus, the happy time as Jesus lived in Nazareth with Joseph and Mary. He was preparing for His public ministry and work of salvation. Using an image of Our Lady of Perpetual Help, explain the story behind the image and telll them that Jesus, even from a young age, was preparing for His work of salvation. Explain to the children that at age 30, Jesus was ready to begin His public work. Today we will learn about the beginning of His ministry.

Develop

1. Read the first four pages of this chapter as a class.

2. From the children's Bible, read the story of the Baptism of Jesus (Mt 3:4–17; Mk 1:4–13; Lk 3:1–23). You may also read the Temptation in the Desert (Mt 4:1–11; Mk 1:12; Lk 4:1–13).

3. Discuss these Bible stories. They may dramatize them. The students should understand the events and people involved in these stories.

4. Ask the children what God the Father said at Jesus' Baptism. "This is My beloved Son, with whom I am well pleased." (This may be an opportunity to review the Trinity.) Explain to the children that at their own Baptism, they became children of God and their Original Sin was washed away. They were also filled with grace. In them, God is well pleased, too.

5. If you have taught the students about the Temptation in the Desert, you may ask them how they, too, can overcome the temptations that they experience. Ask them to name some of their temptations: i.e., to not obey, to not do work, to eat only candy and not vegetables, etc. Ask them how they can follow Jesus' example of saying "no" to the devil. They can practice their sports/music with joy, they can strive to please their parents and obey them, etc.

6. Take time to remind them that God has a plan for each of them. Ask them what they can do now to help them prepare for their future. They can pray, nurture their skills/talents, they can study hard, etc. You may have to help them see what needs to be done to accomplish their goals. Ask them what they want to be when they grow up and what they have to do to reach that goal. So, if Johnny wants to become a priest, he must pray, study religion, go to Mass, maybe become an altar server, etc.

Name:____________________

Color the picture of Jesus' Baptism.

Draw a picture of the Temptation in the Desert.

Faith and Life Series • Grade 2 • Chapter 13 • Lesson 1 45

Reinforce

1. Have the students complete *Activity Book*, p. 45.

2. If the students learned about the Temptation in the Desert, recall that Jesus was in the desert for 40 days. Have the children choose a sacrifice to make or a prayer to say every day for 40 days to unite themselves to Jesus in the desert.

3. Watch "The Baptism of Jesus," video from the series Jesus: A Kingdom Without Frontiers, available through Ignatius Press; 30 minutes.

4. Teach the children to sing "O Love, who drew from Jesus' side," *Adoremus Hymnal*, #562.

Conclude

Lead the children in praying for their intentions, end with the Our Father.

Preview

In the next lesson, we will learn about Jesus' public mission and the choosing of the Apostles.

TITLES AND SYMBOLS OF THE HOLY SPIRIT

Water: The Holy Spirit works through Baptism

Anointing: Christ was anointed by God's Spirit

Fire: The transforming energy of the Holy Spirit

Cloud, Light: Obscures and illuminates God

Seal: The permanence of the Holy Spirit's anointing

Hand, Finger: The laying on of hands, written law

Dove: Symbolizes His descent to earth

NOTES

LESSON TWO: JESUS PREACHES THE GOOD NEWS

Aims

The students will learn that when Jesus came out of the desert, He began to preach to people about the Good News of salvation and the Kingdom of God.

They will learn about the twelve Apostles.

Materials

- Newspaper
- Map of the Holy Land (preferably in Biblical times)
- Children's Bible
- Saint books
- *Activity Book*, p. 46

Optional:
- "O Love, who drew from Jesus' side," *Adoremus Hymnal*, #562

Begin

Display a newspaper for the class, and ask what it is and for what purpose it is used. A newspaper provides information to many people. What other ways can we share information? Mail, television, e-mail, Internet, telephone, fax, satellite, etc. Explain to the children that they did not have these ways of communicating in Jesus' time. Jesus had an important message to give, so He had to go from town to town to tell the people. He also had to rely on the help of His friends to spread His message.

13 Good News

"I baptize you with water for repentance, but he who is coming after me is mightier than I, whose sandals I am not worthy to carry; he will baptize you with the Holy Spirit and with fire."

Matthew 3:11

Jesus grew up and became a man. The time came for Him to leave the house in Nazareth and begin the work that God the Father sent Him to do. He said goodbye to His Mother Mary and started out.

First He went to the Jordan River to see **John the Baptist**. Jesus asked John to baptize Him. When John baptized Jesus the Spirit of God, looking like a dove, came to Him and God the Father spoke:

"This is my beloved Son, with Whom I am well pleased."

He said that so all the people would know that Jesus was the Son of God. Then Jesus went into the desert to pray.

After forty days, Jesus left the desert. He began to preach to people in towns and in the country. He

65

Develop

1. Read paragraphs 5–7 with the students.

2. Ask them how Jesus would have travelled from town to town: by foot, maybe by animal, boat. Show them on the map all the places where Jesus would have gone to preach the Good News.

3. Ask them what the Good News is:
   - That God loves them
   - That God wants them to be with Him forever in Heaven
   - That Jesus is the Savior and their sins can be forgiven

4. How did Jesus teach people about the Good News? He told them stories (parables).

5. Could Jesus speak to everyone? He spoke to large groups of people, and even to small groups of people. He even had a large following so people could learn about Him and His Good News. However, Jesus wanted more people to know. Jesus chose twelve disciples, or Apostles. They would learn more from Jesus than all other people. Jesus taught them so they could go out and preach the Good News.

6. Read from the children's Bible the selection of the Twelve Apostles: Mt 10:1–4; Mk 3:10–19; and/or Lk 6:10–18. Teach the students a way to remember the names of the Apostles. See the Chalk Talk on the opposite page.

7. Using books about saints, research the twelve Apostles (you may need to do this research for them). Create booklets, then have the students draw pictures to match each of the Twelve Apostles.

8. Play "telephone" with the children, so they can understand how word of mouth is passed on. Be very clear, so the message is not distorted.

Name:____________________

Jesus picked twelve men to be His disciples. They would be His special helpers and each would spread His word like mustard seeds throughout the world. The disciples soon learned from Jesus how to preach the Good News. Find in your Bible (Matthew 10:1–4) the names of the disciples and write them under the picture below.

1. Simon Peter
2. Andrew
3. James
4. John
5. Philip
6. Bartholomew
7. Thomas
8. Matthew
9. James
10. Thaddaeus
11. Simon
12. Judas Iscariot

46 *Faith and Life Series • Grade 2 • Chapter 13 • Lesson 2*

CHALK TALK: THE TWELVE APOSTLES

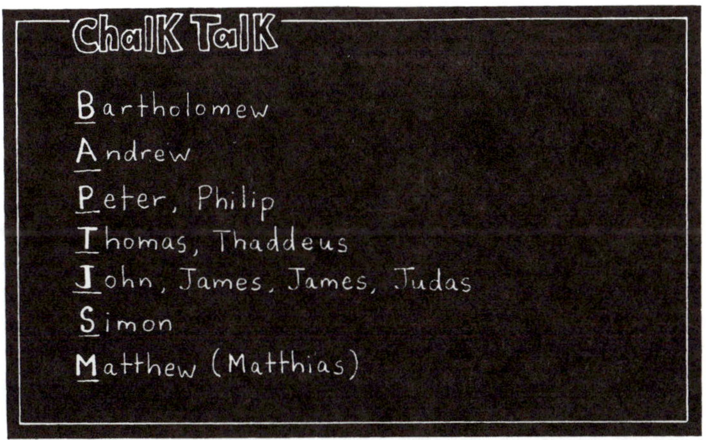

Reinforce

1. Have the students complete *Activity Book*, p. 46.

2. Have them create their own Apostles booklets or present their research on the Apostles.

Conclude

1. Sing with the children "O Love, who drew from Jesus' side," *Adoremus Hymnal*, #562.

2. Lead them in praying their intentions and end with the Our Father.

Preview

In the next lesson, we will learn the parable of the Mustard Seed.

NOTES

LESSON THREE: THE MUSTARD SEED

Aims

The students will learn the parable of the Mustard Seed.

Materials

- Mustard seeds, potting soil, cups
- Picture of mustard plants/bushes
- Children's Bible
- Crayons, pencils
- *Activity Book*, p. 47

Optional:

- "O Love, who drew from Jesus' side," *Adoremus Hymnal*, #562
- "Jesus' Teaching Ministry," video; Jesus: A Kingdom Without Frontiers

Begin

Gather the students and present each child with a tiny mustard seed. Ask them if they know what it is. Explain that it is a tiny mustard seed. Explain that this tiny seed can grow into a large plant or bush. Show them pictures of mustard bushes. Explain that from something so tiny (the seed), a great bush can grow and give homes to birds and small animals. Have the children plant their own mustard seeds in dixie cups with potting soil.

told them that God loved them and wanted them to be with Him in Heaven. He said that God would soon save them from their sins. Jesus told lots of stories that made it easier to understand what God was like.

Jesus picked twelve young men to be His **disciples**. They would be His special helpers and would learn more from Jesus than the other people. The disciples soon learned from Jesus how to preach the **Good News** to others.

Jesus told many stories to teach us about the **Kingdom of God**.

The Mustard Seed

The Kingdom of God is like a mustard seed which someone plants in his field. The mustard seed is one of the smallest seeds but it grows into a very large plant. It grows so big that birds can build their nests in its branches.

66

Develop

1. Read from the textbook, the section on the Mustard Seed, p. 66. You may also read this from a children's Bible (Mt 13:31–32; Lk 13:18–19).

2. Ask them what the mustard seed represents: The Kingdom of God. What is the Kingdom of God (union with God)? The Kingdom can be planted in our hearts by the preaching of the Good News. The Kingdom is Heaven—our union with God forever in Heaven. The Kingdom can be seen in the Church, founded by Christ, which teaches and gives us union with God through the sacraments. The Kingdom of God can be our souls full of grace, the seed having been planted at Baptism.

3. How can the Kingdom (seed) grow into a very large plant for us? Our faith can grow. We can teach it to others. We can live it in charity, so others, too, may be united with God. Can the students think of practical examples?

4. What birds can nest in the branches of the tree of the Kingdom? The poor, the lonely, the humble, those needing God's love and rest from suffering. Can the children think of people they hold in their hearts? Family? Friends? People they have heard about?

5. Ask them how they can plant the seeds of the Kingdom:

- *Give love to others*
- *Learn their faith and teach others about Jesus*
- *Do good works*
- *Invite others to church and class with them*
- *Pray that others will embrace the Kingdom*

6. Tell them that when they pray the Our Father, they pray "Thy Kingdom come . . . " this means that they are planting seeds of faith.

Name:____________________

Jesus taught us about the Kingdom in parables. Draw a picture of one of the parables about the Kingdom.

The kingdom is like Answers will vary.
because ______________________________________

____

Faith and Life Series • Grade 2 • Chapter 13 • Lesson 3 47

Reinforce

1. Have the students complete *Activity Book*, p. 47.

2. Have the children write lists of ways they may be planters of the seeds of the Kingdom.

3. Watch "Jesus' Teaching Ministry," video from the series Jesus: A Kingdom Without Frontiers, available through Ignatius Press; 30 minutes.

Conclude

1. Sing "O Love, who drew from Jesus' side," *Adoremus Hymnal*, #562.

2. Lead the children in praying their intentions and the Our Father.

3. Have them take home their planted mustard seeds.

Preview

In the next lesson, we will learn the parable of the Buried Treasure.

THE RELATIONSHIP OF PERSONS IN THE TRINITY

In Catholic Tradition, certain theological terminology is used to refer to each Person's relation to the other in the Trinity, which is stated in the Nicene Creed. The Church uses the term "substance" (at times "essence" or "nature") to signify the divine being in its unity: the term "person" or "hypostasis" to designate the Father, Son, and Holy Spirit in the real distinction among them; and also the term "relation" to indicate the fact that their distinction lies in the relationship of each to the others. The Father "begets" the Son eternally, and the Father and Son's mutual love results in the "spiration" of the Holy Spirit. See also CCC #249–56.

NOTES

LESSON FOUR: THE BURIED TREASURE

Aims

The students will learn the parable of the Buried Treasure.

Materials

- A box or bag full of treasure (i.e., coin-shaped foil wrapped chocolates)
- Children's Bible
- *Activity Book*, p. 48

Optional:
- "O Love, who drew from Jesus' side," *Adoremus Hymnal*, #562

Begin

Before the children come in, hide a "treasure" for the class. Hide it really well, so they will probably nott find it. You may want to prepare a clue that you keep for yourself. When the children come in, tell them that there is a treasure hidden in the room for them. If after a time, they cannot find the treasure, tell them that you have a clue and that they may buy it from you. What would they give you for this clue? Would they give you something dear to them? Just what would they do to find this treasure. Once they find it, they may share it among themselves.

The Buried Treasure

A man found a buried treasure in a field. He wanted to keep the treasure. But the field belonged to somebody else. So the man took all the money he had in the world. He bought the field so he could have the treasure.

When we learn the secret of how to live forever with God, it is like finding a buried treasure. When the man in the story bought the field, other people might have said, "Why is he spending so much money on an old field?" They did not know about the treasure. In the same way, some people do not understand why we follow God's laws. They do not know how wonderful Heaven is!

Jesus called everyone to live in the Kingdom of God. He taught us how to please God in our daily lives. He came to win us over to a life of friendship with God.

Words to Know:

John the Baptist disciple
Good News Kingdom of God

67

Develop

1. Read from the text book, the parable of the Buried Treasure, p. 67. You may read this from a children's Bible (Mt 13:44).

2. Tell the children that union with God in Heaven is happiness forever. It is worth far more than a real treasure of gold and riches. What would we do to get this treasure? Have the students discuss what they would do.

3. Using a piece of the treasure from the Begin section, give the children an example. Tell them that if you have some chocolate (or whatever the treasure was) and you give it all to someone else, do you have any left? No. Who has it? Someone else does. You may actually give it to a student. However, if you have love, and you give it to another, do you have any love left? Yes. Who else also has it? The other person. What about faith? Is it more like the treasure or love? Love, because if you give it to another, you still have it. Material gifts cannot be multiplied. Spiritual gifts multiply exponentially. So, if you give it to two people, and they each give it to two people—you can see that spiritual gifts grow very fast (like the mustard seed). This kind of treasure is very valuable, not only because it multiplies quickly, but also because it will last forever.

4. Ask the students how they may find the treasure of the Kingdom of God:
- *Study their faith*
- *Pray*
- *Baptism*

5. Ask the students how they may share this treasure.

6. Finish reading the textbook chapter.

Q. 33 *Why was Jesus baptized by Saint John the Baptist?*
Jesus was baptized by Saint John the Baptist so that all people would know that Jesus is the Son of God (CCC 535).

Q. 34 *Why did Jesus preach the Good News?*
Jesus preached the Good News so that everyone could enter the Kingdom of God by accepting His teachings (CCC 543).

68

Reinforce

1. Have the students complete *Activity Book*, p. 48.

2. Have them write their own Kingdom parables. They may draw them, as well, and may share them with the class.

3. Have them research and memorize the Words to Know from this chapter.

Conclude

1. As a class, sing "O Love, who drew from Jesus' side," *Adoremus Hymnal*, #562.

2. Lead them in praying for their intentions and the Our Father.

Preview

In the next lesson, we will review the material covered in this chapter.

CHALK TALK: MATERIAL GIFTS VS. SPIRITUAL GIFTS

Material:

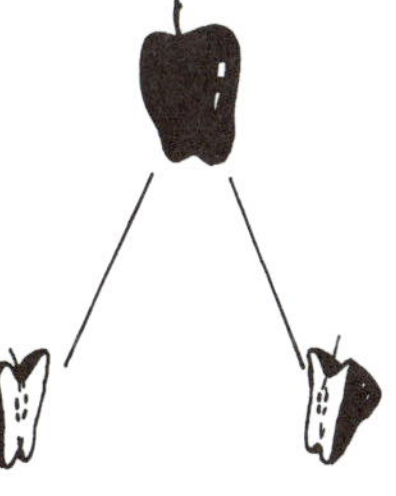

The apple must be divided each time it is shared.

Spiritual:

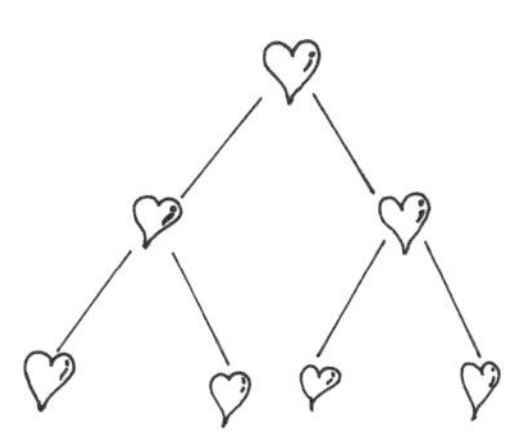

Love can be passed in whole from one person to another and is never used up.

NOTES

CHAPTER THIRTEEN: REVIEW AND ASSESSMENT

Aims

The students' understanding of the material covered this week will be reviewed and assessed.

Materials

- Quiz 13 (Appendix, p. A-19)
- "O Love, who drew from Jesus' side," *Adoremus Hymnal*, #562

Review

1. Review the events of the Baptism of Jesus, and help the students to recognize the three Persons of the Trinity in the Baptism of Christ.

2. Help them to understand that in Baptism they, too, become children of God and are pleasing in His sight.

3. They should know who John the Baptist is, how the Holy Spirit appeared (under what symbol), and where Jesus went after His Baptism.

4. They should know that during His public ministry, Jesus went from town to town preaching the Good News of the Kingdom of God. They should be able to explain what the Kingdom is and the two parables as examples of the Kingdom: the mustard seed and the buried treasure.

5. They should know that the twelve Apostles were selected by Jesus to learn more about the Good News and how to preach it to others.

Name:

The Good News **Quiz 13**

Circle the correct answer.

1. Jesus was baptized by:
   a) Saint Joseph b) Mary, His mother c) John the Baptist
2. Jesus went into the desert for:
   a) one month b) forty days c) three months
3. Jesus went from town to town to:
   a) preach the Good News b) purchase goods for the Kingdom c) bury people
4. Jesus chose ___________ Apostles.
   a) ten b) eleven c) twelve
5. What two parables did you study?
   a) The Pearl and Fisher's Net b) Flour and Leaven and Good Seed c) The Mustard Seed and Buried Treasure

Circle the names of the Twelve Apostles:

Bartholomew Biff Andrew Peter Philip Tim Simon
John James James Judas Thaddeus Thomas Matthew
Bob Sam

Faith and Life • Grade 2 • Appendix A A - 19

Assess

1. Distribute Quiz 13 and answer any questions that the students may have. As the children hand in their quizzes, individually quiz them on the Words to Know from this chapter.

2. After all quizzes have been turned in, review the correct answers.

1. Sing "O Love, who drew from Jesus' side," *Adoremus Hymnal*, #562.

2. Lead the children in praying for their intentions and end with the Our Father.

CHAPTER FOURTEEN
JESUS OUR TEACHER

Catechism of the Catholic Church References

Charity: 1822–29, 1844
Christ the Physician: 1503–5
Jesus as our Teacher and Model of Holiness: 516, 519–21, 561
Love for the Poor and the Works of Mercy: 2443–49, 2462–63
Prayer for the Dead: 1032, 1055
Proclamation of the Kingdom of God: 543–46
Sacrifice: 2099–100
Sickness in Christian Life: 1506–10
Sickness in Human Life: 1500–1501

Scripture References

Good Samaritan: Lk 10:29–37
Corporal Works of Mercy: Mt 25:31–46; Mt 5:1–2

Background Reading: *The Fundamentals of Catholicism* by Fr. Kenneth Baker, S.J.

Volume 2:
"His Mercy Is Everlasting," pp. 71–74

Volume 3:
"A Tribunal of Mercy," pp. 280–82

Summary of Lesson Content

Lesson 1

The story of the Good Samaritan.

Lesson 2

Jesus taught the law of love, and called us to love God and neighbor. The story of the Good Samaritan teaches us who our neighbor is.

Man can love God through loving his neighbor.

Lesson 3

The Corporal Works of Mercy are:
Feed the Hungry.
Give drink to the thirsty.
Clothe the naked.
Shelter the homeless.
Visit the sick.
Visit the imprisoned.
Bury the dead.

Lesson 4

The Corporal Works of Mercy are to be lived by all people.

Optional: The parable of the sheep and goats (last judgment).

LESSON ONE: THE GOOD SAMARITAN

Aims

The students will learn the story of the Good Samaritan.

Materials

- Pictures of different people (various races, religions, ages, genders, etc.)
- Children's Bible
- *Activity Book*, p. 49

Optional:

- "Hail to the Lord's Anointed!" *Adoremus Hymnal*, #354
- "The Story of the Good Samaritan," video; The Beginner's Bible

Begin

Gather the students and ask them who their neighbors are. They may respond that their neighbors are the people who live next door to them. This is correct, but who else? Is it their family? Friends? Only people they have met? Start holding up pictures of different people. Each time ask, "Are these people your neighbors?" How can they know? Explain that all people are our neighbors and that Jesus used the story of the Good Samaritan to teach us about loving our neighbors.

14 Jesus Our Teacher

> Seeing the crowds, he went up on the mountain, and when he sat down his disciples came to him. And he opened his mouth and taught them.
>
> Matthew 5:1–2

One day Jesus told this story:

Once a man was travelling on a very dangerous road. It was a place where robbers would often wait to hurt people and take their belongings. And that is what happened to this man. He lay by the road, too hurt to move, and all his things had been stolen.

Soon a man came riding by. He saw the other man lying there, but he didn't care and rode on by. Another man did the same. Then a third man came. He felt sorry for the man who had been robbed. He took the man to the next town, and he paid for the man to be taken care of.

This, said Jesus, is what it means to love your neighbor. It means to help those in need, and to be kind to everyone. Jesus said that if we do something

69

Develop

1. Read from the text, the first 2 (or 3) paragraphs about the Good Samaritan. (Stop before, "This, said Jesus, is what it means to love your neighbor.") You may read this from the children's Bible: Lk 10:29–37.

2. Watch "The Story of the Good Samaritan," video from the series The Beginner's Bible, available through Ignatius Press; 30 minutes.

3. Discuss with the students, how the three men who came across the hurt man differ. The first two were a priest and a Levite. They were Jews. They were of the same race as the hurt man. Why did they not stop to help? Maybe they were scared to hurt him more. Maybe they thought he was dead. They would both have been labeled as "unclean" in their culture for coming in contact with blood or a dead person, and would have been separated from their community and worship for a time. This would have been a sacrifice to make. Does love require sacrifices? Yes. (Have the children give examples of sacrifices people make because they love another person. For example, their mom sacrifices her time by making them dinner or taking them to a game, etc.)

4. The Samaritan is a man who was not liked by the Jews. They were looked down upon and treated poorly. Why did he stop to help the hurt man? Love requires us to give even to those who have hurt us. It calls us to give of ourselves, even to strangers. Love calls us to see God in our neighbor. Do the children think the Samaritan saw God in the hurt man? Did he make a sacrifice to help him? Did he have to help him? Why did he? Because of love.

5. Make this into a modern day parable, and ask how the children would respond. (Use the idea of a playground bully or another age-appropriate example.) Have the children dramatize their modern day parable.

Name:____________________

Answer the following questions.

1. What did the Good Samaritan do for the man who was robbed? He took the man to the next town, and he paid for the man to be taken care of.
2. Did the Good Samaritan love Jesus in this man? Yes
3. What does it mean to love God? To love your neighbor and to help those in need, and to be kind to everyone.
4. How can you be like the Good Samaritan? Doing something kind for a person who needs our help.
5. List some ways you can love your neighbor. Feed the hungry, give drink to the thirsty, give shelter to the home-less, give clothing to the naked, visit the sick, visit the impris-

Faith and Life Series • Grade 2 • Chapter 14 • Lesson 1 49

Reinforce

1. Have the students complete *Activity Book*, p. 49.

2. If you have not yet done so, watch the "The Story of the Good Samaritan," video from the series The Beginner's Bible, available through Ignatius Press; 30 minutes.

3. Teach and sing "Hail to the Lord's Anointed!" *Adoremus Hymnal*, #354.

Conclude

Lead the children in praying for their neighbors:
Lord of the hungry and thirsty...
Lord of the naked...
Lord of the homeless...
Lord of the sick and imprisoned...
Lord of all who have died and gone to Purgatory
Lord of Heaven...
Lord of our neighbors...
Amen.

Preview

In the next lesson, we will learn more about loving God through loving our neighbor.

SAINT ELIZABETH OF HUNGARY

Saint Elizabeth, the daughter of Alexander II of Hungary, was born in 1207. In 1221, she married Louis of Thuringia, a good man who shared her love of virtue. Despite her royal position, she led an austere life, practiced penance, and devoted herself to works of charity. After Louis' death in the Crusades, Elizabeth left the court, made arrangements for her three children, and in 1228, she renounced the world to become a tertiary of Saint Francis. She died in 1231. Her feast day is November 17. She is the patroness of bakers, countesses, the death of children, the falsely accused, the homeless, nursing services, tertiaries, widows, and young brides.

NOTES

LESSON TWO: LOVE OUR NEIGHBORS

Aims

The students will learn that Jesus taught the law of love and called us to love God and neighbor.

They will learn the story of the Last Judgment and that man can love God through loving his neighbor.

Materials

- Children's Bible: Mt 25:31–46
- Pictures from previous Begin section

Optional:
- "Hail to the Lord's Anointed!" *Adoremus Hymnal*, #354
- "Whatsoever You Do," song by Willard F. Jabusch, often found in Missalettes

Begin

Review who their neighbors are: everyone. Ask them if they do good to their neighbors if they also love God. Yes. We know this because Jesus told us so. We can also know this because God comes to live in His children. So, when we do something good to a child of God, we do something good to God Himself. God is the Father of all people (because they are made in His image), and more perfectly in those who are baptized.

Develop

1. As a class, read the last paragraph on p. 69 together (Paragraph starting: This, said Jesus...).

2. Read from the children's Bible the Last Judgement: Mt 25:31–46. Focus on Mt. 25:40 "Truly, I say to you, as you did it to one of the least of these my brethren, you did it to me." The children may dramatize this story.

Optional: If you have the song: "Whatsoever You Do" by Willard F. Jabusch, teach it to the children and write the words on the board. This song is often found in missalettes or hymnals.

3. Remind the students of the Ten Commandments and that they represent ten ways to love God and neighbor. We can love God and neighbor by keeping God's laws. We also learned the Great Commandments of Love. Ask them if they remember the Commandments. You shall love the Lord your God with all your heart, soul, strength, and mind, and your neighbor as yourself.

4. Holding up the pictures of the different people, ask them how they can love God through them. For example, if you have a picture of a homeless person, they can say that they can love God by giving him food, clothes, a place to stay, by praying for him, etc.

5. Ask them how they can love God through their family members, their friends, and themselves. If possible, do a class project, such as visit the elderly in a nursing home, make cards for homeless people in a shelter or sick children in a hospital, or do a clothes/food/money drive for charity.

kind for a person who needs our help, it is like doing it for Jesus Himself.

Here are some of the things Jesus said we should do, and some ways we can do them. They are called the **Corporal Works of Mercy**.

Feed the Hungry and
Give Drink to the Thirsty

Give money to the missions, bring food to your church Thanksgiving drive, help your mother fix dinner, and eat the food you are given without complaining, as a sacrifice for the hungry.

Clothe the Naked

Send old clothing to the missions, lend your extra coat or gloves if your friend doesn't have his, help your little brother or sister to get dressed.

71

Reinforce

1. Explain the following class activity of loving God through our neighbor, even if it is only making time for prayer for another.

2. Have the students choose one neighbor through whom they will love God, and say how they will accomplish this. This can be a week-long assignment (e.g., I will love God in my mother by helping her do dishes). Have them report back on their works of charity.

Conclude

1. Sing: "Hail to the Lord's Anointed!" *Adoremus Hymnal*, #354.

2. Lead the children in praying for their neighbors:
Lord of the hungry and thirsty...
Lord of the naked...
Lord of the homeless...
Lord of the sick and imprisoned...
Lord of all who have died and gone to Purgatory...
Lord of Heaven...
Lord of our neighbors...
Amen.

Preview

In the next lesson, we will learn the Corporal Works of Mercy.

SAINT SIMON STOCK

Little is known about Saint Simon Stock's early life, though the name "Stock," i.e., tree trunk, derives from the fact that from age twelve he lived as a hermit in the hollow of an oak tree. He became a Carmelite and went on to found many Carmelite communities, specifically in the university towns of Cambridge, Oxford, Paris, and Bologna, and helped to change the order from hermits to mendicants. In 1254, he was elected Superior General of his Order in London. He became well known after a Marian apparition in Cambridge, England, on July 16, 1251, while the Carmelite Order was being oppressed. Our Lady appeared to him holding the brown scapular in one hand.

NOTES

LESSON THREE: CORPORAL WORKS OF MERCY

Aims

The students will learn that the Corporal Works of Mercy are:
Feed the Hungry.
Give Drink to the Thirsty.
Clothe the Naked.
Shelter the Homeless.
Visit the Sick.
Visit the Imprisoned.
Bury the Dead.

Materials

- Children's Bible
- *Activity Book*, p. 50

Optional:
- "Hail to the Lord's Anointed!" *Adoremus Hymnal*, #354

Begin

Review the story of the Last Judgment (Mt 25:31–46). You may re-read this from the children's Bible. List the works of mercy that are mentioned in this passage on the board. Tell the children that these seven works are called the Corporal Works of Mercy. Today, they will learn more about the Corporal Works of Mercy.

Shelter and Welcome the Homeless

If someone new moves to your neighborhood, make him feel welcome. Be a friend to the boy or girl in your class who seems lonely.

Visit and Comfort the Sick and Imprisoned

Go to see friends and neighbors when they are sick. If your classmate is sick, bring his schoolwork home and help him with it. Visit someone who is old and can't go out much; ask if you can help in any way.

Bury the Dead

We should pray every day for those who have died, even if we did not know them, so they will be happy in Heaven with God.

72

Develop

1. Explain to the students that the Corporal Works of Mercy deal with taking care of the physical needs of others. God made us with both a body and a soul; it is, therefore, important to take care of our bodies as well as our souls.

2. Go through each of the Works of Mercy and be sure the children understand what they mean. Can they think of examples of people who can be served (e.g., people who go to a local soup kitchen or homeless shelter)?

- *Give Food to the Hungry and Drink to the Thirsty. This means that all people should have something to eat and drink to nourish their bodies. We need food and drink to live. In some countries, people die from not eating/drinking. In our own country, many people have to miss meals because they cannot afford food.*
- *Clothe the Naked. Clothing is a way of protecting our bodies. Some people have no clothes at all. Others do not have the right kind of clothes; for example, some people do not have winter coats and are very cold in the winter.*
- *Shelter the Homeless. Some people do not have anywhere to live. Some people have no home because they had to leave them for their safety. Others have no money.*
- *Visit the Sick and Imprisoned. Often sick and imprisoned people are not taken care of, or are forgotten about. Sometimes people are scared of them.*
- *Bury the Dead. It is important to bury the dead because it is a way of honoring their bodies, but also a way of preventing illness. We should always pray for the dead so they will be happy with God in Heaven.*

Name:________________

Can you find these words in the puzzle?
Look carefully! The words go across and down.

FEED	DEAD	IMPRISONED
HUNGRY	HELP	LOVE GOD
CLOTHE	GIVE DRINK	LOVE OTHERS
NAKED	THIRSTY	BE KIND
VISIT THE SICK	SHELTER	
BURY	HOMELESS	

```
V I S I T T H E S I C K
L G I V E D R I N K F B
O B U R Y I D E A D E E
V D L X E N O F E D E K
E I M P R I S O N E D I
G M V X P U X X P R T N
O N A K E D R A Y E H D
D X H U N G R Y X F I S
H O M E L E S S S A R R
E N C L O T H E E T S E
L O V E O T H E R S T X
P S H E L T E R V E Y X
```


Reinforce

1. Have the students complete the puzzle on *Activity Book*, p. 50.

2. Have them memorize the Corporal Works of Mercy, and the Words to Know.

Conclude

1. Sing "Hail to the Lord's Anointed!" *Adoremus Hymnal*, #354.

2. Lead the children in praying for their neighbors:
   Lord of the hungry and thirsty…
   Lord of the naked…
   Lord of the homeless…
   Lord of the sick and imprisoned…
   Lord of all who have died and gone to Purgatory…
   Lord of Heaven…
   Lord of our neighbors…
   Amen.

Preview

In the next lesson, we will learn age-appropriate ways to live the Corporal Works of Mercy.

MENDICANT ORDERS

Religious in these orders, by their vow of poverty, rely on their work and the charity of others to survive. This vow is not merely individual, it is also a community vow. Four great mendicant orders from the Middle Ages (the Order of Preachers, the Friars Minor, the Carmelites, and the Hermits of Saint Augustine) were recognized by the Second Council of Lyons in 1274. It is important to realize that receiving charity is often, in itself, charitable, for items may be offered that are not desired. It is vital that a person recognize the hand of God, to trust that He will give what is needed, and always to thank Him for His gifts.

NOTES

LESSON FOUR: LIVING THE WORKS OF MERCY

Aims

The students will learn age-appropriate ways to live the Corporal Works of Mercy.

Materials

- *Activity Book*, p. 51

Optional:

- "Hail to the Lord's Anointed!" *Adoremus Hymnal*, #354

Begin

Review the seven Corporal Works of Mercy. Have students volunteer to come forward and write them on the board. Ask other students to describe what these works mean.

Q. 35 *What are the Corporal Works of Mercy?*
The Corporal Works of Mercy help us to live the Kingdom of God here on earth (CCC 2447). The seven Corporal Works of Mercy are:

1. Feed the hungry.
2. Give drink to the thirsty.
3. Give shelter to the homeless.
4. Give clothing to the naked.
5. Visit the sick.
6. Visit the imprisoned.
7. Bury the dead.

Words to Know:

Corporal Works of Mercy

73

Develop

1. As a class, read pp. 71 and 72 of the textbook.

2. *Ask the students different ways they can live each of the Works of Mercy (practical, age-appropriate examples). Listed below are a few to get them started:*

- *Feed the Hungry/Give Drink to the Thirsty: Share their lunches with a student who has forgotten his*
- *Clothe the Naked: Give their hand-me-downs to younger relatives*
- *Shelter the Homeless: Welcome a new student to the class*
- *Visit the Sick and Imprisoned: Make cards for the sick, pray for those in jail*
- *Bury the Dead: Pray for those who have died*

3. Have the children break into five groups. Each group is assigned a box from the textbook. They may act out one of the examples given or make up their own. They should perform their skit for the rest of the class.

4. Play a review game with the children, giving them examples of works of mercy for which they must name the Corporal Work of Mercy. For example: Martin of Tours gave half his coat to a beggar. (Clothe the Naked) Share your lunch with a student who forgot his. (Feed the Hungry) Make a get well soon card. (Visit/Comfort the Sick). Saint Thérèse prayed for the conversion of a sinner in jail. (Comfort the Imprisoned).

5. Have the students work on a class project for charity, or have a volunteer come in and explain the kind of work they do. This should give the children an example of loving God in their neighbor.

6. Follow up with the children's projects of works of charity.

Name:____________________

CORPORAL WORKS OF MERCY	HOW CAN YOU LIVE THESE WORKS?
1. Feed the hungry	Answers will vary
2. Give drink to the thirsty.	
3. Clothe the naked.	
4. Shelter the homeless.	
5. Visit the sick.	
6. Visit the imprisoned.	
7. Bury the dead.	

Faith and Life Series • Grade 2 • Chapter 14 • Lesson 3 51

Reinforce

1. Have the students complete *Activity Book*, p. 51.

2. Have the students perform their "Corporal Works of Mercy" skits for each other.

3. Work on a class project together.

Conclude

1. Sing "Hail to the Lord's Anointed!" *Adoremus Hymnal*, #354.

2. Lead the students in praying for their neighbors:
Lord of the hungry and thirsty...
Lord of the naked...
Lord of the homeless...
Lord of the sick and imprisoned...
Lord of all who have died and gone to Purgatory...
Lord of Heaven...
Lord of our neighbors...
Amen.

Preview

In the next lesson, we will review the material covered in this chapter.

SAINT CATHERINE OF SIENA

Saint Catherine was born in Siena in 1347, the 25th child of the dyer Giacomo di Benincasa and his wife Lapa. From a young age she began to have mystical experiences, seeing guardian angels as clearly as people. At age 16 she became a Dominican tertiary and her visions of Jesus, Mary, and other saints continued. She experienced a "mystical espousal" in 1366, and she received the stigmata in 1375, visible only after her death in Rome in 1380. She died at age 33, the age of Christ at His death, and her body was found incorrupt in 1430. Her feast day is April 29. She is one of three female Doctors of the Church. She is the patroness of Italy.

NOTES

CHAPTER FOURTEEN:
REVIEW AND ASSESSMENT

Aims

The students' understanding of the material covered this week will be reviewed and assessed.

Materials

- Quiz 14 (Appendix, p. A-20)
- "Hail to the Lord's Anointed!" *Adoremus Hymnal*, #354

Review

1. The students should know and understand the story of the Good Samaritan.

2. They should understand that everyone is their neighbor and that we are called to love him. Love may require sacrifice and even giving to those who have hurt us. We should love family, friends, and all people. The children should know that in loving their neighbors, they are also loving God.

3. They should know and understand the meaning of the seven Corporal Works of Mercy:
   - Feed the hungry
   - Give drink to the thirsty
   - Clothe the naked
   - Shelter the homeless
   - Visit the sick
   - Visit the imprisoned
   - Bury the dead

4. They should be able to give age-appropriate, practical examples of how to live the Corporal Works of Mercy.

Name:

Jesus Our Teacher **Quiz 14**

Answer these questions.

1. Jesus told a story of a good man who helped a stranger in need. Who was this good man? the good samaritan
2. By helping the poor, the needy, and those wanting help, we are helping our neighbor.
3. In loving our neighbor, we are really loving Jesus.

Write how you can live each of the Corporal Works of Mercy:

1. Feed the Hungry: Answers will vary
2. Give Drink to the Thirsty:
3. Clothe the Naked:
4. Shelter the Homeless:
5. Visit the Sick:
6. Visit the Imprisoned:
7. Bury the Dead:

A - 20 *Faith and Life • Grade 2 • Appendix A*

Assess

1. Distribute Quiz 14 and answer any questions that the students may have. As the children hand in their quizzes, individually quiz them on the Words to Know from this chapter.

2. After all have turned in their quizzes, review the correct answers.

Conclude

1. "Hail to the Lord's Anointed!" *Adoremus Hymnal*, #354.

2. Pray for the intentions of the students.

CHAPTER FIFTEEN
LET US PRAY

Catechism of the Catholic Church References

Childlike Trust in Prayer: 2734–41, 2756
Forgiveness: 2842–45, 2862
Holiness of God's Name: 2142–45
Jesus at Prayer: 2598–2606, 2620
Jesus Hears and Answers Prayer: 2616, 2621
Lord's Prayer as Summary of the Whole Gospel: 2761–76
Prayers of Blessing and Adoration: 2626–28, 2645
Prayers of Intercession: 2634–36, 2647
Prayers of Petition: 2629–33, 2646
Prayers of Thanksgiving: 2637–38, 2648
Seven Petitions of the Lord's Prayer: 2803–6, 2857
Summary of Our Father: 2797–2802, 2857–63
What Is Prayer?: 2559–65, 2590, 2644

Scripture References

Our Father: Mt 6:1–16; Lk 11:1–4; Mt 6:9–13
Pharisee and Tax Collector: Lk 18:10–14; Lk 11:9

Background Reading: *The Fundamentals of Catholicism* by Fr. Kenneth Baker, S.J.

Volume 2:
"Prayer and God's Knowledge of the Future," pp. 59–62

Summary of Lesson Content

Lesson 1

The disciples asked Jesus how to pray, and Jesus taught the disciples to pray the Our Father.

[Note: the focus of this lesson is the spirit of prayer and the memorization of the Our Father]

Lesson 2

The petitions of the Our Father.

Lesson 3

Man should pray always and everywhere.

The two types of prayer are vocal and mental prayer.

There are four kinds of prayer:

1. Adoration/Praise
2. Thanksgiving
3. Petition
4. Intercession

Lesson 4

God hears man's prayers and responds according to His will.

[Note: we will spend extra time memorizing common Catholic Prayers.]

LESSON ONE:
TEACH US HOW TO PRAY

Aims

The students will learn that the disciples asked Jesus how to pray and that Jesus taught them.

They will learn with what spirit they should pray.

Materials

- Children's Bible
- *Activity Book*, p. 52

Optional:
- "All hail, adored Trinity!" *Adoremus Hymnal*, #462

Begin

Gather the students and ask them how they pray. What do they do? Do they pray out loud? Do they pray silently? Do they pray only at church? Some will say they kneel beside their beds. Some may hold hands with their families for grace before supper. Explain to the children that the Apostles had the best person to learn from: God Himself in the Person of Jesus. They asked Jesus how they should pray, and Jesus taught them. We too, can learn from what Jesus said.

Develop

1. Read the first paragraph from the textbook with the children.

2. Read from a children's Bible Mt 6:1–8 (Stop before the Our Father—we want to focus on the spirit of prayer).

3. Ask the students what they learned about how they should pray. What did Jesus say?
- *Beware of praying to be seen*
- *Do not seek praise (be humble)*
- *Be generous and pray in secret*
- *Say what you mean, do not use empty words*

4. Discuss what these things mean at an age-appropriate level.

5. To give the children a good example, read from the children's Bible again. This time, read the story of the Pharisee and tax collector who go to the temple to pray: Lk 18:10–14.

6. Ask the children why the tax collector's prayer was better. Who was humble? Who used empty words? Who wanted to be heard and seen? Who turned to God for help? Who was proud? What was the Pharisee saying? What did the tax collector say? What did Jesus say about this?

7. Remind the children that Jesus was preparing for His ministry while living with the Holy Family. They taught Him to pray, and they learned from Jesus, too. We can ask the Blessed Virgin Mary and Saint Joseph to intercede for us, to teach us to pray as they did, and to pray with us.

Name:___________________

Jesus,
Teach me how to pray.

Color the picture.

52 *Faith and Life Series • Grade 2 • Chapter 15 • Lesson 1*

Reinforce

1. Have the students complete *Activity Book*, p. 52.

2. Have them write their own prayers to God. Remind them what Jesus taught them about how to pray.

3. Teach the children to sing "All hail, adored Trinity!" *Adoremus Hymnal*, #462.

Conclude

1. The students may share the prayers that they wrote.

2. Review the Sign of the Cross, the Our Father, the Hail Mary, and the Glory Be.

Preview

In the next lesson, we will learn the Our Father and study its petitions.

THE PHARISEE AND THE TAX COLLECTOR
(Lk 18:10–14)

Pharisee	Tax Collector
• Proud	• Humble
• Praises himself	• Confesses his sins
• Stands fearlessly	• Cannot bear to look up
• Thanks God	• Pleads with God

NOTES

LESSON TWO: OUR FATHER

Aims

The students will learn the petitions of the Our Father.

Materials

- Children's Bible
- *Activity Book*, p. 53

Optional:
- "All hail, adored Trinity!" *Adoremus Hymnal*, #462

Begin

Review how Jesus taught us to pray. He taught them what to pray: the Our Father. Read from a children's Bible: Mt 6:9–13 or Lk 11:1–4.

Ask the children if they recognize this prayer. Orally quiz each child to see if they know the Our Father. You may need to help them. Review the prayer regularly.

15 Let Us Pray

"Pray then like this:
Our Father who art in heaven,
Hallowed be thy name.
Thy kingdom come,
Thy will be done,
On earth as it is in heaven.
Give us this day our daily bread;
And forgive us our debts,
As we have also forgiven our debtors;
And lead us not into temptation,
But deliver us from evil."

Matthew 6:9–13

The disciples knew that when they prayed they were talking to God, praising Him, and asking for what they needed. But they wanted to know how they should pray so they asked Jesus to teach them. Jesus taught them to say the prayer we call the **Our Father**. By giving the disciples that one prayer Jesus was able to teach them how they should pray.

God wants us to call Him *Father*, because we are the children He loves. *Hallowed be Thy Name* is our

75

Develop

1. Read paragraphs 2–6. The students may take turns reading aloud.

2. Go through the prayer of the Our Father line by line. Have them explain the prayer in their own words to give concrete examples.

Our Father, Who art in Heaven
- We can call God our Father because we are the children He loves (Note: we became His children in baptism)
- God is in Heaven and everywhere

Hallowed by Thy Name
- Holy is God's Name (2nd Commandment); we honor God

Thy Kingdom come
- Then everyone will be His children, and we will be united with Him

Thy will be done on earth as it is in Heaven
- God's will, is what He wants. We want what God wants because He is all good and loving, and He wants what is best for us

Give us this day our daily bread
- We are asking for all the things we need, including the Eucharist
- We are also praying for the poor and hungry

Forgive us our trespasses as we forgive those who trespass against us
- We ask God to forgive our sins
- We are reminded that we, too, must forgive people if we expect to be forgiven

Lead us not into temptation
- We ask God to keep us strong when we are tempted to sin.

Deliver us from evil
- We ask God to protect us from all evil

Amen
- This means "so be it" or "we believe this to be true"

Name:____________________

Prayer

Answer the following questions.

1. What is prayer?

Prayer is talking to God, praising Him, and asking Him for what we need.

2. What did the disciples know they were doing when they were praying?

They knew they were talking to God

3. Whom did the disciples ask to teach them how to pray?

Jesus

4. What prayer did He teach them?

The Our Father

5. For what does this prayer teach us to pray? There are seven things. Can you list them and explain them?

1. To call God Father
2. To use God's holy name with honor and respect
3. To know that God has a plan for us
4. To ask for all that we need
5. To forgive those who have done wrong to us
6. To ask God to forgive our sins
7. To ask God to keep us strong when we are tempted to sin

Faith and Life Series • Grade 2 • Chapter 15 • Lesson 2 53

Reinforce

1. Have the students complete *Activity Book*, p. 53.

2. Have them begin memorizing the questions for the chapter.

Conclude

1. Lead the students in singing "All hail, adored Trinity!" *Adoremus Hymnal*, #462.

2. End by praying the Our Father. Take a moment for silent reflection before praying.

Preview

In the next lesson, we will learn more about different kinds of prayer.

JESUS ON PRAYER

In Matthew 6:5–8, Jesus tells his disciples how to pray:

"And when you pray, you must not be like the hypocrites; for they love to stand and pray in the synagogues and at the street corners, that they may be seen by men. . . But when you pray, go into your room and shut the door and pray to your Father who is in secret; and your Father who sees in secret will reward you."

NOTES

LESSON THREE: PRAYING TO GOD

Aims

The students will learn that they can pray always and everywhere.

They will learn about the differences between vocal and mental prayer.

They will learn the four kinds of prayer: adoration/praise; thanksgiving; petition; intercession.

Materials

- *Activity Book*, p. 54

Optional:
- "All hail, adored Trinity!" *Adoremus Hymnal*, #462

Begin

Review with the children the Our Father and Question 36 on p. 78. Explain to the children that God knows everything. He knows who we are, what we do, even what we are thinking. He is all knowing. So, when we pray, we can pray out loud or in our hearts. Prayer is lifting our hearts and minds to God. We can do this vocally or mentally. Write "vocal" on the board and "out loud" beside it. Then write "mental" on the board, and "in your heart" beside it. Tell the children that both ways of praying are good.

wish that everyone use God's holy name with honor and respect.

We want God's Kingdom to come because then everyone will be His children. *Thy will* means the plan God has for us. If we all did what God wanted, as the angels do in Heaven, then earth would be a very happy place for everyone.

When we ask God for our *daily bread* we are really asking for all the things we need. With these words we are also praying for people who are poor and hungry, for those who are sick or lonely. We ask for what our souls need, too.

We beg God to forgive our sins. The words *as we forgive those* remind us that if we want God to forgive us, we should be ready to forgive those who have done wrong to us.

We end the Our Father by asking God to keep us strong when we are tempted to sin. God will help us fight and win over evil.

Jesus told us other things about prayer. He said we should pray always. We can talk to God any time, at home, in school, or at play.

Jesus told us that God will give us what we ask of Him if it is good for us. Sometimes we have to wait a long time before God answers our prayers, but we

76

Develop

1. Read the third paragraph on p. 76 as a class.

2. Explain to the students that there are four kinds of prayer:

- *ADORATION AND PRAISE: In adoration and praise, we see God for Who He is. We tell Him how great He is and how much we love Him. Have the children think of examples of praise and adoration: I love you God; O God, You are so good.*

- *THANKSGIVING: With prayers of thanksgiving, we remember all of the gifts God has given us, like our families, food, love, special gifts, etc., and we take the time to say thank you to God for His generosity. Have the children give examples of Thanksgiving: I thank You God for my family and for helping me with my test.*

- *PETITION: This means "to ask for." When we petition God, we ask for something. We can pray for things we need or want. God will give them to us if He sees that they are for our good. Have the children give you an example of petition: Dear God, if it is Your will, please help me with my studies.*

- *INTERCESSION: This means "to ask in the place of someone else." With this prayer, we can pray for other people and their needs. The saints can intercede for us. Have the children give an example of intercessory prayer: Dear God, please help my sick grandmother get better, etc.*

3. Tell the children that "singing is praying twice." You pray with the words and with the music. Mass is the perfect prayer: it has all four kinds of prayer.

Name:___________________

4 Kinds of Prayer

When we pray, we can pray to God out loud or in our hearts. When we pray, we talk with and listen to God. There are four different kinds of prayer:

1. Adoring or Praise.
With this kind of prayer, we see God for who He is, and tell Him how much we love Him.

2. Thanksgiving.
With this kind of prayer, we thank God for all the gifts He has given to us, such as family, food, and love.

3. Petition. This means "to ask for." With this kind of prayer, we can ask God for all that we need.

4. Intercession. This means "to ask in place of someone else." With this kind of prayer, we can pray for other people and their needs.

54 *Faith and Life Series • Grade 2 • Chapter 15 • Lesson 3*

Reinforce

1. Have the students complete *Activity Book*, p. 54.

2. Have them write prayers of Adoration, Thanksgiving, Petition, and Intercession. Have them label the kinds of prayer: we praise, we thank, we ask, and we intercede.

Conclude

1. Sing: "All hail, adored Trinity!" *Adoremus Hymnal*, #462. (Remember this is praying twice.)

2. Have them review the song and name the types of prayer they can find in the lyrics.

3. End by praying the Morning Offering on p. 78.

Preview

In the next lesson, we will learn that God hears and answers our prayers.

SAINT JOHN BOSCO

Saint John Bosco was born of poor parents in a small town near Piedmont, Italy, on August 16, 1815. At age nine he had a dream about his future vocation. He was ordained a priest in 1841 and settled in Turin. He began his ministry by using his gift of juggling to catch the attention of the young boys in town, after which he would teach them, take them to Mass, and hear their confessions. This apostolate soon developed into the Salesian Order (the order of Saint Francis de Sales). One of his students was Saint Dominic Savio. Later he founded an order of women, the Daughters of Mary Auxiliatrix; for similar work among girls. He died in 1888 at the age of seventy-two. He was canonized in 1934; his feastday is January 31.

NOTES

LESSON FOUR: GOD HEARS OUR PRAYERS

Aims

The students will learn that God hears their prayers.

Note: they will spend extra time memorizing common Catholic Prayers.

Materials

- Children's Bible
- *Activity Book*, p. 55

Optional:
- "All hail, adored Trinity!" *Adoremus Hymnal*, #462

Begin

Review the definition of prayer: lifting one's heart and mind to God.

Review vocal (out loud) and mental (in the heart) prayer.

Review the four kinds of prayer: praise/adoration, thanksgiving, petition, and intercession.

Review that singing is praying twice, and Mass is the perfect prayer.

Ask the students if God hears and answers all their prayers. We will learn more about this today.

shouldn't be afraid to keep asking. Jesus once told a story of a man who went to his friend's house late at night. The man knocked on the door and called out that he needed some bread. Even though the friend didn't want to get up, he finally did, because the man kept asking.

God loves you more than the man loved his friend, Jesus said, so you know that God will answer your prayers.

Words to Know:

Our Father

***"Ask, and it will be given you;
seek, and you will find;
knock and it will be
opened to you."***

Luke 11:9

77

Develop

1. Read the rest of the chapter with the students.

2. From a children's Bible, read Luke 11:5–9.

3. Review the story of the man who knocks on his friend's door late at night. His friend opens the door to give to his friend. Is God like the friend? Surely if we knock, He will open the door.

4. If a child asks his father for a fish, would he give the child a serpent? If he asks for an egg, would he give him a scorpion? No. God is more loving than our earthly fathers, so he will give what we need with perfect generosity and love.

5. Does God hear all our prayers? Yes. Does God answer all our prayers? Yes. Do we always get the answers we like? Not always. Sometimes the answer to a prayer is "no" or "not now." Sometimes it is "Yes," but God always answers according to His will and out of love for us. God knows more than we do, and He knows what is best for us. Sometimes we ask for things that are not the best for us. For example, we might ask to eat only ice cream for lunch. This would taste good and might give us pleasure, but it would probably make us sick and we would not get the nutrients we need. The best answer is to eat a good meal, then maybe we can have ice cream for dessert.

6. Have the children dramatize the importune friend parable, or a modern day version, or simply how God answers their prayers.

7. Spend time with the students reviewing Catholic prayers they should have memorized.

Q. 36 *What is prayer?*
Prayer is lifting our hearts and minds to God to adore Him, to thank Him, and to ask Him for what we need and for the needs of others (CCC 2559, 2626, 2629, 2634, 2637).

We Pray:

MORNING OFFERING

O my God, I offer You every thought
and word and act of today.
Please bless me, my God,
and make me good today. *Amen.*

78

PRAYERS THAT SHOULD BE MEMORIZED

By this point in the class, the children should have memorized the following prayers:

- Our Father (The Lord's Prayer)
- Sign of the Cross
- Glory Be
- Guardian Angel Prayer
- Saint Michael the Archangel Prayer
- Hail Mary

Reinforce

1. Have the students complete *Activity Book*, p. 55.

2. Have them work on memorizing their prayers and the questions for the chapter.

Conclude

1. Sing "All hail, adored Trinity!" *Adoremus Hymnal*, #462.

2. End class with a prayer.

Preview

In the next lesson, we will review the material covered in this chapter.

NOTES

CHAPTER FIFTEEN:
REVIEW AND ASSESSMENT

Aims

The students' understanding of the material covered this week will be reviewed and assessed.

Materials

- Quiz 15 (Appendix, p. A-21)
- "All hail, adored Trinity," *Adoremus Hymnal*, #462

Review

1. Review with the students how they should pray. You may review the story of the Tax Collector and the Pharisee.

2. Review the Our Father and its petitions.

3. Review vocal and mental prayer.

4. Review the four kinds of prayer:
   - Praise and Adoration
   - Thanksgiving
   - Petition
   - Intercession

5. Review that "singing is praying twice" and that Mass is the perfect prayer.

6. Review with them that they can pray any time and any where.

7. Review with them that God hears all our prayers and answers all of them.

8. Review the story of the importune friend.

9. Review various Catholic prayers the students should have memorized.

Name:

Let Us Pray **Quiz 15**

Matching *Place the letter from column 2 in the correct space of column 1.*

Column 1	Column 2
b Our Father Who art in Heaven	a. May what God wants be done so everyone will be happy.
e Hallowed be Thy Name	b. As His children, we can say this.
d Thy Kingdom come	c. May God provide all we need.
a Thy will be done on earth as it is in Heaven.	d. May everyone be united with Him.
c Give us this day our daily bread	e. May we use God's name with respect and honor.
g And forgive us our trespasses as we forgive those who trespass against us	f. Let us not give in to sin, and protect us.
f Lead us not into temptation but deliver us from evil.	g. May our sins be washed away, and may we love one another.

1. Circle how often God hears our prayers:

sometimes usually **(always)** often never

2. Circle why can we trust God to answer our prayers the best way:

(His love) we work hard we bother Him He has to

Faith and Life • Grade 2 • Appendix A *A - 21*

Assess

1. Distribute Quiz 15 and answer any questions that the students may have. As the children hand in their quizzes, individually quiz them on the prayers they memorized.

2. After all quizzes have been turned in, review the correct answers.

Conclude

1. Sing "All hail, adored Trinity!" *Adoremus Hymnal*, #462.

2. End with prayer.

CHAPTER SIXTEEN
WE BELIEVE

Catechism of the Catholic Church References

Jesus as Messiah: 436–40, 453
Jesus as True God and True Man: 464–70, 480–83
Jesus' Miracles: 547–48
Jesus' Mission of Salvation: 456–60
Jesus: Only Son of God: 441–45, 454
Jesus Still Acts in Sacraments: 1084
Miracles and Other Signs of the Kingdom: 547–50, 567

Proclamation of the Kingdom of God: 543–46
Signs and Wonders:
- Accompanying preaching: 542
- Messianic signs: 549
- Witness to mission: 550

"The Kingdom of God is at hand": 541–42, 567

Scripture References

Calming of the Storm: Mt 8:23–27; Mk 4:35–41; Lk 8:22–25
Healing of Blind: Mt 9:27–31
Healing of Paralyzed: Mt 9:27–31
Jairus' Daughter: Mt 9:18, 23–31; Mk 5:22–24, 35–43; Lk 8:40–42, 49–56
Multiplication of Loaves and Fish for 5000: Mt 14:13–21; Mk 6:34–44; Lk 9:11–17; Jn 5:5–15
Wedding at Cana: Jn 2:1–11
John 20:29

Background Reading: *The Fundamentals of Catholicism* by Fr. Kenneth Baker, S.J.

Volume 3:
"Jesus Gave Thanks," pp. 226–28

Summary of Lesson Content

Lesson 1

Jesus' first public miracle was the changing of water into wine at the wedding at Cana.

Mary interceded for the bride and groom.

Miracles evoke faith.

Lesson 2

Jesus was able to calm a storm at sea (nature miracle).

The disciples were in awe of the authority of Christ even over nature.

Lesson 3

Jesus multiplies five loaves and two fish to feed 5000 men (women and children aside).

This miracle leads to the Bread of Life discourse, referring to Jesus present in the Eucharist.

Lesson 4

Jesus' miracles also directly healed people: the blind, the paralyzed, the sick, and the hurt.

Jesus was even more powerful than death, demonstrated by the raising of Jairus' daughter from the dead.

LESSON ONE: THE WEDDING AT CANA

Aims

The students will learn that Jesus' first public miracle was the changing of water into wine at the wedding at Cana.

They will know Mary interceded for the bride and groom.

Materials

- Paper, 2 paper clips
- Pitcher of water, sugar, juice crystals, cups
- Children's Bible
- *Activity Book*, p. 56

Optional:
- "Faith of our fathers!" *Adoremus Hymnal*, #603
- "The Wedding at Cana," video; Jesus: A Kingdom Without Frontiers

Begin

Gather the children around and ask them what magic is? It is a trick, where the hand should to be faster than the eye. Demonstrate for them a magic trick (any will do—see opposite page for a suggestion). Sometimes with magic, things are changed so we may believe they are different, even though it was only a trick done by a human. For example, take a pitcher of water, add 1 cup sugar and 1 package Kool-Aid crystals. Voila, you have a drink. Was it magic? Not really. There was nothing to it. What is the difference between magic and a miracle? We'll learn today.

16 We Believe

Jesus said to him, "Have you believed because you have seen me? Blessed are those who have not seen and yet believe."

John 20:29

Jesus wanted people to believe that He was the promised Savior and the Son of God. To help them believe, Jesus worked many **miracles**. By working these miracles He showed that He could do all things. Jesus is God, just as His Father is God.

The first miracle Jesus worked was at a wedding party. They had run out of wine to drink. Mary, Jesus' Mother, asked Him to help. Jesus took some water and changed it into wine.

Another time, Jesus and the disciples were in a boat on a lake. The wind started blowing hard. Soon big waves were crashing into the boat. The disciples were afraid. They woke up Jesus, Who was sleeping down inside the boat. "Lord, save us! The boat will sink!" Jesus got up and said "Be still" to the wind and water. At once the storm ended. The disciples were surprised to see the wind obey Jesus.

79

Develop

1. Ask the students who does magic. Usually a magician, who wants money or fame. Why does he do magic? For entertainment. Can he do miracles? No. Magic is a trick done with the things we have; miracles are an act of God, and they lead us to faith in God.

2. Explain to the students that this week they will be learning about miracles. Have the students look up the word "miracle" in the glossary. They should pay attention to whether or not a miracle they learn about could be a magic trick, or if it is truly a miracle, and if it is a miracle, it should strengthen their faith.

3. Have the students read the first two paragraphs of this chapter.

4. Read the account of the Wedding at Cana from the children's Bible (Jn 2:1–11). Ask the children about this story:

- What did Jesus do? What did He change, and into what?
- Where does wine usually come from? How long does it take to make wine?
- Who asked Jesus to do this miracle? What did she ask for?
- What did she tell the servants to do?
- Did anyone come to believe in Jesus because this happened?
- Was this a miracle, or magic?

5. Review the role of the Blessed Virgin Mary as intercessor. What prayer do we know that asks Mary to intercede for us? The Hail Mary: Holy Mary, Mother of God, pray for us sinners . . .

6. What does this miracle teach us about Jesus?
- *He can perform miracles.*
- *He is the Son of God.*
- *He loves others.*
- *He answers prayers.*

Name:___________________

Jesus made the lame to walk and the blind to see.

56 *Faith and Life Series • Grade 2 • Chapter 16 • Lesson 1*

Reinforce

1. Have the students complete *Activity Book*, p. 56.

2. Teach and sing "Faith of our fathers!" *Adoremus Hymnal*, #603.

Conclude

Lead the children in praying for their intentions. Pray the prayer found on the top of p. 83, and the Hail Mary.

Preview

In the next lesson, we will learn about the Calming of the Storm.

NOTES

____

____

____

____

____

INSTRUCTIONS FOR A SIMPLE MAGIC TRICK

Materials: two paper clips and a sheet of paper.

Fold the sheet of paper in three.

Fasten a paper clip at the two places indicated.

Pull the ends of the paper outward and the two paper clips will be interlocked.

LESSON TWO: THE CALMING OF THE STORM

Aims

The students will learn that Jesus was able to calm a storm at sea and that the disciples were in awe of the authority of Christ over nature.

Materials

- Weather section of newspaper
- Children's Bible
- *Activity Book*, p. 57

Optional:
- "Faith of our fathers!" *Adoremus Hymnal*, #603

Begin

Show the students the weather section of a newspaper. Ask the children if the weather prediction is always right. Certainly not. We cannot always accurately predict the weather. We also cannot change the weather. How often have we wanted good weather and it rained, or we want snow (so we can miss school) but it just will not snow? Only God can determine the weather. Changing the weather would take a miracle.

Develop

1. Read paragraph 3 with the students.

2. Read the Calming of the Storm from a children's Bible: Mt 8:23–27; Mk 4:35–41; Lk 8:22–25.

3. Discuss this story with the students:
   - Who was in the boat?
   - What was Jesus doing?
   - Why were the disciples afraid? Were they in danger?
   - What happened?
   - Is this a magic trick?
   - Why can we say this is a miracle?
   - What does it say about Jesus?

4. You may take time to discuss the picture on p. 80 of the text. What is happening? What are the disciples doing? Do they look happy/sad? Is the boat big? Do they look like they are in danger? Does Jesus look scared?

5. *Do the students think Jesus was not aware of the storm? He was sleeping. Who asked Jesus to perform this miracle? (The disciples). As the communion of saints they, too, can pray for us. Why did Jesus wait for the disciples to ask for His help? Maybe to show that he answers our prayers. Would Jesus have allowed the boat to sink? Why did the disciples have to ask? Jesus wanted them to believe. Why did the disciples turn to Jesus? They had faith that Jesus could help them. We, too, should have this kind of faith.*

6. What did the disciples say? Who is this that even the wind obeys? Surely, the disciples recognized that Jesus was not just a man, but the Son of God. Their faith was made stronger.

Name:____________________

Miracles

1. What did Jesus want people to believe?

That He was the promised Savior and the Son of God

2. Why did Jesus work miracles?

To show that He could do all things and to show that He is God

3. What different miracles did Jesus do?

He changed water into wine, ended a storm, made enough food to feed five thousand people, made the blind see, made the lame walk, and cured the sick

4. What happened during a storm? Why were the disciples surprised?

Jesus stilled the wind and the water. They were surprised because the wind obeyed him.

Color the picture.

Faith and Life Series • Grade 2 • Chapter 16 • Lesson 2 57

Reinforce

1. Have the students complete *Activity Book*, p. 57.

2. Have them dramatize the miracles about which they have learned.

3. Have them memorize the definition of miracle.

4. Compare the two miracles they have learned by using the chart.

Conclude

1. Sing "Faith of our fathers!" *Adoremus Hymnal*, #603.

2. Lead in praying for their petitions. Ask for the intercession of the Blessed Virgin Mary and the Apostles (by name) as a litany. End with the prayer on the top of p. 83.

Preview

In the next lesson, we will learn about the multiplication of loaves and fish.

BENEDICT AND SCHOLASTICA

Benedict and Scholastica are brother and sister saints of the sixth century. Both were dedicated to the monastic houses they had founded, but they met sometimes for spiritual conferences in a house halfway between them. On the very last of these conferences, when it was getting late and Benedict wished to return to his monastery, Scholastica begged him to stay. Benedict refused, as he never spent a night outside his monastery. Scholastica prayed that he might be forced to stay and, as she finished her prayer, a terrific storm began raging outside, forcing Benedict to spend the night in continued spiritual conference with his sister. She was to die very soon. God's answer to her prayer was a consolation.

NOTES

LESSON THREE: MULTIPLICATION OF LOAVES AND FISH

Aims

The students will learn the story of the multiplication of five loaves and two fish to feed 5000 men (not including the women and children).

Materials

- Small loaf of uncut bread, butter/jam (butter knife), napkins
- Children's Bible
- *Activity Book*, p. 58

Optional:
- "Faith of our fathers!" *Adoremus Hymnal*, #603
- Construction paper, pipe cleaners, or S&S craft kits
- "Jesus Feeds the Multitudes," video; Jesus: A Kingdom Without Frontiers

Begin

Present the loaf of bread. Ask the students if there is enough there for all of them. There may or may not be. If the loaf must be divided among many, the servings will be small. Divide the bread. Everyone should have only a small piece, and there should be none left. Count how many people, and how many loaves. Any leftovers? No. Ask if this one loaf could feed one thousand people. No, remember material goods, when given away, are gone, unlike spiritual goods. Feeding one thousand people with one loaf of bread would require a miracle.

One day Jesus was teaching a great big crowd all day. He felt sorry for them because they didn't have anything to eat so he told the disciples to feed the people. The disciples told Jesus, "We have only five loaves of bread and two fish. That will not feed five thousand people! And there are no stores nearby, either." Jesus took the bread and fish and, by blessing them, made them into enough food to feed all five thousand. There was so much food that twelve baskets of scraps were left over!

Most of the miracles of Jesus were to help people who were sick or hurt and to show that He loves them. He made blind people see again. If someone couldn't walk, Jesus said, "Get up," and he could walk again.

81

Develop

1. Read the first paragraph from the next chapter on p. 81.

2. Read the multiplication of loaves and fish from the Children's Bible (Mt 14:13–21; Mk 6:34–44; Lk 9:11–17; Jn 6:5–15).

3. Discuss this story with the children.
   - Why were there so many people to feed?
   - How much food did they have to share?
   - What did Jesus do before sharing the bread and fish?
   - How many people did it feed? Were there any leftovers?
   - Is it possible that this was a trick? Maybe everyone had his own food.
   - Did people come to believe in Jesus?

4. With your children's Bible, continue reading from John 5:16–17, 25–35. Jesus Himself is the Bread of Life. He gives us His very Body and Blood to consume in the Eucharist (the bread and wine changed into Himself). Just as Jesus had the power to change water into wine, to calm the storm, and make five loaves into enough to feed 5000, He has the power to change bread and wine into His Body and Blood.

5. Often we see the symbol of a fish, used to declare our faith in Jesus as the Son of God and Savior. Miracles help us to understand the same truth—that Jesus is the Son of God and our Savior.

6. Watch "Jesus Feeds the Multitudes," video from the series Jesus: A Kingdom Without Frontiers, available through Ignatius Press; 30 minutes.

Name:____________________

Write about the miracle that Jesus did with loaves and fish

Answers will vary

58 *Faith and Life Series • Grade 2 • Chapter 16 • Lesson 3*

Reinforce

1. Have the students complete *Activity Book*, p. 58, and then share their work with the class.

2. Have the students make Christian fish symbols (S&S Craft makes craft kits), or another craft on the Eucharist, the Bread of Life.

Conclude

1. Sing "Faith of our fathers!" *Adoremus Hymnal*, #603.

2. Lead the children in praying for their intentions. End with a litany to the Blessed Virgin Mary and the Apostles. End with the prayer on p. 83.

Preview

In the next lesson, we will learn the story of Jairus' daughter.

THE SYMBOLISM OF THE FISH

*The symbol of the fish in Christian art may have been suggested by the miraculous multiplication of the loaves and fish, or by the Apostles' breakfast of fish on the shore of the Sea of Galilee after the Resurrection (Jn 21:9–14). However, its popularity among Christians is likely the result of the acrostic forming the Greek word for fish (*Ichthys*), which briefly but clearly describes the character and divinity of Christ:* Iesous Christos Theou Yios Soter, *i.e.,* Jesus Christ, Son of God, Savior. *This word, as well as the representation of the fish were thus a brief profession of faith. Tertullian called Christians "little fishes," who, after the image of the Ichthys, are born in the water.*

NOTES

LESSON FOUR: JAIRUS' DAUGHTER

Aims

The students will learn about the different miracles Jesus did.

They will learn about the raising of Jairus' daughter from the dead.

Materials

- Children's Bible
- *Activity Book*, p. 59
- "The Miracles of Jesus," video; Jesus: A Kingdom Without Frontiers

Optional:
- "Faith of our fathers!" *Adoremus Hymnal*, #603

Begin

Compare and contrast the different miracles of Jesus. Note which miracles are done using materials provided, which are nature miracles, how many people witnessed the miracles, etc. Have the children break into groups and dramatize some of these miracles.

One day a man named Jairus came up to Jesus. "Please come to my house," he said. "My little girl is very sick. I'm afraid she will die. But if you come and lay your hands on her, I know she will get better."

Jesus went with Jairus. When they got to the house, everyone was crying. "It's too late," they said. "She is dead."

But the power of Jesus was stronger than death. He went inside and took the girl's hand. "Get up, little girl," He said, and with that she opened her eyes and got up, alive and well!

Words to Know:

miracles

Q. 37 *Why did Jesus work miracles?*
Jesus worked miracles so that people would have faith and recognize Him as the Son of God (CCC 515).

82

Develop

1. Finish reading the chapter from the text.

2. Read the story of the raising of Jairus' daughter from the children's Bible (Mt 9:18, 23–31; Mk 5:22–24, 35–43; Lk 8:40–42, 49–56).

3. Discuss this story with the students.
   - Who came to Jesus for a miracle?
   - How old was his daughter?
   - Was she alive or dead?
   - What did Jesus do and say?
   - What happened to the girl?
   - Who else do we know that Jesus raised from the dead? (They may know about Lazarus, and Jesus Himself.)
   - What about us, will we rise from the dead, too? Yes.

4. Reread paragraph 5, and, in the chart on the board, is some of the other miracles Jesus has performed: healed the sick and hurt, given sight to the blind, made the lame walk. Ask the students why Jesus performed these miracles. This will show them how much He loves us, and to help us believe.

5. Ask the students if they believe in all these miracles. Why? What do they believe about Jesus? Why? Can other people perform miracles? Not of their own power; they can intercede and ask Jesus to do a miracle, such as Saint Scholastica, Saint Thérèse, Saint Francis, as the Blessed Virgin Mary did.

6. What about magic or coincidence—are these miracles? Why or why not? Reaffirm the difference, primarily, that miracles cannot be performed by man and that miracles give us faith in God.

7. Watch "The Miracles of Jesus," video from the series Jesus: A Kingdom Without Frontiers, available through Ignatius Press; 30 minutes.

Name:____________________

"Get up, little girl."

Jesus is God and His power is stronger than death!

Faith and Life Series • Grade 2 • Chapter 16 • Lesson 4 59

Reinforce

1. Have the students complete *Activity Book*, p. 59.

2. They may make a mural of all the different miracles Jesus performed, or perform skits covering the miracles of which they are familiar.

3. Play a game to review the material, such as tic tac toe, or Bible baseball.

4. Have them memorize the definition of miracle.

Conclude

1. Sing with the children "Faith of our fathers!" *Adoremus Hymnal*, #603.

2. Lead them in praying their intentions. Lead them in a litany to the Blessed Virgin Mary and the Apostles. End with the prayer on p. 83.

Preview

In the next lesson, we will review the material covered in this chapter.

SPEAKING OF GOD IN THE MASCULINE

Although God is pure spirit, has no body, and therefore has no sex, the Church has always called God "Father" This tradition follows Christ's example in Scripture of calling God not only "Father," but also "Abba," that is, "Daddy."

"In no way is God in man's image. He is neither man nor woman. God is pure spirit in which there is no place for the difference between the sexes. But the respective 'perfections' of man and woman reflect something of the infinite perfection of God: those of a mother and those of a father and husband" Cf. *Isa* 49:14–15; 66:13; *Ps* 131:2–3; *Hos* 11:1–4; *Jer* 3:4–19 as quoted in the *Catechism of the Catholic Church*, #370.

NOTES

____

____

____

____

____

____

____

____

____

____

____

CHAPTER SIXTEEN:
REVIEW AND ASSESSMENT

Aims

The students' understanding of the material covered this week will be reviewed and assessed.

Materials

- Quiz 16 (Appendix, p. A-22)
- Unit 4 Test (Appendix, pp. A-23 and A-24)
- "Faith of our fathers!" *Adoremus Hymnal*, #603

Review

1. Using the chart on the board, review the different miracles. Note: after the review, erase the chart from the board.

2. Review the details of:
   - The Wedding at Cana
     * Mary intercedes
   - The Calming of the Storm
     * Nature Miracle
     * Apostles asked Jesus and believed
   - The Multiplication of Loaves and Fish
     * fed 5000 men
     * Jesus is the Bread of Life
     * the fish is a symbol of Christ
   - Various healing miracles
     * Jesus loves His people
   - The Raising of Jairus' daughter
     * Jesus is more powerful than death

3. The students should know the difference between miracles, magic, and coincidence.

4. The students should know why Jesus performed miracles so that we may believe and to help us.

Name: ____________________

We Believe **Quiz 16**

Place an M beside the miracles, and an X beside the events which are not miracles.

_X_ 1. Mom buys your favorite cookies without being asked.
_M_ 2. A person is raised from the dead.
_M_ 3. A person walks on water.
_X_ 4. A rabbit is pulled from a hat.
_M_ 5. The sun sets.
_X_ 6. A lost pet is returned home.
_M_ 7. After prayers to God, a person is healed.
_X_ 8. A pizza arrives at your door, but you did not order it!
_M_ 9. A man escapes from an accident unharmed.
_X_ 10. A person skates on ice.

Answer the following questions in complete sentences.

1. Why did Jesus do miracles?
To show that He could do all things and that He is God

2. How could Jesus do miracles? By what power?
Because He is God, just as His Father is God

3. Name three miracles Jesus did.
   i) Calming of the storm
   ii) Multiplication of the bread and fish
   iii) Make the blind see

(There are other possible answers for the above)

A - 22 *Faith and Life • Grade 2 • Appendix A*

Assess

1. Distribute Quiz 16 and answer any questions that the students may have. As the children hand in their quizzes, individually quiz them on the Words to Know from this chapter.

2. After all quizzes have been turned in, review the correct answers.

3. Repeat 1 and 2 with the unit test.

Conclude

1. Sing "Faith of our fathers!" *Adoremus Hymnal*, #603.

2. End class by praying for the intentions of the students.

CHAPTER SEVENTEEN
ASKING FORGIVENESS

Catechism of the Catholic Church References

Confession of Sins: 1455–58, 1493
Contrition: 1451–54, 1492
Definition of Sin: 1849–51, 1871
Forgiveness: 2839–45, 2862
God Alone Forgives Sin: 1441–42
Mercy and Sin: 1846–48

Penance, Sacrament of:
- Confession of Sins: 1456–58
- Effects: 1422, 1468–70, 1496
- Essential parts: 1491
- Structure: 1480

Scripture References

The Prodigal Son: Lk 15:11–32; Ps 103:8

Background Reading: *The Fundamentals of Catholicism* by Fr. Kenneth Baker, S.J.

Volume 1:
"True Morality is Based on Objective Principles," pp. 135–38

Volume3:
"Importance of Confession," pp. 292–94

Summary of Lesson Content

Lesson 1

When man breaks God's laws intentionally, he sins.

There are two types of sin: mortal and venial

God hates sin, but loves the sinner.

God can, and is ready to, forgive sins.

Lesson 2

The story of the Prodigal Son.

Lesson 3

By sinning, man turns away from God.

Sin offends God.

God always calls us back to Him. We must respond by being sorry for our sins and asking forgiveness.

Lesson 4

God's mercy is greater than any sin.

By confessing our sins and seeking His forgiveness, we are reconciled with God.

LESSON ONE: SIN

Aims

They will review the Ten Commandments and the types of sin: mortal and venial.

The students will learn that God hates sin, but loves the sinner and that God can, and is ready to, forgive sins.

Materials

- List of the Ten Commandments (Poster or set of index cards for each)
- *Activity Book*, p. 60

Optional:
- "Jesus, Lover of my soul," *Adoremus Hymnal*, #604

Begin

Begin the class by reviewing the Ten Commandments and definitions of mortal and venial sins. This review may be accomplished through a game.

Ask them if they remember what love is. It is a feeling. It is when you put another first, it is sacrificial. It is very good. Can they think of examples of people who love them? Who loves the most? God. He knows us, accepts us for who we are, and made the greatest sacrifice for us. His sacrifice was so great, nothing can compare to it—that's how much He loves us.

Develop

1. Read the first two paragraphs from the chapter with the students. Review the first paragraph line by line, asking questions. What are God's laws? The Ten Commandments, the commandment to love, the corporal works of mercy, etc. What is a sin? When we know something is wrong, and we still choose to do it. What are the types of sin? Have the students explain the difference between mortal and venial sin. What happens then? What happened to Adam and Even when they sinned? Sin offends God and leads to sadness. We turn away from God. What does God do? He is offended, but He still loves us. What should we do? Tell Him we are sorry.

2. Explain that no matter what we do, God still loves us. His love is so great and merciful that we cannot make Him stop loving us. Even the worst sin does not make God stop loving us.

3. Explain that God hates sin. Hate is a strong word! Sin not only breaks laws, it breaks hearts. It causes hurt between people and puts a distance between God and man. God remains constant, but when we sin, it is like we step away from God. Demonstrate. Stand at the front of the class with the students in a line. As you list good acts, have them step closer. As you list venial sins, have them take small steps backwards. As you say a mortal sin, have them turn around and walk as far away as possible from you. Ask the children if you moved? No. It is the same with sin: it is we who move away from God.

4. Ask the students how many times God can forgive us. He may forgive every time we need His forgiveness and ask for it. He died for all of our sins, so He has a treasury of grace that He gives to us if we ask for it. There is enough grace for ALL of our sins, and more. There is even enough grace to make us overcome our sins.

Name:____________________

SIN

Fill in the blanks with the words below.

sorry Laws loves sin

Sometimes we break God's Laws. We commit a sin.

Although God hates sins, He loves you very much. He is always ready to forgive you when you are sorry for the sins you committed.

60 *Faith and Life Series • Grade 2 • Chapter 17 • Lesson 1*

Reinforce

1. Have the students complete *Activity Book*, p. 60.

2. Teach them to sing "Jesus, Lover of my soul," *Adoremus Hymnal*, #604.

3. Have them begin to memorize the Act of Contrition, p. 87 of the text.

Conclude

1. As a class, ask God for His forgiveness, using the Ten Commandments as a guide:
For our sins against the First Commandment, we ask your forgiveness Lord, ...

2. End by praying the Act of Contrition.

Preview

In the next lesson, we will learn about the story of the Prodigal Son.

CHALK TALK: THE TEN COMMANDMENTS

1. You shall have no other gods before me
2. You shall not take the name of the Lord your God in vain
3. Remember the Sabbath day, and keep it holy
4. Honor your father and your mother
5. You shall not kill
6. You shall not commit adultery
7. You shall not steal
8. You shall not bear false witness against your neighbor
9. You shall not covet your neighbor's wife
10. You shall not covet your neighbor's goods

NOTES

____
____
____
____
____
____
____
____
____
____

LESSON TWO: THE PRODIGAL SON

Aims

The students will learn the story of the Prodigal Son.

Materials

- Children's Bible
- Props for a skit on the Prodigal Son.
- *Activity Book*, p. 61

Optional:
- "Jesus, Lover of my soul," *Adoremus Hymnal*, #604
- "The Prodigal Son," video; Jesus: A Kingdom Without Frontiers

Begin

Tell the students that sin not only breaks laws, it breaks hearts. Ask the students what this means. You may use examples, such as: If I lied to you would you be upset? Does this break a law? Yes. What does it do to our relationship? Could you trust me? Now it is harder for us to love one another, isn't it? What if I stole from you, or said mean things to you? It would take a very generous person, a very loving person to forgive another, or to ask forgiveness because this is hard, too. Jesus teaches us about God's love for us with the following story.

17 Asking Forgiveness

The LORD is merciful and gracious,
slow to anger and abounding in steadfast love.

Psalm 103:8

Sometimes we break God's Laws. We commit a sin. What happens then? What does God do, and what should we do?

Although God hates sin, He loves you very much. He is always ready to forgive you when you are sorry for the sins you committed. Jesus told this story to show how God loves and forgives.

There was once a rich farmer who had two sons. The younger son said, "Father, I know that someday when you die, my brother and I will get all your money. Well, I want my half right now." So the father gave him the money. The son ran away and spent the money unwisely. Soon he had wasted it all, and he was now poor and hungry. He found a job herding pigs, but he was still hungry and lonely. One day, he said, "I've been so bad that my father won't

85

Develop

1. Read paragraphs 3–4 with the students.

2. Read the story of the Prodigal Son from a children's Bible (Luke 15:11–32), or an illustrated story book.

3. Ask the children about the story:

How would the Father have felt when his son asked for his share of the money that he would get when his father died? The father would be sad. It was as though the son had wished him to be dead, so he could have the money. He put the money before his own father. How sad. What did the father do? Why did he give his son the money? Because of his love.

What happened to the son? He ended up in a far-off land, feeding pigs. He was sad. Is this this like Adam? He left Eden because of his sin. Even worse. Feeding pigs was horrible because they were so unclean. He would have been an outcast from his friends. Why did he return to his father? He knew he was wrong and that his father's care was very good. What did he expect from his father? To be treated as a hired hand, maybe to be punished.

What happened when he returned? Was his father waiting for him? Yes. The son said he was sorry and asked for forgiveness. The father forgave him, gave him clothes, a ring, and a party.

(If your story includes the second brother, ask about him as well: How did he feel? What reward did he get for being faithful to his father?)

4. Have the students dramatize this story. They may make it a modern day version if they like. They may perform it for each other.

Name:___________________

"Father, I have sinned against Heaven and against you."

The son had sinned and turned away from the father. When the son was sorry for his sin, he returned to the father, who was very happy to see his son. He forgave his son and embraced him in love and mercy.

Draw the father and son, at the moment the son comes home.

Faith and Life Series • Grade 2 • Chapter 17 • Lesson 2 61

Reinforce

1. Have the students complete *Activity Book*, p. 61.

2. They may interview the characters in the Prodigal Son story.

3. They may write what they would say to the father if they were the prodigal son.

4. Show "The Prodigal Son," video from the series Jesus: A Kingdom Without Frontiers, available through Ignatius Press; 30 minutes.

Conclude

1. Sing with the children: "Jesus, Lover of my soul," *Adoremus Hymnal*, #604.

2. Lead the students by praying the Act of Contrition. Test them in small groups on their memorization progress.

Preview

In the next lesson, we will learn about what we do when we sin.

"OFFER IT UP"

Many Catholics are familiar with this phrase. While some children are told to "offer up" a discomfort, what is really being offered up is the *comfort*. In a non-religious sense, sacrifice is understood as a surrender of some good for the sake of something better, in this case for personal edification or the benefit of others (e.g., for the souls in Purgatory). What we offer up goes into the Treasury of the Church.

NOTES

LESSON THREE: TURNING FROM GOD

Aims

The students will learn that by sinning, man turns away from God, and that sin offends God.

They will also learn that God always calls sinners back to Him. We should respond by being sorry for our sins and asking forgiveness.

Materials

• *Activity Book*, p. 62

Optional:
• "Jesus, Lover of my soul," *Adoremus Hymnal*, #604

Begin

Have the students begin the class by recounting the story of the Prodigal Son. Ask the children to retell the story with God as the Father, and each of them in the role of the Prodigal Child. Give them an example of a sin, such as telling God that television is more important than obeying Him. How can they turn back to God? Will God be waiting for them? Does He forgive them? and more? What other gifts will He give to them? (Grace.) The students may want to dramatize their own version of this Prodigal Child with God as Father and a student as the repentant sinner.

want me for his son anymore. But maybe I can get a job on his farm. At least that way, I'll be near my home."

The son was wrong. His father saw him coming. He was so happy that he did not care about how bad his son had been. The son said, "Father, I have sinned against Heaven and you. I am not good enough to be your son." But the father was happy to have him back. He knew that his son was sorry. He forgave his son and showered his love upon him. He invited all his friends to a big party to celebrate his son's return.

Our Heavenly Father is just like the father in the story. Sometimes we sin and "run away" from God like the younger son. That makes us sad because when we sin we offend God Who loves us very much. But God wants us to be happy. He wants us to come back to Him. All we have to do is admit that what we have done is wrong. And then we must feel real sorrow that we have offended God. God will be waiting for us with open arms.

God will always **forgive** us. There is nothing we can do that is so bad that God won't forgive if we are truly sorry. It shows God that we really love Him when we tell Him we are sorry for having offended Him and want to be forgiven.

86

Develop

1. Read paragraph 5 from the textbook.

2. Ask the students what it means to "offend" God? It means to make Him sad and displeased. Does God stop loving us? No. He will always love us. Does He hate our sins? Yes. But He loves us.

3. Explain to them that because God loves us, He wants us to be with Him forever in Heaven, where we will be happy. This union with God is why we were created. If we go against our design, we will not be happy. For example, if we have a jigsaw puzzle, but we put the pieces together wrong, it will not look like a picture. It is only when it is assembled according to the plan that it looks like a picture.

4. God not only waits for us with open arms, He calls us back by name. Does He use the telephone? Or the Internet? No. But He speaks to us in our hearts. How do we know this? We feel sorry for our sins. We want to tell God we are sorry. We feel bad for what we have done. Sometimes, God works through other people, too, so, for example, if I were to sin, my friend might say, "I'm going to receive the Sacrament of Penance at the church, do you want to come along?" Sometimes God speaks in our hearts to find a confession time, or helps us to pray to say we are sorry.

5. Play the game that was played in Lesson One, listing actions (good and bad) to make the students come closer and move farther away. As they move away, call to them saying, "come back to me" and then have them run and gather around you. Do this every time they take a step backward (big or little, or even run away).

6. Remind the students that they can choose to not return to God, or to move far away. Each one has this freedom. At the end of the game, if they come near, give them a reward.

Name:____________________

When we sin, we offend God.
But, He wants us to be happy.
He wants us to come back to Him.

Color the picture.

God loves me and lets me choose to do good or bad. I love God, so I choose to do good!

62 *Faith and Life Series • Grade 2 • Chapter 17 • Lesson 3*

Reinforce

1. Have the students complete *Activity Book*, p. 62. They may draw themselves into the picture.

2. They may write lists of ways they may show God that they love Him, and ways that show that they do not love God above all.
For example,

Loving God	Not Loving God
• Obey my parents	• Disobey my parents
• Do not lie	• Lie to teacher
• Go to Mass	• Misbehave at Mass

Conclude

1. Sing with the children: "Jesus, Lover of my soul," *Adoremus Hymnal*, #604.

2. Pray, asking God to help them to show Him how much they love Him, and to ask forgiveness for the times they have not done so. End by praying the Act of Contrition.

Preview

In the next lesson, we will learn about God's merciful love.

SAINT VINCENT DE PAUL

Saint Vincent was born about the year 1580 to poor parents in the village of Pouy, France. In 1596, he went to the University of Toulouse to study theology, and four years later he was ordained a priest. In a 1605 sea voyage, he was captured by African pirates and carried to Tunis where he was a a slave for two years. After his providential escape from captivity, he returned to France where he began to preach missions and to lay the foundations for a congregation that afterward became the Congregation of the Mission, the Lazarists. He was most well known for his charity to all people. His feast day is September 27, and he is the patron of charitable societies.

NOTES

LESSON FOUR: RETURNING TO GOD

Aims

The students will learn that God's mercy is greater than any sin.

They will learn that by confessing our sins and seeking His forgiveness, we are reconciled with God.

Materials

- Bucket of water, dark colored food coloring
- *Activity Book*, p. 63

Optional:
- "Jesus, Lover of my soul," *Adoremus Hymnal*, #604

Begin

Begin the class by gathering the students, and explain what Saint Faustina taught about God's mercy being like an ocean (see opposite page, bottom). Using a pail full of water, have the students remember that this is only a very small amount of water, and that we could not empty the ocean with buckets. Next have the students imagine the food coloring as sin, even really bad mortal sin. Drop one drop into the pail. It cannot be seen. This exercise is an example of God's merciful love: it washes away even the greatest of sin.

Words to Know:

sorrow forgive

Q. 38 *What is sorrow for sins?*
Sorrow for sins is the sadness we have for the sins we have done, and the wish to never do them again. We have sorrow for sins because we are sad that we have offended God, or because we fear His just punishments (CCC 1451–53).

We Pray:

ACT OF CONTRITION

O my God, I am heartily sorry for having offended You. I detest all my sins because of Your just punishments, but most of all because they offend You, my God, Who are all good and deserving of all my love. I firmly resolve, with the help of Your grace, to confess my sins, to do penance, and to amend my life. *Amen.*

87

Develop

1. Finish reading the chapter from the textbook with the students.

2. Ask them if God will always forgive us our sins. Yes, if we are truly sorry for them. What about mortal sins? Yes, if we are truly sorry for them. Is there any sin so bad that God cannot or will not forgive? What about stealing a car? What about badly hurting someone in a fight? What about purposely missing Mass? Yes, God can and will forgive all these sins, if the sinner is truly sorry.

3. Have the students read Question 38 on p. 87 of the text: What is sorrow for sin? Discuss the answer.

4. Remind them that sin breaks laws and hearts. When we seek God's forgiveness, does God withhold His love from us? No, in seeking His forgiveness, we are reconciled with Him. Write the word "reconciled" on the board. Have the children figure out what it means:

re = again, such as in the words renew, reappear, repeat, etc.
con = with, such as contact, content, conviction, etc.
cil = eyelash (to see eye to eye)
ed = past tense
ation = action in the present, such as renovation, motivation, incorporation, separation, etc.
What about reconciliation?
This is what we seek when we seek God's forgiveness, to be restored, right now, to a relationship (see eye to eye) with God. How do we see reconciliation in the story of the Prodigal Son?

5. Discuss ways of coming to be sorry for their sins. (Often in sin, we are seeking a good, so sometimes, we do not feel bad yet). An example is meditating upon the crucifixion of Our Lord, or thinking of another's feelings.

Name:________________

I. Do you remember the Ten Commandments?
1. You shall not have other gods besides me.
2. You shall not use God's name in vain.
3. Remember to keep God's day holy.
4. Honor your mother and father.
5. You shall not kill.
6. You shall not commit adultery.
7. You shall not steal.
8. You shall not lie.
9. You shall not covet your neighbor's wife.
10. You shall not covet your neighbor's goods.

2. What is sin? Any wrong that we do. Sin turns us away from God.

3. What is Mortal Sin? A very big sin that kills all life of grace in a soul

4. What is Venial Sin? A small sin that makes a soul less pleasing to God

5. Who forgives sin? God

6. Does God love you even if you sin? Yes

7. What should we do if we sin and want to be forgiven? Admit that what we have done is wrong, feel real sorrow that we have offended God, and tell God that we are sorry.

Faith and Life Series • Grade 2 • Chapter 17 • Lesson 4 63

Reinforce

1. Have the students work on *Activity Book*, p. 63.

2. Have them memorize Question 38 of the textbook and the Words to Know from this chapter.

3. Quiz each child on their progress in memorizing the Act of Contrition.

Conclude

1. Sing with the children "Jesus, Lover of my soul," *Adoremus Hymnal*, #604.

2. Have the children think of examples of sorrow, such as: if Betty lied to get out of going to school, if John is sorry he fought with his brother. Note: Be sure that they give good examples, not sorrow because they missed-out on something they would have liked, such as a field trip or a game. End by praying the Act of Contrition.

Preview

In the next lesson, we will review the material covered in this chapter.

SAINT FAUSTINA

Saint Faustina was born in 1905 in Poland. Even in her childhood, Faustina demonstrated admirable prayerfulness, willingness to work, and compassion for the poor. As a nun in the Congregation of the Sisters of Our Lady of Mercy, Faustina had a vision of Jesus' Divine Mercy on February 22, 1931. Jesus described His Mercy as a sea from which graces flow infinitely. Sin is overwhelmed by the ocean of Jesus' Divine Mercy. Jesus demanded that Faustina and all men perform at least one act of mercy each day. Faustina was canonized on the first Sunday after Easter, April 30, 2000, on what will forever be known in the Church as Divine Mercy Sunday.

NOTES

CHAPTER SEVENTEEN: REVIEW AND ASSESSMENT

Aims

The students' understanding of the material covered this week will be reviewed and assessed.

Materials

- Quiz 17 (Appendix, p. A-25)
- "Jesus, Lover of my soul," *Adoremus Hymnal*, #604

Review

1. Review the answers to the questions in the *Activity Book*, p. 63.

2. Review the story of the Prodigal Son.

3. Ask the children what happens when they sin:
- They turn away from God
- They offend God
- They break God's laws
- They break hearts (hurt each other, themselves, and their friendship with God)
- They choose not to love God

4. Ask the children what God does when they sin:
- He remains present
- He calls us back
- He is ready to forgive us (even for big sins!)

5. Ask the children how they can be forgiven?
- They must be sorry for their sins (what is sorrow for sins? see Q. 38).
- We must go to God and tell Him we are sorry (Later they will learn that this means receiving the Sacrament of Penance, but they may already know this.)

6. Review the Act of Contrition.

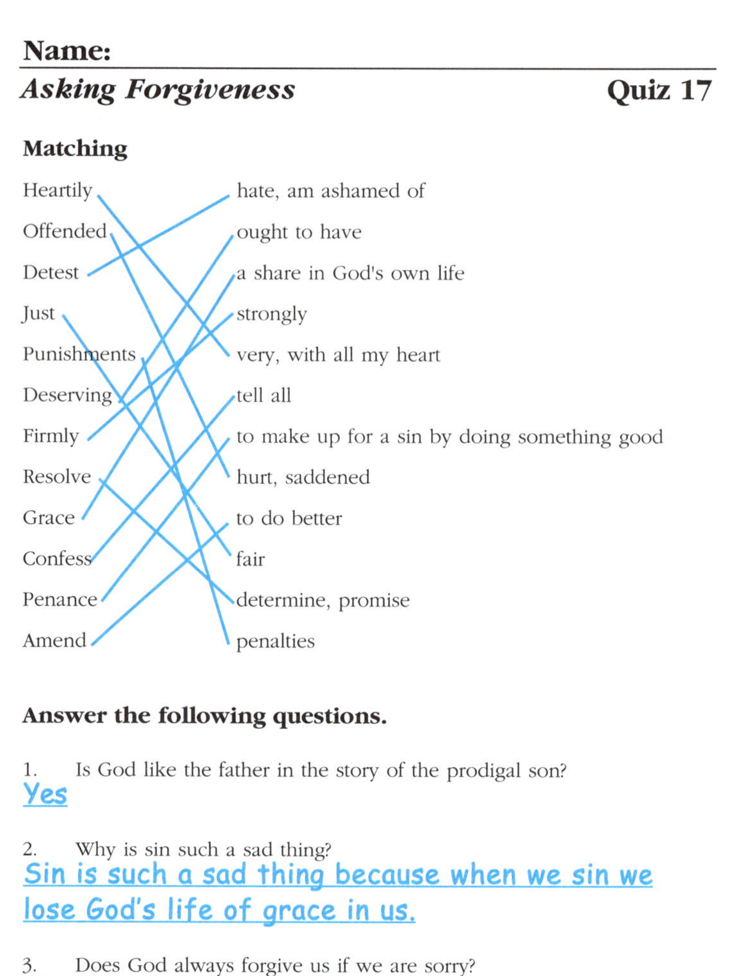

Name:

Asking Forgiveness **Quiz 17**

Matching

Heartily	hate, am ashamed of
Offended	ought to have
Detest	a share in God's own life
Just	strongly
Punishments	very, with all my heart
Deserving	tell all
Firmly	to make up for a sin by doing something good
Resolve	hurt, saddened
Grace	to do better
Confess	fair
Penance	determine, promise
Amend	penalties

Answer the following questions.

1. Is God like the father in the story of the prodigal son?
Yes

2. Why is sin such a sad thing?
Sin is such a sad thing because when we sin we lose God's life of grace in us.

3. Does God always forgive us if we are sorry?
Yes

Faith and Life • *Grade 2* • *Appendix A* *A - 25*

Assess

1. Distribute Quiz 17. As they turn in their quizzes, individually quiz them on the Act of Contrition, Question 38, and the Words to Know.

2. When all quizzes have been turned in, review the correct answers.

Conclude

1. Sing as a class "Jesus, Lover of my soul," *Adoremus Hymnal*, #604.

2. End with prayer.

CHAPTER EIGHTEEN
JESUS FORGIVES

Catechism of the Catholic Church References

Confession of Sins: 1455–58, 1493
Contrition: 1451–54, 1492
Conversion of the Baptized: 1427–29, 1490
Definition of Sin: 1849–51, 1871
Different Names for the Sacrament of Penance: 1423–24
Effects of the Sacrament of Penance: 1468–70, 1496
Forgiveness: 2839–45, 2862
God Alone Forgives Sin: 1441–42
Mercy and Sin: 1846–48
Minister of the Sacrament of Penance: 1461–67, 1495
Need for a Sacrament of Reconciliation after Baptism: 1425–26, 1486–89
Rite of Penance: 1449–69, 1480, 1491
Sacrament of Penance Instituted by Jesus: 1446, 1485
Sacrament of Penance as Sacrament of Forgiveness: 1446–49

Scripture References

The Healing of the Paralytic: Luke 5:17–32
Sacrament of Penance: Mt 16:19, 18:18; Jn 20:23
Institution of Penance: John 20:21–23

Background Reading: *The Fundamentals of Catholicism* by Fr. Kenneth Baker, S.J.

Volume 3:
"Who Can Hear Confessions?," pp. 304–6

Volume 3:
"Reconciliation with God," pp. 301–3

Summary of Lesson Content

Lesson 1

Jesus cured the sick in body.

Jesus also forgave sins (cured the sick in soul).

Jesus will forgive sin when the sinner is sorry for having offended Him.

Lesson 2

Only God can forgive sins. Jesus is God.

Jesus made the disciples His first priests and gave them the power to forgive sins. God forgives sins through them, as the priests act in the person of Jesus.

When a priest forgives sins, it is called the Sacrament of Penance.

Lesson 3

There are five steps to a good confession:
1. Examination of Conscience
2. Contrition
3. Resolve to not sin again
4. Confess sins to a priest
5. Penance

The formula of absolution is: "I absolve you from your sins in the Name of the Father and of the Son and of the Holy Spirit. *Amen.*"

Lesson 4

The Sacrament of Penance takes away our sins and gives us grace.

Grace gives us a share in God's life, and it helps man to be stronger against sin.

The priest is bound by the seal of the Sacrament.

LESSON ONE: JESUS FORGIVES SINS

Aims

The students will learn that Jesus cured the sick in body. They will also learn that Jesus also forgave sins (cured the sick in soul).

They will understand that Jesus will forgive sins when the sinner is sorry for having offended Him.

Materials

- Children's Bible
- *Activity Book*, p. 64

Optional:
- "Help, Lord, the souls that thou has made," *Adoremus Hymnal*, #571

Begin

Review the different miracles of Jesus: Which ones concern the body and which ones concern the soul? The students themselves may write this list on the board and explain the result of each miracle.

Have the students recognize that Jesus had authority over the material and the spiritual world.

Develop

1. Begin the class by reading the first paragraph of the chapter. Have the students think about ways Jesus could cure the sick. Remember that a sick soul needs a cure, too.

2. Read from a children's Bible the story of the healing of the paralytic (Lk 5:17–32). The children may dramatize this story. Emphasize that Jesus shocked everyone who heard him say, "Your sins are forgiven," because they thought Jesus was just a man. They knew that only God can forgive sins. Jesus performed this miracle to show that He is God and that He can forgive sins.

3. Ask the students about the Bible reading. Why did the people think Jesus was just a man? Did He look different from other men? Did He glow or have a halo like we see in pictures? What did Jesus prove by giving the man the ability to walk? Can only God forgive sins? What does this say about Jesus?

4. Return to the first paragraph of the textbook. Stress that Jesus is always ready to forgive our sins when we are sorry for them, and sorry for offending Him. Ask the children questions like: Can Jesus forgive big sins? Can Jesus forgive many sins? Can Jesus forgive your sins and my sins? Will Jesus forgive sins of people who do not want His forgiveness? etc.

5. Review what a sin is. It is when something is wrong, we know it is wrong, and we choose to do it anyway. Mortal sin is very serious. Venial sin is less serious. Does all sin offend God? Yes. Does all sin hurt us? Yes. Does all sin break God's laws? Yes. Should we ever want to sin? No. Why? Because we love God. How can we show God we love Him? By not sinning and by choosing to do good.

Name:____________________

Lord Jesus, You cured the sick and forgave sinners. Forgive me and keep me and keep me in Your love.

Draw Jesus curing a sick person

Draw Jesus healing a person with a sick soul because of sin.

64 *Faith and Life Series • Grade 2 • Chapter 18 • Lesson 1*

Reinforce

1. Have the students complete *Activity Book*, p. 64.

2. They may draw pictures of the healing of the paralytic.

3. Have them work on memorizing the prayer on the bottom of p. 91.

4. Teach them to sing "Help, Lord, the souls that thou has made," *Adoremus Hymnal*, #571.

Conclude

1. Lead them in praying for their sick family members and friends, asking the Lord to heal them.

2. End with the prayer on p. 91.

Preview

In the next lesson, we will learn more about the Sacrament of Penance.

SAINT CHARLES BORROMEO

Saint Charles, the son of Count Gilbert Borromeo and Margaret Medici, was born at the family castle in Italy in 1538. In 1559, his uncle was elected Pope Pius IV, and at age 22, Charles was named a cardinal and the Pope's Secretary of State. Charles was influential in the Council of Trent and oversaw the resulting catechism, missal, and breviary. He was ordained a priest and consecrated bishop of Milan in 1563. He was a towering figure of the Reformation, and brought many lapsed Catholics to the Church, all in great humility. He died in 1584, was canonized in 1610, and his feast day is November 4. He is the patron of learning and the arts.

NOTES

____

____

____

____

____

____

____

____

____

____

LESSON TWO: HOW JESUS FORGIVES

Aims

The students will understand that only God can forgive sins. Jesus is God.

They will learn that Jesus made the disciples His first priests and gave them the power to forgive sins. God forgives sins through them, as the priests act in the person of Jesus.

They will learn that when a priest forgives sins, it is called the Sacrament of Penance.

Materials

- Children's Bible
- *Activity Book*, p. 65

Optional:
- "Help, Lord, the souls that thou has made," *Adoremus Hymnal*, #571

Begin

Ask the students to review what they learned in the previous lesson. How did Jesus show that He had the authority to forgive sins? Why was this a shock to people? Who has the authority to forgive sins? What does this say about Jesus?

The students may dramatize the story of the healing of the paralytic.

18 Jesus Forgives

"But that you may know that the Son of man has authority on earth to forgive sins"—he said to the man who was paralyzed—"I say to you, rise, take up your bed and go home."

Luke 5:24

There were many times when Jesus cured sick people. There were also many times when He forgave their sins. Jesus is always ready to forgive us when we are sorry for having offended Him.

Only God can forgive sins. Jesus showed that He was God by curing people and forgiving their sins. Jesus made some of the disciples His first priests. He gave them special powers. One of these is the power to forgive sins. Priests today have this power, too. God forgives our sins through them.

When God uses a priest to forgive our sins, it is called the **Sacrament** of Penance. It is also called Confession because we "**confess**," or tell, our sins to the priest.

89

Develop

1. Read the rest of p. 89. Have the students take turns reading aloud.

2. Ask questions based on this reading:
   - Who can forgive sins?
   - How did Jesus show He was God?
   - What did Jesus give to His disciples?
   - How does God forgive our sins today?
   - What is this sacrament called?
   - What role does the priest play in the Sacrament of Penance?
   - Who hears and forgives your sins?

3. From a children's Bible, read Jn 20:21–23. Ask the children about this passage:
   - Why did Jesus say, "peace be with you"?
   - What power did He give to the disciples?
   - What do we receive when our sins are forgiven? (peace)
   - By what authority did Jesus give the disciples this power?

4. *Ask the children to think of times they have told someone that they are sorry. Was this easy? How did they know they were "sorry"? Were they scared to tell that person? How does it feel to hear the words, "you are forgiven"? These are powerful words. They make us happy again. Can we forgive sins? No, but we can forgive each other the wrongs we have done. A sin is an offense against God. Sometimes we seek forgiveness for things that are not sins, things like accidents: "I'm sorry, I accidentally broke your toy," "I'm sorry you're mad at me, but I spoke the truth." It is very important to begin using these words regularly. Have each student think of a person he can say he is sorry to and a person he can forgive. You may assign that they practice this lesson.*

5. Ask the students to write skits telling someone they are sorry, asking forgiveness, and being forgiven. Ask the students to write skits telling God they are sorry, too.

Name:____________________

Jesus Forgives

Fill in the blanks with the words below. Some words are used more than once.

God	forgiving	Sacrament	Confession
powers	Apostles	Penance	today
priest	forgive	through	sins

Only God can forgive sins. Jesus showed that He was God by curing people and forgiving their sins. Jesus made some of the disciples His first Apostles. He gave them special powers. One of these is the power to forgive sins. Priests today have this power too. God forgives our sins through them.

When God uses a priest to forgive our sins, it is called the Sacrament of Penance. It is also called Confession because we "confess," or tell our sins to the priest.

Faith and Life Series • Grade 2 • Chapter 18 • Lesson 2 65

Reinforce

1. Have the students complete *Activity Book*, p. 65. They may use their text to help them.

2. Have the students memorize Questions 39 and 40, p. 91.

Conclude

1. As a class, sing "Help, Lord, the souls that thou has made," *Adoremus Hymnal*, #571.

2. Lead the students in praying the Our Father, focussing on "Forgive us our trespasses, as we forgive those who trespass against us."

3. End with the prayer on p. 91.

Preview

In the next lesson, we will learn about the steps to a good confession.

THE SACRAMENT OF PENANCE

Christ instituted this sacrament after His Resurrection (see Mt 16:19, 18:18, and Jn 20:23) to forgive post-baptismal sins and to impart grace to the soul through the priest's absolution to penitents, who with true sorrow, confess their sins and promise to do penance. The penitent is at once the accuser, the person accused, and the witness, while the priest, in the person of Christ, pronounces judgment and sentence. This sacrament is supported in Scripture. It is not enough for a Catholic to confess his sins to himself or to a layman. Sincere sorrow is also necessary in order to receive the priest's absolution.

NOTES

LESSON THREE: STEPS TO FORGIVENESS

Aims

The students will learn that the five steps to a good confession are:

1. Examination of Conscience
2. Contrition
3. Resolve to not sin again
4. Confess sins to a priest in the Sacrament of Penance
5. Penance

They will also learn the formula of absolution.

Materials

- *Activity Book*, p. 66

Optional:
- "Help, Lord, the souls that thou has made," *Adoremus Hymnal*, #571

Begin

Teach the students the specifics of the Sacrament of Penance: its different names, matter, form, minister, etc. Later, they will learn more about the rite, but they need to first know WHAT the Sacrament of Penance conveys. They should memorize this information. You may have the students write it down for themselves. See the opposite page for details.

The priest takes the place of Jesus. When we confess our sins it is Jesus Who hears us and Who forgives us.

Before we go to confess our sins, we must get ready. We should think about our sins and be sorry for them. Then we tell our sins to the priest. He forgives us by saying:

> "I **absolve** you from your sins in the Name of the Father, and of the Son, and of the Holy Spirit. *Amen.*"

The Sacrament of Penance does more than take our sins away. It gives us grace. Grace gives us a share in God's life, and helps us to be stronger against sin.

The priest will never tell our sins to anyone. He only wants to bring us God's forgiveness. He wants to help us to be good.

Words to Know:

Sacrament confess absolve

"If you forgive the sins of any they are forgiven."

John 20:23

90

Develop

1. As a class, read the top of p. 76, including the formula of absolution. Have the students memorize this formula.

2. *Make a chart of the steps to a good confession and fill in examples:*

Step 1: Know what my sins are: think of all your sins
e.g., I told 3 lies, I was disobedient 6 times, I fought with my brother twice, I failed to say my daily prayers twice

Step 2: Be sorry for my sins: try to be sorry for having offended God, or at least be sad because of God's just punishment.
e.g., I could look upon a Crucifix and know Jesus died because of my sins. For this I am sorry.

Step 3: Make up my mind to not sin again:
e.g., I will do my best to never do this again because I know it is wrong. I know it offends God, and I know of God's just punishments.

Step 4: Tell my sins to the priest in the Sacrament of Penance: This is when you actually receive the Sacrament of Penance (As a class, you may want to begin "practicing" confessions —be sure the students make up sins.)

Step 5: Do the penance the priest gives me:
e.g., 5 Hail Marys

Note: the students should have memorized various prayers: Our Father, Act of Contrition, Hail Mary, Glory Be, etc.

3. Have the students make their own examples or lists. They should memorize the five steps to a good confession.

Name:___________________

5 Steps to the Sacrament of Penance:

1. Know what my sins are.
2. Be sorry for my sins.
3. Make up my mind not to sin again.
4. Tell my sins to the priest.
5. Do the penance the priest gives me.

Draw the five steps to Confession.

66 *Faith and Life Series • Grade 2 • Chapter 18 • Lesson 3*

Reinforce

1. Have the students complete *Activity Book*, p. 66.

2. Play a review game, covering the Sacrament of Penance (including all the material covered in this chapter and lesson).

3. Have them spend time memorizing:
   - Formula of Absolution
   - Questions 39 and 40
   - Words to Know
   - Steps to a good confession
   - Matter/Form/Minister/Titles of the Sacrament of Penance

Conclude

1. As a class, sing "Help, Lord, the souls that thou has made," *Adoremus Hymnal*, #571.

2. Lead the students in the prayer on p. 91 of the text.

* You may want to begin discussing whether or not the students are nervous or excited about receiving the Sacrament of Penance. Often students are not nervous, but the adults are. There is no need to make the students nervous about the Sacrament of Healing.

Preview

In the next lesson, we will learn about the effects of the Sacrament of Penance.

CONFESSION/PENANCE/RECONCILIATION

What is the Sacrament of Penance? The telling of our sins to an authorized priest for the purpose of obtaining forgiveness.

Sacrament of Healing

Matter: Confession of Sins
Form: "I absolve you from your sins in the Name of the Father and of the Son and of the Holy Spirit."

Minister: The Priest

Note: we must confess at least once a year if we are in the state of mortal sin. We must always confess mortal sins before going to Holy Communion.

NOTES

____
____
____
____
____
____
____
____
____
____
____

LESSON FOUR: WHY CONFESS?

Aims

The students will learn of the effects of the Sacrament of Penance: it takes away our sins and gives us grace to strengthen us against sin.

They will learn that the priest is bound by the seal of confession.

Materials

- *Activity Book*, p. 67
- *Hymnal*, #571

Optional:
- "Help, Lord, the souls that thou has made," *Adoremus*
- Note: arrange for a tour of the confessionals at your church

Begin

Begin the class with a review game on the materials covered in this chapter. Review with the students:
- Jesus cured the sick and forgave sins
- Only God can forgive sin
- Jesus gave the power to forgive sins to His Apostles, and through them to priests
- The sacrament is called the Sacrament of Penance or Reconciliation and is a Sacrament of Healing
- The matter, form, minister of the sacrament
- The five steps to a good confession
- Questions 39 and 40, Words to Know

Q. 39 *What is the Sacrament of Penance?* The Sacrament of Penance is also called the Sacrament of Reconciliation or the Sacrament of Confession. In this sacrament we confess to a priest the sins that we have done and we are forgiven by the power of Jesus Christ. Grace is restored in our souls and we are given a penance to make up for the wrongs we have done (CCC 1440–41, 1456).

Q. 40 *What words must a priest say for your sins to be forgiven in the Sacrament of Penance?* For your sins to be forgiven in the Sacrament of Penance, the priest must say: "I absolve you from your sins in the Name of the Father, and of the Son, and of the Holy Spirit. *Amen*" (CCC 1449).

We Pray:

Lord Jesus, You cured the sick and forgave sinners. Forgive me and keep me in Your love.

91

Develop

1. Ask the children if they know why they should receive the Sacrament of Penance? They will likely answer: to have their sins forgiven. Explain to the students that the Sacrament of Penance is a Sacrament of Healing, and in this sacrament, their sins are forgiven, but much more occurs.

2. Read the rest of the chapter from the textbook. Emphasize that the Sacrament of Penance not only heals us from our sins, but it also makes us stronger in our fight against sin by giving us grace. Do the students remember what grace is? A share in God's own life! Use the example of medicine to explain this concept to the students. Sometimes when we are sick, we go to the doctor for medicine. The medicine will make us better. It often also makes us stronger so that we will not get sick again.

3. Go through the effects of the Sacrament of Reconciliation with the students:
- *Forgives our sins*
- *Fills us with God's grace (restores life to our souls)*
- *Reconciles us with God and the Church*
- *Gives us penance to make up for our sins*
- *Gives us peace and spiritual consolation*
- *Prepares us for our final judgment before God*

4. Take the children for a tour of the confessionals. If your confessionals have both anonymous and face-to-face options, show the children how they may choose either way to confess their sins. Let the students each have a chance to kneel behind the screen, or sit in the face-to-face chair. You may sit in the priest's chair to let them know what it is like to have someone there. Explain the words for all of the parts of the confessional: screen, kneeler, chair, Bible/Crucifix/Act of Contrition if on display, etc.

5. Review with the children from their text the sacramental seal: a priest cannot repeat anything confessed.

Name:__________________

In Confession, God forgives my sins and heals my soul! He fills me with His love and mercy and makes me stronger with His grace.

In the picture above ...

1. Color the kneeler brown.
2. Circle a crucifix in red.
3. Color the priest's hair black.

Draw yourself after being forgiven of your sins.

Faith and Life Series • Grade 2 • Chapter 18 • Lesson 4 67

Reinforce

1. Have the students complete *Activity Book*, p. 67.

2. Play a review game, covering the materials listed in the Begin section, as well as the effects of the Sacrament of Penance and the seal of confession.

3. Have them work on memorizing Questions 39 and 40, the Words to Know, and the five steps to a good confession.

Conclude

1. Sing with the children "Help, Lord, the souls that thou has made," *Adoremus Hymnal*, #571.

2. End by asking God to help them prepare for a good confession and look forward to the effects of this sacrament. End with the prayer on p. 91 of the text.

Preview

In the next lesson, we will review the material covered in this chapter.

PADRE PIO: CONFESSOR

Perhaps the most famous confessor of the twentieth century, Padre Pio, heard confessions daily for ten to twelve hours. During his life, he received the visible signs of the stigmata, or wounds of Christ, upon his hands. His strong connection to our Lord, demonstrated by this miracle, found its greatest benefit to humanity in the confessional. As a confessor, Padre Pio would understand the hearts of the penitent and give the exact words of counsel each one needed to hear to mend his life. Padre Pio's funeral was attended by 100,000 mourners.

NOTES

CHAPTER EIGHTEEN:
REVIEW AND ASSESSMENT

Aims

The students' understanding of the material covered this week will be reviewed and assessed.

Materials

- Quiz 18 (Appendix, p. A-26)
- "Help, Lord, the souls that thou has made," *Adoremus Hymnal*, #571

Review

1. Review the story of Jesus healing the paralytic. What does this teach about Jesus? Can Jesus only heal bodies? How does Jesus heal souls? How can Jesus forgive sins, if only God can forgive sins?

2. Discuss the sacrament itself:
- Matter, form (the students should have memorized the formula of absolution)
- Minister (how did the priests receive the power to forgive sins? From Whom?)
- Names for this sacrament
- What kind of sacrament is this (Healing)
- What are the five steps to a good confession:
  1. know your sins
  2. be sorry for them
  3. decide to not sin again
  4. confess your sins to a priest
  5. do the penance
- What are the effects of the sacrament:
  1. sins forgiven
  2. grace received to overcome sin
  3. reconciled with God and Church
  4. peace and consolation
  5. preparation for judgment
- Seal of confession (priest cannot tell what was confessed)
- Review sin: what it is, mortal vs. venial

Name:

Jesus Forgives **Quiz 18**

Answer the following questions.

1. How can Jesus heal your soul?
By the forgiveness of sins and the restoration of grace

2. Who gave priests the power to forgive sins?
Jesus

3. What is the sacrament called, in which Jesus hears our sins and forgives them through a priest? (Three names)
   a. Sacrament of Penance
   b. Sacrament of Reconciliation
   c. Sacrament of Confession

4. What is the Sacrament of Penance?
In the Sacrament of Penance, we confess our sins to a priest and are sins are forgiven by the power of Jesus Christ. Also, grace is restore in our souls.

5. What are the five steps to a good confession?

Step 1: Know what my sins are

Step 2: Be sorry for my sins

Step 3: Make up my mind not to sin again

Step 4: Tell my sins to the priest in the Sacrament of Penance

Step 5: Do the penance the priest gives me

6. What are three effects of the Sacrament of Reconciliation?
   a. the forgiveness of sins
   b. the restoration of grace in my soul
   c. the strength to be a good Christian

A - 26 *Faith and Life • Grade 2 • Appendix A*

Assess

Distribute Quiz 18. Answer any questions that they may have. As the students hand in their quizzes, individually test them on the Memorization Questions and the Words to Know. After all the quizzes have been turned in, review the answers.

Conclude

1. Sing "Help, Lord, the souls that thou has made," *Adoremus Hymnal*, #571.

2. End by praying the Act of Contrition.

CHAPTER NINETEEN
THE SACRAMENT OF PENANCE

Catechism of the Catholic Church References

Celebration of the Sacrament of Penance: 1480–84, 1497
Confession Rite:
- Absolution: 1449
- Confession: 1456, 1458
- Effects: 1496
- Essential parts: 1491
- Fundamental structure: 1480
- Instituted by Christ: 1446, 1485
- Minister: 1461, 1495
- Preparation: 1454

Confession of Sins: 1455–58, 1493
Contrition: 1451–54, 1492
Definition of Sin: 1849–51, 1871
Different Names for the Sacrament of Penance: 1423–24
Effects of the Sacrament of Penance: 1468–70, 1496
Forgiveness: 2839–45, 2862
Forms of Penance in Christian Life: 1434–39
God Alone Forgives Sin: 1441–42
Mercy and Sin: 1846–48
Minister of the Sacrament of Penance: 1461–67, 1495
Need for a Sacrament of Reconciliation after Baptism: 1425–26, 1486–89
Sacrament of Penance as a Sacrament of Forgiveness: 1446–49

Scripture References

The Institution of the Sacrament of Penance: Jn 20:19–23; Lk 19:8

Background Reading: *The Fundamentals of Catholicism* by Fr. Kenneth Baker, S.J.

Volume 3:
"Perfect Contrition," pp. 286–88

Volume 3:
"Imperfect Contrition," pp. 289–91

Summary of Lesson Content

Lesson 1

The first step to a good confession is an examination of conscience. It is an assessment of one's moral life, taking stock of one's sins that need to be brought to God for forgiveness.

Lesson 2

The second step to a good confession is contrition.

There are two types of contrition: perfect and imperfect. Perfect contrition is when one is sorry for his sin because he is truly sad that he has offended God. Imperfect contrition is when one is sorry for his sin because of fear of God's just punishment.

The third step is to decide to not sin again.

Lesson 3

The fourth step to a good confession is to receive the sacrament: the confessing of sins to a priest and making an Act of Contrition.

This lesson will review the new rite of Penance.

Lesson 4

The fifth step to a good confession is to do the assigned penance.

A penance helps the sinner to make up for his offenses against God and neighbor.

LESSON ONE: EXAMINATION OF CONSCIENCE

Aims

The students will review the first step to a good confession, an examination of conscience.

They will practice this step.

Materials

- Suitcase full of things that may be taken on a trip and things you wouldn't take
- *Activity Book*, p. 68

Optional:

- "Lord Jesus, think on me," *Adoremus Hymnal*, #364
- Appendix, pp. B-16 and B-17

Begin

Have an empty suitcase and things that could be packed in it—some silly things, too. Have items like clothes, toothbrush, shoes, etc, but also things like a wrench, a toaster, a rock, etc. Ask the students what things you should pack for your trip. Do you need to pack everything? No, only those things you need for your trip. Some things, like the rock, wrench, and toaster, would be silly to take. So, too, we must decide what things we will take with us to the Sacrament of Penance. We won't need to take everything, only our sins.

Develop

1. Begin by reading the first two paragraphs of the chapter from the textbook.

2. *Explain to the students that in order to receive the Sacrament of Penance, you must first know your sins. Have the students define sin (for an action to be a sin it must be three things: it must be something wrong (against God's Law); you must know it is wrong; and you must choose to do it anyway). Review mortal (serious) and venial (less serious) sins.*
Mortal sins: three things required
   - *Gravely wrong*
   - *Knowledge of it being gravely wrong*
   - *Choosing to do it anyway*

Venial sin: less grave, or grave without full knowledge or free consent

3. Explain the difference between an accident and a sin. An accident is when you do not intend for something to happen, such as accidentally breaking a vase vs. purposely breaking a vase to be mean.

4. To know your sins (examination of conscience), teach the students to pray to the Holy Spirit for guidance, think about what sins they have committed, and how many times they sinned. Explain to them that they need only confess their mortal sins, and the number of times (or frequency) they committed them. It is also a good practice to confess venial sins, too. If they have no mortal sins, they should confess their venial sins. They do not need to confess their venial sins by numbers.

5. Give the students examples of venial sins, mortal sins, and accidents, and ask the students to identify what they are, and explain why.

6. Hand out an age appropriate examination of conscience and lead them in this exercise (Appendix, pp. B-16 and B-17).

Name:____________________

If you were going on a trip, you would get ready and pack everything you need. You need to get ready for Confession! What kind of things would you "pack" to take with you into the Sacrament of Penance?

Draw lines connecting what you would take with you to Confession to the suitcase.

Accidentally spilled cereal

Lied to my Mother

Hit my brother

Forgot to feed the cat

Sneezed at Mass

Disobeyed my Father

Cheated on a test

Stole a candy bar

Was very angry about something silly

Destroyed someone's work on purpose

Swallowed bubble gum

Was mean to a boy/girl

68 *Faith and Life Series • Grade 2 • Chapter 19 • Lesson 1*

Reinforce

1. Have the students complete *Activity Book*, p. 68.
2. Have them work on their examination of conscience.
3. Play a review game of mortal vs. venial sin vs. accidents.
4. Teach the students to sing "Lord Jesus, think on me," *Adoremus Hymnal*, #364.
5. Have them continue memorizing the steps to a good confession.

Conclude

Lead the children in praying the Act of Contrition. Add a prayer of thanksgiving, anticipating the effects of the Sacrament of Penance.

Preview

In the next lesson, we will learn more about the second and third steps to a good confession.

DAILY EXAMINATION OF CONSCIENCE

A valuable spiritual exercise recommended by Saint Ignatius of Loyola is the daily examination of conscience before bed. By recalling our sins at the very end of the day, we are more likely to remember our sins, and less likely to make the same mistakes on the following day.

NOTES

LESSON TWO: SORROW FOR SIN

Aims

The children will learn that the second step to a good confession is contrition.

They will know that there are two types of contritions: perfect and imperfect. Perfect contrition is when one is sorry for his sins because he is truly sad that he has offended God. Imperfect contrition is when one is sorry for his sins because of fear of God's just punishments.

They will learn that the third step to a good confession is to decide to not sin again.

Materials

- Crucifix
- *Activity Book*, p. 69
- Diorama of the Crucifixion, Appendix, pp. B-22 and B-23, shoe boxes

Optional:
- "Lord Jesus, think on me," *Adoremus Hymnal*, #364

Begin

Review the first step to a good confession. Do they need to confess everything they feel sorry for? What about accidents? What sins must be confessed? Do they have to tell the number of times and/or frequency? Do they know what is a mortal or venial sin? What is the first step to a good confession? What is the second step? What is the third step? They will learn more about these steps today.

19 The Sacrament of Penance

"Receive the Holy Spirit. If you forgive the sins of any, they are forgiven; if you retain the sins of any, they are retained."

John 20:22–23

When you are going to do something special, you have to get ready for it. If you are going away on a trip, you don't just get in the car and ride away. First you think about the things you want to take with you. Then you find the things and pack them.

You also have to get ready before you receive the **Sacrament of Penance**. First, you should ask God the Holy Spirit to help you remember your sins. Think about what you have done wrong, and how many times you did it.

Then, try to be sorry for your sins. Think of how your sins hurt Jesus. Make up your mind not to sin again. Say an Act of Contrition, which tells God that you are sorry.

After this, it is time to receive the Sacrament. The priest will welcome you. You then make the Sign of the Cross. The priest may then read to you from the Bible.

93

Develop

1. Read the third paragraph as a class. Ask the students why they should be sorry for their sins:
   - What they have done is wrong
   - Their sins offend Jesus/God
   - Their sins hurt other people
   - Jesus died on the Cross for our sins

2. They should understand that by meditating upon the Crucifix, they may foster perfect contrition, knowing that Jesus suffered and died for their sins.

3 . *The students should be taught to recognize two forms of contrition: perfect and imperfect.*
   - *Perfect contrition is when we are truly sorry for our sins, because they have offended God*
   - *Imperfect contrition is when we are sorry for our sins because we fear God's just punishments*

4. The students should know that either form of contrition is acceptable for receiving the Sacrament of Penance, but that perfect contrition is the better form of sorrow.

5. Let them know that if they are truly sorry for their sins, they will decide that they do not want to sin again. This is the third step. It is helpful to pray an Act of Contrition.

6. Ask them if they do sin again, does this mean that they were not sorry? No. Because of Adam and Eve's sin, we are always tempted to sin. We are weakened because of Original Sin. We can still choose to do good, but often we seek what seems like a good, even when it is not (e.g., we want a toy, but instead of buying it, we steal it). The third step is to decide that we will do our very best to not sin again.

Name:____________________

I'm sorry for my sins, O God. Forgive me, a sinner.

Faith and Life Series • Grade 2 • Chapter 19 • Lesson 2 69

Reinforce

1. Have the students complete *Activity Book*, p. 69.

2. They may make dioramas for themselves using shoe boxes, and Appendix, pp. B-22 and B-23. Give them plenty of time so that they can do a good job.

3. Teach them a prayer to say to help them prepare for a good confession. Review the Act of Contrition.

Conclude

1. Sing "Lord Jesus, think on me," *Adoremus Hymnal*, #364.

2. Lead the students in praying the Act of Contrition.

3. Have the students take home their dioramas.

Preview

In the next lesson, we will learn about the fourth step to a good confession.

A CHILDREN'S EXAMINATION OF CONSCIENCE

- Do you obey your parents?
- Do you fulfill your household chores?
- Do you speak respectfully to those in authority over you?
- Do you remember to pray for your parents?
- Do you ask permission to do things that are not part of your ordinary life?
- Do you humbly accept correction from your parents?

NOTES

LESSON THREE: CONFESSION OF SINS

Aims

The students will learn about the rite of the Sacrament of Penance and will practice the rite.

Materials

- *Activity Book*, p. 70

Optional:
- "Lord Jesus, think on me," *Adoremus Hymnal*, #364

Begin

Review with the students the first three steps to a good confession including:
- Examination of conscience
- Mortal and venial sins vs. accidents
- What to confess (sins, number/frequency)
- Sorrow for sin: perfect and imperfect
- Decide to not sin again

Ask the students what the next step to the Sacrament of Penance is:
- Tell your sins to a priest.

This is what they will learn about today.

Next you say how long it has been since your last Confession. Then you tell the priest your sins. When you have finished, say, "For these and all my sins, I am sorry." The priest will talk to you and give you a penance.

A penance is what the priest tells you to do to help you make up for the wrong you have done to God, to others, and to yourself. Sometimes the penance may be to say a few prayers or to do something for someone.

The priest may then ask you to pray an Act of Contrition. After that, he will forgive you in the name of Jesus: "I absolve you from your sins in the Name of the Father, and of the Son, and of the Holy Spirit." You will answer: "Amen."

The priest may then say: "Give thanks to the Lord for He is good." Your answer is: "His mercy endures forever."

The Sacrament of Penance helps us to be strong and holy Christians. It keeps us in God's friendship.

We Pray:

Give thanks to the Lord for He is good
and His mercy endures forever.

94

Develop

1. Read from the textbook paragraphs 4–8. Review the rite of Penance with the students.

2. Go into the confessional (behind the screen or face-to-face). Have the students each say how they will receive this sacrament the first time. Both ways are acceptable.

3. Remind them that the priest will then welcome them. He may something like: "May the Lord be in your heart and on your mind, as you make a good confession."

4. Next the student will make the Sign of the Cross (review it with the students), and they will say how long it has been since they last received the Sacrament of Penance. Have the students review saying "Bless me Father, for I have sinned; this is my first confession" or "Bless me Father, for I have sinned, it has been (insert time here) since my last confession." Have them rehearse as you give them different times (e.g., what if it is your first confession? What if you went 3 months ago, etc.).

5. The priest may read from the Bible.

6. Tell the priest your sins. You may teach the students to go in order of the Ten Commandments, or to say their mortal sins first. Let them know that when they have finished saying their sins, they should say, "For these and all my sins, I am sorry."

7. The priest may talk, give some advice, or ask questions (which the student should answer honestly), then the priest will give a penance—what one should do to help him make up for his sins.

8. The priest will ask you to say an Act of Contrition. He will then say the words of absolution. The student should make the Sign of the Cross and say, "Thanks to be God" and "Thank you, Father," and exit. He will then dismiss you.

Name:___________________

Answer the following questions.

1. What are the five steps to a good Confession?

1. Know what my sins are.
2. Be sorry for my sins.
3. Make up my mind not to sin again.
4. Tell my sins to the priest.
5. Do the penance the priest gives me.

3. What is a penance?

It is what the priest tells you to do to help you make up for the wrong you have done to God, to others, and to yourself.

4. What are the effects of the Sacrament of Penance?

It helps us to be strong and holy Christians. It keeps us in God's friendship.

70 *Faith and Life Series • Grade 2 • Chapter 19 • Lesson 3*

Reinforce

1. Have the students rehearse confessions in pairs. Have the students make up three sins, then each take a turn playing the penitent and the priest. Observe carefully to make sure the students have a good understanding.

2. Have them complete *Activity Book*, p. 70.

3. You may want to re-visit the confessionals and practice there, with you playing the priest.

Conclude

1. Sing "Lord Jesus, think on me," *Adoremus Hymnal*, #364.

2. Pray, asking God to help the students to make good confessions, to help them prepare well, and to give them joy in knowing that their sins will be forgiven and that they will be filled with grace. End with the We Pray on p. 94.

Preview

In the next lesson, we will learn about the fifth step to a good confession.

INDULGENCES

An indulgence is the remission before God of temporal punishment due to sin when the guilt has already been forgiven (i.e., in Confession). A properly disposed Catholic, following the prescribed conditions of the Church, can obtain an indulgence. A plenary indulgence removes all temporal punishment. If some of the punishment remains, the indulgence was partial.

NOTES

LESSON FOUR: PENANCE

Aims

The students will learn about the fifth step to a good confession: to do the assigned penance.

They will learn that a penance helps the sinner to make up for his offenses against God and neighbor.

Materials

- Raw egg, some newspapers
- *Activity Book*, p. 71

Optional:
- "Lord Jesus, think on me," *Adoremus Hymnal*, #364

Begin

Lay out on the floor some newspaper. Be sure this covers a few square yards. Gather the students around and do a presentation for them. Explain that sinning will be demonstrated by dropping a raw egg. It makes a mess! (Drop the egg.) Can I say I'm sorry for dropping the egg? Yes. Can I be forgiven? Yes. Does that clean up the mess? No. This is what penance is for. How can we fix the egg mess and undo the damages? We can buy a new egg, and clean up the mess. We could even try to put the egg back together! Penance is like undoing the damage.

"May the Lord be in your heart and help you to confess your sins with true sorrow."

Rite of Penance

Q. 41 *What are the five steps to make a good Confession in the Sacrament of Penance?*
1. Know what my sins are
2. Be sorry for my sins
3. Make up my mind not to sin again
4. Tell my sins to the priest in the Sacrament of Penance
5. Do the penance the priest gives me (CCC 1451, 1454, 1456, 1459–60).

Q. 42 *What are the effects of a good Confession?*
With a good Confession, my sins will be forgiven, and I will receive grace into my soul and the strength to be a good Christian (CCC 1468–69).

Words to Know:

Sacrament of Penance

95

Develop

1. Explain to the children that penance is a way of making up for our sins. In confession, the priest will tell you to do a penance to help you make up for the wrong you have done to God, others, and to yourself. Sin always affects all three. God, others, and you. Sometimes the penance is a work of charity, a reading, or saying some prayers.

2. The effects of the Sacrament of Penance are the forgiveness of sins and the restoration of grace. This grace will help us to overcome our sins. Penance helps us, too.

3. Penance can help us to overcome our sins by teaching us to behave better, to be more charitable, and to think about our sins (especially before we do them).

4. We can do more penance than what the priest gives us, as a sign of our love for God, and our desire to overcome our sins.

5. We can also do penance that will help us. For example, if we have a habit of being mean to our brothers and sisters, we could do penances, like doing nice things for them, not saying bad things and telling them that we are sorry when we hurt them. These are sacrifices we can make to help us grow in overcoming sin. Can the students think of appropriate penances to help them overcome various sins? List some sins for them:
- Lying
- Stealing
- Being disobedient
- Not paying attention at Mass
- Using God's Holy Name in vain
- Reading bad books/watching bad movies

6. Finish reading the chapter.

Name:____________________

Word Search

SACRAMENT	REMEMBER SINS	CONTRITION
HOLY	ABSOLVE	GOOD DEED
FORGIVE	SON	FRIENDSHIP
FATHER	CONFESSIONS	MERCY
PENANCE	SORROW FOR SIN	SIN

R E M E M B E R S I N S
C O N T R I T I O N F A
O M E R C Y T E E P R C
N E L T E U X L M E I R
F O R G I V E S B N E A
E C E S U L E X E A N M
S F A T H E R N R N D E
S I N E A A R Y A C S N
I E H O L Y S P I E H T
O A B S O L V E R M I S
N G O O D D E E D X P O
S O R R O W F O R S I N

Faith and Life Series • Grade 2 • Chapter 19 • Lesson 4 71

Reinforce

1. Continue practicing confessions.
2. Have the students work on their puzzles, found on *Activity Book*, p. 71.
3. Play a review game on all the materials they have learned so far on the Sacrament of Penance, including the Ten Commandments, confession (matter, form, minister, effects, etc.), sin, the steps to a good confession, the rite, etc.

Conclude

1. Sing "Lord Jesus, think on me," *Adoremus Hymnal*, #364.
2. End by praying the Act of Contrition and the We Pray, on p. 94.

Preview

In the next lesson, we will review the material covered in this chapter.

THE BROWN SCAPULAR: OUR LADY'S GARMENT

The brown scapular is a miniature model of the Carmelite Order's religious habit. Tradition holds that in the 13th century, Our Lady appeared to Saint Simon Stock, Superior General of the Order and gave him the brown scapular. She told him that whomever wore it would be preserved from eternal damnation and that on the first Saturday after his death, she would take that person to Heaven. A person must be enrolled, or "invested," in the scapular in a special ceremony at which a priest presides. Our Lady of Mount Carmel's feast day is July 16.

NOTES

CHAPTER NINETEEN:
REVIEW AND ASSESSMENT

Aims

The students' understanding of the material covered this week will be reviewed and assessed.

Materials

- Quiz 19 (Appendix, p. A-27)
- "Lord Jesus, think on me," *Adoremus Hymnal*, #364

Review

1. Review specifics of the Sacrament of Penance:
   - Matter, form, minister, effects
   - Where they go to confess their sins
   - Ways to confess sins (face to face or behind screen)
   - What they confess

2. Review the five steps to a good confession:

Step 1: examination of conscience:
- What is sin? what is mortal vs. venial sin?
- What must be confessed? (sin/number)
- What can be used as a guide? (Ten Commandments, Law of love)

Step 2: be sorry for sins:
- Perfect vs. imperfect contrition
- Know their sins have offended God, and Jesus died on the Cross for them

Step 3: decide to not sin again:
- Do their very best

Step 4: tell sins to a priest
- Review the rite:
  * welcome
  * Sign of the Cross (Maybe Bible reading)
  * say how long it has been
  * tell sins
  * get penance
  * say Act of Contrition, receive Absolution
  * dismissal

Step 5: do the penance given by the priest

Name:

The Sacrament of Penance **Quiz 19**

Part 1. Place the steps to a good confession in the correct order.

4 Tell your sins to a priest.
1 Know your sins.
5 Do the Penance the priest gives you.
2 Be sorry for your sins.
3 Make up your mind not to sin again.

Part 2. Fill in the blanks.

Cross	sorry	Amen
sins	Bible	confession
kneel	penance	Contrition

Go in and sit in the chair or kneel behind the screen.
Make the Sign of the Cross.
Tell the priest how long it has been since your last confession.
Tell your sins to the priest.
Say: "For these and all my sins, I am sorry."
The priest will talk to you and give you a penance.
The priest may read from the Bible.
Make an Act of Contrition.
Receive absolution, and say "Amen."

Faith and Life • Grade 2 • Appendix A *A - 27*

Assess

1. Distribute Quiz 19. Answer any questions that they may have. When they turn in the quizzes, individually quiz them on the Memorization Questions for this chapter.

2. After all the quizzes have been turned in, review the answers with the class.

Conclude

1. Sing "Lord Jesus, think on me," *Adoremus Hymnal*, #364.

2. Pray an Act of Contrition and a Hail Mary.

CHAPTER TWENTY
MAKING UP FOR OUR OFFENSES

Catechism of the Catholic Church References

Cardinal Virtues:
- Fortitude: 1808, 1837
- Justice: 1807, 1836
- Prudence: 1806, 1835
- Temperance: 1809, 1838

Consequences of Sin: 1472–73, 1487–88
Contrition: 1451–54, 1492
Conversion of the Baptized: 1427–29, 1490
Forgiveness: 2839–45, 2862
Forms of Penance in Christian life: 1434–39
Grace: 1996–2005, 2021–24
Grace Conferred by the Sacraments: 1127–29, 1131
Passions: 1768
Sacrifice: 2099–100
Satisfaction for Sin: 1459–60, 1494
Theological Virtues:
- Charity: 1822–29, 1844
- Faith: 1814–16, 1842
- Hope: 1817–21, 1843

Truthfulness: 2468, 2505
Virtues and Grace: 1810
Works of Penance: 1430, 1460

Scripture References

Zacchaeus: Lk 19:1–10

Background Reading: *The Fundamentals of Catholicism* by Fr. Kenneth Baker, S.J.

Volume 3:
"Punishment is not Popular," pp. 298–300

Volume 3:
"Reconciliation with God," pp. 301–303

Summary of Lesson Content

Lesson 1

The story of Zacchaeus.

Lesson 2

Jesus redeemed us from our sins and atones for our sins with God by His death on the Cross.

Lesson 3

Forgiveness is when our relationship is made right with another after one is offended, and the other says they are sorry.

Penance is making up for our sins, or a removal of our punishment. It restores what was lost due to sin.

Lesson 4

Receiving the Sacrament of Penance frequently, will give man the grace to overcome sin.

Man should also do regular penance to overcome sin.

Penance should be done out of love for Christ.

LESSON ONE: ZACCHAEUS

Aims

The students will learn the story of Zacchaeus.

Materials

- Children's Bible
- *Activity Book*, p. 72

Optional:
- "Lord, who throughout these forty days," *Adoremus Hymnal*, #360
- "The Story of Zacchaeus," video; Jesus: A Kingdom Without Frontiers

Begin

Begin with reviewing:
- Specifics about the Sacrament of Penance (matter, form, minister, effects)
- 5 Steps to a good confession
- Sin: Ten Commandments, mortal/venial
- Rite of the Sacrament of Penance

This review may be accomplished as a game, such as Bible Baseball or Tic Tac Toe (see Appendix, p. B-1 for rules).

Develop

1. Ask the students what the fifth step to a good confession is? (Do penance)

2. They will learn about a man who can teach us about penance; his name is Zacchaeus. Read the first paragraph from the chapter with the students.

3. Read the story of Zacchaeus from a children's Bible (Lk 19:1–10), or a Bible story book.

4. Ask the students about the story of Zacchaeus.
   - Was Zacchaeus tall? How do we know?
   - Why did Zacchaeus want to see Jesus?
   - Was Zacchaeus a good man? Did he steal?
   - What did Jesus ask of Zacchaeus?
   - Why was Zacchaeus sad?
   - How did Zacchaeus make up for his sins?
   - How is Zacchaeus a good example for us?

5. Watch "The Story of Zacchaeus," video from the series Jesus: A Kingdom Without Frontiers, available through Ignatius Press; 30 minutes.

6. Have the students think of penance they can do to make up for their sins. List them on the board. Find various examples.

7. *Zacchaeus made generous penance. If he stole $1.00, he gave back $4.00. How can we follow his example. Should we just do the bare minimum? How can we follow his example after receiving the Sacrament of Penance? What if the priest tells us to say 3 Hail Marys? What can we do? What about daily penance? What kind of things can we do? Should we do acts of charity or try to do good to people we have hurt?*

8. Have the students think of ways they can do good to restore a wrong they have done (e.g., told a lie, stole a pencil, told gossip, were rude, were bullies, were disobedient, etc.).

Name:____________________

Zacchaeus

Fill in the blanks

One day, a big crowd of people was with Jesus. A little man named Zacchaeus went up in a tree so he could see. Jesus saw him and called out "Zacchaeus, I would like to come to eat dinner at your house." Zacchaeus was happy, but also sad. He knew that his sins offended Jesus. So Zacchaeus told Jesus he would make up for his sins. He paid people four times the money he had taken from them!

72 *Faith and Life Series • Grade 2 • Chapter 20 • Lesson 1*

Reinforce

1. Have the students work on *Activity Book*, p. 72.

2. If you have not yet done so, watch "The Story of Zacchaeus," video from the series Jesus: A Kingdom Without Frontiers, available through Ignatius Press; 30 minutes.

3. Teach the students to sing "Lord, who throughout these forty days," *Adoremus Hymnal*, #360.

4. Continue practicing confessions.

Conclude

1. Lead the students in prayer, asking God to inspire them to do penance to make up for their sins.

2. End by praying the Act of Contrition.

Preview

In the next lesson, we will learn that Jesus died to make up for our sins, and we can make up for our sins, too.

THE PROMISE OF THE BROWN SCAPULAR

"Whoever dies wearing this scapular shall not suffer eternal fire."

The brown scapular (there are nearly twenty approved types of scapulars) is a sacramental, that is, a sacred sign resembling a sacrament and by means of which spiritual effects are obtained through the prayers of the Church. The promise attached to the scapular is contingent on living a chaste life.

NOTES

LESSON TWO: MAKING UP FOR OUR SINS

Aims

The students will learn that Jesus redeemed us and atoned for our sins with God by His death on the Cross.

They will learn that they, too, can make up for their sins.

Materials

- *Activity Book*, p. 73
- *Adoremus Hymnal*, #360

Optional:

- "Lord, who throughout these forty days,"
- "Fatima: The Day the Sun Danced," video

Begin

Review with the students the second step for a good confession: sorrow for sin. Ask the children what they could meditate upon in order to help them be sorry for their sins (the Crucifixion of Jesus). Explain to the students that Jesus died for our sins, to make up for our sins. Jesus was true God and true man. He was perfect. He was like us in all things but sin. By dying on the Cross, Jesus saved us from sin, for Himself. Because He was perfect, He made perfect satisfaction of our sins. He was the perfect Sacrifice, paying for all our sins by making up for them.

20 Making Up For Our Offenses

> And Zacchaeus stood and said to the Lord, "Behold, Lord, the half of my goods I give to the poor; and if I have defrauded any one of anything, I restore it fourfold."
>
> Luke 19:8

One day, a big crowd of people was with Jesus. A little man named Zacchaeus went up in a tree so he could see. Jesus saw him and called out, "Zacchaeus, I would like to come to eat dinner at your house." Zacchaeus was happy, but also sad. He knew his sins offended Jesus. So Zacchaeus told Jesus he would make up for his sins. He paid people four times the money he had taken from them.

Jesus died for us to make up for our sins. We can help to make up for our sins, too.

Once a boy was playing in his house. He was throwing a ball around, even though his mother had said not to throw balls inside. The ball hit a beautiful vase and broke it. The boy told his mother what had happened. He said he was sorry and would never

97

Develop

1. Read paragraphs 2–4 with the students.

2. Ask the students about the reading:
   - What did the boy do wrong?
   - How did he sin?
   - What did he break?
   - Was he sorry?
   - Did his mother forgive him?
   - Did her forgiveness fix the vase?
   - How did the boy try to make up for his wrong doing?
   - Why did the boy want to make up for his wrong doing?
   - What good did his cleaning up and picking flowers for his mother do?
   - Why is it good to make up for our wrong doing?
   - What is another word for making up for wrong doing?
   - What Bible story did we learn about yesterday that taught us more about making up for what we do wrong?
   - What can we learn from this?

3. *Have the students break into small groups and perform skits. Have each group act out a wrong doing and then act out a penance that is appropriate for that wrong doing. Have the students explain why they chose the penance they did. You may provide a list of wrong doings:*
   - *Breaking a friend's toy*
   - *Lying to get out of trouble*
   - *Fighting with a sibling*
   - *Being a bully at school*
   - *Cheating on a test*
   - *Not paying attention at Mass*

4. Watch "Fatima: The Day the Sun Danced" video (available through Ignatius Press; 30 minutes), making note of the sacrifices of the children. Teach the children to make sacrifices, united with Jesus' sufferings on the Cross, as a way to make up for their sins and for the sins of the whole world.

Name:____________________

Jesus dies to make up for our sins. We can make up for our sins too!

1. How can you make up for your sins?
You can do the penance the priest gives you when you go to confession and you can give up things you like.
2. Why do you do penance?
To make up for sins.
3. What does our textbook give as examples of penances?
Not watch TV for a day, help mother and father, play with brother or sister, or give up things you like
4. Sometimes we have habits of sin. What should we do about this?
By going to confession often, we will have the grace to stay away from sin.

Faith and Life Series • Grade 2 • Chapter 20 • Lesson 2 73

Reinforce

1. Perform the skits discussed in #3 of Develop section.

2. If you have not yet done so, watch "Fatima: The Day the Sun Danced," video, available through Ignatius Press; 30 minutes.

3. Have the students complete *Activity Book*, p. 73.

4. Continue practicing confessions.

Conclude

1. Sing "Lord, who throughout these forty days," *Adoremus Hymnal*, #360.

2. End with the prayer of reparation taught to the children of Fatima and by praying the Act of Contrition.

Preview

In the next lesson, we will learn more about penance.

OUR LADY OF FATIMA

Our Lady appeared six times to three shepherd children between May 13th and October 13th, 1917, near Fatima, Portugal. She asked the children to pray the rosary daily, to wear the brown scapular, and to perform acts of sacrifice and reparation. The children were given a terrifying vision of Hell and, through Mary, predicted the fall of Russia from Christianity and the future outbreak of World War II. Our Lady asked that the faithful attend Mass on five consecutive first Fridays in her honor. She performed the Miracle of the Sun on October 13, 1917. May 13 is the feast of Our Lady of Fatima.

NOTES

____

____

____

____

____

____

____

____

____

____

____

LESSON THREE: FORGIVENESS AND PENANCE

Aims

The students will learn the need for both forgiveness and penance, and understand how these two concepts are complementary, but different.

Materials

- *Activity Book*, p. 74

Optional:
- "Lord, who throughout these forty days," *Adoremus Hymnal*, #360

Begin

Review what a penance is: a way of making up for a wrong-doing or a sin. Why should we do this? Because sin affects God, others, and yourself. When we offend someone, we can say we are sorry and they can forgive us. This means that the the relationship is restored. To show the other that we are sorry and that we want to do better, we can do a penance to make up for our wrong-doing. Use again the example of the vase from the textbook. Help the students to understand how forgiveness and penance are related, but different.

throw the ball inside again. "That's all right. I forgive you," said his mother.

But the boy wanted to make up for what he did. He picked up all the broken pieces. Then, instead of going to play, he went and picked some flowers. His mother looked so happy when he gave her the flowers. That made the boy feel glad.

How can you make up for your sins? First, you can do the penance the priest gives you when you go to Confession. Because you love God, you can do something more. You could not watch TV for one day and use that time to help your mother or father. You could play with your little brother or sister instead of your friends. It is hard to give up things you like, but it will make you strong. It will help you to say "No" to what is wrong.

Sometimes there is one sin that you commit more than others. It may be lying, or disobeying, or fighting with others. You should try hard to stop this bad habit, and to start a good habit. By going to confession often, you will have the grace to stay away from sin.

Remember: the reason why you want to make up for your sins is to please Jesus. If you think of that, it will be easier to do something that is hard for you to do.

98

Develop

1. Read paragraph 5 with the students.

2. Ask the students these questions, relating them to the reading:
   - Why should we do penance? (to show God we love Him, to help us become strong so we will not sin)
   - What are some examples of penance given from our textbook? (no T.V., help mother and father, play with brother or sister).
   - Is penance easy? (No, it is hard to give up things we like)
   - Should we do the penance a priest gives us in the Sacrament of Penance? Yes, we must do this penance.
   - Should we do more than the penance that a priest gives us in the Sacrament of Penance? Yes, to show God we are sorry for our sins, how much we love Him, and that we want to be better.

3. Make a list of penances on the board that the students can do. What did the children of Fatima do? Can they do these things? Have the students create this list. List as many various penances as possible on the board (this will be useful for their activity page).

4. Ask the students how a penance may make them learn to say "no" to sin:
   - *It reminds them how it offends God*
   - *It reminds them how sin has consequences*
   - *It reminds them that they need to overcome sin*
   - *It helps them become strong by not putting themselves first*
   - *It helps them to understand how their sin affects God, others, and themselves*

5. Together, as a class, make an act of penance from the list on the board, i.e., prayer for someone or for an intention, or do an act of charity, etc.

Name:____________________

Make a list of Penances you can do!

Answers will vary

____

____

____

____

____

____

74 *Faith and Life Series • Grade 2 • Chapter 20 • Lesson 3*

Reinforce

1. Have the students complete *Activity Book*, p. 74.

2. Do a group penance project with the class.

3. Continue to practice confessions.

Conclude

1. Sing "Lord, who throughout these forty days," *Adoremus Hymnal*, #360.

2. End with the prayer of reparation taught to the children of Fatima and the the Act of Contrition.

Preview

In the next lesson, we will learn about vices and virtues, and that penance is done to please Jesus.

SUGGESTED BACKGROUND READING ON FATIMA

Roses, Fountains, and Gold, by John Martin, pp. 213–33, Ignatius Press, 1998.

PUBLIC VS. PRIVATE REVELATION

Public revelation is the property of the entire Church and, if approved, must be believed for one's salvation (i.e., the doctrine of the Trinity, the Incarnation, the Eucharist). Public revelation ended with the death of the last Apostle, John. Since then, every apparition is considered private, and though they may be approved by the Church, they are never necessary for salvation, though the Church may encourage their practice or devotion for personal sanctity. Apparitions are never granted Church approval until they have ceased.

NOTES

LESSON FOUR: OVERCOMING SIN

Aims

The students will learn about vices and their opposing virtues.

They will learn that penance will help them overcome their sins and that penance should be done to please Jesus.

Materials

- *Activity Book*, p. 75

Optional:
- "Lord, who throughout these forty days," *Adoremus Hymnal*, #360

Begin

Review penance with the students. What is penance? What does penance help us to do? What are penatents? Who are good examples of doing penance? (Zacchaeus and the children of Fatima). Why should we do penance?

Remember: Tell the children that doing Penance is a way to tell Jesus that they love Him and that they want to make up for their sins. They may offer their penances in union with His sufferings on the Cross.

Can You Answer?

1. When does a person sin? (Chapter 9)
2. How do you know what is right or wrong? (Chapter 9)
3. Why should you be sorry for your sins? (Chapter 17)
4. Does God love you even when you sin? (Chapter 17)
5. What does it mean to be truly sorry? (Chapter 17)
6. Why do we go to Confession? (Chapter 18)
7. Who takes away your sins? (Chapter 18)
8. Whose place does the priest take in Confession? (Chapter 18)
9. What does the priest say to forgive you? (Chapter 18)
10. What must you do to make a good confession? There are five steps. (Chapter 19)
11. The priest gives you a penance. What is this penance for? (Chapter 20)
12. Besides being forgiven, what happens to you when you go to Confession? (Chapter 20)

99

Develop

1. Gather the students around the chalkboard and read the second to last paragraph of the textbook. Explain that a repeated habit of sin, a bad habit, is called a vice. Write on the board: "vice: a habit of doing bad."

2. Ask them what the vices listed in the textbook are (lying, disobeying, fighting). List these vices under the definition. What are some other vices? Pride, laziness, jealousy, gluttony, saying mean things, selfishness etc. The children may make suggestions to the list.

3. Ask them if tpracticing vices is loving God and neighbor as they should. No. They are putting themselves first and breaking God's laws.

4. The textbook says that we should try hard to stop our bad habits, and to start good ones. A virtue is a habit of doing good. Under the definition of virtue, list the opposing virtue written on the board, list the opposing virtue for the listed vice.

5. Tell them that growing in virtue is hard; it requires work, and much effort. With God's grace, the Sacrament of Penance, and penance, we may overcome our vices and replace them with virtues. We may become so good at virtue that we will enjoy it and find it easy. Better yet, as we grow in one virtue, we will grow in other virtues, too. For example, if I become virtuous by overcoming meanness, I'll become gentle-hearted, charitable, and less selfish, as well. Remind the students that to grow in virtue, we need to work at it. We must take our sins and vices to the Sacrament of Penance and do penance. We may also pray to grow in a particular virtue, and God will help us.

6. Reread the last paragraph of the chapter. Remind the children that as they grow in virtue and do penance, they will become more pleasing to Jesus.

Q. 43 *What is penance?*
Penance is a prayer, offering, work of mercy, service to neighbor, act of self-denial, sacrifice, work of charity, or acceptance of our cross. It helps us to become like Jesus, and to make up for our sins (CCC 1459–60).

100

Reinforce

1. Have the students copy the vice/virtue chart onto lined paper so they may study it.

2. Have them complete *Activity Book*, p. 75.

3. Read aloud the questions (Can You Answer) on p. 99. Have them answer these questions orally or write them out so that they may study them.

Conclude

1. Sing "Lord, who throughout these forty days," *Adoremus Hymnal*, #360.

2. Lead the children in praying to God, asking for His grace to help overcome vices and to grow in the opposing virtues. End by praying the Act of Contrition.

Preview

In the next lesson, we will review the material covered in this chapter.

CHALK TALK: VICE VS. VIRTUE

Vice: a habit of doing bad	**Virtue**: a habit of doing good
lying	speak the truth
disobeying	obeying
fighting	gentleness/charity
pride	humility
laziness	diligence, fortitude
jealousy	wanting good for others
gluttony	temperance (moderation)
speaking mean	speaking kindly
selfishness	put others first

NOTES

CHAPTER TWENTY: REVIEW AND ASSESSMENT

Aims

The students' understanding of the material covered this week will be reviewed and assessed.

Materials

- Quiz 20 (Appendix, p. A-28)
- Unit 5 Test (Appendix, pp. A-29 and A-30)
- "Lord, who throughout these forty days," *Adoremus Hymnal*, #356

Review

1. Review the story of Zacchaeus and how he is a good example of one performing generous penance.

2. Remind them that Jesus died to make up for their sins, and that they, too, can make up for their sins. What is this called? Penance.

3. Have them explain the differences between:
   - Being sorry
   - Being forgiven
   - Doing a penance

   What is their relation?

4. What are some penances the children can do?

5. What did the children of Fatima do for penances? Why?

6. What is a vice? What is a virtue? How can one replace a vice with a virtue?
   - Hard work
   - Take vice and sins to the Sacrament of Penance
   - Do penance
   - Pray to grow in virtue

7. Ask the children why they should do penances?
   - To show Jesus how much they love Him and that they are sorry for their sins

Name:

Making up for Our Offenses **Quiz 20**

Multiple Choice *Circle the correct answer.*

1. Zacchaeus make up for his sins by repaying people how many times the money he had taken from them?
   a) three
   (b)) four
   c) five

2. Who can make up for our sins?
   a) Jesus
   b) We can
   (c)) a and b

3. Penance is:
   a) when we are sorry for our sins
   b) when we make up for our sins
   (c)) when we repair our relationship with another

4. A habit of doing bad is overcome by:
   (a)) work, confession, penance, and prayer
   b) time and growing up
   c) pretending we do not have a bad habit

5. You should want to make up for your sins to:
   a) be happy
   b) please Jesus
   (c)) a and b

List five penances you can do:

1. Answers will vary
2.
3.
4.
5.

A - 28 *Faith and Life • Grade 2 • Appendix A*

Assess

1. Distribute Quiz 20. Answer any questions that they may have. When they turn in their quizzes, individually test them.

2. When all the quizzes have been turned in, review the correct answers.

3. Do the same with the Unit 5 Test.

Conclude

1. Sing "Lord, who throughout these forty days," *Adoremus Hymnal*, #360.

2. End with praying an Act of Contrition and a Hail Mary.

CHAPTER TWENTY-ONE
THE GOOD SHEPHERD

Catechism of the Catholic Church References

Bearing Witness to the Truth: 2171–74, 2506
Charity: 1822–29, 1844
Christ's Redemptive Death in the Divine Plan of Salvation: 599–605, 619–20
Christ's Life as an Offering to the Father: 606–618, 621–23
Christian Holiness: 2012–16, 2028–29
Duties of Children toward Parents: 2214–20, 2247–48, 2251
Forgiveness: 2839–45, 2862
Jesus as Our Teacher and Model of Holiness: 516, 561
Jesus' Messianic Entrance into Jerusalem: 559–60, 570
Kingship of Christ: 671
Lamb of God: 608
Living in the Truth: 2465–70, 2505
Messianic Kingship: 440, 680, 1060
Obedience: 144–49, 176
Parables of Christ: 546
Prayer: 2559–67, 2590–91, 2644

Scripture References

Entrance into Jerusalem: Mt 21:1–11; Jn 12:12–16
Good Shepherd: Jn 10:1–21
Passion Sunday: Jn 12:12–16
Lost Sheep: Mt. 18:10–14; Is: 40:11
"The Lord is my Shepherd": Ps 23
Crucifixion: Lk: 23

Background Reading: *The Fundamentals of Catholicism* by Fr. Kenneth Baker, S.J.

Volume 2:
"Jesus Died Not for Himself but for All Men," pp. 295–98
"Jesus' Sacrifice on the Cross," pp. 289–92

Summary of Lesson Content

Lesson 1

Jesus knew that He would die for the sins of mankind.

On Palm Sunday, Jesus rode into Jerusalem as the Messianic King.

Jesus was not to be a king of this world, but to be the Savior and lead people to Heaven.

Lesson 2

Jesus is the "Good Shepherd"; His sheep are all people.

Lesson 3

Jesus nourishes man's soul in the sacraments; the sacraments strengthen man spiritually.

Jesus guards man from sin and evil and calls man back to His love when man sins.

Lesson 4

Jesus is the Way to Heaven. Man must become like Him, especially in the virtues of obedience, humility, forgiveness, prayerfulness, and mercy.

Jesus lays down His life for the life of the world.

LESSON ONE: JESUS IS KING

Aims

The students will understand that Jesus knew that He would die for our sins.

They will learn that on Palm Sunday, Jesus rode into Jerusalem as the King of Heaven and earth.

Materials

- Children's Bible
- Picture of a coronation
- Palm Branch
- Pictures of Christ the King
- *Activity Book*, p. 76

Optional:
- "The King of love my shepherd is," *Adoremus Hymnal*, #580
- "Triumphant Entry into Jerusalem," video; Jesus: A Kingdom Without Frontiers

Begin

Read about or show a picture (or video) of a coronation. The coronation of Queen Elizabeth II is a good example. Many preparations were made. Flags and flowers were placed in the streets. Ask the children what a ruler does. He protects (sometimes going to war), takes care of his people, goes to other places to prepare for friendly visits, etc. Jesus was a King, too, though not quite the same kind. However, when He came into Jerusalem, the people treated Him like a king. Compare Jesus to modern-day kings.

21 The Good Shepherd

He will feed his flock like a shepherd,
he will gather the lambs in his arms,
he will carry them in his bosom,
and gently lead those that are with young.

Isaiah 40:11

The time came when Jesus knew He would soon die for us. He rode on a donkey into the city of Jerusalem. Nobody else knew Jesus was going to die. Many people came to honor Jesus as king. They threw palm branches and coats onto the road where He was coming. They shouted for joy.

The people were right to think Jesus was King. But He was not the kind of king they wanted. Jesus is King of Heaven as well as earth. He did not come to live in a palace and wear a crown. He came to be the Savior Who would die for our sins and lead us to Heaven.

"I am the **Good Shepherd**," said Jesus. "I know my sheep and they know me. They hear my voice. I know them and they follow me."

101

Develop

1. Read the first two paragraphs from the textbook.

2. Read the story of Palm Sunday from a children's Bible (Jn 12:12–16). Show the students a palm branch. Teach them about the tradition of Palm Sunday, when every Catholic receives a blessed palm and places it behind the Crucifix in their home.

3. Have them dramatize the story of Palm Sunday.

4. Ask them to think of why the Israelites would have been so excited to see Jesus coming into Jerusalem on a donkey. They had been told that this would be a sign of the King (Zec 9:9). What did these people expect from their king?
- No taxes
- Protection from the Romans
- Conquering of enemies
- Peace and joy
- Represent His people to foreign lands

5. Was Jesus like the king they expected? No. Why not?
- Jesus did not come to fight wars, but to bring peace
- Jesus did not come to rule in this world, but to be King of Heaven and earth
- Jesus came to represent His people, not before other kings, but before God—to take our place and die for our sins

6. What does Jesus being King mean to all of us?
- *Jesus died for our sins, so we can go to Heaven*
- *If He is King of Heaven, and we are His brothers through Baptism, then we will inherit the Kingdom of Heaven*
- *He will share His riches with us, which are grace and the sacraments*

7. Look at pictures of Christ the King.

Name:____________________

Jesus Christ Is Our King!

The time came when Jesus knew He would soon die for us. He rode a donkey into the city of Jerusalem. Nobody else knew that Jesus was going to die. Many people came to honor Jesus as king. They threw palm branches and coats onto the road where He was coming. They shouted for joy.

The people were right to think Jesus was King. But He was not the kind of king they wanted. Jesus is King of Heaven as well as earth. He did not come to live in a palace and wear a crown. He came to be the Savior who would die for our sins and lead us to Heaven.

76 *Faith and Life Series • Grade 2 • Chapter 21 • Lesson 1*

EXPECTATIONS OF THE MESSIAH

Among the Jewish people of the first century, it was widely expected that the Messiah would be a military leader who would free Judah from Roman imperialism and re-establish the old, pre-Roman theocratic order. Certain Jewish sects, including the radical Zealots, were not opposed to the use of violence in defense of their faith and homeland. The Zealots were in a high state of anticipation for the Messiah at the time of Jesus and were likely disappointed in Jesus' message of love and peace. During the unsuccessful rebellion of 79 A.D. the Holy City of Jerusalem was sacked by Rome and the Temple destroyed.

Reinforce

1. Have the students complete *Activity Book*, p. 76.

2. Show "Triumphant Entry into Jerusalem," video from the series Jesus: A Kingdom Without Frontiers, available through Ignatius Press; 30 minutes.

3. Teach the students to sing "The King of love my shepherd is," *Adoremus Hymnal*, #580.

Conclude

Lead the students in prayer, asking Jesus to bring us into His Kingdom one day. End by praying the Our Father.

Preview

In the next lesson, we will learn of Jesus as the Good Shepherd.

NOTES

LESSON TWO: THE GOOD SHEPHERD

Aims

The students will learn that Jesus is the "Good Shepherd" and that we are His sheep.

They will learn the qualities of the Good Shepherd.

Materials

- Picture of Jesus the Good Shepherd (use p. 102 of text as needed)
- Drawing paper, crayons
- *Activity Book*, p. 77

Optional:
- "The King of love my shepherd is," *Adoremus Hymnal*, #580

Begin

Ask the students what a shepherd does. A shepherd is one who cares for sheep. He takes care of them, keeps them safe, sees that they eat well, etc. Do the students know any shepherds? Jesus is the Good Shepherd. Turn to p. 102 of the text and have the students look at the picture and tell you what is going on. Jesus is carrying a sheep. He has a staff. He looks as though He loves the sheep, and they trust Him.

Develop

1. Read paragraphs 3 and 4 with the students.

2. Ask them if they know the Good Shepherd. Who is He? (Jesus.) Do they hear His voice? How? Through prayer, through their authorities, through things going on around them. Have the students give examples, such as feeling called to prayer or to do a good deed, etc.

3. Ask them how they follow Jesus. Do they pray? Do they keep His Commandments? Do they live the virtues? Do they strive to do what is right always and love their neighbor? Can they give examples of how they follow Jesus?

4. Ask them how they are like sheep. Do they need food and shelter? Do they need the care of a shepherd? Do they go in groups and follow a leader?

5. Ask the students how Jesus can watch over them day and night. He is all knowing and can watch over every person at all times. He knows what we need and want and what will make us happy.

6. *You may read the 23rd Psalm to the children, and have them pick out the imagery and symbolism, or draw pictures that reflect this psalm.*

7. If time permits, explain to them that Jesus is also a role model for us (as sheep) by being the Lamb of God (cf, Jn 1:29). Ask the children how Jesus is a role model for them and how they can imitate Him:
- Be obedient
- Be humble
- Be forgiving
- Be prayerful
- Be merciful (see p. 104 of text)

Name:_______________

"I Am the Good Shepherd"

1. What does Jesus tell us about being a Good Shepherd?
Jesus is the Good Shepherd.

2. What does a shepherd do?
He watches over his sheep night and day. He gives them food and keeps them safe.

3. What would a good sheep do?
Follow the shepherd

4. Who is the Good Shepherd?
Jesus is the Good Shepherd

5. Who are His sheep?
We are His sheep

Faith and Life Series • Grade 2 • Chapter 21 • Lesson 2 77

Reinforce

1. Have the students complete *Activity Book*, p. 77. They may need to read John 10 for help.

2. Have them work on pictures of Psalm 23.

Conclude

1. Sing together "The King of love my shepherd is," *Adoremus Hymnal*, #580.

2. End with the prayer on p. 105.

Preview

In the next lesson, we will learn more about the works of the Good Shepherd.

PSALM 23

The Lord is my shepherd, I shall not want; he makes me lie down in green pastures.
He leads me beside still waters; he restores my soul.
He leads me in the paths of righteousness for his name's sake.
Even though I walk through the valley of the shadow of death, I fear no evil; for Thou art with me; thy rod and thy staff, they comfort me.
Thou preparest a table before me in the presence of mine enemies; thou anointest my head with oil,
my cup overflows.
Surely goodness and mercy shall follow me all the days of my life; and I shall dwell in the house of the Lord
for ever.

NOTES

LESSON THREE: JESUS FEEDS US

Aims

The students will learn that Jesus nourishes men's souls in the sacraments, which strengthen man's spiritually.

They will understand that as the Shepherd, Jesus guards man from sin and evil and calls man back to His love when man does sin.

Materials

- Appendix, B-24, cotton balls, glue
- Children's Bible
- *Activity Book*, p. 78

Optional
- "The King of love my shepherd is," *Adoremus Hymnal*, #580
- "The Good Shepherd," video; Jesus: A Kingdom Without Frontiers

Begin

You will need a picture of a sheep (Appendix, p. B-24) for each child. Have cotton balls for the children to glue to the picture. This is a review game. As the children get a correct answer, they may glue a cotton ball to their sheep. Ask the children questions such as "Who is the Good Shepherd?" "Does Jesus know His sheep?" "Does Jesus take care of us?" Ask the children how He cares for us, etc., and with each answer, they may glue on a cotton ball to make nice "healthy" looking sheep, well cared for by their personal shepherd.

We are the sheep that Jesus speaks of. Just like a shepherd, Jesus watches over us night and day. He knows all about each one of us. He knows everything we say and do. Jesus even knows what we want and what will make us happy.

A shepherd must feed his sheep. Jesus gives us food for our souls in the sacraments. This food makes us strong so we will be good.

A shepherd protects his sheep from the wolves and other dangers, and he finds those sheep that have gotten lost. Jesus guards us against evil and sin. But even when we turn away from Jesus by sinning, He will always come after us, calling us back to His love.

A shepherd leads his sheep to green pastures where they will be happy. Jesus came to lead all of us on the way to Heaven—the only place where we will be truly happy. He taught us that He is the Way and that we must become like Him to go to Heaven.

"The Good Shepherd lays down His life for His sheep." Jesus was brave enough to lay down His life for us. He died so that we all could live forever. Even if you were the only boy or girl in the world, Jesus would have died just for you. He loves you that much.

103

Develop

1. From the text book, read paragraphs 3–7 with the students. As you read this passage, write on the board all the things Jesus does as a shepherd:
- *Knows His sheep*
- *Leads His sheep*
- *Watches over His sheep*
- *Feeds His sheep*
- *Protects His sheep*
- *Guards His sheep*

2. Discuss each of the things Jesus does as the Good Shepherd:
- How does Jesus know His sheep? He knows each of us. He is God.
- How does Jesus lead His sheep? Jesus opened the doors to Heaven and leads us to His Father's Kingdom by giving us His example and telling us how to get there.
- How does Jesus feed His sheep? Teach the children about the seven sacraments. Baptism gives the soul grace and makes us part of God's Family. Eucharist feeds us with Jesus' Body and Blood. Confession gives us grace to overcome our sins. Confirmation gives us the gifts of the Holy Spirit to live as Catholics. Holy Orders gives priests and deacons the power to feed the souls of the sheep in the Church. Matrimony gives us grace to help one another be faithful to God. Anointing of the Sick gives us grace to unify ourselves with Christ.
- How does Jesus watch over His sheep? Jesus knows what we are doing, what we need, and what dangers we may face. He guards us from dangers, protects us from evil, and keeps us safe in His love.

Name:___________________

Complete this chart.

WHAT A SHEPHERD DOES	WHAT JESUS DOES
1. A shepherd knows his sheep.	Answers will vary slightly
2. A shepherd watches over his sheep.	
3. A shepherd knows what his sheep want and need.	
4. A shepherd feeds his sheep.	
5. A shepherd protects his sheep.	
6. A shepherd looks for his lost sheep.	
7. A shepherd leads his sheep to green pastures.	
8. A shepherd cares for the injured sheep.	

78 *Faith and Life Series • Grade 2 • Chapter 21 • Lesson 3*

Reinforce

1. Have the students work on *Activity Book*, p. 78. They may refer to John 10 for help.

2. Write sentences with blanks on the board and have the children supply appropriate answers. The sentences at the bottom of this page offer an example.

3. Watch "The Good Shepherd," video from the series Jesus: A Kingdom Without Frontiers, available through Ignatius Press; 30 minutes.

Conclude

1. Sing "The King of love my shepherd is," *Adoremus Hymnal*, #580.

2. Together, pray p. 105 of the text.

Preview

In the next lesson, the children will learn about the Good Shepherd's love for each of them and how they may imitate His love.

CHALK TALK: THE GOOD SHEPHERD

Chalk Talk

Jesus is called the (Good Shepherd).
A good shepherd (finds) his lost sheep.
We are the (sheep) of Jesus' flock.
A good shepherd (protects) his flock from dangers.
Jesus is the (Way) to heaven.
Jesus died so that we could (live) forever.

NOTES

LESSON FOUR:
JESUS, OUR WAY

Aims

The students will learn that Jesus is the Way to Heaven. He laid down His life for each of us so that we may go to Heaven.

They will learn to become like Jesus by living the virtues of obedience, humility, forgiveness, prayerfulness, and mercy.

Materials

- Crucifix or pictures of the crucifixion
- Children's Bible
- *Activity Book*, p. 79

Optional:
- "The King of love my shepherd is," *Adoremus Hymnal*, #580
- "Jesus Dies on the Cross," video; Jesus: A Kingdom Without Frontiers

Begin

Tell the students the story of Saint Francis de Sales (opposite page). Ask what it meant for a shepherd to risk his life for his sheep. How did his neighbor show charity toward this shepherd? What did Saint Francis de Sales learn? What can we learn from this story? How is Jesus like the shepherd? How is He like the neighbor? How should we be?

"I am the way, and the truth, and the life; no one comes to the Father, but by me."
John 14:6

Jesus Is the Way—We Must Become Like Him

obedient:	Always do what pleases God. Obey cheerfully.
humble:	Tell the truth. Never lie.
forgiving:	Love your enemies. Forgive those who hurt you.
prayerful:	Say your daily prayers. Always be mindful of God's presence.
merciful:	Be kind to everyone. Be helpful and generous.

Words to Know:

Good Shepherd

104

Develop

1. Finish reading the text from this chapter.

2. Ask the students how Jesus laid down His life for His sheep. He suffered and died on the Cross for us. Show the children a Crucifix or pictures of the crucifixion. Explain to the children that Jesus died on the Cross for our sins, so we could live forever. He opened the gates of Heaven, and died for each and every one of us. Even if it were just (child's name) and (child's name), He would have died for just them! He loves us so much. Optional: you may read the crucifixion story from the children's Bible (Lk 23).

3. Jesus was the Lamb of God, the perfect Sacrifice to the Father. He is our example and role model for being a humble sheep or lamb. We must become like Him.

4. Read the box on p. 104. Read each virtue, and ask the children how Jesus exemplified each virtue:

- *Jesus was obedient to the Father by suffering and dying on the Cross for our sins. He was obedient to God the Father in all things.*
- *Jesus was humble by speaking the truth about God, His love, and His Kingdom.*
- *Jesus loved His enemies and prayed for them. He forgave and asked the Father to forgive them, even from the Cross.*
- *Jesus was prayerful. At many times, He went off to pray, and He even taught the Apostles how to pray. He was also always aware of God's presence.*
- *Jesus was kind, helpful, and generous to everyone. Can the children remember some of His miracles that attest to this?*

5. Ask them how they can become more like Jesus by living each virtue. Write their answers on the board. Their answers may be made into a chart.

Q. 44 *Why can we call Jesus the Good Shepherd?*
Jesus is the Good Shepherd because He loves His sheep, cares for them, gives them food, protects them from evil, and even lays down His life for them. We are His sheep, and the Church is His sheepfold (CCC 754).

We Pray:

Jesus, meek and humble of heart,
make our hearts like unto Yours.

105

Reinforce

1. Have the students work on *Activity Book*, p. 79.

2. You may show "Jesus Dies on the Cross," video from the series Jesus: A Kingdom Without Frontiers, available through Ignatius Press; 30 minutes.

Conclude

1. Sing "The King of love my shepherd is," *Adoremus Hymnal*, #580.

2. End with the prayer on p. 105.

Preview

In the next lesson, we will review the material covered in this chapter.

SAINT FRANCIS DE SALES

Tell the students about Saint Francis de Sales. He wrote to his friend, Saint Jane de Chantal, about coming to a town where there were many shepherds. This place was a land of snow and ice, he said. It happened that while looking for a stray sheep, one shepherd fell into a crevice that was seventy feet deep. The only way he was found was that a neighbor happened to find his hat near the place where he had fallen. This neighbor was lowered by other men into the crevice and found the dead body. He took hold of the body and called to the men to haul him up before he, himself, died of the cold. These men buried the body of the unfortunate shepherd, who had willingly gone to very dangerous places just to find his sheep. Then he saw, too, the charity of the neighbor who risked his life for the sake of his friend.

NOTES

CHAPTER TWENTY-ONE: REVIEW AND ASSESSMENT

Aims

The students' understanding of the material covered this week will be reviewed and assessed.

Materials

- Quiz 21 (Appendix, p. A-31)
- "The King of love my shepherd is," *Adoremus Hymnal*, #580

Name:

The Good Shepherd **Quiz 21**

Matching:

Obedient	Say your daily prayers.
Humble	Always do what pleases God.
Forgiving	Be kind to everyone.
Prayerful	Love your enemies.
Merciful	Tell the truth.

Answer the following questions in complete sentences.

As the Good Shepherd, how does Jesus…

1. … lead His sheep?
Answers will vary
2. … feed His sheep?
3. … protect His sheep?
4. …know His sheep?
5. …lay down His life for His sheep?

Faith and Life • Grade 2 • Appendix A *A - 31*

Review

1. Review the events of Palm Sunday. What kind of king did everyone expect Jesus to be? What kind of king is Jesus?

2. Review the readings on the Good Shepherd. How is Jesus like a Shepherd? How are we like His sheep? Use *Activity Book*, p. 78 as a review page. You may play a review game, such as Bible Baseball or Tic Tac Toe.

3. Review the virtues on p. 104 of the text. Have the children give examples of each virtue, how they live them, and how Jesus exemplified them (obedience, humility, forgiveness, prayerfulness, mercy).

Assess

1. Distribute Quiz 21. Read through the questions with the children and answer any questions that they may have.

2. Administer the quiz. After all the quizzes have been turned in, review the answers with the children orally. As the children turn in their quizzes, individually quiz them on the virtues they learned.

Conclude

1. Sing "The King of love my shepherd is," *Adoremus Hymnal*, #580.

2. End by praying the prayer on p. 105 of the text.

CHAPTER TWENTY-TWO
THE LAST SUPPER

Catechism of the Catholic Church References

Eucharist:
- As a Memorial: 1356–57, 1409
- Instituted by Christ: 1341–44

Fruits of Communion: 1391–1401, 1416
Holy Communion: 1355, 1382–90, 1415, 1417
Institution of the Eucharist: 1337–40
Last Supper: 610–11, 621
Presence of Christ in the Eucharist: 1373–81, 1410, 1418

Reception of Communion:
- Admission: 1244
- In Every Mass: 1388
- Preparation: 1385–87

Signs of Bread and Wine in the Eucharist: 1333–36, 1412
Sunday Eucharist: 2177–79
- Two parts: 1346, 1408

Scripture References

Bread of Life: Jn 6:35–59
Fish and Loaves: Mt 14:13–21; Jn 6:1–15

Last Supper: Mk 14:22–25; Mt 26:26–29; Lk 22:11–39; I Cor 11:23–26; Jn 13

Background Reading: *The Fundamentals of Catholicism* by Fr. Kenneth Baker, S.J.

Volume 3:
"My Flesh Is Real Food and My Blood Is Real Drink," pp. 232–35

Volume 3:
"The Mass Is a True Sacrifice," pp. 259–61

Summary of Lesson Content

Lesson 1

The Israelites celebrate the feast of Passover annually, commemorating the exodus from Egypt.

The night before Jesus died, He celebrated His Last Supper, the Passover meal, with His Apostles.

Jesus wanted to stay with all those who loved Him.

Lesson 2

At the Last Supper, Jesus instituted the Eucharist.

With the words of Jesus, bread and wine were changed into His Body, Blood, Soul, and Divinity, really and truly present under the appearance of bread and wine. No longer bread or wine, but truly Jesus.

At the Last Supper, the Apostles received Jesus into their souls, sacramentally. This event was the first Communion.

Lesson 3

The sacrament of Christ's Body and Blood is the Holy Eucharist.

Jesus gave the power to the Apostles (and through them to every priest) to change bread and wine into His Body and Blood when He said, "Do this in memory of Me."

Lesson 4

The miracle of the multiplication of loaves and fish prefigured the Eucharist.

Jesus is the Living Bread from Heaven.

LESSON ONE: THE LAST SUPPER

Aims

The students will learn the story of the Passover.

They will learn that on the night before Jesus died, He celebrated His Last Supper, the Passover meal, with His Apostles.

They will learn that Jesus wanted to stay with all those who loved Him.

Materials

- Children's Bible
- *Activity Book*, p. 80
- "The Exodus," video; In the Beginning: Stories from the Bible

Optional:

- "Jesus, my Lord, my God, my all!" *Adoremus Hymnal*, #516
- Seder meal, see Appendix, pp. B-3–B-7

Begin

Optional: If possible, celebrate the seder meal as a class. Explain the Passover through celebrating the seder. You may want to invite in a Rabbi to explain the meal and Passover.

If a seder meal is not possible, begin with reading from the children's Bible the Passover Story (Ex 1–20).

Develop

Optional: Show "The Exodus," video from the series In the Beginning: Stories from the Bible, available through Ignatius Press; 30 minutes.

1. If you celebrate or read the Passover story, review the story itself, having the children place events in the correct order, or retell the story in their own words. They may dramatize the story or have a seder meal (Appendix, pp. B-3–B7).

2. Read paragraphs 1 and 2 from the chapter.

3. Explain to the children that just as Moses led the people from slavery at Passover, so, too, Jesus freed us from our sins through dying on the Cross. We share in His Passover meal every time we go to Mass. You may want to parallel Jesus being the Lamb of God with the Passover Lamb (connecting this lesson to the last chapter).

4. Reread the last sentence of the second paragraph. Explain to the children that Jesus wanted to stay with us always, and so He gave us a special gift called the "Eucharist." Write this on the board. Explain that this word means THANKSGIVING. The Eucharist is Jesus really and truly present, hidden under the appearances of bread and wine. At Mass, the priest, through Jesus Christ, changes bread and wine into Jesus; it is no longer bread or wine, but really Jesus—His Body, Blood, Soul, and Divinity. This change is called "transubstantiation," which means a change in what it is (from bread and wine into Jesus). Jesus gave us this special gift at the Last Supper, which we will learn more about this miracle in the next lesson.

5. Explain that Jesus is present in the Eucharist so He can stay with us. He remains present in the church after Mass in the "tabernacle." You may take the children to the tabernacle and teach them to genuflect. Take time for silent prayer, emphasizing that they are praying to Jesus really and truly present.

Name:_______________

Jesus is with us always. He comes to live in us.

1. What is the Eucharist? The sacrament of the real Body and Blood of our Lord, Jesus Christ
2. When did Jesus give us the Eucharist? At the Last Supper
3. What is "transubstantiation"? The change of the Eucharistic bread and wine into the Body and Blood of Jesus
4. Into what are the bread and wine changed? The real Body and Blood of Jesus

80 *Faith and Life Series • Grade 2 • Chapter 22 • Lesson 1*

Reinforce

1. Have the students work on *Activity Book*, p. 80.

2. Teach them to sing "Jesus, my Lord, my God, my all!" *Adoremus Hymnal*, #516. They may sing this to Jesus in the tabernacle.

3. Have the children start memorizing the questions for this chapter.

Conclude

1. Have the students spend some time in prayer with Jesus in the tabernacle.

2. Finish the class by praying the Our Father.

Preview

In the next lesson, we will learn about transubstantiation.

THE TABERNACLE

Consecrated Hosts are reserved in a tabernacle made of non-transparent material and locked to prevent profanation. The interior walls must either be lined with fine fabric or gilded. A mantle should be hung in front of it. A lamp or wax candle, usually in red glass, must burn perpetually nearby as a sign of the Real Presence.

NOTES

LESSON TWO: THE EUCHARIST

Aims

The students will review that at the Last Supper, Jesus instituted the Eucharist.

They will learn about transubstantiation: with the words of Jesus, bread and wine were changed into His Body, Blood, Soul, and Divinity, really and truly present under the appearances of bread and wine. The Eucharist is no longer bread or wine, but truly Jesus.

Materials

- Pictures of the Last Supper (see p. 106 of the text)
- Children's Bible
- *Activity Book*, p. 81

Optional:

- "Jesus, my Lord, my God, my all!" *Adoremus Hymnal*, #516
- "The Prince of Egypt," video, Dreamworks

Begin

If you watch the "Prince of Egypt," it will take half of the class time. In the second half, review the Passover, read the first two paragraphs of the text, and complete steps 4 and 5 from the previous lesson, p. 212. Visit Jesus in the tabernacle.

Other: Look at a picture of the Last Supper, and make the parallel to the Passover Meal.

Review: Eucharist, transubstantiation, tabernacle, and genuflection.

22 The Last Supper

"I am the living bread which came down from heaven; if any one eats of this bread, he will live for ever; and the bread which I shall give for the life of the world is my flesh."

John 6:51

Every year, the Jews had a great feast called Passover. This was to remember the time when God led Moses and the Israelites, God's chosen people, out of slavery.

The night before Jesus died, He celebrated the Passover dinner with His twelve disciples. Jesus felt very sad to be leaving His friends. He wanted there to be a way that He could always stay with them, and with all those who loved Him.

While they were eating, Jesus took some bread. He prayed to His Father, blessed the bread, and broke it. He gave it to the disciples and said,

"This is My Body, which is being given up for you."

107

Develop

1. Read p. 107 and the top of p. 108 of the text. You may read the Last Supper narrative from the children's Bible (Mt 26:18–30; Mk 14:13–26; Lk 22:11–39; 1 Cor 11:23–26; Jn 13). The students may dramatize the Last Supper. Be sure to include the washing of feet and the departure of Judas.

2. Explain the facts of the Sacrament of the Eucharist (as found on the opposite page). They should know the matter, form, and minister of this sacrament.

3. Explain to them that Jesus is really and truly present: Body, Blood, Soul, and Divinity. Jesus is present under the appearances of bread and wine. In the Host, Jesus is present Body and Blood; in the Precious Blood, His Body is also present. Also, if a Consecrated Host is broken in two, Jesus is wholly present. Jesus is present in each of the Hosts.

4. The students should understand that after the words of Jesus are said by the priest, it is no longer bread or wine, but Jesus' Body and Blood. The bread and wine are no longer present, though the Body and Blood appear like bread and wine.

5. Explain to them that when the disciples ate the consecrated bread and wine, the Eucharist, Jesus came to live in their souls. When we receive the Eucharist, Jesus comes to live in our souls.

6. Explain that another name for the Eucharist is the Blessed Sacrament. When we receive the Eucharist, it is called Holy Communion; Communion means "in union with," so we are in union with Jesus or we are together with Jesus. This union is a special way we can be with Jesus because He loves us so much. We can also tell Him how much we love Him when we receive Holy Communion.

Then Jesus took a cup of wine and said,

"This is the cup of My Blood. . . . It will be shed for you so that sins may be forgiven."

With those words, the bread and wine became the Body and Blood of Jesus. It was not bread and wine anymore, but Jesus. When the disciples ate it, Jesus came to live in their souls. This was the first time anyone had received Holy Communion.

Living Bread

Remember when Jesus fed the crowd of five thousand people with only five loaves of bread and two fish? The people were all amazed and wanted Jesus to do it for them again. But Jesus told them that He would give them food that would make them live forever. He told them that He was that living bread.

Jesus gave this living bread for the first time to His disciples at the Last Supper and He gives it to us in Holy Communion.

108

Reinforce

1. Have the students color *Activity Book*, p. 81.

2. Take the students to visit Jesus in the tabernacle again, and have them take time to pray, telling Jesus how much they look forward to receiving Him in the Eucharist. They may make a spiritual communion.

3. Have the students work on their Memorization Questions for this chapter, the Words to Know, and the matter/form/minister of the Eucharist.

Conclude

1. Sing "Jesus, my Lord, my God, my all!" *Adoremus Hymnal*, #516.

2. End with the prayer of Spiritual Communion: My Jesus, as I cannot receive You now in the Most Holy Blessed Sacrament, I ask You to come into my heart and make it like Thine own. *Amen.*

Preview

In the next lesson, we will learn that the priests have the power, through Jesus, to consecrate the Eucharist.

THE SACRAMENT OF THE EUCHARIST FACTS

- Matter: bread and wine
- Form: "This is my body" and "This is the cup of my blood"
- Minister: priest

Names: Eucharist, Blessed Sacrament, Holy Communion (when received)

Effects: see index p. 788 of the CCC, 2nd ed.

NOTES

____

____

____

____

____

____

____

____

____

____

____

LESSON THREE: DO THIS . . .

Aims

The students will learn that Jesus gave the power to the Apostles (and through them to every priest), to change bread and wine into His Body and Blood when He said, "Do this in memory of Me." These events are re-presented at Mass.

Materials

- Missalettes
- Children's Bible
- *Activity Book*, p. 82

Optional:
- "Jesus, my Lord, my God, my all!" *Adoremus Hymnal*, #516

Begin

Distribute missalettes to the students. Explain to the students that the words of the Mass are found in missalettes. Go through the Mass parts, asking the children to recite the parts they know (this will give you a good assessment of what they need to learn about the Mass itself). Have the students find the words of Consecration in each of the Eucharistic prayers.

We call the Sacrament of Christ's Body and Blood the **Holy Eucharist**. At the **Last Supper** Jesus said to His disciples, "Do this in memory of me." At every Mass the priest says the words of Jesus, and so the bread and wine are changed into Jesus' Body and Blood.

Words to Know:

Holy Eucharist   Last Supper

Q. 45 *What is the Eucharist?*
The Eucharist is the sacrament of the real Body and Blood of our Lord, Jesus Christ (CCC 1333).

Q. 46 *When did Jesus give us the Eucharist?*
Jesus gave us the Sacrament of the Eucharist at the Last Supper (CCC 1340).

109

Develop

1. Read the top of p. 92 with the students. You may also review the Last Supper in a children's Bible (Mt 26:18–30; Mk 14:13–26; Lk 22:11–39; 1 Cor 11:23–26; Jn 13).

2. Explain to them that at the Last Supper, when Jesus said "Do this in memory of me," He made His disciples priests and gave them the power, through Him, to change bread and wine into the Body and Blood of Jesus Himself. What is this change called? (Transubstantiation.)

3. Explain to the students that this power has been passed on from the Apostles, down through time, to all bishops and priests. Therefore, at every Mass, when the priest says the words of Jesus over the bread and wine, they become the Body and Blood of Jesus in the Holy Eucharist. The part of the Mass when the priest says the words of Jesus and changes the bread and wine into Jesus' Body and Blood is called the "Consecration."

4. Explain to them that with God, there is no time, and that this is a great mystery. So, the Last Supper, the sacrifice of the Cross, and the Mass are all the same sacrifice: Jesus giving Himself for us. At the Last Supper, Jesus gave Himself for us in the first Eucharist. On the Cross, Jesus gave Himself for us by dying for our sins. At the Mass, Jesus gives Himself for us as a sacrifice and meal in the Eucharist. The Mass is both the Last Supper and the Crucifixion of Our Lord. It is called the Pascal Mystery.

5. Review with them: the name of the sacrament (Eucharist, Blessed Sacrament, Holy Communion); the matter (bread and wine); form ("this is My Body, This is the cup of My Blood"); and the minister (the priest). Also review the words: Eucharist, transubstantiation, tabernacle, genuflection, Consecration, Communion, and the questions from the chapter. Do a review with Bible Baseball or Tic Tac Toe.

Name:__________________

This is My Body which is being given up for you. This is the cup of My Blood. It will be shed for you and for all so that sins may be forgiven.

Draw a chalice and a host.

82 *Faith and Life Series • Grade 2 • Chapter 22 • Lesson 3*

Reinforce

1. Have the students work on *Activity Book*, p. 82. Discuss as a class how the Last Supper, Crucifixion, and the Sacrifice of the Mass are related. Have the children write: "Do this in remembrance of me" on the bottom of the page.

2. Play a review game.

Conclude

1. Sing "Jesus, my Lord, my God, my all!" *Adoremus Hymnal*, #516.

2. Visit Jesus in the Blessed Sacrament or, if possible, attend Mass as a class. Have a priest come in and explain the parts of the Mass.

Preview

In the next lesson, we will learn about Jesus as the "Bread of Life."

SAINT TARSICIUS

Saint Tarsicius was a young acolyte or deacon in Rome in the third century. Little is known about his life other than a poem written by Pope Saint Damasus I in the fourth century. It relates that Saint Tarsicius, while carrying the Blessed Sacrament to some Christians in prison, was attacked by a mob on the Appian Way. Rather than surrender the Body of Christ to be desecrated, he fought his attackers as they beat and stoned him to death. His martyrdom probably occurred during a persecution against Christians in Rome. He was buried in the catacombs of Pope Saint Callistus on the Appian Way. He is the patron saint of first communicants, altar boys, and teenagers.

NOTES

LESSON FOUR: BREAD FROM HEAVEN

Aims

The students will learn how the miracle of the multiplication of loaves and fish prefigured the Eucharist.

They will know that Jesus is the Living Bread from Heaven.

Materials

- Children's Bible
- Missalettes
- *Activity Book*, p. 83

Optional:
- "Jesus, my Lord, my God, my all!"

Adoremus Hymnal, #516

- "Jesus Feeds the Multitudes," video; Jesus: A Kingdom Without Frontiers

Begin

Begin class by reading from the children's Bible the story of the multiplication of loaves and fish (Jn 6:1–15).

Discuss this miracle with the children and how Jesus feeds His sheep.

Q. 47 *How can a priest change the bread and wine into the Body and Blood of Christ?*
When a man becomes a priest, he receives the power from Jesus to change the bread and wine into the Body and Blood of Jesus. Jesus first gave this power to His disciples when He said, at the Last Supper, "Do this in memory of Me" (CCC 1339–41, 1356).

Q. 48 *What words must a priest say at Mass for the bread to become the Body of Christ?*
"This is My Body" (CCC 1365).

Q. 49 *What words must a priest say at Mass for the wine to become the Blood of Christ?*
"This is the cup of My Blood" (CCC 1365).

110

Develop

1. Read the Living Bread box from p. 108 of the text with the students.

2. Read from the children's Bible the Bread of Life text, found in John 6:25–69. Explain that people had a hard time understanding how they could eat Jesus' flesh, but He did not deny that He meant just that. They did not understand that He would give them the Eucharist. The Eucharist is how we eat Jesus' Body and Blood.

3. Review with them the events from Palm Sunday to the Resurrection of Jesus. Have them understand that this is all one event: the giving of Jesus for all of us. This sacrifice also happens at Mass.

4. Using the missalettes, go to the the Eucharistic prayer most commonly used at your parish. Review the prayer of Consecration, and emphasize that it is no longer bread and wine, but Jesus really present. Explain the importance of reverence at the time of Consecration at Mass. Teach the children that they should kneel (even if they can barely see over the pew in front of them). They should have their hands folded in prayer and they should be paying close attention. When the priest changes, through Jesus Christ, the bread and wine, teach them to say little prayers from the heart, such as "My Lord and my God," or "I adore you, my Savior," or "I give myself to You, my Jesus, in the Most Holy Blessed Sacrament of the altar."

5. In church, practice genuflecting and kneeling with hands folded in prayer. Have them spend a few minutes in prayer before the tabernacle. Say a prayer of spiritual communion.

6. Review the names for Jesus in this sacrament: Eucharist, Blessed Sacrament, Holy Communion, and add Living Bread.

Q. 50 *After the prayer consecrating the Eucharist, is it still bread and wine?* After the prayer of consecration, it is no longer bread and wine. It is Jesus really and truly present in the Eucharist (CCC 1365).

111

Reinforce

1. Have the students work on *Activity Book*, p. 83.

2. When you visit the Church, you may want to point out the altar, tabernacle, sanctuary lamp, tabernacle veil (if there is one), kneelers, pews, reservation chapel (if there is one), etc. The children should be very familiar with these terms.

Conclude

1. Sing "Jesus, my Lord, my God, my all!" *Adoremus Hymnal*, #516.

2. End by praying for Spiritual Communion.

Preview

In the next lesson, we will review the material covered in this chapter.

ADDITIONAL RESOURCES

For the students:
Know Him in the Breaking of the Bread by Fr. Francis Randolph, Ignatius Press. This book explains the ceremonies of the Mass and their meaning for lay people, including the young.

For the teacher:
Ceremonies of the Modern Roman Rite by Msgr. Peter Elliott, Ignatius Press, 1995. This work describes the Rites of the Eucharist and Liturgy of the Hours.

Liturgical Question Box by Msgr. Peter Elliott, Ignatius Press, 1998. This work examines and answers some common questions about the celebration of the Mass and the sacraments.

NOTES

____

____

____

____

____

____

____

____

____

____

____

CHAPTER TWENTY-TWO:
REVIEW AND ASSESSMENT

Aims

The students' understanding of the material covered this week will be reviewed and assessed.

Materials

- Quiz 22 (Appendix, p. A-32)
- "Jesus, my Lord, my God, my all!" *Adoremus Hymnal*, #516

Review

1. Review the Passover, the events and, specifically, that Jesus was celebrating the Passover meal as the Last Supper.

2. Review that Jesus remains with us in the Eucharist.

3. Review the matter, form, and minister of the Sacrament of the Eucharist.

4. Review the real presence of Jesus, under the appearances of Bread and Wine, in all parts of the Consecrated Host and Wine. Jesus is present, Body, Blood, Soul, and Divinity in the Blessed Sacrament.

5. They should know different names for this sacrament.

6. Review that Jesus gave the power to consecrate the Eucharist to His disciples, and through them, to all priests when He said, "Do this in memory of me."

7. They should be able to recount the multiplication of loaves and fish and the bread of life discourse.

Name:

The Last Supper **Quiz 22**

Circle the correct answer.

1. Jesus celebrated the Last Supper
   a. with all of His friends
   (b.) during the feast called Passover
   c. every time He had dinner

2. When the words of Jesus are said over the bread and wine by a priest
   a. they are no longer bread and wine
   b. they become the Body, Blood, Soul, and Divinity of Jesus really and truly present
   (c.) both a and b

3. The Sacrament of Christ's Body and Blood is called
   (a.) the Eucharist
   b. the Passover
   c. the Last Supper

4. The priest at Mass says the words of Jesus in the prayer of
   a. tabernacle
   b. communion
   (c.) Consecration

5. What is transubstantiation?
   (a.) When the bread and wine are changed into Jesus' Body and Blood.
   b. The place where the Eucharist is stored in the Church.
   c. The first time the Apostles received Holy Communion.

What words must be said by a priest over the bread and wine for them to change into Jesus' Body and Blood? This is My Body, which is being given up for you. This is the cup of My Blood....It will be shed for you so that sins may be forgiven."

A - 32 *Faith and Life • Grade 2 • Appendix A*

Assess

1. Distribute Quiz 22. Answer any questions that they may have. When they turn in their quizzes, individually quiz them on the Memorization Questions and the Words to Know.

2. When all the quizzes have been turned in, review the correct answers.

Conclude

1. Sing "Jesus, my Lord, my God, my all!," *Adoremus Hymnal*, #516.

2. End by praying for Spiritual Communion.

CHAPTER TWENTY-THREE
JESUS DIES FOR US

Catechism of the Catholic Church References

Burial of Jesus: 624–26
Christ's Redemptive Death in the Divine Plan of Salvation: 599–605, 619–20
Christ's life as an Offering to the Father: 606–18, 621–23
- Jesus Embraces the Father's Redemptive Love: 609
- Last Supper: 610–11
- Agony at Gethsemane: 612
- Death of Christ as Definitive Sacrifice: 613–14
- Jesus' Obedience for Our Disobedience: 615
- Jesus' Sacrifice on the Cross: 616–17
- Our Participation in Christ's Sacrifice: 618

Agony in the Garden: 612
Death of Jesus: 619, 627, 629
Jesus' Sufferings: 572
Jesus' Trial: 574–75, 585

Scripture References

Bread of Life: Jn 6:35–58
Passion of Jesus, Part I: Mt 26:30–46; Mk 14:26–42; Lk 22:39–47
Passion of Jesus, Part II: Mt 26:30—27:49; Mk 14:26—15:25; Lk 22:39—23:33, Jn 19:23–42
Passion of Jesus, Part III: Mt 27:35–54; Mk 15:25–42; Lk 23:33–48; Jn 19:16–35

Background Reading: *The Fundamentals of Catholicism* by Fr. Kenneth Baker, S.J.

Volume 3:
"The Mass and the Cross," pp. 262–64

Volume 3:
"Where Is the Sacrifice?" pp. 265–67

Summary of Lesson Content

Lesson 1

After the Last Supper, Jesus and the disciples went to the Garden of Olives, where Jesus experiences the agony in the garden.

Jesus prays and accepts the Will of God.

Lesson 2

Jesus was arrested. He was condemned to death by Pontius Pilate.

Jesus was scourged, crowned with thorns, made to carry His Cross, and was crucified.

Lesson 3

Jesus was crucified. He prayed for the forgiveness of the sins of mankind.

On the Cross, Jesus gave Mary to all mankind to be the Mother of God's children.

Jesus was obedient to His Father unto death.

Lesson 4

Jesus died upon the Cross and opened the gates of Heaven.

The death of Jesus bought back man's friendship with God.

The Stations of the Cross.

LESSON ONE: THY WILL BE DONE

Aims

The students will learn how after the Last Supper, Jesus and the disciples went to the Garden of Olives.

They will learn that in the Garden, Jesus prayed and accepted the Will of God.

Materials

- Picture of the Garden of Olives
- Children's Bible
- Olives, olive branch, olive oil
- *Activity Book*, p. 84

Optional:

- "O Cross of Christ, immortal tree," *Adoremus Hymnal*, #361

Begin

Begin with looking at the picture in the text of Jesus in the Garden of Olives. Ask the children about this picture: What is Jesus doing? Who is with Him? What are they doing? When did this occur? What kind of trees are around Jesus? (olive trees). If you have an olive branch, or some cured olives, let the children pass them around and taste the olives. Explain to the children that olive trees live a very long time. In fact, the same trees Jesus prayed under are still alive in this garden. Show the children the picture of the garden. Explain that olive oil is used in some sacraments to show our eternal life, which Jesus won for us through His suffering, death, and Resurrection.

Develop

1. Remind the students that Jesus and His disciples had just celebrated the Last Supper on Holy Thursday. You may review the events of the Last Supper with them. You may want to emphasize that with the Consecration of the Precious Blood, Jesus said "which *will* be given up for you" (future tense).

2. Read the first paragraph of Chapter 23 as a class. You may also read this passage from a children's Bible (Mt 26:30–46; Mk 14:26–42; Lk 22:39–47).

3. Teach them that this story is commemorated as the first Sorrowful Mystery of the Rosary.

4. Explain that Jesus knew that He would die for our sins. He knew that the Father wanted Him to lay down His life out of love for mankind. How would Jesus have felt?

5. *Reread: He felt sad when He thought about our sins. Jesus knew all of our sins. He knew each and every person that lived then, and now, and throughout time. He died for all of us—and for all our sins. Even if there were just me and my sins, or Suzy and her sins, or Johnny and his sins, Jesus would have suffered and died because He loves us so much.*

6. Explain that Jesus had to pray to God the Father to make Him strong and brave. Ask the children if there is anything that they have had to do for which they needed strength or bravery, such as going to the dentist or having to help someone in need. We, too, need God's help.

7. Explain that because of fear, it would have been hard for Jesus to lay down His life, but He accepted God's will. We should, too. We can pray for this in the Our Father: Thy will be done.

Name:____________________

Answer the following questions

1. Where did Jesus and His disciples go after the Last Supper? Garden of Olives
2. Why was Jesus sad? Because he thought about our sins
3. What did Jesus tell His Father? "I will do what You want."
4. What happened after Jesus was arrested? Pilate said that Jesus should die.

Draw Jesus in the Garden. Add yourself praying with Jesus.

84 *Faith and Life Series • Grade 2 • Chapter 23 • Lesson 1*

Reinforce

1. Have the students work on *Activity Book*, p. 84. As the students work on coloring the picture of Jesus in the garden, remind them that Jesus asked them to pray with Him. They may draw themselves praying with Jesus in the garden.

2. Teach the students to sing "O Cross of Christ, immortal tree," *Adoremus Hymnal*, #361.

Conclude

1. Pray together the Our Father, stressing "Thy will be done." Ask the children to list the things for which they ask God's help, and for God's gift of strength and courage for different things in their lives. For each petition, add: Lord hear our prayer.

2. End with a general prayer, asking God to help us to do what He wants us to do.

3. You may pray the decade of the Rosary from the Sorrowful Mysteries, the Agony in the Garden.

Preview

In the next lesson, we will learn about the trial of Jesus and the Way of the Cross.

CONSECRATION OF THE CHRISM

Chrism—Balsam and olive oil—used in Baptism, Confirmation, and Holy Orders, is consecrated by the bishop on Holy Thursday. Following is one of the consecratory prayers said by the bishop:

God, our maker, source of all growth in holiness, accept the joyful thanks and praise we offer in the name of your Church.

In the beginning, at your command, the earth produced fruit-bearing trees. From the fruit of the olive tree you have provided us with the oil for holy chrism.

The prophet David sang of the life and joy that the oil would bring us in the sacraments of your love.

After the avenging flood, the dove returning to Noah with an olive branch announced your gift of peace. This was a sign of a greater gift to come (continued p. 225).

NOTES

____

____

____

____

____

____

____

____

____

____

LESSON TWO: JESUS SUFFERED

Aims

The children will become familiar with the Apostles' Creed, and focus of how Jesus was arrested and condemned to suffer and die by Pontius Pilate.

Jesus was scourged, made to carry His Cross, and was crucified.

Materials

- Crucifix
- Children's Bible
- Pictures of the Stations of the Cross (use p. 115 of text)
- *Activity Book*, p. 85
- stickers

Optional:

- "O Cross of Christ, immortal tree," *Adoremus Hymnal*, #361
- Children's Way of the Cross

Begin

Begin with reviewing the events of the Last Supper (stressing: This is the cup of My Blood, which will be given up for you) then the Agony in the garden. Ask the children how Jesus went from the garden to the Cross. Do any of them know? If Jesus was innocent of any sin or crime, then why did He die on the Cross, which was a punishment for criminals? Show the Crucifix to the children. They may all hold and reverence the cross. Remind the children how much Jesus loves them.

23 Jesus Dies for Us

Then Jesus, crying with a loud voice, said, "Father, into thy hands I commit my spirit!"

Luke 23:46

After the Last Supper, Jesus and the disciples went to the Garden of Olives. He asked them to pray with Him, but they were tired and fell asleep. So, all by Himself, Jesus began to pray. He felt sad when He thought about our sins. Jesus asked His Father to make Him strong and brave. He told His Father, "I will do what You want."

Soldiers came to arrest Jesus. Pilate said that Jesus should die. The soldiers hit Jesus and beat Him with whips. They put a crown of thorns on His head and slapped Him, saying, "Hail, King of the Jews."

Jesus had to carry a heavy **Cross** through the streets. The weight of our sins made it even more heavy. Sometimes Jesus fell down.

At Mount **Calvary** Jesus was nailed to the Cross. Even then He did not stop loving everyone. He prayed for the people who wanted to kill Him, "Father, forgive them." He forgave the good thief.

113

Develop

1. Read paragraphs 1–3 of Chapter 23 with the students. You may reread this from the children's Bible (Mt 26:30—27:29; Mk 14:26—15:25; Lk 22:39—23:33; Jn 19:23–42).

2. Begin teaching them the Way of the Cross. Place pictures around the classroom or, if possible, pray in the Church before the permanent Stations of the Cross. They will need p. 115 of their text book.

3. Pray the stations with the children. They may begin by singing "O Cross of Christ, immortal tree," *Adoremus Hymnal*, #361. As you move to each station, you may lead the children in an age-appropriate meditation. There are many published children's Ways of the Cross, or you may simply explain what is happening in each picture. Ask them about each image. What is happening? Who is in the picture? Teach the children that by meditating upon the Stations of the Cross, it is as though they are there with Jesus, and He is consoled that they are with Him.

4. Have the students read the title of each station, pray the We Pray on the bottom of p. 114 (some genuflect each time this is prayed, some kneel for the 12th station), and if time permits, pray an Our Father, Hail Mary and Glory Be at each station.

5. If time permits, when you return to class, ask them what they thought of the Stations of the Cross, and answer any questions they may have.

Name:__________________

The Apostles' Creed

I believe in God, the Father Almighty, Creator of Heaven and earth, and in Jesus Christ, His only Son, our Lord, Who was conceived by the Holy Spirit, born of the Virgin Mary, suffered under Pontius Pilate, was crucified, died, and was buried. He descended into hell; on the third day He rose again. He ascended into Heaven and sits at the right hand of God, the Father Almighty; from thence He shall come to judge the living and the dead. I believe in the Holy Spirit, the holy catholic Church, the Communion of Saints, the forgiveness of sins, the resurrection of the body, and life everlasting. *Amen*.

You will have to study hard to learn this creed. Say it often and write it out. Ask Jesus to help you to learn this statement of our Holy Faith. Mark the days in which you say the Apostles' Creed this week.

Monday	Tuesday	Wednesday	Thursday	Friday	Saturday	Sunday

Faith and Life Series • Grade 2 • Chapter 23 • Lesson 2 85

Reinforce

1. Pray the Stations of the Cross with the students.

2. Have the students work on *Activity Book*, p. 85. They may break into pairs and begin memorizing the Apostles' Creed. Have them underline the parts of the prayer on which they need more study. Give them stickers to reward them for each day's prayers (to put into the boxes at the bottom).

3. The children may draw one of the Stations of the Cross. You may have them work on a class set.

Conclude

1. Sing "O Cross of Christ, immortal tree," *Adoremus Hymnal*, #361.

2. Teach the children to pray the Apostles' Creed. Explain it line by line. Have the children stand up while you recite it slowly. Have them say "Amen" at the end.

Preview

In the next lesson, we will learn about the crucifixion of Our Lord.

A CONSECRATORY PRAYER FOR CHRISM

(Continued from p. 223)

Now the waters of baptism wash away the sins of men, and by the anointing with olive oil, you make us radiant with your joy.

At your command, Aaron was washed with water, and your servant Moses, his brother, anointed him a priest.
This too foreshadowed greater things to come.

After your Son, Jesus Christ our Lord, asked John for baptism in the waters of Jordan, you sent the Spirit upon him in the form of a dove and by the witness of your own voice you declared him to be your only, well-beloved Son. In this you clearly fulfilled the prophecy of David, that Christ would be anointed with the oil of gladness beyond his fellow men.

Amen.

NOTES

____

LESSON THREE: JESUS DIED FOR US

Aims

The students will learn that Jesus was crucified and that He prayed for the forgiveness of the sins of mankind.

They will learn about obedience.

Materials

- Children's Bible
- Picture of Jesus on the Cross with Mary and John
- *Activity Book*, p. 86

Optional:
- "O Cross of Christ, immortal tree," *Adoremus Hymnal*, #361

Begin

Gather the students around the diorama or picture of Jesus on the Cross with Mary and John. Explain how Jesus must have been consoled by their presence as He hung upon the Cross, just as He is consoled when we pray the Stations of the Cross. Review the Stations of the Cross, reading them in order, asking the children what happened at each station. This exercise will be a review from the previous lesson.

He gave His Mother, Mary, to be the Mother of all God's children.

Some people called out, "If you are the Son of God, come down from the Cross!" Because Jesus was God, He could have done this. But He wanted to suffer His **Passion** and die because He loved us. He wanted to obey His Heavenly Father.

Finally, Jesus died. At that moment the gates of Heaven were opened. We were brought back to the friendship of God, which Adam and Eve had lost.

Words to Know:

Cross Calvary Passion

Q. 51 *What did Jesus Christ do to save us from our sins?*
Jesus Christ died for the forgiveness of our sins by suffering and dying on the Cross, so we can be with Him forever in Heaven (CCC 613).

We Pray:

We adore You, O Christ, and we bless You, because by Your Holy Cross You have redeemed the world.

114

Develop

1. Read paragraphs 4–6 from the chapter with the students. You may also read these events from the children's Bible (Mt 27:35–54; Mk 15:25–42; Lk 23:33–48; Jn 19:16–35).

2. Review with them the definition of obedience. It means to do what our authorities ask us of us. Jesus was obedient to God the Father, even unto death. Sometimes we know how hard it is to be obedient, especially when it is something we do not want to do (e.g., do our homework, clean our rooms, etc.). Jesus was obedient out of love for all of us.

3. Jesus was obedient but was so full of love that He wanted to be obedient. He even forgave the people who hurt Him. He forgave all of us for our sins (for we know not what we do). His forgiveness is always there, waiting for us—we simply need to ask Him for His forgiveness when we sin against Him.

4. On the Cross, people wanted to test Jesus to see if He was the Son of God. Would He come down off the Cross? He could have, but Jesus knew that His death on the Cross would give us life everlasting. He loves us so much, He wants us to spend forever with Him in Heaven. What can we do to try to get to Heaven? (Not sin, pray, be obedient to God's laws, etc.)

5. Review Jesus' obedience and contrast it with Adam's disobedience. Adam, when he sinned, closed the gates of Heaven. Jesus, in His obedience, opened the gates of Heaven. Adam displeased God, but Jesus pleased God by His obedience. Adam acted out of love for himself. Jesus acted out of love for all of us. Adam lost God's life for all of us. Jesus won it back.

6. Just as Jesus is the New Adam, Mary is the New Eve, Mother of the living. She is our Mother, too.

Name:____________________

We adore You, O Christ, and we bless You, because by Your Holy Cross, You have redeemed the world.

86 *Faith and Life Series • Grade 2 • Chapter 23 • Lesson 3*

Reinforce

1. Have the students color *Activity Book*, p. 86. Explain the picture on p. 86. Remind them of the connection of the Last Supper and the Crucifixion: they are really one event, just as they are at Mass. Tell them that we share in Jesus' sacrifice and receive His life when we receive Him in Holy Communion (just as the Apostles did at the Last Supper).

2. Have them work on memorizing the questions for the chapter.

Conclude

1. Sing "O Cross of Christ, immortal tree," *Adoremus Hymnal*, #361.

2. Review the Stations of the Cross, by praying: We thank you God, that ___________(station). (e.g. We thank you God that Jesus is condemned to death.) Then pray the We Pray. (Note that the children will be expected to know the Stations of the Cross, and in the correct order.)

Preview

In the next lesson, we will review the crucifixion of Jesus.

THE APOSTLE JOHN

John, the son of Zebedee and Salome, was the younger brother of James the Greater. Christ called these brothers the "Sons of Thunder" (Mk 3:17). With their father, they fished on Lake Genesareth, became followers of John the Baptist, then Apostles of Jesus. John witnessed the raising of Jairus' daughter (Mk 5:37), the Transfiguration (Mt 17:1), and the Agony in Gethsemane (Mt 26:37). He and Peter were sent into Jerusalem to prepare for the Last Supper (Lk 22:8), during which his place was next to Christ upon Whose breast he leaned (Jn 13:23, 25). John, of all the Apostles, remained at the foot of the Cross and took Mary into his care at the request of Christ (Jn 19:25–27). After the Resurrection, John, with Peter, was the first disciple to hasten to the tomb, and he was the first to believe that Christ had truly risen (Jn 20:2–10). When Jesus appeared at the Sea of Tiberias, John was the first Apostle present to recognize his Master standing on the shore (Jn 21:7). John wrote the fourth Gospel, three Epistles, and the Book of Revelation. Tradition relates that by order of the Emperor Diocletian, he was cast into a cauldron of boiling oil. Emerging unharmed, John was then exiled to the island of Patmos for a year. He died at an advanced age in Ephesus about the year 100, the last of the Apostles. A church was built over his tomb, which was afterwards converted into a mosque. His feast day is December 27. He is the patron saint of Asia Minor.

LESSON FOUR: THE CROSS

Aims

The students will review that Jesus died upon the Cross and opened the gates of Heaven.

They will understand that the death of Jesus bought back man's friendship with God.

They will begin to learn how the Last Supper and Crucifixion are present at the Mass.

Materials

- Children's Bible
- Missals
- *Activity Book*, p. 87

Optional:
- "O Cross of Christ, immortal tree," *Adoremus Hymnal*, #361

- "Jesus Dies on the Cross," video; Jesus: A Kingdom Without Frontiers
- Prayer cards of the San Damiano Cross with the Prayer before the Crucifix on the back

Begin

Begin by showing "Jesus Dies on the Cross," video from the video series Jesus: A Kingdom Without Frontiers, available through Ignatius Press; 30 minutes.

If you do not have an appropriate video, have the children put on a play of the Last Supper, Passion, and Crucifixion of Jesus.

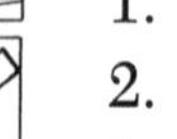

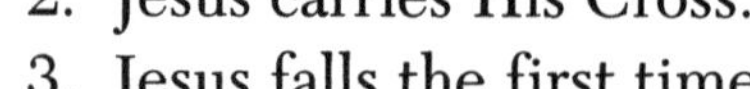

Stations of the Cross

1. Jesus is condemned to death.
2. Jesus carries His Cross.
3. Jesus falls the first time.
4. Jesus meets His Mother.
5. Jesus is helped by Simon.
6. Veronica wipes the face of Jesus.
7. Jesus falls a second time.
8. Jesus speaks to the women.
9. Jesus falls a third time.
10. Jesus is stripped of His clothes.
11. Jesus is nailed to the Cross.
12. Jesus dies on the Cross.
13. Jesus is taken down from the Cross.
14. Jesus is placed in the tomb.

115

Develop

1. Review the content of this week's lessons with the students. Help them to see the connection between the Last Supper and the Crucifixion—that it is all one event. It is one and the same sacrifice (of His Body and Blood for the life of the world). This event explains the Bread of Life discourse (Jn 6:35–58). You may need to review this discourse with the children. You can do so by reading it from a children's Bible.

2. Remind them that God made time, so He may work outside of it. At the Mass, we are present for the Last Supper (the priest acts in the person of Christ, says His words, and changes bread and wine into Jesus' Body and Blood).

3. Review with them what a sacrifice is: when something is given up. Jesus was sacrificed on the Cross, and gave up His life, Body and Blood, for our sins. He died and was sacrificed to God for us. Every sacrifice happens on an altar. Do they remember the sacrifices in the Old Testament (i.e., Isaac)? The Cross was Jesus' altar. Now, in every church we have an altar, and the Sacrifice of Jesus is made present when the priest consecrates the Eucharist. The Mass is not a new sacrifice, or Jesus sacrificed over and over. It is the exact same sacrifice. We are present for it by participating in the Mass.

4. Reread the last paragraph of this chapter with the students. Jesus' suffering and death restored our friendship with God. If we share in His sacrificial meal and have His life in us, we are sharing in God's friendship. His life in us is what Communion is: when Jesus comes to live in us, and unites us with (com = with, union = unites us) God in His friendship. All of this happens at the Mass.

5. Review Mass etiquette.

Name:____________________

Word Search

JESUS	SHEEP	WATCHES	BODY
KING	OBEDIENT	PROTECT	BREAD
SHEPHERD	HUMBLE	FEED	BLOOD
SACRAMENTS	FORGIVING	SON	WINE
LOVE	MERCIFUL	GARDEN	MEMORY

P E M E J K E S S S I O
R W E F E I H A L H S B
O A R O S N U C O E H E
T T C R U G M R V E E D
E C I G S V B A E P P I
C H F I U L L M E A H E
T E U V B G E E R M E N
B S L I R A Y N A E R T
L W H N E R B T I M D F
O I B G A D O S R O S E
O N O O D E D E D R O E
D E R R O N Y O R Y N D

Faith and Life Series • Grade 2 • Chapter 23 • Lesson 4 87

Reinforce

1. Have the students work on the puzzle on *Activity Book*, p. 87. Have them find these words in their textbooks.

2. If possible, arrange a church tour and vessels presentation. Be sure to point out the tabernacle, altar, Crucifix (and Stations of the Cross) during your tour.

3. Have the children work on memorizing the questions for the chapter and the Words to Know.

Conclude

1. "O Cross of Christ, immortal tree," *Adoremus Hymnal*, #361.

2. Review the Stations of the Cross, by praying: We thank you God, that ___________(station). (e.g. We thank you God that Jesus is condemned to death.) Then pray the We Pray. (The children will be expected to know the Stations of the Cross in the correct order.)

Preview

In the next lesson, we will review the material covered in this chapter.

DEVOTION TO THE WAY OF THE CROSS

According to tradition, Our Lady visited the scenes of Christ's Passion every day. After Constantine legalized Christianity in the year 312, this pathway, called the Via Dolorosa, was marked with stations. Saint Jerome, living in Bethlehem in the early fifth century, attested to the many international pilgrims who visited those holy places and followed the Way of the Cross. Shortly thereafter, an interest developed in the Church to reproduce these holy places elsewhere so that pilgrims did not have to travel to the Holy Land. Promotion of this devotion began in earnest with the Franciscans, who were given custody of these places in the Holy Land in the 14th century. Today there are fourteen stations which can be found in most churches.

NOTES

CHAPTER TWENTY-THREE: REVIEW AND ASSESSMENT

Aims

The students' understanding of the material covered this week will be reviewed and assessed.

Materials

- Quiz 23 (Appendix, p. A-33)
- "O Cross of Christ, immortal tree," *Adoremus Hymnal*, #361
- Box, Crucifix

Review

1. Have the students recount the story of the Passion and death of Our Lord—this may be dramatized.

2. Have them review the Stations of the Cross and be able to put them in order. You may play a game by giving the children two of the Stations and having them tell you which one occurred first.

3. Review that Mary is our Mother and that Jesus gave her to us as He hung on the Cross. The beloved disciple John acted in our place.

4. They should know that Jesus won back God's friendship for us and opened the gates of Heaven by his death on the Cross.

5. They should understand the connection between the Last Supper and the Crucifixion and that they are present to us in the Mass.

6. They should be able to name everything presented to them in the church tour and/or vessels presentation.

Name:

Jesus Dies for Us **Quiz 23**

1. Place the Stations of the Cross in the correct order:

5 Jesus is helped by Simon.
10 Jesus is stripped of His clothes.
14 Jesus is placed in the tomb.
2 Jesus carries His Cross.
8 Jesus speaks to the women.
3 Jesus falls the first time.
13 Jesus is taken down from the Cross.
4 Jesus meets His Mother.
7 Jesus falls a second time.
1 Jesus is condemned to death.
12 Jesus dies on the Cross.
6 Veronica wipes the face of Jesus.
9 Jesus falls a third time.
11 Jesus is nailed to the Cross

2. Please answer in complete sentences:

1. Why did Jesus want to suffer and die on the Cross?

Answers will vary

2. How are the Last Supper and the Crucifixion connected to the Mass?

3. Why can we say that Mary is our Mother?

4. What did Jesus win for us by dying on the Cross?

5. Jesus asks us to pray with Him. How can we do this?

Faith and Life • Grade 2 • Appendix A *A - 33*

Assess

1. Distribute Quiz 23. Answer any questions that they may have.

2. As the children turn in their quizzes, individually quiz them on the Memorization Questions and the Words to Know.

3. When all quizzes are turned in, review the answers with the class.

Conclude

1. Sing "O Cross of Christ, immortal tree," *Adoremus Hymnal*, #361.

2. Pray a prayer before a Crucifix.

3. Before the end of class, gather the children around, place a Crucifix in a box, and lock it. Tell them this is for safe-keeping.

CHAPTER TWENTY-FOUR
HE IS RISEN, ALLELUIA!

Catechism of the Catholic Church References

Apparitions of the Risen One: 641–44
Easter as Central Christian feast: 638, 1169
Historical and Transcendent Event of Resurrection: 639, 656
 Christ's Authority: 649, 651, 653
 Empty Tomb: 640, 657
 Fulfillment of Old Covenant: 652
Resurrected Body of Christ: 645–46
Resurrection as Transcendent Event: 647
Resurrection as a Work of the Holy Trinity: 648–50
Resurrection's Meaning and Consequences for Salvation: 651–55, 658
Sunday as Day of Resurrection: 2174

Scripture References

Christ appears to Apostles: Mt 27:57—28:10; Mk 15:42—16:6; Lk 23:30—24:8, 24:36–48; Jn 19:39–20:10, 20:19–29
Great Commission: Mt 28:5–20
Emmans: Lk 24:25–34
Appears to Mary Magdalane: Jn 20:11–18
Breakfast on Shore: Jn 21:19–22

Background Reading: *The Fundamentals of Catholicism* by Fr. Kenneth Baker, S.J.

Volume 2:
"Jesus' Glorious Resurrection," pp. 304–7

Summary of Lesson Content

Lesson 1

The Sunday after Jesus died, women went to the tomb of Jesus, but it was empty.

Angels told the women that Jesus was risen.

Lesson 2

The women told the disciples who disbelieved, even though Jesus predicted His own death and Resurrection.

Some other of Jesus' disciples saw the risen Lord.

Lesson 3

Jesus appeared to the disciples in the upper room. He ate with His disciples to verify that He was not a ghost.

Lesson 4

Jesus gave His Apostles His peace. Jesus's peace comes to all who receive Jesus into their lives.

Easter is the season to celebrate the Resurrection of Jesus and the grace He won for man, so man can live forever.

At Easter a candle is lit to signify Christ, the Light of the World.

LESSON ONE: THE EMPTY TOMB

Aims

The students will learn about Easter Sunday: On the Sunday after Jesus died, women went to the tomb of Jesus and saw it was empty.

They will learn how the angels told the women that Jesus was risen.

Materials

- Box without Crucifix in it.
- Children's Bible
- *Activity Book*, p. 88
- Paper, crayons/markers

Optional:
- "Jesus Christ is risen today," *Adoremus Hymnal*, #410

Begin

Begin by asking the students what was the last thing they did after their quiz. They put a Crucifix in a box for safe keeping. Today, ask one of the children (or a few of the children) to go to the box and get the Crucifix. The box should be empty. This will parallel the empty tomb experience. How do the children feel? Sad that the Crucifix is gone? Worried about what happened to it? Excited as to where they might find it?

Develop

1. Explain to the students that after the crucifixion of Jesus, His Body was laid in a tomb. Some friends had prepared Him for burial, and some guards were placed outside the tomb to keep watch. Because it was the Passover feast, people could not come in contact with a dead body, until Sunday. That morning, the women were going to go to the tomb to anoint His body with fragrances and oils, as is the Jewish custom. What do you think they were expecting? (To find Jesus.)

2. Read the first two paragraphs with the children. You may also read this from the children's Bible (Mt 27:57—28:7; Mk 15:42—16:6; Lk 23:50—24:8; Jn 19:39—20:10). They may dramatize these events or draw pictures of them.

3. Ask them what they would have thought had they gone to the tomb and found it empty. How would they feel? What would they think if they saw an angel? What would they do? Would they believe what the angel told the disciples? How was it possible that Jesus would be risen from the dead? What does this say about Jesus? (He is God!)

4. The angel told the women: Go and tell the others. Who can you tell about this Good News? Have the children think of people. What would they say? How could they convince others that they were telling the truth? (Jesus said He was going to die and rise from the dead). Proof: the tomb is empty. They will need to believe your words, just like we believe the words recorded in the Bible. Belief takes faith.

5. Have the children perform skits telling others about the Resurrection of Jesus. What would they say? How would they convince others?

Name:____________________

Jesus Christ Is Risen Today!

Write how you would feel if you went to the tomb and found it empty. Also write about meeting the angel and knowing that your Lord is Risen!

Answers will vary

88 *Faith and Life Series • Grade 2 • Chapter 24 • Lesson 1*

Reinforce

1. Have the students work on *Activity Book*, p. 88.

2. Have the children look up and memorize the Words to Know, as well as the question for the chapter.

3. Teach the children to sing: "Jesus Christ is risen today," *Adoremus Hymnal*, #410.

Conclude

End with praying p. 119 and an Our Father, a Hail Mary, and the Glory Be.

Preview

In the next lesson, we will learn of encounters with the Risen Lord.

EASTER SYMBOLS

- Bunny (leaps up – sign of rising)
- Egg (life from within the shell – out of the tomb)
- Butterfly (life from within the cocoon – out of the tomb)
- Yellow and Purple: Yellow or Gold – light. Purple – color of kings
- Bread: yeast makes bread rise – rising from dead
- Hot Cross Buns: Cross – Crucifix, raisins and bread – bread and wine consecrated

NOTES

LESSON TWO: HE IS RISEN!

Aims

The students will learn that the women told the disciples about Jesus' Resurrection, and they disbelieved, even though Jesus predicted His own death and Resurrection.

They will learn about some of the encounters with the Risen Lord.

Materials

- Children's Bible
- *Activity Book*, p. 89
- Paper, crayons/markers

Optional:
- "Jesus Christ is risen today," *Adoremus Hymnal*, #410
- "The Resurrection of Jesus," video; Jesus: A Kingdom Without Frontiers

Begin

Pre-arrange for a student to tell the class that he saw Jesus in the Church. (You may take the student to go see Jesus in the tabernacle so he will not be lying).

As you begin today's class, say that a student has an announcement to make. Have the student say that he saw Jesus in the Church. Ask the students if they believe this student or not, and why.

24 He Is Risen, Alleluia!

"Why do you seek the living among the dead? He is not here, but has risen."

Luke 24:5

Early in the morning the Sunday after Jesus died, some women came to visit His tomb. All the way over they worried about the big stone that closed the tomb. "Who will roll it away for us?" they wondered.

But when they got there, the stone was already rolled back. A beautiful angel was sitting on it. "Why do you look in a tomb for someone Who is alive?" he said. "Jesus is not here. He is risen. Go and tell the others."

Very surprised and a little afraid, the women ran off. The disciples did not believe them, even though Jesus used to tell them that He would die and rise again. But soon different friends of Jesus saw Him. Mary Magdalen and the other women saw Him first.

A few days later, the disciples were together in one room. The door was locked. All at once Jesus was there with them! "Peace be with you," He said. Jesus talked and ate with them so they could see

117

Develop

1. Read the third paragraph with the children.

2. From the children's Bible read various accounts of Jesus' encounters with His disciples after the Resurrection. Discuss each with the children:

Mt 28:5–20: Great Commission
- *Disciples doubted*
- *They went to Galilee where Jesus ordered them to go*
- *Jesus told them to baptize all nations and teach what He had taught them*

Lk 24:25–34: Road to Emmaus
- *Jesus told the disciples how the Bible said this would happen*
- *Jesus broke bread (said Mass) with the disciples*
- *Jesus vanished*

Jn 20:11–18: Mary Magdalene at the tomb
- *Mary was sad*
- *Jesus appeared to her, but she did not recognize Him*
- *He spoke her name, and she knew it was Him*
- *He said He has not yet gone to the Father*

Jn 21:19–22: Breakfast on the Shore
- *Jesus was recognized first by the beloved disciple, but Peter swam to shore*
- *Jesus has prepared breakfast for them*
- *Jesus asked Peter if he loved Him, and told him to take care of His followers*

Note: What these encounters reveal:
- *Jesus' desire that all be taught about faith and baptized*
- *The Mass – Liturgy of the Word and Eucharist (Emmaus)*
- *Jesus would go back to the Father*
- *Jesus left Peter in charge of His Church*

Name:____________________

Put these events in order:

PART I:

__3__ Jesus taught us about loving God and our neighbor and worked many miracles.
__2__ Jesus was baptized by John the Baptist.
__1__ Jesus was born of the Virgin Mary in Bethlehem.
__4__ Jesus gave us the Eucharist.

PART II

__9__ Jesus carried a heavy cross to Mount Calvary.
__11__ Jesus forgave the good thief.
__5__ Jesus rode into Jerusalem on a donkey.
__7__ Jesus went to the Garden of Olives to pray.
__6__ Jesus celebrated the Last Supper with His disciples.
__10__ Jesus was nailed to the Cross.
__12__ Jesus rose from the dead on Easter Sunday.
__8__ Soldiers came to arrest Jesus.

Faith and Life Series • Grade 2 • Chapter 24 • Lesson 2 89

JESUS AS THE NEW ADAM

ADAM	NEW ADAM
• Disobedient	• Obedient
• Selfish sin	• Self-sacrifice
• Loss of grace	• Won back grace
• Loss of Heaven	• Opened Heaven
• Death	• Eternal Life

Reinforce

1. Have the students work on *Activity Book*, p. 89. When they have finished, review the correct answers.

2. Have them draw one of the Resurrection encounter stories.

3. Show "The Resurrection of Jesus," video from the series Jesus: A Kingdom Without Frontiers, available through Ignatius Press; 30 minutes.

Conclude

1. Sing: "Jesus Christ is risen today," *Adoremus Hymnal*, #410.

2. Pray p. 119 with the students.

3. They may show and tell about their pictures.

Preview

In the next lesson, we will learn about the encounter with Jesus in the upper room.

NOTES

____
____
____
____
____
____
____
____
____
____
____

LESSON THREE: JESUS WITH US AGAIN

Aims

The students will learn about the time Jesus appeared to the disciples in the upper room. He ate with His disciples, verifying that He was not a ghost.

They will learn how Jesus gave the power to forgive sins to the Apostles.

Materials

- Children's Bible.
- *Activity Book*, p. 90

Optional:
- "Jesus Christ is risen today," *Adoremus Hymnal*, #410

Begin

Review the other Risen Lord encounters. What does each of them teach about Jesus and what He wants us to know? What do they say about His Risen Person—His body?

that He was not a ghost, but really alive. How happy the disciples were! Jesus was risen from the dead.

"Peace be with you." The disciples no longer felt any fear or sadness when Jesus was with them. We, too, will have peace when we let Jesus come into our lives.

That is why **Easter** is such a joyful time. We celebrate because Jesus is alive and has won for us the life of grace. Now we can live forever!

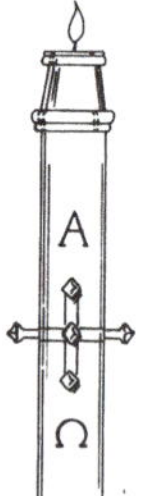

Jesus Christ is risen today, alleluia,
Our triumphant holy day, alleluia,
Who did once upon the Cross, alleluia,
Suffer to redeem our loss, alleluia.

Hymns of praise then let us sing, alleluia,
Unto Christ our Heavenly King, alleluia,
Who endured the Cross and grave, alleluia,
Sinners to redeem and save, alleluia.

On Easter Sunday we light a special candle in the church. It is called a Paschal Candle. We light it on Easter to remind us of Jesus' **Resurrection**.

Sometimes we call Jesus the Light of the World. The Paschal Candle is a symbol for Jesus.

118

Develop

1. Read paragraphs 4 and 5 with the students.

2. Read from the children's Bible Jn 20:19–22, and Lk 24:36–48.

3. Emphasize to the students that the room was locked. Jesus came in even though it was locked! Jesus ate with the disciples. He allowed them to touch Him. What was His body like? Remember that, earlier, both Mary Magdalene at the tomb and the disciples on the way to Emmaus saw Jesus and did not recognize Him!

4. The resurrected body of Our Lord was beautiful. It still bore the wounds of the Crucifixion—Saint Thomas touched them. He was not a ghost: He was touchable and ate with the disciples. He could pass through walls and be in different places with great speed. He would not die again or suffer. These are all qualities of the risen body that we, too, will experience at the end of time.

5. Note that after Jesus wished peace to His Apostles, He breathed on the Apostles. He gave them the power to forgive sins. It is in the Sacrament of Reconciliation, or Confession, that Jesus forgives our sins through His priests. This power has been passed down to all priests and bishops, so we can receive Jesus' forgiveness and peace. This forgiveness is a great gift from Jesus.

6. When our sins are forgiven through the Sacrament of Confession, we receive God's grace, and Jesus comes to live in our souls again. This sacrament gives us peace and joy, like the Apostles experienced when they encountered the Risen Lord.

7. You may want to review the Sacrament of Reconciliation, the five steps, and, if possible, take the class to receive the sacrament.

Name:__________________

Our Lord is risen from the dead. He won for us eternal life! Jesus is true God and true man. He is a divine Person who took on a human nature. We show this by the color of His clothes. Jesus often is shown wearing a blue robe (divinity) and a red coat (humanity). Can you color His clothes?

90 *Faith and Life Series • Grade 2 • Chapter 24 • Lesson 3*

Reinforce

1. Have the students read, and color *Activity Book*, p. 90.

2. Have the students break into groups and act out the Resurrection encounters with Our Lord.

3. Have them work on the memorizing Words to Know and questions for this chapter.

Conclude

1. Sing: "Jesus Christ is risen today," *Adoremus Hymnal*, #410.

2. End with the prayer on p. 119 of the student text.

Preview

In the next lesson, we will learn more about Easter traditions, and specifically the Paschal Candle.

THE RESURRECTION

Mt 28:1–10 Mk 16:1–13
Lk 24:1–43 Jn 20:1–29

THE FIVE GLORIOUS MYSTERIES

1. The Resurrection of Christ
2. The Ascension of Christ
3. The Descent of the Holy Spirit
4. The Assumption of Mary
5. The Coronation of Mary

NOTES

____

____

____

____

____

____

____

____

____

____

____

LESSON FOUR: PEACE BE WITH YOU

Aims

The students will learn about Easter traditions and the Paschal Candle.

Materials

- Easter Candle or one prepared for class demonstration (prayers)
- *Activity Book*, p. 91
- Craft materials, hard-boiled eggs, white candles, cloves

Optional:
- "Jesus Christ is risen today," *Adoremus Hymnal*, #410
- Supplies for an Easter party (remember in the Church year, this celebration is bigger than Christmas)
- "The Story of Easter," video; The Beginner's Bible

Begin

Begin by asking the children how they celebrate Easter. Many of them will celebrate with the Easter bunny, new outfits, a big family gathering and feast. Ask them to share some of their fondest Easter memories. You, in turn, may share yours.

Words to Know:

Easter Resurrection

Q. 52 *After His death, what did Jesus Christ do?*
On the third day after His death, Jesus rose from the dead, took up His body, and won for us the life of grace (CCC 640, 645, 654).

We Pray:

May the Light of Christ,
rising in glory,
dispel the darkness
of our hearts and minds.

119

Develop

1. Finish reading the chapter as a class.

2. Ask the students which is a bigger celebration, Christmas or Easter. According to the Church, Easter is. It is the time we celebrate Jesus rising from the dead, conquering death. It is the time we celebrate sharing in God's life. We celebrate grace and our hope for eternal life.

3. You may want to explain some of the Easter Celebrations in the Church. At Easter Vigil Mass, people are baptized, confirmed, and receive the Holy Eucharist; they are received into the Church. The priest lights the Easter Candle (which the students will learn more about). The priest also sings the Exsultet – a beautiful hymn summarizing salvation history.

4. On Easter Sunday, many families celebrate together with feasts. Many people bring their bread to the church for blessing. Also, blessed chalk is often distributed, so people may take it for the blessing of their homes.

5. Teach them about the paschal candle. Read p. 118 with the students. With the prayers said by the priest, read to the class what is said with the blessing and assembly of the Easter candle. Explain the symbolism. The flame reminds us of Christ our Light. (In a dark room, it illumines much—it allows us to see and be seen.) The Alpha means the beginning, the Omega means the end. The date is put on the candle telling us how many years of Christian life there have been. The five cloves remind us of the wounds of Christ. The wax reminds us of ourselves, and that we are to become molded into the likeness of Christ. If possible, visit the Paschal candle in the church.

6. Celebrate with an Easter party.

Name:____________________

The Paschal Candle is lit on Easter Sunday. It is a white candle with special marks on it. Can you draw these marks?

1. There is a large red cross on the candle (See page *118* in your text book for a pattern).

2. At the top of the Cross is an "A", or in greek this is called an alpha. It means the beginning.

3. At the bottom of the Cross is a upside down horseshoe. In Greek this is a letter called an omega. It means the end. The alpha and omega remind us that Jesus is the Beginning and the End —that He is the Eternal God.

4. Usually in the corners of the cross, are the numbers of the date, e.g., for the year 2003 we would see:

20
\+
03

The center and four points of the cross are marked with cloves, reminding us of Christ's wounds.

Faith and Life Series • Grade 2 • Chapter 24 • Lesson 4 91

Reinforce

1. Have the students work on *Activity Book*, p. 91.

2. Celebrate with a party. You may show "The Story of Easter" video from the series The Beginner's Bible, available through Ignatius Press; 30 minutes. Paint eggs, make Easter Candles, Easter cards, etc.

Conclude

1. Sing: "Jesus Christ is risen today," *Adoremus Hymnal*, #410.

2. The children may dramatize the Easter Story.

Preview

In the next lesson, we will review the material covered in this chapter.

EASTER CUSTOMS – CÁSCARONES

In some parts of Mexico and the United States, families celebrate Easter with eggs that are not hardboiled. For weeks these families save the shells (cáscaras) of the eggs that they intend to cook. They make a hole in the top just large enough to release the yolks and egg whites. After washing and drying the egg shells, the children color and decorate them. Once the dyed shells have dried, their parents fill them with confetti, often homemade, and using a paste made of flour and water they cover the opening with a small piece of tissue or napkin. After Easter morning Mass, the families hide the cáscarones in the yard and the children find them, then chase each other and crack the eggs in their hands and rub the confetti in each other's hair.

NOTES

CHAPTER TWENTY-FOUR: REVIEW AND ASSESSMENT

Aims

The students' understanding of the material covered this week will be reviewed and assessed.

Materials

- Quiz 24 (Appendix, p. A-34)
- Unit 6 Test (Appendix, pp. A-35 and A-36)
- "Jesus Christ is risen today," *Adoremus Hymnal*, #410

Review

1. The students should be able to recount the events of the Resurrection.

2. They should be able to recount stories of encounters with the Risen Lord:
   - Mt 28:5–20: Great Commission
   - Lk 24:25–34: Road to Emmaus
   - Jn 20:11–18: Mary Magdalene at the tomb
   - Jn 21:19–22: Fish on the Shore
   - Jn 20:19–22, and Lk 24:36–48: Upper Room

3. Review what these encounters teach about our faith:
   - Jesus' desire that everyone be taught about faith and be baptized
   - The Mass—Liturgy of the Word and Eucharist (Emmaus)
   - Jesus would go back to the Father
   - Jesus left Peter in charge of His Church

4. Review what do we know about the Resurrected Body.

5. They should be able to speak about Easter traditions, celebrations, and the Paschal Candle.

Name:

He Is Risen, Alleluia! **Quiz 24**

Circle the correct answer:

1. The women went to the tomb of Jesus on:
   a) Good Friday
   b) Holy Saturday
   c) Easter Sunday

2. Whom did the women see at the tomb?
   a) soldiers
   b) angel
   c) Jesus

3. After His death, what did Jesus Christ do?
   a) rose from the dead.
   b) appeared as a ghost.
   c) gave up His body.

4. What did Jesus give to the Apostles in the upper room?
   a) money
   b) peace
   c) gifts

5. Easter reminds us of Jesus':
   a) death
   b) suffering
   c) Resurrection

Please answer in complete sentences:

What was Jesus like after the Resurrection? Was He a ghost?
Answers will vary. He was not a ghost!

To whom did Jesus appear after the Resurrection?
Mary Magdalene, the other women at the tomb, and the disciples

A - 34 *Faith and Life • Grade 2 • Appendix A*

Assess

1. Distribute Quiz 24. Answer any questions that they may have. When they turn in their quizzes, individually quiz them on the Memorization Questions and the Words to Know.

2. When all quizzes have been turned in, review the correct answers.

3. Do 1 and 2 the same for the unit test.

Conclude

1. Sing "Jesus Christ is risen today," *Adoremus Hymnal*, #410.

2. Pray for the student intentions.

CHAPTER TWENTY-FIVE
THE HOLY MASS

Catechism of the Catholic Church References

Eucharist as Sacrifice: 1356–58, 1414
- Eucharist: Thanksgiving/Praise to the Father: 1359–61
- Eucharist as Sacrificial Memorial of Christ and of His Body, the Church:1341–44, 1362–72, 1414
- Eucharistic Presence of Christ: 1373–81, 1410, 1418

Obligation to Participate, Mass: 1389, 2180
Significance of Sunday Celebration: 2177–79
Structure of Movement of the Mass:
- An Action of Ministerial Priesthood: 1552
- Corresponds to Paschal Meal and Risen Lord: 1347
- Two Parts: 1346, 1408

Sunday—Day of the Resurrection: 2174, 2191
Sunday—Fulfillment of the Sabbath: 2175–76, 2190
Sunday Obligation: 2180–83, 2192
- Day of Grace and Rest from Work: 2184–88, 2193–95
- Worship: 2096–97, 2135–36

Scripture References

The Last Supper: Lk 22:14–23; 1 Cor 11:23–27; Mt 26:20–29; Mk 14:17–26
O.T. Sacrifices:
Abraham: Gen 15,
Elijah: 18:22–39

Crucifixion as Sacrafice Mt 27:22–32; Mk 15:15–39; Lk 23:33–46; Jn 19:16–37; Heb 7:26–27
Resurrection: Mt 27:60—28:10; Mk 16:1–8; Lk 23:53—24:9; Jn 20:1–18

Background Reading: *The Fundamentals of Catholicism* by Fr. Kenneth Baker, S.J.

Volume 3:
"Where Is the Sacrifice?," pp. 265–67

Volume 2:
"Adore God, and Him Alone," pp.138–41

Summary of Lesson Content

Lesson 1

We celebrate Mass in obedience to the Commandments and to follow Jesus' instruction "Do this in memory of me."

At the Last Supper, Jesus instituted the Eucharist and the priesthood.

The power to consecrate the Eucharist has been passed on to all validly ordained priests.

Lesson 2

At Mass, the same sacrifice of Christ is offered to the Father for our sins. It is the same sacrifice offered on the Cross.

This is not the same sacrifice offered over and over again, but one time for all, made sacramentally present on the altar.

Lesson 3

At the Mass, the Resurrection is also celebrated.

Mass is celebrated on Sunday, the day of the Resurrection.

Lesson 4

Mass is the perfect prayer, including praise and thanksgiving, petition and intercession.

Man is called to actively participate in Mass.

The Third Commandment is reviewed.

LESSON ONE: DO THIS . . .

Aims

The students will learn that we celebrate Mass in obedience to the Commandments and to follow Jesus' instruction "Do this in memory of me."

They will understand that at the Last Supper, Jesus instituted the Eucharist and the priesthood.

Materials

- Ten Commandments
- Picture of the Last Supper, Picture of the Mass (see p. 126).
- Children's Bible
- *Activity Book*, p. 92

Optional:
- "O saving Victim," *Adoremus Hymnal*, #519/520

Begin

Begin by writing the Ten Commandments on the board. Ask the children which of the Ten Commandments they are obeying by going to Mass on Sunday. The first three:

- I am the Lord your God, you shall have no other gods besides Me (this means worship God)
- You shall not take the Name of the Lord in vain (This means to honor God)
- You shall honor the Lord's Day (Go to Mass)

Ask the children if Jesus Himself said we should go to Mass. (Yes: Do this in memory of me).

Develop

1. Read paragraphs 1–2 from the chapter.

2. Read the Last Supper accounts from the children's Bible (Mt 26: 20–29; Mk 14:17–26; Lk 22:13–20; 1 Cor 11:23–27). The students may act out this reading.

3. Compare a picture of the Last Supper and a picture of the Mass (you may use pp. 106 and 126 of text). What is going on in each picture?
   - Who is present?
   - Is there an altar in each picture?
   - Is there a cup? bread?
   - What is happening to the bread and wine?
   - Is the Last Supper a Mass? (it is the first Mass)
   - Is Jesus present at our Mass?
   - What role does the priest have? (He acts in the Person of Christ)
   - Where are the Apostles in the Last Supper picture?
   - Where do we belong at Mass?
   - Have the students ever been to a Mass with many priests celebrating?

4. Jesus said: "Do this in remembrance of me." In the Jewish culture, to remember means to "make present." It is not just thinking of something that happened a long time ago, but ir ia making it present now. Jesus wants us to be present with Him now through the Mass. By saying "Do this" to His Apostles, Jesus made them priests. All priests have the power, through Jesus, to change bread and wine into the Body and Blood of Jesus, to make Him present now at the Mass. We should want to be there for this great event! When we go to Mass, we are at the Last Supper, with Jesus on the Cross, and at the Resurrection; we are united with Jesus through Holy Communion.

5. If possible, have the class interview a priest.

Name:____________________

Sunday is God's Day

List ways to make the Lord's Day special.

Answers will vary

Draw yourself honoring God on Sunday.

92 *Faith and Life Series • Grade 2 • Chapter 25 • Lesson 1*

Reinforce

1. Have the students work on Activity Book, p. 92.

2. Teach the children to sing "O saving Victim," *Adoremus Hymnal*, #519/520.

Conclude

1. End the day with praying the Our Father.

2. You may review the responsory parts of the Mass.

Preview

In the next lesson, the students will learn about the Sacrifice of the Mass.

SUNDAY TRADITIONS

The Christian day of rest and worship is Sunday, rather than the traditional Jewish sabbath of Saturday, because Jesus was resurrected on Sunday. Each Sunday, therefore, is in some sense a re-enactment of the first Easter Sunday, with a part in the joy of God's greatest gift.

It is customary for Catholic families to celebrate each Sunday with family time, relaxation time, time for preparing for the rest of the week, and time for attending Mass. Sunday Mass is an obligation that cannot be missed, except for very serious reasons.

NOTES

LESSON TWO: THE SACRIFICE OF THE MASS

Aims

The sudents will learn that at Mass, the same sacrifice of Christ is offered to the Father for our sins. It is the same sacrifice Jesus offered on the Cross.

Materials

- Picture on p. 120 of text
- Children's Bible
- *Activity Book*, p. 93

Optional:
- "O saving Victim," *Adoremus Hymnal*, #519/520

Begin

Begin by writing "sacrifice" on the board. Ask the students if they can explain what this word means (make sure they know how to pronounce it first). Use the picture on p. 120 of the text to help explain what a sacrifice is. A sacrifice is when we give our best to God without taking it back. In the times before Jesus, for example, people would take their best crops or animals and burn them on an altar, leaving nothing for themselves. It is to give something totally to God. Ask the children how Jesus is a sacrifice. What was His altar? (Cross/altar at Mass.)

25 The Holy Mass

And he took bread, and when he had given thanks he broke it and gave it to them, saying, "This is my body which is given for you. Do this in remembrance of me." And likewise the cup after supper, saying, "This cup which is poured out for you is the new covenant in my blood."

Luke 22:19–20

Every Sunday we go to church to do what Jesus told the disciples to do when He said, "Do this in memory of Me." You see, the Last Supper was the very first **Mass**.

At the Last Supper, Jesus changed bread and wine into His Body and Blood. He gave the disciples the power to do this, too. The disciples gave that power to other men. That is why our priest today can change bread and wine into the Body and Blood of Christ at every Mass.

At Mass we offer the same sacrifice that Jesus offered for our sins. That is the **sacrifice** which Jesus

121

Develop

1. Read the third paragraph from this chapter with the students.

2. Go through the chalk talk at right with them. This exercise may be done on the board.

3. Find examples of sacrifices in the Bible, such as Isaac in Genesis 15, Elijah 1, Kings 18:22–39.

4. Read the crucifixion of Jesus and point out how it, too, is a sacrifice (Mt 27:22–32; Mk 15:15–39; Lk 23:33–46; Jn 19:16–37):
- Offered to the Father
- Jesus was the victim and the priest
- Withheld nothing, not even His life
- Atoned for our sins

5. Ask them how the sacrifice of Jesus on the Cross can be present at Mass more than 2000 years later. With God, there is no time. How do we tell time? With the sun, moon, rotation of the earth, etc. God made all these things; therefore, He is outside of them. At Mass, the same Victim is being offered to the Father. The victim is Jesus, His Body and Blood, Soul and Divinity. He is being offered for our sins. It is the same sacrifice as on the Cross, only celebrated in the unbloody Eucharist. Ask the children if Jesus is being sacrificed over and over again at each Mass. No. (See Heb 7:26–27.) He was sacrificed once for all and for all time.

6. Ask them why it is important that we go to Mass. If Jesus has died for our sins as a sacrifice to the Father, and if we are united with Him in Communion, we are offering ourselves to God, too. We become living sacrifices, giving ourselves and all we have and do to God. This sacrifice is very pleasing to Him.

Name:___________________

Make a poster inviting people to Mass.

Reinforce

1. Have the students complete *Activity Book*, p. 93.

2. Play a game in which they list what sacrifices they may make to God. For example:

Child 1: I will sacrifice to God my prayers today.
Child 2: [Child 1] will sacrifice to God his prayers, and I will sacrifice my soccer game.
Child 3: [Child 1] will sacrifice . . . [Child 2] will sacrifice . . . and I will sacrifice my homework to God.

Conclude

1. Sing: "O saving Victim," *Adoremus Hymnal*, #519/520.

2. Remind them that Jesus is the victim of a Sacrifice of Love. Teach the children to pray a spiritual communion, uniting themselves to the Father with Jesus' sacrifice.

3. Pray the Our Father.

Preview

In the next lesson, we will learn that Sunday is a celebration of the Resurrection.

CHALK TALK: THE HOLY MASS

Chalk Talk

(Provide a "word bank")

Jesus gave (Himself) up to the Father for us.

Jesus (sacrificed) Himself for us.

At Mass we (worship) God, we (thank) Him, we make up for our (sins), and we (ask) God for things we need.

The most perfect prayer is the (Mass).

NOTES

LESSON THREE: WE CELEBRATE THE RESURRECTION

Aims

The students will learn that at the Mass, the Resurrection is also celebrated.

They will learn that we celebrate Mass on Sunday, the day of the Resurrection.

Materials

- Ten Commandments
- Children's Bible
- *Activity Book*, p. 94

Optional:
- "O saving Victim," *Adoremus Hymnal*, #519/520

Begin

Begin by asking the students what the Third Commandment is. You shall honor the Sabbath/ Lord's Day. Ask the children if they know what day the Jewish people honor as the Sabbath. Saturday. Why do we celebrate Mass on Sunday? Ask the children if they know what day of the week Jesus rose from the dead. Sunday. So, we celebrate the Lord's Day on Sunday because that is the day Jesus conquered death by rising from the dead.

offered to the Father when He died on the Cross. Sacrifice means giving up something completely. Jesus gave Himself up to God the Father for us. This is the sacrifice we offer at every Mass.

We also celebrate the Resurrection. That is why we go to Mass on Sunday, because Jesus rose from the dead on a Sunday. Each Sunday is a "little Easter." This is a community celebration and that is why we all come together on Sunday.

Why do we go to Holy Mass?
We go to **praise** our God, Who is great and good.
We go to say "thank you" to God for all the good things He has given us.
At Mass we tell God we are sorry for our sins, and we ask His help to be better.
We also pray for the things we need, and for the needs of others.

If we listen carefully to the Mass and try to say the prayers, God will give us His grace and blessing. Taking part in the Mass will help to prepare you for your First Communion.

122

Develop

1. Read paragraph 4 from the text with the students.

2. Read from a children's Bible the account of the Resurrection (Mt 27:60—28:10; Mk 16:1–8; Lk 23:53—24:9; Jn 20:1–18). The children may discuss why the Resurrection is a time of celebration.

3. Discuss with the children ways of celebrating Easter
   - Feasts and family gatherings
   - Easter bread, special foods
   - New clothes, etc.

4. Easter is a special time in the Church to pray and to praise God. We thank Him for the death and Resurrection of Jesus. We thank God for the life He shares with us, the life Jesus won for us by rising from the dead. We thank god for all these things at every Mass.

5. Review the meaning of prayer and the different kinds of prayer. Explain that the Mass is the perfect prayer offered to God because in the Mass not only do we offer praise and thanks to God, but we also ask for the forgiveness of sins and for other things, all through Jesus Christ, God's own Son. Jesus makes our prayers perfect because they are united to His. Our sacrifices are united to His perfect Sacrifice.

6. If Easter is such a time of celebration, and Mass is a little Easter, how should we approach Mass?
   - Should we worry about work we need to do?
   - Should we pay attention?
   - Should we dress up?
   - Should we prepare for Mass? How?
   - Should we be thankful and participate? How?

7. Ask the children if their families have any Sunday traditions.

Name:________________________

Can you fill in the blanks?

Every Sunday we go to church to do what Jesus told us to do when He said, "Do this in remembrance of Me." You see, the Last Supper was the very first Mass.

At the Last Supper, Jesus changed bread and wine into His Body and Blood. He gave the disciples the power to do this too. The disciples gave that power to other men. That is why our priests today can change bread and wine into the Body and Blood of Christ at every Mass.

At Mass, we offer the same sacrifice that Jesus offered for our sins. That is the sacrifice which Jesus offered to the Father when He died on the Cross. A sacrifice is the total giving up of something. Jesus gave Himself up for us to God the Father. This is the sacrifice we offer at every Mass.

94 *Faith and Life Series • Grade 2 • Chapter 25 • Lesson 3*

Reinforce

1. Have the students work on *Activity Book*, p. 94.

2. Have them work on memorizing the questions on p. 124. They should also look up and memorize the Words to Know. They may race to find the words in the glossary.

3. Review types and kinds of prayer:
   - Adoration/Blessing
   - Thanksgiving
   - Petition
   - Intercession
   - Vocal
   - Mental

Conclude

1. Sing: "O saving Victim," *Adoremus Hymnal*, #519/520.

2. Have the children discuss what they most look forward to when going to Mass. What do they look forward to about their First Communion Mass? Should they be this excited about every mass in which they may receive Jesus?

3. End by praying the Our Father and the Glory Be.

Preview

In the next lesson, we will learn more about Mass as prayer.

SAINT ROBERT BELLARMINE

The third of ten children, Saint Robert was born in Italy in 1542. His mother was the niece of Pope Marcellus II, and he was dedicated to almsgiving, prayer and fasting. He entered the newly formed Society of Jesus in 1560. In 1576 he was appointed chair of theology at the Roman College, and named a cardinal in 1598. He was the spiritual father of Saint Aloysius Gonzaga, helped Saint Francis de Sales obtain formal approval of the Visitation Order, and, in his prudence, opposed the severe treatment of Galileo. He died in 1621 and was canonized in 1930. His feast day is September 17. He is the patron of catechists and a Doctor of the Church.

NOTES

LESSON FOUR: THE PERFECT PRAYER

Aims

The children will learn that Mass is the perfect prayer.

They will learn that we are called to actively participate in Mass.

They will review the Third Commandment.

Materials

- *Activity Book*, p. 95
- Poster-board, crayons

Optional:
- "O saving Victim," *Adoremus Hymnal*, #519/520

Begin

Review with the children why Sunday is the Lord's Day, and why Mass is so important:
- Sunday (not Saturday) is the Lord's Day because it is the day of the Resurrection
- We are present for the sacrifice of the Lord to the Father, and we unite ourselves with the perfect sacrifice of Jesus
- We obey God's Commandments
- Jesus told us to do this in remembrance of Him

Sunday is God's Day

The Third Commandment says: Remember to keep holy the Lord's Day. By going to Mass on Sunday we are obeying God's Law and keeping His Day holy. But we should do more than just go to Mass on Sunday to honor God. We should make it a special day and we can do that by:

— not doing any work that can be done on another day.
— wearing our best clothes when we go to church.
— not going shopping.
— having a special meal with our family.
— spending time together with our family.
— spending more time thinking and talking about God.

Words to Know:

Mass sacrifice praise

123

Develop

1. Finish reading the chapter with the students.

2. Ask the children the questions in the text, and have them write their answers on the board:
- Why do we go to Mass?
- How do we praise God? And for what?
- How do we thank God? And for what?
- What will God give us at Mass?
- How can we prepare for First Communion?

Add the memorization questions:
- What is the Mass?
- Why is the Mass offered to God?

3. Together, read the "Sunday is God's Day" box.

4. Ask them in what ways their families make the Lord's Day special.

5. Review the Third Commandment:
- No (unnecessary) work
- Go to Mass
- No (unnecessary) shopping
- A meal with the family
- Time together with family (and friends)
- Time to rest
- Time for prayer and talking about God

Be sure to review what one should do, as well as what one should not do. You may write these on the board.

6. Review the responsory parts of the Mass. Encourage the children to listen for these parts the next time they attend Mass.

Q. 53 *What is the Mass?*
The Mass is the sacrifice of Jesus on the Cross, and the gift of Himself in the Eucharist. The priest offers the Eucharist in church (CCC 1362, 1366–67).

Q. 54 *Why is the Mass offered to God?*
The Mass is offered to God to worship Him, to thank Him, to make up for our sins, and to ask for His help (CCC 1357, 1360, 1367).

124

Reinforce

1. Have them students complete *Activity Book*, p. 95.

2. Have them make posters showing how they should celebrate the Lord's Day (and why).

Conclude

1. Sing "O saving Victim," *Adoremus Hymnal*, #519/520.

2. End with making a spiritual communion and praying the Our Father and the Glory Be.

Preview

In the next lesson, we will review the material covered in this chapter.

PATRON SAINTS

- Schools: Saint Catherine (November 25)
- Science: Saint Catherine (November 25)
- Silence: Saint John Nepomucen (May 16)
- Spies: Saint Guido
- Spinsters: Saint Catherine of Siena (April 29)
- Sufferers from Unjust Lawsuits: Saint Aya (April 18)

NOTES

CHAPTER TWENTY-FIVE
REVIEW AND ASSESSMENT

Aims

The students' understanding of the material covered this week will be reviewed and assessed.

Materials

- Quiz 25 (Appendix, p. A-37)
- "O saving Victim," *Adoremus Hymnal*, #519/520

Review

1. Review that the Last Supper was the first Mass; in it Jesus instituted the Eucharist and the priesthood.

2. Review that Jesus gave the power to the Apostles, so that through Him, they could change bread and wine into His Body and Blood. This power has been passed on to all validly ordained priests.

3. Review that at Mass, we offer to the Father the same sacrifice that Jesus offered for our sins when He died on the Cross. A sacrifice is totally giving up something for God. We can offer ourselves to the Father by uniting ourselves to the Sacrifice of Jesus.

4. Review that at Mass, we also celebrate the Resurrection of Jesus. Jesus rose from the dead on Sunday, so we celebrate Mass on Sunday. Every Sunday Mass is like a little Easter.

5. Review that we go to Mass to praise God, to thank Him, to tell Him we are sorry for our sins, and to pray for our needs and the needs of others.

6. Review that we are encouraged to actively participate in the Mass.

7. Review that to obey the Third Commandment we should:
- Go to Mass
- Not work or shop
- Spend time with family and friends
- Rest

Name:

The Holy Mass **Quiz 25**

Circle the correct answer:

1. At the Last Supper, Jesus gave the Church
   a) The Eucharist b) The Priesthood
   (c) The Eucharist and the Priesthood

2. The Sacrifice of the Mass is
   (a) The same sacrifice of Jesus on the Cross offered to the Father for our sins.
   b) The sacrifice of Jesus offered over and over again.
   c) A new sacrifice of ourselves instead of Jesus, for the forgiveness of our sins.

3. We go to Mass on Sunday because
   a) It is the day the Jewish people celebrate.
   b) It is the day chosen by the early Christians.
   (c) It is the day Jesus rose from the dead.

4. The perfect prayer is
   a) The Our Father, as taught to us by Jesus Himself.
   b) The Rosary. (c) The Mass.

5. By going to Mass, we honor which of the Ten Commandments?
   (a) The Third Commandment b) The Fifth Commandment
   c) The Eighth Commandment

Place a red "X" beside things we should not do on Sunday, and a green "O" beside things we should do on Sunday, in order to honor God's Law.

_O_ Go to Mass
_X_ Go shopping
_O_ Spend time with family
_X_ Do homework
_X_ Fight with brothers and sisters
_O_ Read the Bible
_O_ Pray
_X_ Misbehave at Church
_O_ Help our neighbor
_O_ Sing songs praising God

Faith and Life • Grade 2 • Appendix A *A - 37*

Assess

1. Distribute Quiz 25. Answer any questions that they may have. When the students turn in their quiz, individually quiz them on the Memorization Questions and Words to Know that they learned this week.

2. When all quizzes have been turned in, review the correct answers.

Conclude

1. Sing "O Saving Victim," *Adoremus Hymnal*, #519/520.

2. Pray the Our Father.

CHAPTER TWENTY-SIX
WHAT WE DO AT MASS

Catechism of the Catholic Church References

Altar: 1383
Creeds: 185–97
Eucharist as Sacrifice: 1356–58, 1414
Eucharist as Thanksgiving/Praise to the Father: 1359–61
Eucharist as Sacrificial Memorial of Christ and of His Body, the Church: 1341–44, 1362–72, 1414
Presence of Christ in the Eucharist: 1373–81, 1410, 1418
Liturgical celebration of the Eucharist
Celebration through the Ages: 1345–47
Movement of the Celebration: 1348–55, 1408
The Mass: 1345–1405 (or in brief: 1406–19)

Scripture References

Jesus Establishes the Mass: Luke 24:27–31

Background Reading: *The Fundamentals of Catholicism* by Fr. Kenneth Baker, S.J.

Volume 3:
"Power of the Mass," pp. 268–70

Summary of Lesson Content

Lesson 1

There are two main parts to the Mass: The Liturgy of the Word and the Liturgy of the Eucharist.

The first lesson covers the introductory rites.

Lesson 2

The second lesson covers the Liturgy of the Word

Lesson 3

The third lesson covers the Liturgy of the Eucharist.

The students will also learn from an altar presentation.

Lesson 4

The fourth lesson covers the closing rites.

The children will learn more about the overall structure of the Mass.

LESSON ONE: THE MASS AND INTRODUCTORY RITES

Aims

The students will learn the two main parts to the Mass: the Liturgy of the Word and the Liturgy of the Eucharist.

They will become familiar with the introductory rites.

Materials

- Chart of the parts of the Mass (see opposite page). This can be drawn onto posterboard with each column a different color.
- Posters of the prayers
- Missalettes
- Paper/pencils
- *Activity Book*, p. 96

Optional:
- "Father, we thank thee who hast planted," *Adoremus Hymnal*, #515

Begin

Begin by displaying the chart of the parts of the Mass. Have the students distinguish the four parts of the Mass. Explain that the two main parts are the Liturgy of the Word and the Liturgy of the Eucharist. The other two parts simply give an introduction and conclusion.
Ask the children if they can recognize any of the parts, e.g., the I Confess, or the Gloria. Explain that today they will learn more about the introductory rites.

26 What We Do at Mass

Praise the LORD!
Sing to the LORD a new song,
his praise in the assembly of the faithful!

Psalm 149:1

The Liturgy of the Word has many parts leading up to the coming of Jesus in the Eucharist. They prepare us to meet and receive our Lord.

We begin the Mass by singing a hymn or saying a prayer while the priest goes to the altar. Then we make the Sign of the Cross.

Next the priest asks us to think of the ways we have hurt God and others. We say the *I Confess* prayer which asks forgiveness. This prayer also asks Mary, the saints, and those in church to pray for us. Then comes a song of praise, *Glory to God*.

The Liturgy of the Word begins and we sit down to hear the *Word of God*. The lector and the priest read to us from the Bible. We learn about God's chosen people, and about the life of Jesus. The priest gives a **homily** to help us understand the Bible and lead good lives.

125

Develop

1. Read the first three paragraphs as a class. Compare the parts listed in the text with the parts listed on the chart:
   - Opening Hymn
   - Greeting
   - Sign of the Cross
   - Penitential Rite and I Confess prayer
   - Kyrie (Lord have mercy)
   - Gloria
   - Opening Prayer

2. Have the students find these parts of the Mass in the missalettes. Teach the students to follow along in the book as you read the I Confess and the Gloria.

3. The students should know how to respond to the Lord have mercy. Quiz them on the response.

4. *Give special attention to each student's memory work in prayers and parts of the Mass. You may find that some will need reinforcement at home. If you discover that some of your students are not attending Mass, you may need to have their parents come in for an interview. You may have the students sign a Mass contract, or ask them about the Homily at Mass as a way of testing whether or not they have gone. Do not embarrass a child or single them out for not attending Mass because they cannot get themselves there. If there is a Mass attendance problem, discuss this with the director or religious education, parish priest, and parents to find a suitable remedy. It is however, not acceptable for a child to make First Communion if he is not familiar with the Mass itself.*

5. Have the students write out the parts of the introductory rites, including the prayers they need to memorize. This exercise will create a missal for them to use at Mass.

Name:____________________

Word Search

Can you find these words in the puzzle?
Look carefully! The words go across and down.

ALTAR	CHALICE	ENTRANCE
BIBLE	CIBORIUM	FORGIVE
BLESSED	COMMUNION	JESUS
BLOOD	CREED	
BODY	CRUETS	

96 *Faith and Life Series • Grade 2 • Chapter 26 • Lesson 1*

Reinforce

1. Have the students begin working on *Activity Book*, p. 96. While they are working you may quiz them on their memory work of the week.

2. Have the students memorize the I Confess prayer and the Gloria.

3. Quiz them on responses for the Mass, e.g., The Lord be with you, and also with you; Lord have mercy, Lord have mercy; etc.

4. Teach the students to sing "Father, we thank thee who hast planted," *Adoremus Hymnal*, #515.

Conclude

Have the students recite the prayers for memorization.

Preview

In the next lesson, we will learn about the Liturgy of the Word.

Introductory Rites:	Entrance Song, Greeting (the Sign of the Cross), Penitential Rite (the Confiteor), Kyrie, Gloria, and Opening Prayer
Liturgy of the Word:	First Reading, the Responsorial Psalm, the Second Reading, the Alleluia, the Gospel, the Homily, Credo (Profession of Faith), and the General Intercessions
Liturgy of the Eucharist:	Offertory (Preparation of the Altar and the Gifts), Offertory Hymn, Prayer over the Gifts, Preface, Sanctus, the Eucharistic Prayer, and the Consecration
Communion Rite:	Lord's Prayer, Sign of Peace, the Agnus Dei, Communion, the Communion Hymn, and the Prayer after Communion
Concluding Rite:	The Blessing, and Dismissal

LESSON TWO: THE LITURGY OF THE WORD

Aims

The students will learn about the Liturgy of the Word

They will also learn the names of the places in the church. This lesson may be accompanied by a church tour.

Materials

- *Activity Book*, p. 97
- Chart from previous lesson
- List of places in the church: altar, presider's chair, etc., with space for the children to draw pictures.

Optional:
- "Father, we thank thee who hast planted," *Adoremus Hymnal*, #515

Begin

Begin by reviewing the Introductory Rites, and by quizzing the students on their memorization work. You may need to recite the prayers with the students (they will often remember them if someone says it with them).

Ask the students what is the next part of the Mass: the Liturgy of the Word. Today they will learn more about this part of the Mass.

Develop

1. Read paragraphs 4 and 5 with the students and list the parts of the Liturgy of the Word:
   - First Reading
   - Responsory Psalm
   - Second Reading
   - Alleluia (Gospel Acclamation)
   - Gospel
   - Homily
   - Creed (Profession of Faith)
   - General Intercessions

2. Have the children continue working on their memorization of the I Confess and the Gloria. They should know the response used in their parish to the General Intercessions, e.g., Lord Hear Our Prayer. They should also memorize the Creed. Be sure to go through the rubrics of "Glory to You Lord" as you explain that we make a small cross on our foreheads, lips, and hearts and silently say, "May the Lord be on our minds, on our lips and in our hearts." Ask the students what this gesture means. We should think about God, speak of God, and love God.

4. You may give each student a list of the places in the church and go for a church tour. As you show the children where each of these places are, have them draw how it looks in their church. If you have examples from other churches, it would also be helpful to show them that churches can look different (often seven year olds have never been to another church, so they think all altars are the same, etc.)

5. Give them ample time to complete their task. When finished, they may continue their memory work (including the names of the parts of the Mass).

Name:___________________

This year we receive our First Communion!

Color the picture.

Faith and Life Series • Grade 2 • Chapter 26 • Lesson 2 97

Reinforce

1. Have the students complete their pictures of the places in the church.

2. Have the students continue their memory work.

3. The students may work on *Activity Book*, p. 97, and if they have not completed p. 96, they may continue to work on the word find.

Conclude

1. Together, recite the prayers for memorization.

2. You may have the students offer God their petitions, using the same formula used at Mass, e.g., Lord, hear our prayer.

3. Sing "Father, we thank thee who hast planted," *Adoremus Hymnal*, #515.

Preview

In the next lesson, we will learn more about the Liturgy of the Eucharist.

DRAW THESE PLACES IN YOUR CHURCH

1. Altar
2. Ambo
3. Presider's Chair
4. Tabernacle
5. Pew
6. Choir
7. Sanctuary
8. Baptistry
9. Vestry
10. Confessionals

NOTES

____

____

____

____

____

____

____

____

____

____

____

LESSON THREE: LITURGY OF THE EUCHARIST

Aims

The students will learn about the Liturgy of the Eucharist.

They will also learn about the altar and sacred objects.

Materials

- *Activity Book*, p. 98
- Altar Presentation (see opposite page)
- Large paper table cloth, crayons
- Vessels used during Mass

Optional:
- "Father, we thank thee who hast planted," *Adoremus Hymnal*, #515

Begin

Begin by reviewing the Introductory Rites and the Liturgy of the Word. You may review their memorization prayers, rewarding those who have successfully memorized the prayers.

Ask the students what the third part of the Mass is called: the Liturgy of the Eucharist. Explain to the students that this is the part of the Mass when the priest changes the bread and wine into Jesus' Body and Blood. Explain that they will learn more about this today.

We stand to say the *Creed*. The Creed tells what we believe as Catholics. It tells what our parents promised we would believe at our Baptism. Then, as a Church, we pray for the needs of God's people.

The Liturgy of the Eucharist begins with the *Offertory*, when the bread and wine are brought to the altar. We offer ourselves as a gift to God. Also, we give our money to help our church.

Then we kneel down, and the priest says a long prayer to prepare us for the *Holy Eucharist*. He says the words of Jesus:

> *"This is My Body."*
> *"This is the cup of My Blood."*

And the bread and wine become Jesus, our Savior.

After this we stand and say the *Our Father*, then give the sign of peace to one another. Then the people go to receive our Lord in *Holy Communion*. They kneel down and spend some time talking to Jesus, Who now lives in their souls.

The priest ends Mass with a *Blessing*, and says, "The Mass is ended. Go in peace." We leave the church, and we try to spend the rest of the day in a way that is pleasing to God.

127

Develop

1. Read paragraphs 6–8 with the students, and list on the board all the parts of the Liturgy of the Eucharist:
   - Offertory (often with a hymn and a collection)
   - Preparation of the bread and wine
   - Prayer over the gifts
   - Eucharistic Prayer (there are four main ones)
   - Preface
   - Acclamation: Holy, Holy, Holy (Sanctus)
   - Consecration:
     * This is My Body
     * This is the cup of My Blood
   - Memorial Acclamation
   - Memorial prayer
   - Intercessions
   - Doxology
   - Great Amen
   - Lord's Prayer
   - Sign of Peace
   - Breaking of the Bread
   - Lamb of God (Agnus Dei)
   - Prayers before Communion
   - Reception of Communion
   - Communion Song/Hymn (reposition of the Blessed Sacrament: Jesus goes to the Tabernacle)
   - Prayer after Communion

2. If possible, having a priest say an explanatory Mass would be wonderful.

3. As you explain the rite and all of its parts, you may also explain the vessels used during the Mass (see opposite page; also see Appendix, pp. C-4 and C-5).

4. Play a review game of the parts of the Liturgy of the Word, the Liturgy of the Eucharist, and the places and vessels used during the Mass.

Name:____________________

Instrument	What it Is	Draw It
Altar		
Chalice		
Ciborium		
Cruets		
Missal		
Paten		
Tabernacle		
Monstrance		

98 *Faith and Life Series • Grade 2 • Chapter 26 • Lesson 3*

Reinforce

1. Have the students complete *Activity Book*, p. 98.

2. Lay out a paper table cloth, and have the students draw everything used during the Mass:
   - Corporal
   - Sacramentary
   - Cruets of water and wine
   - Finger basin and towel
   - Paten
   - Purificator
   - Chalice (wine) and paten (hosts/bread)
   - Pall
   - Chalice veil and burse

Conclude

1. Say the prayers and the responses of the Mass

2. Sing "Father, we thank thee who hast planted," *Adoremus Hymnal*, #515.

Preview

In the next lesson, we will learn more about the Concluding Rite of the Mass.

ALTAR PRESENTATION

Items Needed:

- Altar
- Altar cloth
- Candles
- Crucifix
- Corporal
- Paten
- Purificator
- Cruets
- Bell
- Burse
- Candle snuffer
- Matches
- Small plate used for matches
- Storage tray for Mass materials
- Chalice
- Pall
- Chalice Veil
- Finger bowl
- Finger towel

See also Appendix, pp. C-4 and C-5.

NOTES

____
____
____
____
____
____
____
____
____
____
____

LESSON FOUR: CONCLUDING RITES

Aims

The students will learn more about the overall structure of the Mass, especially the Concluding Rite.

They will learn how the priest and the laity participate in the Mass.

Materials

- Chart of the Mass parts
- Missalettes
- Table cloth from previous day
- Cards with the parts of the Mass on them
- Vestments
- *Activity Book*, p. 99

Optional:
- "Father, we thank thee who hast planted," *Adoremus Hymnal*, #515

Begin

Review the three parts of the Mass and the prayers and responses said during these parts of the Mass. The students may follow along in the missalettes.

Using the chart on p. 128, have the students review the basic structure of the Mass, learning what the priest does and what we do during these parts of the Mass.

Parts of the Mass	What the Priest Does	What We Do
Entrance:	goes to the altar gives greeting	sing a hymn or say opening prayer ask forgiveness for our sins
Readings:	reads from the Bible	listen to the Word of God
Offertory:	offers the bread and wine to God	offer ourselves to God
Consecration:	changes the bread and wine into the Body and Blood of Jesus	offer Jesus as sacrifice to the Father
Communion:	gives the people the Body and Blood of Jesus	receive the Body and Blood of Jesus
Blessing:	blesses and dismisses the people	receive God's blessing

128

Develop

1. Finish reading the chapter from the text book.

2. Review the Concluding Rite with the students:
   - Greeting
   - Blessing
   - Dismissal
   - Closing Hymn

3. Using the table cloth from the previous day, have the students point to each of the items drawn as you point to them. If the word is also listed on p. 129, have them read to you what it says.

4. Have the students break into groups of four. Give each group a set of cards which has one part of the Mass on each card. Have them place these cards on the table/floor in the correct order of the Mass. Each group may need a bit of help. You may break the students into 4 groups, and have each group place cards in the correct order for each of the four parts of the Mass.

5. If possible, have a priest come in and show the children his vestments, and how he vests. See Appendix, pp. C-6 and C-7 for more information.

6. Explain to the children the liturgical year and colors used:
- *Purple: penance and preparation (Advent and Lent)*
- *White: feasts of the Lord, saints, Baptisms/funerals*
- *Green: hope and growth (ordinary time)*
- *Red: fire and blood (feasts of the Holy Spirit and martyrs, Palm Sunday)*
- *Rose: used twice a year for subdued penance with joy, once during Advent, and once during Lent*
- *Black: used for All Souls day, and sometimes for funerals*

Name:____________________

PARTS OF MASS	WHAT THE PRIEST DOES	WHAT WE DO
Entrance:		
Readings:		
Offertory:		
Consecration:		
Communion:		
Blessing:		

5aith and Life Series • Grade 2 • Chapter 26 • Lesson 4 99

Reinforce

1. Have the students complete *Activity Book*, p. 99.

2. Have the students draw and color the priest's vestments according to the current time of the year. They should label their picture.

3. Review the general overview of the Mass and what the priest and laity do during each of these parts (chart on p. 128 of text).

4. Continue working on the memorization material.

Conclude

1. Play a review game.

2. Pray the prayers of the people during Mass, e.g., the Lord's Prayer.

3. Sing "Father, we thank thee who hast planted," *Adoremus Hymnal*, #515.

Preview

In the next lesson, we will review the material covered in this chapter.

Vestments and Liturgical Colors Presentation

- Alb
- Amice
- Cinture
- Stole
- Chasuble

others:

- Cassock & surplice
- Humeral veil and cope

Colors: red, green, white, rose, purple, and sometimes black.

(See Appendix, pp. C-6 and C-7.)

NOTES

CHAPTER TWENTY-SIX
REVIEW AND ASSESSMENT

Aims

The students' understanding of the material covered this week will be reviewed and assessed.

Materials

- Quiz 26 (Appendix, p. A-38)
- "Father, we thank thee who hast planted," *Adoremus Hymnal*, #515

Review

1. The students should know the four parts of the Mass (Introductory Rites, Liturgy of the Word, Liturgy of the Eucharist, and the Concluding Rites).

2. They should be able to recognize all the prayers and responses said during the Mass, including:
   - I Confess
   - Gloria
   - Our Father
   - Holy, Holy, Holy
   - The Lord be with you. And also with you.

3. They should be able to recognize the priest's words of Consecration.

4. They should know the names of the places and vessels used during the Mass.

5. They should know what the priest does and what we do during the Mass, according to the chart on p. 128 of the text.

6. The students should understand why they go to Mass:
   - To worship God
   - To be nourished with God's word in the readings and in the Eucharist
   - To receive God's grace

Name:

What We Do at Mass **Quiz 26**

Fill in the chart below.

PARTS OF THE MASS	WHAT THE PRIEST DOES	WHAT WE DO
Entrance:	Goes to the Altar Gives the greeting	sing a hymn or say opening prayer and ask forgiveness of our sins
Readings:	reads from the Bible	Listen to the word of God
Offertory:	Offers the bread and wine to God	offer ourselves to God
Consecration:	changes the bread & wine into the Body and Blood of Jesus	Offer Jesus as sacrifice to the Father
Communion:	Gives the people the Body and Blood of Jesus	receive the Body and Blood of Jesus
Blessing:	blesses and dismisses the people	receive Gods' blessing

Matching:

a. Altar — d The bottles that hold the water and wine.

b. Chalice — f The plate of precious material that holds the bread which becomes the Body of Jesus at Mass.

c. Ciborium — a The table Mass is offered on.

d. Cruets — e The book with the prayers of the Mass.

e. Missal — c The cup of precious material that holds the Body of Christ which people receive at Communion.

f. Paten — b The cup of precious material that holds the wine which becomes the Blood of Jesus at Mass.

A - 38 *Faith and Life • Grade 2 • Appendix A*

Assess

1. Distribute Quiz 26. Answer any questions that they may have. When the students turn in their quiz, individually quiz them on the memorization of vocabulary and prayers that they learned this week.

2. When all quizzes have been turned in, review the correct answers.

Conclude

1. "Father, we thank thee who hast planted," *Adoremus Hymnal*, #515.

2. Pray an Our Father.

CHAPTER TWENTY-SEVEN
JESUS COMES TO US

Catechism of the Catholic Church References

Adoration of Jesus in the Eucharist: 1178, 1183, 1378–81, 1418, 2691, 2696
Altar: 1383
Christ's Presence in the Eucharist: 1088, 1373–77, 1413
Consecration of the Mass: 1352–54, 1413
Fruits of Communion: 1391–1401, 1416
Holy Communion: 1355, 1382–90, 1415, 1417
Prayer as Expression of Adoration: 2098
Presence of Christ in the Eucharist: 1373–81, 1410, 1418

Scripture References

Call of Children: Mt. 19:13–15
Bread of Life: Jn 6:35–56

Background Reading: *The Fundamentals of Catholicism* by Fr. Kenneth Baker, S.J.

Volume 3:
"My Flesh Is Real Food and My Blood Is Real Drink," pp. 232–35

Volume 3:
"The Eucharist: A Pledge of Future Glory," pp. 247–50

Summary of Lesson Content

Lesson 1

The Consecration is the part of the Mass when the bread and wine become the Body and Blood of Jesus.

Lesson 2

Jesus comes to man through Holy Communion.

The Eucharist is heavenly food for the soul.

Lesson 3

Jesus beckoned the children to come unto Him.

Lesson 4

Jesus waits for man to come to Him in the Eucharist.

LESSON ONE: THE CONSECRATION

Aims

The students will learn that the Consecration is the part of the Mass when the bread and wine become the Body and Blood of Jesus.

They will learn the four acclamations said after the Consecration.

Materials

- Flash cards with the words of Consecration, the four acclamations, and the prayer of Saint Thomas
- *Activity Book*, p. 100
- Paper, colored pencils

Optional
- "O Lord, I am not worthy," *Adoremus Hymnal*, #512

Begin

Show the students a flashcard with the word "Consecration" on it. Ask them what the Consecration is. It is the part of the Mass when the priest changes the bread and wine into the Body and Blood of Jesus. Do the children know when the Consecration takes place during the Mass?

Can the students recognize the words of the Consecration? If they can, begin with the develop section. If so, add the flash cards with the words of Consecration under the flashcard labeled Consecration.

Develop

1. Read paragraphs 1–3, p.131, with the students (ending with By praying this . . .).

2. Be sure the students can recognize the words of Consecration. Ask them who says these words (the priest). Ask the children how the bread and wine change. Explain that we must have the proper person saying them; only a priest, through Jesus Christ, can change bread and wine into Jesus' Body and Blood. He must have the right matter: bread and wine. He cannot use chips and soda, or pasta and juice. The priest must also say the right words. He cannot say just anything, it must be "This is my Body . . ." and "This is My Blood . . ."

3. Write on the board:
Minister: Priest
Matter: Bread and wine.
Form: This is My Body . . . , This is My Blood . . .
When these things are present, then Jesus becomes present on the altar in the Eucharist. This change is called "transubstantiation."

4. Quiz the students:
- Who must consecrate the Eucharist? (The priest.)
- What matter must be used?
- What must be said?
- What if you had a priest, and bread and wine, but he said "Now you're Jesus"? Is Jesus present? No.
- What if a priest said "This is My Body" and "This is My Blood," over muffins and apple juice? No.
- What if I had bread and wine and said, "This is My Body," and "This is My Blood"? No.

5. How should we respond to Jesus being made present on the altar in the Eucharist? We should tell Him that we believe.

Name:____________________

The Words of the Mass

Use your crayons to underline words from this prayer of the Mass. Follow these instructions:

- With a red crayon, underline the words that the priest says to consecrate the bread.
- With a brown crayon, underline the words that the priest says to consecrate the wine.
- With a blue crayon, underline the words calling on the Holy Spirit.
- With an orange crayon, underline the words that tell why Jesus died for us.

"Lord, You are holy indeed, the fountain of all holiness. Let Your Spirit come upon these gifts to make them holy, so that they may become the Body and Blood of Our Lord, Jesus Christ.

Before He was given up to death, a death He freely accepted, He took bread and gave You thanks. He broke the bread, gave it to His disciples and said:

> Take this, all of you, and eat it: this is My Body which is given up for you.

When supper was ended, He took the cup. Again He gave You thanks and praise, gave the cup to His disciples, and said:

> Take this, all of you, and drink from it: this is My Blood, the Blood of the new and everlasting covenant. It will be shed for you and for all so that sins may be forgiven. Do this in memory of me.

100 *Faith and Life Series • Grade 2 • Chapter 27 • Lesson 1*

Reinforce

1. Have the students complete *Activity Book*, p. 100.

2. Have them create a chart of the minister, matter, and form of this sacrament, and then draw a picture with these elements.

3. Have them memorize the question on p. 133 of their text.

4. Teach the children to sing "O Lord, I am not worthy," *Adoremus Hymnal*, #512.

Conclude

End by praying some of the prayers from the Mass and have the children say their own prayers, telling Jesus that they believe He is present in the Eucharist.

Preview

In the next lesson, we will learn how to receive Jesus and how He nourishes our souls.

THE EUCHARISTIC DISCOURSE

"Truly, truly, I say to you, unless you eat the flesh of the Son of man and drink his blood, you have no life in you; he who eats my flesh and drinks my blood has eternal life, and I will raise him up at the last day. For my flesh is food indeed, and my blood is drink indeed. He who eats my flesh and drinks my blood abides in me, and I in him. As the living Father sent me, and I live because of the Father, so he who eats me will live because of me. This is the bread which came down from heaven, not such as the fathers ate and died; he who eats this bread will live for ever."

Jn 6:53–58

NOTES

LESSON TWO: FOOD FOR THE SOUL

Aims

The students will learn how to receive Jesus.

They will learn that Jesus is food for man's soul.

Materials

- Unconsecrated hosts
- *Activity Book*, p. 101

Optional
- "O Lord, I am not worthy," *Adoremus Hymnal*, #512

Begin

Review the minister, matter, and form of the Sacrament of the Eucharist. Ask the children if Jesus in the Eucharist is the same Jesus Who walked the earth 2000 years ago. Yes. Is this the same Jesus Who performed many miracles? Yes. Is this the same Jesus Who is God? Yes. Is the Eucharist just blessed bread? No. What is the Eucharist? The Body, Blood, Soul, and Divinity of Jesus Christ. When, during Mass, does the change from bread/wine to Body/Blood occur? Consecration. What is this change called? Transubstantiation. Where can we find Jesus in our church? In the tabernacle (perhaps in a reservation chapel).

27 Jesus Comes to Us

"This is the bread which came down from heaven, not such as the fathers ate and died; he who eats this bread will live for ever."

John 6:58

A very important part of the Mass is called the **Consecration**. This is when the priest takes the bread and wine and says:

"This is My Body."
"This is My Blood."

At that moment, Jesus is there on the altar. We should all adore Jesus. We can pray the words of St. Thomas, the Apostle, when he met the risen Jesus:

"My Lord and My God."

By praying this, we are telling God that we really believe that Jesus is present.

When you receive Holy Communion, it will be one of the greatest things that ever happens to you. At Baptism you received a share in God's life. When

131

Develop

1. Read p. 131 and the top of p. 132 (until "you tell Him,") with the students.

2. Ask them if they are looking forward to their First Communion. Most will be. Ask them if they are doing any special preparations. Have them share what they are doing.

3. Reread the beginning of the last paragraph. Just as food makes our bodies grow, Holy Communion makes our souls strong and beautiful. Using the chalk talk (at right), make a chart comparing regular food and Jesus as food for our souls. You may add, under Holy Communion, Food For Our Souls:

- We are united with Jesus and His Church in a special way.
- We receive grace
- We become committed to serving the poor
- We pray for the coming of Jesus at the end of time
- We receive a pledge of the glory that will come
- We have our venial sins forgiven

4. Ask them if they know how to receive Holy Communion. They may receive either in the hand or on the tongue. If they receive in the hand, have the students cup their left hand inside the right hand, and lift their hands as high as their shoulders. They should make a throne or a manger for Jesus. When they receive, they should take Jesus with their right hand (from their left hand) and consume Our Lord in the presence of the priest (or extraordinary minister) and then make the Sign of the Cross. If they receive on their tongues, they should have their hands folded as in prayer, tilt back their heads, open their mouths wide and stick out their tongues. After consuming Our Lord, they should make the Sign of the Cross.

5. Have them practice receiving unconsecrated hosts. Hold up the host and say "The Body of Christ." They should respond: "*Amen.*" Then have them receive either in the hand or on the tongue. Practice many times, and frequently.

Name:____________________

Draw a picture of yourself spending time with Jesus after having received Him in the Holy Eucharist

When you receive First Holy Communion, it will be one of the greatest things that ever happens to you. At Baptism you received a share in God's life. When you receive Holy Communion, you will have even more of God's life. Jesus, Himself, will be with you.

Just as food makes our bodies grow, Holy Communion makes our bodies strong and beautiful. Jesus will be closer to you than ever before. He will listen to everything you tell Him.

Faith and Life Series • Grade 2 • Chapter 27 • Lesson 2 101

CHALK TALK: FOOD FOR OUR BODIES AND FOOD FOR OUR SOULS

Chalk Talk

Food for our bodies	Holy Communion Food for our souls
1. keeps us alive, must have to live	1. Must have to live God's life
2. Makes us strong, builds muscles	2. Makes us strong to resist temptation
3. Helps us grow up	3. Helps us become saints
4. Helps us stay healthy	4. Helps us to do what is right

Reinforce

1. Have the students complete *Activity Book*, p. 101.

2. Have them answer review questions, and if they get one right, they may practice receiving an unconsecrated host.

Conclude

1. Have them visit Jesus in the tabernacle, and sing "O Lord, I am not worthy," *Adoremus Hymnal*, #512.

2. End with some of the prayers from the Mass.

Preview

In the next lesson, we will learn of Jesus' desire for children to come to Him.

NOTES

LESSON THREE: LET THE CHILDREN COME

Aims

The students will learn that Jesus beckoned the children to come unto Him.

Materials

- Candy
- Children's Bible and picture of Jesus blessing children
- *Activity Book*, p. 102
- *Activity Book*, p. 103

Optional
- "O Lord, I am not worthy," *Adoremus Hymnal*, #512

Begin

You may begin the class by having the students practice receiving unconsecrated hosts. Be sure they can be heard saying "*Amen*" and that they receive the host reverently. Be sure that they do not grab for the host. Be sure that they do not use both hands to put the host in their mouths. Be sure they are making the Sign of the Cross correctly. If they do very well, reward them with a candy. If they need more practice, they may rejoin the line and practice until they merit a candy.

you receive Holy Communion you will have even more of God's life. Jesus, Himself, will be with you.

Just as food makes our bodies grow, Holy Communion makes our souls strong and beautiful. Jesus will be closer to you than ever before. He will listen to everything you tell Him.

One day, when Jesus was out teaching, lots of children came to see Him. The disciples started to say, "No, boys and girls, don't bother Jesus now." Jesus told the disciples that they were wrong. "Let the children come to me, and don't stop them. The Kingdom of Heaven is for them." Then Jesus began talking and playing with the children. He put them on His lap and blessed them.

Jesus is waiting for you to come to Him. He wants very much to hold you close and bless you.

Words to Know:

Consecration

When we eat this Bread and drink this Cup we proclaim Your death, Lord Jesus, until You come in glory.

Words from Mass

132

Develop

1. Read the third paragraph on p. 132 with the students.

2. From a children's Bible, read the account of Jesus calling the children to Him (Mt 19:13–15).

3. Ask them how they can go to Jesus:
   - They can visit Him in the tabernacle
   - They can receive Him in Communion
   - They can love Him
   - They can read about Him in the Bible, and listen to His words at Mass

4. Show a picture of Jesus blessing the children. Explain that Jesus said we are all called to become like children (Mt 18:1–6). You may read this account from the children's Bible, too.

Ask them why they think that Jesus wants all people to become as children:
- *Because of their faith*
- *Because of their love*
- *Because of their humility and obedience, etc.*

This is a good time to review the virtues proper to children, and how their hearts should be disposed to receive Jesus.

5. Give them a homework assignment (*Activity Book*, p. 102). Explain to them that they are to interview someone about his First Communion. This person may be a parent or godparent, a family friend, a teacher, or anyone else. The person should answer all the questions on the sheet and any other ones the child may have. They will be expected to make presentations during the next class based on their interviews. Answer any questions the students may have about one assignment.

6. If possible, make a visit to Jesus in the Blessed Sacrament for some time in silent prayer.

Name:____________________

My Lord and My God!

Color the picture.

Faith and Life Series • Grade 2 • Chapter 27 • Lesson 3 103

Reinforce

1. Have the students work on *Activity Book*, p. 103.

2. Distribute *Activity Book*, p. 102 for their interview assignments.

3. Have the students work on their memorization questions and Words to Know.

Conclude

1. Visit Jesus in the Blessed Sacrament.

2. Sing: "O Lord, I am not worthy," *Adoremus Hymnal*, #512.

3. Have them say whom they will interview, and pray for these people. End with praying an Our Father.

Preview

In the next lesson, we will learn about how Jesus wants us to come to Him in the Blessed Sacrament.

CATHOLIC TEACHING

- The Eucharist is no longer bread and wine
- Jesus is only under the *appearance* of bread and wine
- The Eucharist is the Real Presence
- Christ's presence remains
- He is present in every part of the Eucharist, even if the Host is broken
- The Chalice and Host each contain the entire True Presence of Christ

NOTES

____

____

____

____

____

____

____

____

____

____

____

LESSON FOUR: COME TO ME . . .

Aims

The students will present their homework interview assignments.

They will learn how Jesus waits for man to come to Him in the Eucharist.

Materials

- *Activity Book*, p. 104
- Children's Bible
- Paper, colored pencils
- Hosts, candy

Optional:
- "O Lord, I am not worthy," *Adoremus Hymnal*, #512

Begin

Have the children make their interview presentations. Be sure to praise each child for his work. Ask the children what they learned from doing the interviews and what they most liked about interviewing someone about his First Communion.

This should take most of the class time.

The Bread of Life

Holy Communion is food for our souls.

It gives us life — God's life and love.

It makes us grow — as children of God.

It keeps us healthy — by helping us do what is right.

Q. 56 *When do the bread and wine become the Body and Blood of Jesus?*
The bread and wine become the Body and Blood of Jesus when the priest says the words of Jesus: "This is My Body" and "This is the Cup of My Blood" over the bread and wine during the prayer of Consecration. This change is called transubstantiation (CCC 1375–76).

133

Develop

1. Finish reading the text from the chapter.

2. Read from the children's Bible Jn 6:35–56. Stress, "Whoever eats my flesh and drinks my blood remains in me, and I in him."

3. Explain to the students that "Communion" means "in union with." By receiving Jesus in Holy Communion, we are placed in union with Jesus. He comes to live in our souls, He brings us God's life. We are united to Jesus in such a special way; we are filled with His love. This union is so great and holy, we meet God within our hearts. Ask the children to share their excitement about being united with Jesus. You may find some examples of saints and what they said about being united with Jesus in the Eucharist (see opposite page).

4. Review the box at the top of p. 133: The Bread of Life. Have the students read this aloud, and then have them take a piece of paper, fold it in three parts, and draw each of these statements.

5. Play a review game with all the material covered in the last few chapters, including names of places in the church, things used during Mass, prayer and responses at Mass, minister/matter/form of the Eucharist, words of Consecration, etc. Reward the children for their correct answers.

6. Continue practicing receiving unconsecrated hosts. Be sure the children are doing this correctly and reverently.

Name:____________________

Write a letter to Jesus inviting Him into your soul.

Dear Jesus,

Answers will vary

____

____

____

____

____

____

____

____

____

Love,

____

104 *Faith and Life Series • Grade 2 • Chapter 27 • Lesson 4*

Reinforce

1. Have the students complete *Activity Book*, p. 104. They may share their letters with the class.

2. As a class, visit Jesus in the tabernacle for prayer time.

Conclude

1. Sing: "O Lord, I am not worthy," *Adoremus Hymnal*, #512.

2. End with prayer.

Preview

In the next lesson, we will review the material covered in this chapter.

THOUGHTS ON THE EUCHARIST

From: *Hidden Treasure: The Riches of the Eucharist* by Louis Kaczmarek, Trinity Communications, Manasses VA 22110, © 1990 ISBN 0-937495-38-7

"The Eucharist is that love which surpasses all loves in Heaven and on earth" (Saint Bernard, p. 51).
"It is not possible to have a union of love more profound and more total: He in me and I in Him; the one in the other. What more could we want?" (Saint Gemma Galgani, p. 52)
"Holy Communion is paradise on earth" (Saint Madeleine Sophie Barat, p. 52).
"The Eucharist is the point where God and the soul meet – God with all His graces, the soul with all its wants" (Bishop Fulton J. Sheen, p. 52).
"Sacrifice all earthly goods rather than a single communion" (Saint Mary Magdalene of Pazzi, p. 52).

NOTES

____

____

____

____

____

____

____

____

____

____

____

CHAPTER TWENTY-SEVEN
REVIEW AND ASSESSMENT

Aims

The students' understanding of the material covered this week will be reviewed and assessed.

Materials

- Quiz 27 (Appendix, p. A-39)
- "O Lord, I am not worthy," *Adoremus Hymnal*, #512

Review

1. The students should review that the Consecration is the part of the Mass when the priest, through Jesus Christ, changes the bread and wine into the Body and Blood of Jesus. The words He uses are: This is My Body, and This is My Blood. This change is called transubstantiation. When Jesus is made present on the altar, we should let Him know that we believe He is present.

2. The students should be able to compare food for our bodies and food for our souls:

BODY	SOUL
keeps us alive	gives us God's life
makes us strong	makes us strong to resist sin
helps us to grow up	help us become saints
keeps us healthy	helps us to do what is right and good

3. They should know that Jesus wants the children to come to Him. He waits for all people in the Eucharist.

4. The students should know how to receive Holy Communion reverently.

Name:

Jesus Comes to Us **Quiz 27**

Please answer with complete sentences.

1. What is the part of the Mass called when the priest changes bread and wine into the Body and Blood of Jesus? (1 point)
Consecration

2. What is this change called? (1 point)
Transubstantiation

3. What are the words that change the bread and wine? (2 points)
This is My Body and This is the Cup of My Blood

4. How is the Eucharist food for our souls? (1 point)
It gives us God's life and love, It makes us grow as children of God, and it keeps us healthy by helping us to do what is right

5. Who is the minister of the Sacrament of the Eucharist? (1 point)
The priest

6. Jesus wants us to come to Him. How can we do this (two ways). (2 points)
Receive Holy Communion and praying to Him.

7. What are two ways we can receive Jesus in Holy Communion? (2 points)
Either in the hand or on the tongue

Faith and Life • Grade 2 • Appendix A *A - 39*

Assess

1. Distribute Quiz 27. Read through the questions with the children and answer any questions that they may have. When they turn in their quizzes, individually test them on the Memorization Questions and Word to Know that they learned this week.

2. When all quizzes have been turned in, review the correct answers.

Conclude

1. Sing: "O Lord, I am not worthy," *Adoremus Hymnal*, #512.

2. End class with a prayer.

CHAPTER TWENTY-EIGHT
JESUS, MY LORD AND MY GOD

Catechism of the Catholic Church References

Adoration of Eucharistic Species: 1378, 1418
Christian Initiation: 1212, 1322
Christ's Presence in the Eucharist: 1088, 1373–75, 1413
Eucharist as Our Daily Bread: 2837, 2861
Eucharist as the Source and Summit of Ecclesial Life: 1324–27, 1406–7
Fruits of Communion: 1391–1401, 1416
Holy Communion: 1355, 1382–90, 1415, 1417
Presence of Christ in the Eucharist: 1373–81, 1410, 1418
Reception of Communion: 1415, 1417
Transubstantiation: 1373–77, 1413
Union with Heavenly Liturgy: 1326, 1370

Scripture References

Doubting Thomas: Jn 20:24–29

Background Reading: *The Fundamentals of Catholicism* by Fr. Kenneth Baker, S.J.

Volume 3:
"Reception of the Holy Communion," pp. 253–56

Summary of Lesson Content

Lesson 1

The first step to receiving Holy Communion is to ensure that one is not in mortal sin.

Lesson 2

The second step is to observe the Eucharistic fast.

During the Mass, one should also activity participate in the Mass.

Lesson 3

The third step is to consider Whom one is about to receive in Holy Communion and to receive Him reverently.

Lesson 4

The fourth step is to thank Him for the gift of Himself in Holy Communion.

LESSON ONE: A HEALTHY SOUL

Aims

The students will learn that the first step to receiving Holy Communion worthily is to be sure that one is not in mortal sin (has a healthy soul).

Materials

• *Activity Book*, p. 105

Optional:
• "Godhead here in hiding," *Adoremus Hymnal*, #511

Begin

Ask the students what preparations are made when you have a special guest come to your house. Do you clean? Do you put on your good clothes? Do you prepare your best food? Do you have to play outside or quietly inside? Do you have to think of what to say? etc. We, too, must prepare when we receive Jesus, our Special Guest into our souls. This week we will learn what preparations we must make before we receive our Special Guest.

Develop

1. Read the first three paragraphs from the chapter.

2. Review these paragraphs with the students and let them know that they need to get ready for their First Communion, but that they also need to prepare themselves for *every* Communion.

3. Ask them what it means to have mortal sin on their souls. There are three conditions:
i) the sin must be serious
ii) you must know the sin is serious
iii) you must freely choose to sin
(generally, breaking any of the Ten Commandments is serious matter)

What must we do if we have mortal sin on our souls? Go to Confession. Review the steps to a good Confession.
1. Know your sins
2. Be sorry for your sins
3. Decide not to sin again
4. Tell your sins to a priest in the Sacrament of Penance
5. Do your penance

You may want to arrange for your class to go to Confession.

4. In what ways can we show that we love Jesus?
- *Say our prayers*
- *Be kind to people around us*
- *Choose not to sin*
- *Obey our parents*
- *Learn our faith*
- *Pay attention at Mass, etc.*

5. Explain that if we do these things, be free from mortal sin, and show in our lives that we love Jesus, we will have healthy souls ready for Holy Communion.

Name:___________________

Write a prayer to Jesus in the Blessed Sacrament.

Dear Jesus,

Answers will vary

Love,

2aith and Life Series • Grade 2 • Chapter 28 • Lesson 1 105

Reinforce

1. Have the students work on *Activity Book*, p. 105. They may write a prayer to Jesus, telling Him how they will prepare for a good First Communion.

2. Teach the children to sing "Godhead here in hiding," *Adoremus Hymnal,* #511.

Conclude

1. If everyone has not yet had a chance to go to Confession, make arrangements for the rest of the students to receive this sacrament.

2. Help the children pray, asking God to help them to receive Him worthily in their First Communion. End by praying the Act of Contrition.

Preview

In the next lesson, we will learn about the Eucharistic fast, and remembering Whom we are about to receive in the Holy Eucharist.

HERESIES ABOUT THE EUCHARIST

Consubstantiation: The bread and wine remain as bread and wine with Jesus inside of them

Symbolism: The Eucharist is only a symbol and not the Real Presence

Temporary: The Real Presence eventually leaves and the Eucharist becomes bread and wine again

NOTES

LESSON TWO: PREPARE FOR JESUS

Aims

The students will learn that to help them prepare to receive Jesus in the Eucharist, they need to observe the Eucharistic fast.

They will learn that during the Mass, they should actively participate, and consider Whom they are about to receive in Holy Eucharist.

Materials

- Cards listing the movement of the Mass
- *Activity Book*, p. 106

Optional:
- "Godhead here in hiding," *Adoremus Hymnal*, #511

Begin

Review the first step to a worthy Holy Communion: having a healthy soul. Write on the board:

Step 1: Make sure your soul is healthy.

Have the students write under this heading what they must do, including: have no mortal sins and show in our daily lives that we love Jesus.

28 **Jesus, My Lord And My God**

"I made known to them thy name, and I will make it known, that the love with which thou hast loved me may be in them, and I in them."

John 17:26

There are things we should do to get ready for our First Communion.

First, we must make sure our souls are healthy. We may never receive **Holy Communion** if we have a mortal sin on our souls. We must receive the Sacrament of Penance first. It is a good idea to go to Confession often, even if we only have small sins. This will give us grace and make us strong enough to keep away from mortal sin.

We should try to show in our lives that we love Jesus. This means that we say our prayers morning and night, and that we obey our parents. It means being kind and loving to all those around us.

We also prepare to receive Jesus by not eating or drinking one hour before Holy Communion.

135

Develop

1. Read p. 135 and the first paragraph on p. 136.

2. *Ask the students if they are allowed to snack right before dinner or before a family gathering; Usually no. Why not? It will spoil their supper. They will not be hungry. Before receiving Holy Communion, we should not eat or drink anything for one hour. This is a sacrifice we make to show Jesus that we want to receive Him above all else. This sacrifice is called a "Eucharistic fast." (Write it on the board.) We are allowed only medicine and water during this time (the sick or very elderly and those caring for them are exempt from this fast).*

3. The next step is to pay attention during Mass and listen to Jesus. We should think about Whom we are about to receive and be aware that we are about to receive Our Lord in the Eucharist in Holy Communion. We should be reverent.

4. We should actively participate in the Mass. Actively participating means singing the hymns, saying the prayers, and making all the responses. You may want to review the prayers and responses and the movement of the Mass with the students.

5. Before we receive Jesus in Holy Communion, we should let Him know how much we want to receive Him. We can say our own prayers to Jesus and let Him know that we love Him so very much.

6. Ask the children what they would like to tell Jesus before they receive Him in Holy Communion for the first time. Let each child answer.

7. Review the first three steps to making a worthy Communion:
- Have a healthy soul
- Observe the Eucharistic fast
- Know Whom you are about to receive

Name:___________________

The steps to receiving the Blessed Sacrament worthily.

STEP 3
We must consider Whom we are about to receive. Pay attention at Mass and say the responses. Pray to Jesus. Show in you daily life that you love Jesus by your words and actions. Tell Jesus you know He is present in the Eucharist and want to receive Him.

STEP 2
We must fast for one hour before receiving Holy Communion. We may not eat or drink anything except water before Communion. (We may drink water and take medicine if we need to before Communion.) It is good to prepare to receive Jesus.

STEP 1
Make sure your soul is healthy. We may never receive Communion if we have mortal sins on our souls. Examine your conscience and go to the Sacrament of Penance first if you need to. It is good to confess venial sins, too.

106 *Faith and Life Series • Grade 2 • Chapter 28 • Lesson 2*

Reinforce

1. Have the students complete *Activity Book*, p. 106.

2. Have them continue to go to Confession (if they have not all received the sacrament).

3. Rehearse Mass prayers and responses.

Conclude

1. Teach them a prayer before Holy Communion and pray.

2. Sing with the children: "Godhead here in hiding," *Adoremus Hymnal*, #511.

3. End by praying an Act of Contrition.

Preview

In the next lesson, we will review how to receive Holy Communion, worthily.

SAINT PATRICK OF IRELAND

Saint Patrick was born around the year 385 to Roman parents living in Britain who were in charge of the Roman colony in Britain. Around the age of fourteen he was captured and taken to Ireland as a slave and shepherd, at a time when Ireland was a land of Druids and pagans. He learned their language and customs, then at age twenty escaped to the coast where sailors returned him to Gaul. He became a priest and then a bishop, and he returned to Ireland in 433. Patrick preached the Gospel, converted thousands, and built churches all over Ireland. He used the shamrock to teach about the Trinity. He is the patron saint of Ireland. His feast day is March 17.

NOTES

____

LESSON THREE: RECEIVE HIM WELL

Aims

The students will learn that they must receive Holy Communion reverently and prayerfully.

They will again practice receiving unconsecrated hosts.

Materials

- Hosts
- *Activity Book*, p. 107

Optional:
- "Godhead here in hiding," *Adoremus Hymnal,* #511

Begin

Ask the students what they say if they want to receive something. They should say "please." What do they say after they receive something? They should say "thank you." Teach the students that they should let Jesus know how much they want to receive Him before Holy Communion. They should ask to receive Him worthily and all the graces He wants to give them. After Communion it is also important to pray thanking Jesus for His gift of Himself and all His graces.

In church we get ready for Jesus by paying attention to the Mass and making the responses. During quiet times in the Mass, we can say our own prayers to Jesus. We can tell Him how glad we are that He will soon come to us.

We should walk up to receive Communion quietly. This is not the time to look around at the other people. It is time to think about Jesus. We should receive Jesus with love and respect.

When we get back to our seats we kneel down and close our eyes. We can tell Jesus anything we want. He is glad to hear it all. We can ask Him to make us more like Him and to help us not to sin. We can ask Him to bless our family and friends.

Sometimes instead of talking to Jesus, it is nice to quietly enjoy having Jesus in our hearts. He does not need to hear lots of words from us. Just say "I love you, Jesus." That is what Jesus wants to hear most of all.

Words to Know:

Holy Communion

136

Develop

1. Read paragraphs 2 and 3 on p. 136 with the students.

2. Have the students go into the church and sit in the pews. Review proper church etiquette, including genuflecting on the right knee and sitting properly in the pew.

3. Have them verbalize some of the things they may pray before they receive Holy Communion. What can they say to Jesus?
- Please, help me to make a worthy Holy Communion
- Please bring to me Your graces
- I believe You are present, my Jesus, in the Holy Sacrament of the altar
- I want to receive You because I love You!

4. Have the students practice coming forward for Communion in line. They should have their hands folded, ready to receive in the hand or on the tongue. Each child should be able to tell you how they will receive their First Communion. Note: children receiving Holy Communion in the hand should not wear gloves (it makes dropping Our Lord too easy). Be sure the students do not talk or look around. They should be thinking about Jesus.

5. Have them practice receiving unconsecrated hosts.

6. Have them return to their pews, kneel, and pray. Again, they should not be talking or looking around, but taking time to talk with Jesus.

7. Have them say out loud some of the things they can say to Jesus after receiving Him in Holy Communion.
- Thank You for coming to me
- I love You, my Lord and my God

Name:________________

What can you pray before you receive Holy Communion?

Answers will vary

What can you pray after you receive Holy Communion?

Answers will vary

Faith and Life Series • Grade 2 • Chapter 28 • Lesson 3 107

Reinforce

1. Have the students complete *Activity Book*, p 107.

2. Add to the list of the steps to a worthy First Communion:
Step 4: Receive Our Lord reverently
Step 5: Thank Jesus for coming to us in Communion

3. Have the students work on memorizing the question on p. 138.

Conclude

1. Together sing "Godhead here in hiding," *Adoremus Hymnal,* #511.

2. Spend time in front of Jesus in the tabernacle, asking Him to help the students to make a worthy First Communion.

Note: if the students are receiving Communion this week, you may want to review and practice First Communion rules: e.g., dress code, etc.

Preview

In the next lesson, we will review the steps to a worthy Holy Communion, and how we should spend our time with Jesus once we have received Him.

THE CHURCH AND SACRIFICE

Sacrifice is important in the Church, for at every Mass Christ offers Himself in sacrifice to the Father. The Son sacrificed Himself on the Cross so that we might have eternal life. The word "sacrifice" is derived from two Latin words, *sacrum* and *facere*, meaning "to make holy." It is the act of offering something precious to God; the gift is thus set apart from profane items and made holy. A true sacrifice must be a visible and/or precious item, have a priest or authorized representative presiding, have as its purpose the recognition of the supreme sovereignty of God, and it must visibly represent the invisible or inner sacrifical disposition. See also *Fundamentals of Catholicism*, Fr. Kenneth Baker, Volume 3, pp. 265–67; Ignatius Press.

NOTES

LESSON FOUR: THANK JESUS

Aims

The students will review the steps to a worthy Holy Communion.

They will also consider how they should spend their time with Jesus after they have received Him.

Materials

- *Activity Book*, p. 108.
- Book: *The Caterpillar That Went to Church*

Optional:
- "Godhead here in hiding," *Adoremus Hymnal*, #511

Begin

Have the students review the steps to a worthy Holy Communion:
1. Have a healthy soul (no mortal sin and show in your daily life that you love Jesus)
2. Eucharistic fast (no food or drink 1 hour before receiving)
3. Consider Whom you are about to receive and pay attention at Mass
4. Receive Him reverently
5. Thank Jesus for coming to you in Holy Communion

Have the children explain each step and give examples.

Before Holy Communion:

Think about Jesus and how much He loves you. Pray to Him telling Him that you:

— believe in Him.

— hope in Him.

— love Him.

— are sorry for ever offending Him.

— want Him to come to you.

After Holy Communion:

Pray to Jesus to:

— thank Him for coming to you.

— tell Him that you love Him and always want Him to be with you.

— ask Him to help you and other people.

137

Develop

1. Finish reading the text from this chapter.

2. Ask the students what happens when a guest arrives in our home. Help them to see that a guest receives all our attention. We talk with him, we look at him, we listen to him. We do things together. We do not ignore him or leave him by himself. Explain that when Jesus comes to us, we should return to our places, close our eyes, and speak only to Him. We should not be looking at our friends or talking with our neighbor. This time is for Jesus alone.

3. Ask them what are some of the things they can tell Jesus at this time:
- They can thank Him for coming to them in Communion
- They can tell Him they love Him.
- They can pray for friends and family
- They can pray for things they need
- They can tell Jesus anything; He wants to share their hearts with them

4. Read the two boxes on p. 137 of their text book. Have the students create their own lists of Before Holy Communion and After Holy Communion prayers. As they give their responses, write them on the board.

5. Tell them that just as Jesus is giving Himself to them in Holy Communion, they too, can give themselves to Jesus. In Communion, we are in union with Jesus. We can offer ourselves to the Father in union with Jesus in the Eucharist. This is the best gift we can give to God—our very selves. We should tell God that we want to do whatever He wants of us, we want to be pleasing to Him, and we ask His help that we may be His faithful servants.

6. Review the content of this chapter and this unit with the students with a game, such as Bible Baseball.

Name:____________________

Receiving Jesus

Fill in the blanks with the words below to complete the sentences.

respect one listening thank healthy

We Receive Jesus:

1. First I will ask myself if my soul is healthy.
2. I will make sure I do not eat or drink anything one hour before I receive Holy Communion.
3. I get ready for Jesus by listening and praying during Mass.
4. I receive Jesus in Holy Communion with love and respect.
5. When I get back to my seat I will thank Jesus for coming to me.

108 *Faith and Life Series • Grade 2 • Chapter 28 • Lesson 4*

Reinforce

1. Have the students complete *Activity Book*, p. 108.

2. You may read an appropriate book to the children, such as: *The Caterpillar That Went to Church.*

Conclude

1. Sing "Godhead here in hiding," *Adoremus Hymnal,* #511.

2. Have the students pray for their intentions and that they will be ready to receive Holy Communion worthily at their First Communion Mass.

Preview

In the next lesson, we will review the material covered in this chapter.

SAINT JOHN BAPTIST DE LA SALLE ON THE EUCHARIST

"Be convinced that there is in all your life no more precious time than that of Holy Communion and the moments following, during which you have the happiness to be able to speak face to face, heart to heart with Jesus."

– Saint John Baptist de la Salle
Hidden Treasure: The Riches of the Eucharist
by Louis Kaczmarek
Trinity Communications
Manasses, VA 22110
© 1990
ISBN 0-937495-38-7

NOTES

CHAPTER TWENTY-EIGHT
REVIEW AND ASSESSMENT

Aims

The students' understanding of the material covered this week will be reviewed and assessed.

Materials

- Quiz 28 (Appendix, p. A-40)
- Unit 7 Test (Appendix, pp. A-41 and A-42)
- "Godhead here in hiding," *Adoremus Hymnal,* #511

Review

1. The students should know the five steps to a worthy reception of Holy Communion.

Step 1: Have a healthy soul (in a state of grace)
- No mortal sins
- Show in your daily life that you love Jesus

Step 2: Observe the Eucharistic fast
- No food or drink for 1 hour
- Only water and medicine
- Elderly and those caring for elderly are exempt

Step 3: Know Whom you are about to receive
- Participate in the Mass
- Say the prayers and responses
- Sing the hymns
- Tell Jesus you believe He is present and you want to receive Him

Step 4: Receive Communion reverently
- Stay focused on Jesus (do not look around or talk to others)
- Receive in the hand or on the tongue

Step 5: Thank Jesus
- Spend this time with Our Lord, Who is a guest in your soul

Name:

Jesus, My Lord and My God **Quiz 28**

Write in complete sentences the five steps to a good Holy Communion.

1. We should have a healthy soul.
2. We should observe the Eucharistic fast
3. We should know Whom we are about to receive
4. We should receive Our Lord reverently.
5. We should thank Jesus for coming to us in Communion.

Write T for True and F for False

T 1. If we are in mortal sin, we must go to confession before we receive Holy Communion.

F 2. Eucharistic fast means not eating or drinking for 10 hours before receiving Holy Communion.

F 3. We must say only memorized prayers to Jesus.

T 4. We should not look around or talk to others when receiving Communion (or before or after).

T 5. We can offer ourselves to God in union with Jesus in Holy Communion.

F 6. We need to follow the steps to a worthy communion for our First Communion only.

T 7. We receive God in Holy Communion.

T 8. Jesus' Body and Blood are present in the Consecrated Host.

T 9. Jesus stays with us after Holy Communion.

T 10. Receiving Jesus in Holy Communion is the greatest thing you can do in this life.

A - 40 *Faith and Life • Grade 2 • Appendix A*

Assess

1. Distribute Quiz 28. Answer any questions that they may have. When the students turn in their quizzes, individually test them on the Memorization Questions they learned this week.

2. Review the correct answers.

3. Repeat 1 and 2 for unit test.

Conclude

1. Sing "Godhead here in hiding," *Adoremus Hymnal*, #511.

2. End by praying an Act of Contrition.

CHAPTER TWENTY-NINE
JESUS RETURNS TO THE FATHER

Catechism of the Catholic Church References

Apostles Commissioned by Christ: 2, 858–60
Ascension: 659–67
Final Apparition: 659
Jesus and the Holy Spirit: 727–30, 746
Jesus as Judge of the Living and the Dead: 678–79, 681–82
Jesus Will Return in Glory: 668–77, 680
Mission of the Apostles: 858–60, 869
Pope and the Bishops: Successors to Peter and the Apostles: 861–62, 880–87, 935–38
Vocation of the Laity: 782–86, 897–913, 940–43

Scripture References

Ascension: Acts 1:1–11
Fishers of Men and Feed my Sheep: Jn 21:1–19
Great Commission: Mt 28:16–20
Resurrection: Mt 28:16–20; Mk 16:12–20; Lk 24:13–49; Jn 20:1–13
Jesus Founded the Church: Mt 16:13–19
Denial of Jesus by Peter: Jn 13:36–38, 18:15–27; Mt 26:55–75; Mk 14:53–72; Lk 22:54–62

Background Reading: *The Fundamentals of Catholicism* by Fr. Kenneth Baker, S.J.

Volume 3:
"Who Can Hear Confessions?" pp. 304-306

Volume 3:
"The Primacy of St. Peter," pp. 107-110

Summary of Lesson Content

Lesson 1

After the Resurrection, Jesus remained on earth for 40 days.

Jesus gave His Apostles the power to forgive sins.

Jesus commissioned His Apostles to evangelize.

Lesson 2

Jesus appeared to the Apostles on the shore after the Resurrection.

Lesson 3

Jesus asked Peter three times if he loved Him. Jesus told him to feed His sheep.

Peter became the first Pope.

Lesson 4

Jesus returned to the Father; this is called the Ascension.

Jesus promised to send the Holy Spirit.

Jesus gave the Apostles the commission to teach and baptize.

Jesus will come again to judge the living and the dead.

LESSON ONE: JESUS STAYS FORTY DAYS

Aims

The students will learn that after the Resurrection, Jesus remained on earth for 40 days.

They will learn that Jesus gave His Apostles the power to forgive sins.

They will learn that Jesus sent His Apostles to teach the Good News to all people.

Materials

- Situations on cards (see opposite page)
- Paper, color pencils
- Children's Bible
- *Activity Book*, p. 109

Optional:

- "See the Conqueror mounts in triumph," *Adoremus Hymnal*, #431

Begin

Review the life of Jesus: His conception, birth, adult ministry (miracles), Last Supper, crucifixion and Resurrection. Ask them to draw the major events in Jesus' life to make a pictorial timeline. Hang this timeline around the classroom. When they get to the Resurrection, ask the children what happened next. Do they know? If Jesus was raised from the dead, did He die again? No. We will learn more about what happens today.

Develop

1. Read the first paragraph from this chapter with the children.

2. Ask them what they imagine Jesus did after the Resurrection. Did He spend time with friends and family? Did He continue teaching them about the Kingdom of God? Did He prepare His Apostles to continue His work?

3. Read from a children's Bible some of the Resurrection accounts (i.e., Mt 28:16–20; Mk 16:12–20; Lk 24:13–49; Jn 20:1–31). The children may draw or dramatize these various post-Resurrection accounts with the Lord.

4. What are some of the works Jesus continued for 40 days after His Resurrection?:

- *He explained the Scriptures and how He fulfilled them*
- *He showed He was really resurrected from the dead (He allowed people to touch Him and He ate food)*
- *He told the Apostles to go out and teach the Good News*
- *He gave the Apostles the power to forgive sins*
- *He told the Apostles to baptize all people*
- *He said He would ascend to the Father (What does ascend mean? (It will be taught in Lesson 4.)*

5. Read from the Bible Mt 16:13–19. Explain to them that because Jesus founded His Church with Peter as the head, He had to teach the Apostles (including Peter) how to run Her. The Bible had to be written, and all that Jesus had taught had to be passed down from generation to generation. It was important for Jesus to teach the Apostles all that was necessary for the Church and for the salvation of man.

6. Jesus sent out the Apostles to teach and do His work for the Church. You may discuss missionary work in the world.

Name:___________________

The Apostles

Draw a picture of Jesus sending His Apostles.

After He rose from the dead, Jesus stayed on earth for forty days. He appeared to His disciples many times. He gave the Apostles the power to forgive sins. He told them how to bring the Good News to places all over the world. An Apostle is one "who is sent." Jesus was sending them to teach all people about His saving love.

Faith and Life Series • Grade 2 • Chapter 29 • Lesson 1 109

Reinforce

1. Complete the pictures for the timeline of Jesus' life and display them around the room.

2. Have the students complete *Activity Book*, p. 109.

3. Have them discuss ways they can be Apostles (see the list of situations below for suggested discussion topics).

4. Teach them to sing "See the Conqueror mounts in triumph," *Adoremus Hymnal*, #431.

Conclude

Have the children pray to become better Apostles in the world. You may pray the First Glorious Mystery of the Rosary to conclude.

Preview

In the next lesson, we will learn about the joy of encountering Jesus.

SITUATIONS:

1. You are with a friend at lunch time, and he begins to eat without saying grace.
2. You are watching your sister/brother while your mother is inside cleaning, and some friends ask you to come and play.
3. Your friends wants you to steal some candy with them from a store.
4. You pass by an open church on your way to a ball game with some friends.
5. Your friend asks you why you go to Mass on Sunday and why you want to receive Holy Communion.
6. You hear your sister/brother lie to get out of trouble.
7. Your friend asks you who Jesus is, and why you celebrate Easter.
8. You see some poor children at school, who have no food for lunch and no mittens in the winter.

NOTES

____

____

____

____

____

____

____

____

____

____

LESSON TWO: THE JOY OF MEETING JESUS

Aims

The students will learn about the joy of meeting Jesus from the example of the Apostles on the shore after the Resurrection.

They will learn that meeting Jesus causes us to respond in love.

Materials

- Children's Bible
- *Activity Book*, p. 110

Optional:
- "See the Conqueror mounts in triumph," *Adoremus Hymnal*, #431
- Clay, buttons, paint, beads

Begin

If the students have received their First Communion, ask them what it was like to receive Jesus—to meet Him in this sacrament. Were they happy? Were they peaceful? Do they want to receive Him again? Did it change their lives?

Ask the children how meeting Jesus should affect them. What if they met Jesus when He walked the earth more than 2000 years ago? What would they have done? How can they bring this excitement to their prayer and adoration?

29 **Jesus Returns To the Father**

> To them he presented himself alive after his passion by many proofs, appearing to them during forty days, and speaking of the kingdom of God.
>
> Acts 1:3

After He rose from the dead, Jesus stayed here on earth for forty days. He appeared to His disciples many times. He gave the Apostles the power to forgive sins. He told them how to bring the Good News to places all over the world. Apostle means one "who is sent." Jesus was sending them to teach all people about His saving love.

One day, the Apostles were out in a boat, fishing. They could not find many fish. A voice from the shore called, "Throw your nets to the right side." It was Jesus, but they didn't know it. They did what He said and pulled up so many fish that they could not lift the net.

Then John, the Apostle, knew Who was on the shore. "It's the Lord," he shouted. Peter was so excited that he jumped into the water and swam to the beach.

140

Develop

1. Read paragraphs 2 and 3 with the students.

2. Read the same account from the children's Bible: Jn 21:1–14. They may discuss this reading:
   - Did the Apostles know it was Jesus on the shore?
   - How did they recognize Him?
   - Were they having a hard time catching fish?
   - Why were they fishing? (especially when they were taught by Jesus to begin the Church!)
   - How did they trust Jesus? (by throwing in their nets to the right)
   - What was the result?

3. Ask the children how they are like the fish in this story. If the Apostles were fishermen, and they were fishing for believers, we are the believers: we are the fish caught by faith. (Optional craft: see opposite page).

4. The word "Ichthys" means fish; its letters were made in Greek to stand for "Jesus Christ, Son of God, Savior" by the early Christians. The children may adapt their fish to be Ichthys fish to show that they are believers in Christ.

5. *Discuss how the students can be fishers of men and be Apostles, too.*

6. *How did the Apostles respond to their meeting with Jesus? What did Peter do? How would the children respond if they saw Jesus on the shore? Would meeting Jesus change their lives? How should we respond (short-term and long-term)?*
   - *We should act as Christians*
   - *We would worship as Catholics and pray more*
   - *We would love our neighbors*
   - *We would act as believers, live in charity, etc.*

Name:____________________

It is the Lord!

One day, the Apostles were out in a boat, fishing. They could not find many fish. A voice from the shore called, "Throw your nets to the right side." It was Jesus, but they didn't know it. They did what He said and pulled up so many fish that they could not lift the net.

Then, John, the Beloved Disciple, knew Who was on the shore. "It's the Lord," he shouted. Peter was so excited that he jumped into the water and swam to the beach.

What would you do if you knew Jesus was close by?
Answers will vary

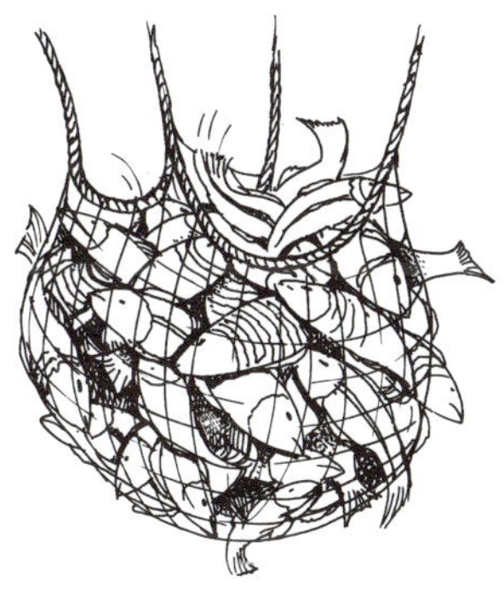

110 *Faith and Life Series • Grade 2 • Chapter 29 • Lesson 2*

CAUGHT BY FAITH: WE'RE THE FISH

Make fish from modeling clay, decorating them with buttons/glitter/beads, etc. for eyes, scales, and other features.. The children may paint them, or even write their names on them.

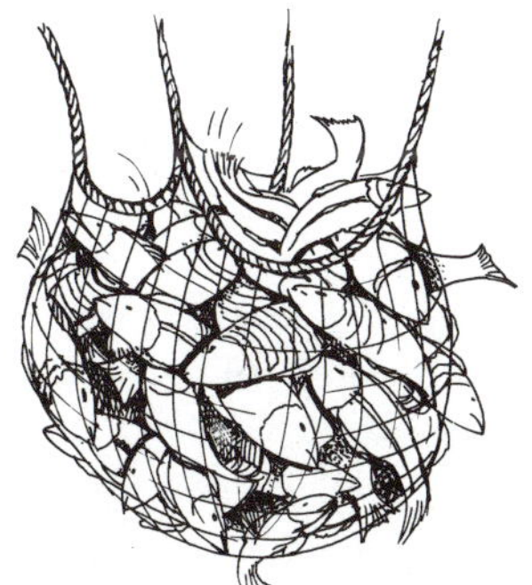

Reinforce

1. Have the students complete *Activity Book*, p. 110.
2. Have them create their fish (optional).

Conclude

1. Sing as a class: "See the Conqueror mounts in triumph," *Adoremus Hymnal*, #431.
2. End by praying the Acts of Faith, Hope, and Charity.

Preview

In the next lesson, we will learn more about the Church Jesus founded.

NOTES

LESSON THREE: FEED MY SHEEP

Aims

The students will learn that Jesus called Peter to ministry as the main servant of His Church.

They will learn the story of Jesus and Peter on the shore after the Resurrection.

Materials

- Children's Bible
- Lineage of Popes
- *Activity Book*, p. 111

Optional:
- "See the Conqueror mounts in triumph," *Adoremus Hymnal*, #431

Begin

Review the events surrounding Jesus' trial, when Peter denied Jesus three times. You may read this from a children's Bible: (Jn 13:36–38, 18:15–27; Mt 26:55–75; Mk 14:53–72; Lk 22:54–62). Ask them how many times Peter denied Jesus. Three. Ask them how they would feel if they loved someone and that person denied that he knew them. Would they be hurt? Yes. From his denial, it would seem that the one they loved did not love them in return. This idea is important so that they may understand the passage in today's lesson.

There on the shore, a fire was built. Fish were being cooked. Jesus asked the Apostles to eat. After they ate, Jesus asked Peter three times, "Do you love Me?" Each time Peter said, "You know that I love you." Then Jesus said, "Feed my sheep. Feed my lambs." This meant that Jesus wanted Peter to take care of all His followers. Peter became the first Pope.

Soon the time came for Jesus to go back to His Heavenly Father. The Apostles were sad that He was going. They did not feel ready to go and preach without Jesus at their side. But Jesus promised to send the Holy Spirit. He would show them what to do and make them strong enough to do it.

Jesus walked up a mountain with His friends. "Go and teach everyone. Baptize them in the Name of the Father, and of the Son, and of the Holy Spirit. I will be with you always, even to the end of time."

Then Jesus rose up into the sky and went back to Heaven. This was the **Ascension**. Jesus is King of Heaven and earth. He has prepared a place in Heaven for all those who love Him. Someday, at the end of the world, Jesus will come again to judge the living and the dead.

Words to Know:

Apostles Ascension

141

Develop

1. Read paragraph 4 with the students. Explain that this event happened right after yesterday's reading when Peter jumped from the boat and swam to the shore to meet Jesus.

2. How do they think Peter felt, seeing Jesus, after having denied Him three times? Did he feel sad? Guilty? How did Jesus speak to Peter? Was He angry? Did He tell Peter that He did not love Peter?

3. Read from a children's Bible the whole account found in Jn 21:1–14. Have the children discuss this passage:
- Why did Jesus ask Peter if he loved Him? How many times did He ask Peter?
- What was Peter's response?
- What did Jesus say after Peter told Jesus that he loved Him?
- What did Jesus mean by saying: "Feed my sheep, Feed my lambs."? Who are the sheep and lambs? (We are.)
- Why did Jesus ask Peter to feed his sheep and lambs, when Peter had denied Our Lord?
- What job did Peter have? (He was the first Pope.) What does a Pope do?
- What other time did we see Peter being given the job of taking care of Jesus' followers? (Mt 16:13–19, you may want to reread this from the children's Bible)

4. Discuss our current Pope. Who is he? What does he do? Explain how he is a successor of Peter. You may want to show a list of Popes dating from the present day all the way back to Peter. (This list can often be found in a Catholic Encyclopedia or source book).

5. Discuss the image of sheep. Jesus is the Good Shepherd. What are sheep like? They follow their shepherd and know his voice. They are fed and lead to safety. How are we like sheep in the Church with the Pope as a shepherd?

Name:____________________

Do you love me?

Draw Peter swimming to meet Jesus on the shore.

You know that I love you.

Faith and Life Series • Grade 2 • Chapter 29 • Lesson 3 111

Reinforce

1. Have the students color *Activity Book*, p. 111.

Conclude

1. Have the children pray that they may be faithful sheep, following Christ through His Church.

2. Sing "See the Conqueror mounts in triumph," *Adoremus Hymnal*, #431.

3. End by praying the Acts of Faith, Hope, and Charity.

Preview

In the next lesson, we will learn about the events surrounding the Ascension.

PAPAL INFALLIBILITY

Papal infallibility is implied in Scripture, though it was not defined until 1870 at the First Vatican Council. This is not to say that the Church did not hold this to be true, for any doctrine that the Church proclaims is not new but becomes their official teaching. In this case, Christ granted a charism (a specific gift or grace of the Holy Spirit which may directly or indirectly benefit the Church) to the Successors of Peter so that in declaring doctrine regarding faith and morals, the Holy Spirit protects him from error. This does not apply to everything the Pope says, such as his daily teaching as the bishop of Rome. Infallibility applies only to the doctrines he officially proclaims for the Universal Church on matters of faith and morals.

NOTES

LESSON FOUR: THE ASCENSION

Aims

The students will learn that Jesus returned to the Father. This is called the Ascension.

They will learn that before the Ascension, Jesus promised to send the Holy Spirit. Jesus also gave the Apostles the commission to teach and baptize.

They will learn that Jesus will come again.

Materials

- Children's Bible
- *Activity Book*, p. 112

Optional:

- "See the Conqueror mounts in triumph," *Adoremus Hymnal*, #431
- "Jesus Ascends into Heaven," video; Jesus: A Kingdom Without Frontiers

Begin

Recount the story of Jesus appearing to Mary Magdalene at the tomb (found in Jn 20:1–17). This passage ends with "I have not yet ascended to My Father." Ask them if they know what this means. Do they think the Apostles or Mary Magdalene knew what He meant? Write the word "Ascension" on the board, and explain that the Ascension is when Jesus rose up into the sky, body and soul, and returned to His Father. Ask the children if this happens often. Have they ever seen anyone lift himself off the ground and disappear into the sky? No. This was an amazing event.

"Go into all the world and preach the gospel to the whole creation."

Mark 16:15

Q. 58 *What did Jesus Christ do after His Resurrection?*
After His Resurrection, Jesus Christ remained on earth for forty days. Then He ascended into Heaven (CCC 659).

142

Develop

1. Read the rest of the chapter with the students. Go through these paragraphs with them, asking questions:
   - What do we mean by "Jesus would go back to the Father"? Where is the Father? (Heaven)
   - Why were the Apostles sad?
   - Were the Apostles ready to do Jesus' work? Did they feel ready?
   - What did Jesus promise to send to them?
   - Why is the Holy Spirit important? What will He help the Apostles do?
   - What did Jesus say to the Apostles on the mountain?
   - What is Baptism? Explain the rite, and the effects (washes away Original Sin, adopts us into God's family, fills us with grace)
   - What are ways Jesus is with us until the end of time? In prayer, in the Church, in a special way in the Eucharist.
   - Where did Jesus go? What is He doing there?

2. Read the same account from the children's Bible: Acts 1:1–12. What did the angels say about Jesus? When will Jesus come again? How should we live while we wait for Him to come again?

3. Have the children look at the picture on p. 139 of their text books. What would it have been like to have been at the Ascension?

4. Watch "Jesus Ascends into Heaven," video from the series Jesus: A Kingdom Without Frontiers, available through Ignatius Press; 30 minutes.

5. Discuss the feast of Christ the King. If Christ is the King, and we are His family, will we inherit the Kingdom of God? How must we live in order to get into the Kingdom? How were we adopted into God's family? Remind the students of the importance of Baptism.

Name:________________

Color the picture of Jesus' Ascension.

As the Apostles watched, Jesus rose up into the sky and went back to Heaven. There He is King of Heaven and earth. He has prepared a place in Heaven for all who are faithful to Him. He is at the right hand of the Father. With the Father, He sent the Holy Spirit.

112 *Faith and Life Series • Grade 2 • Chapter 29 • Lesson 4*

Reinforce

1. Have the students complete *Activity Book*, p 112.

2. You may have a celebration of Christ the King, with a litany to Jesus, King of Heaven and earth, and a crowning of Our Lord (if you have a statue).

3. Have the students work on the memorization questions and the Words to Know.

Conclude

1. Sing "See the Conqueror mounts in triumph," *Adoremus Hymnal*, #431.

2. Pray the Second Glorious Mystery of the Rosary.

3. End with praying the Acts of Faith, Hope and Charity.

Preview

In the next lesson, we will review the material covered in this chapter.

ELIJAH: PRE-FIGURING THE ASCENSION

Elijah, a Tishbite, was a great prophet of the Old Testament whose life is recounted almost entirely in the First Book of Kings. Elijah wore a garment of animal skins and dwelt in caves or clefts in the mountains. One of the more well-known incidents in his life is the contest between the priests of Baal and their god, and the True God, Yahweh, on Mount Carmel. All of their pleading could not illicit a response from Baal, while Yahweh answered immediately (I Kings 18:17–40). God took Elijah from this earth alive. One day, while speaking to one of his followers, a chariot of fire with fiery horses appeared from the sky and carried him away in a whirlwind to Heaven (2 Kings 2:11). Tradition holds that Elijah will return as a prophet at the end of the world.

NOTES

CHAPTER TWENTY-NINE:
REVIEW AND ASSESSMENT

Aims

The students' understanding of the material covered this week will be reviewed and assessed.

Materials

- Quiz 29 (Appendix, p. A-43)
- "See the Conqueror mounts in triumph," *Adoremus Hymnal*, #431

Review

1. The students should know that Jesus remained here on earth for 40 days after the Resurrection. (They should know what the Resurrection is.)

2. Review that Jesus gave His Apostles the power to forgive sins and told them how to bring the Good News to all people. An apostle is one "who is sent."

3. They should be able to give various accounts of the Risen Lord, and what He did during those 40 days:
   - He explained the Scriptures and how He fulfilled them
   - He showed He was really Resurrected from the dead (He allowed people to touch Him, and He ate food, too)
   - He told the Apostles to go out and teach the Good News
   - He gave the Apostles the power to forgive sins
   - He told the Apostles to baptize all people
   - He said He would ascend to the Father. What does this mean?

4. They should know that Jesus established Peter as the first Pope, and how.

5. They should be able to recount the events of the Ascension, including:
   - Jesus promised to send the Holy Spirit
   - Jesus told His Apostles to teach and baptize all people
   - Jesus will come again!

Name:

Jesus Returns to the Father **Quiz 29**

Circle the correct answer.

1. After the Resurrection, Jesus stayed on earth for how long?
   a) 40 days b) 4 months c) 4 years

2. After the Resurrection, Jesus gave the Apostles the power to:
   a) Consecrate the Eucharist b) forgive sins c) ascend into Heaven

3. How many times did Jesus ask Peter if he loved Him?
   a) one time b) two times c) three times

4. Jesus had to go:
   a) to Galilee b) to be with Mary c) back to the Father

5. Jesus promised to send:
   a) many followers b) the Holy Spirit c) angels

6. On the mountain, Jesus told His Apostles to:
   a) teach and heal b) teach and baptize c) fish and baptize

7. How long will Jesus be with us?
   a) for many years b)until the Holy Spirit comes c) always

8. We call Jesus' rising into the sky:
   a) the Resurrection b) the Ascension c) the Assumption

9. In Heaven, Jesus is:
   a) having a well-deserved holiday
   b) preparing a place for those who love Him
   c) all alone

10. When will Jesus come again?
    a) only the Apostles know the time b) never c) at the end of time

Faith and Life • Grade 2 • Appendix A *A - 43*

Assess

1. Distribute Quiz 29 and answer any questions that the students may have. When the students turn in their quizzes, individually test them on the Memorization Questions and Words to Know from the week.

2. When all quizzes have been turned in, review the correct answers with the class.

Conclude

1. Sing "See the Conqueror mounts in triumph," Adoremus Hymnal, #431.

2. Pray for the students' intentions.

CHAPTER THIRTY
THE COMING OF THE HOLY SPIRIT

Catechism of the Catholic Church References

Christ's Spirit in the Fullness of Time: 717–30, 745–46
Church Manifested by the Holy Spirit: 767–68
Gifts of the Holy Spirit: 768, 798–801, 1830–31, 1845
Holy Spirit in the Old Testament: 702–16, 744
Holy Spirit: 683–88, 742
 In Baptism: 1266
 At Confirmation: 1303
Names, Titles, and Symbols of the Holy Spirit: 691–701
Pentecost: The Holy Spirit and the Church: 731–41, 746–47, 767–68
Sacramental Economy: 1076
Sacraments of Christ and Church: 1114–21

Scripture References

Pentecost: Acts 2:1–4

Background Reading: *The Fundamentals of Catholicism* by Fr. Kenneth Baker, S.J.

Volume 2:
"The Origin of the Holy Spirit," pp. 96–99

Volume 3:
"A Sacrament Is a Sacred Sign," pp. 163–66

Summary of Lesson Content

Lesson 1

After the Ascension, the Apostles stayed in the upper room with Mary, preparing for the coming of the Holy Spirit.

After nine days, the Holy Spirit came; this is called Pentecost.

Lesson 2

The Holy Spirit came upon the Apostles and filled them with strength and courage.

The Apostles went out to teach about Jesus.

Around 3000 people were baptized that day.

Lesson 3

The Holy Spirit is the Third Person of the Holy Trinity.

The Holy Spirit comes to man at Baptism. He helps man to pray and to love. He gives us grace.

On Pentecost Sunday we celebrate the descent of the Holy Spirit, also recognized as the birthday of the Church.

Lesson 4

There are seven sacraments: Baptism, Penance, Eucharist, Confirmation, Marriage, Holy Orders, and Anointing of the Sick.

LESSON ONE: PENTECOST

Aims

The students will learn how Mary and the Apostles prepared for the coming of the Holy Spirit.

They will learn that after nine days or praying, the Holy Spirit came. This event is called Pentecost.

Materials

- Candle, matches, fan
- Children's Bible
- *Activity Book*, p. 113

Optional:
- "Come, Holy Ghost, Creator blest," *Adoremus Hymnal*, #443

Begin

Have the students gather around a fan that is turned on and ask them to describe the wind:
- It makes some noise
- It is strong
- It is present everywhere
- It may make the children happy

Write these words on the board. (See Chalk Talk on facing page.)
Have the students gather around a lit candle and have them describe the flame.
- It is warm/hot
- It gives light (try this in the dark)
- It melts the wax

Write their descriptions on the board as well.

30 The Coming of The Holy Spirit

And suddenly a sound came from heaven like the rush of a mighty wind, and it filled all the house where they were sitting. And there appeared to them tongues of fire, distributed and resting on each one of them.

Acts 2:2–3

After the Ascension the Apostles stayed in a house with Mary. They prayed together for nine days. Then, all at once, the sound of a great wind filled the house. Little flames of fire came and rested on each of them.

The Apostles were filled with the Holy Spirit. They were not afraid anymore. They left the house and began to teach about Jesus. The Holy Spirit had given them many gifts. One was that people from all over the world could understand what the Apostles were saying. The Holy Spirit helped them to preach so well that many people believed in Jesus. Three thousand people were baptized that day!

The Holy Spirit that came to the Apostles is the Third Person of the Holy Trinity. The Holy Spirit

143

Develop

1. Read the first paragraph of the chapter on p. 143.

2. From a children's Bible, read the account of Pentecost: Acts 2:1–4.

3. Have the students discuss the picture on p. 144 of the text.
   - Who is in the picture?
   - What is the dove? Whom does it represent? (Add the third column of Chalk Talk to the first two of wind and fire on the board). Describe a dove (sign of peace, gentle, graceful, etc.)
   - What is everyone doing?
   - What is on top of everyone's head?
   - Are the people happy?

4. Quiz the students on the events of Pentecost.
   - How did Mary and the Apostles prepare for the coming of the Holy Spirit?
   - Where did they go?
   - What did they do?
   - For how long?

5. *Explain to them Who the Holy Spirit is. The Holy Spirit is God, the Third Person of the Holy Trinity. Jesus and the Father sent the Holy Spirit. He helps the Church to remember all that Jesus taught the Apostles, and keeps the Church faithful in her teachings. The Holy Spirit brings us God's life, called grace. The Holy Spirit makes us become holy. The Holy Spirit is often depicted as the wind, fire or light, a dove, and sometimes as the finger or hand of God.*

6. You may explain the practice of novenas, which are nine day prayers for a special intention. The first novena was the preparation, praying for the coming of the Holy Spirit at Pentecost. There are many novenas to use as examples.

Name:____________________

Pentecost

Color the picture of the Pentecost

Faith and Life Series • Grade 2 • Chapter 30 • Lesson 1 113

Reinforce

1. Have the students color *Activity Book*, p. 113. Can they name the Apostles? (They may look them up in Mt 10:2–4.)

2. Teach the children to sing "Come, Holy Ghost, Creator blest," *Adoremus Hymnal*, #443.

Conclude

1. You may want to pray a novena as a class, e.g., the novena to the Holy Spirit.

2. Pray to the Holy Spirit (p. 147 text), or the Third Glorious Mystery of the Rosary.

Preview

In the next lesson, we will learn how the coming of the Holy Spirit helped the Apostles.

CHALK TALK: THE COMING OF THE HOLY SPIRIT

NOTES

____

____

____

____

____

____

____

____

____

____

LESSON TWO: THE BIRTHDAY OF THE CHURCH

Aims

The students will learn that the Holy Spirit came upon the Apostles and filled them with strength and courage.

They will learn that the Apostles went out to teach about Jesus. Three thousand people were baptized that day.

Pentecost is the birthday of the Church.

Materials

- Doll, basin, water, scoop, white gown, candle, Baptism rite
- *Activity Book*, p. 114

Optional:
- "Come, Holy Ghost, Creator blest," *Adoremus Hymnal*, #443
- "The Acts of the Apostles," video; Jesus: A Kingdom Without Frontiers

Begin

Review how the Holy Spirit came at Pentecost. They should know that Mary and the Apostles went into the upper room and prayed for nine days, then the Holy Spirit came as in a wind, and descended like flames onto the Apostles. They should also know that images of the Holy Spirit include: wind, fire, and the dove (and why – e.g., the Holy Spirit came into the upper room as a strong wind and He gives us the strength to do God's will, but He works as the wind works, without being seen, etc.)

Develop

1. Review with the students that the Apostles and Mary went into the upper room to pray because they were told to prepare for the coming of the Holy Spirit. They were also afraid of the people outside, who had just recently killed Jesus, their leader. Perhaps they were scared for their lives. Maybe they were also sad because Jesus had left them again.

2. Read the second paragraph of Chapter 30 with the students. Discuss this reading with the students:
   - What happened to the Apostles? Were they scared any more?
   - What were some of the gifts the Holy Spirit gave to the Apostles?
   - How many people were baptized that day?

3. Explain that Baptism is necessary for the forgiveness of sins and that we are filled with grace when we are baptized. You may want to review the rite with a pretend Baptism of a doll.

4. Explain to the children that at Baptism, the Holy Spirit comes to us and brings us His gifts, too. They are found in the box on the opposite page. Have the students give you examples of how they can use each gift as you explain each of the gifts to them. For example:
   - *Wisdom: to see God's plan in choosing our parents*
   - *Understanding: to love our neighbors, even when they hurt us*
   - *Counsel: to choose to obey God through His Laws*
   - *Knowledge: to study our faith in class*
   - *Fortitude: to pray every night, even when we do not want to*
   - *Piety: to love God with all our hearts, and try to show Him all the time the love we have for Him*
   - *Fear of the Lord: never to want to sin*

5. Have them share which of the gifts of the Holy Spirit they use and how.

Name:____________________

Word Find

APOSTLE	THIRD PERSON	PRAYED
BAPTIZED	FIRE	TEACH
HOLY SPIRIT	GIFTS	TRINITY
PENTECOST	JESUS	WIN
PREACH	MARY	

B A P T I Z E D W I N P
S T H I R D P E R S O N
A P R E A C H C I S T P
C J M A R Y R T N C R E
R E P R A Y E D T A I N
I S B R E A D M E P N T
F U C H U R C H R L I E
I S L I G R A C E E T C
T E A C H G I F T S Y O
E I G I F T S F I R E S
H O L Y S P I R I T L T
D E R C O A P O S T L E

114 *Faith and Life Series • Grade 2 • Chapter 30 • Lesson 2*

Reinforce

1. Have the students work on *Activity Book*, p. 114.

2. You may show "The Acts of the Apostles," video from the series Jesus: A Kingdom Without Frontiers, available through Ignatius Press; 30 minutes.

Conclude

1. Pray the novena prayer and/or the prayer to the Holy Spirit, p. 147 of the text.

2. Sing "Come, Holy Ghost, Creator blest," *Adoremus Hymnal*, #443.

Preview

In the next lesson, we will learn more about the Holy Spirit and Pentecost Sunday.

GIFTS OF THE HOLY SPIRIT

- Wisdom – to see things as God does
- Understanding – to have a caring heart
- Counsel – to make good decisions
- Knowledge – to know our faith
- Fortitude – to do what is right, even when it is hard
- Piety - to love God and our neighbor
- Fear of the Lord - to know God is present

NOTES

____
____
____
____
____
____
____
____
____
____

LESSON THREE: COME HOLY GHOST

Aims

The students will review that the Holy Spirit is the Third Person of the Holy Trinity.

They will learn about Pentecost Sunday. It is the day in the Church year when we celebrate the descent of the Holy Spirit. It is also recognized as the birthday of the Church.

Materials

- Picture of red vestments or a display of red vestments
- Birthday cake, candles, matches
- *Activity Book*, p. 115

Optional:

- "Come, Holy Ghost, Creator blest," *Adoremus Hymnal*, #443
- "The Acts of the Apostles," video; Jesus: A Kingdom Without Frontiers

Begin

Ask the students about their birthdays. When are they? Why do they celebrate them? The day they were born into this world is special. Did they have life before they were born? Yes, when they were inside their mothers, they would move, yawn, and even suck their thumbs!

So, too, the Holy Spirit existed before Pentecost. We saw the Holy Spirit at the Annunciation and at the Baptism of Jesus. When the Holy Spirit came into the world at Pentecost we had the first "birthday" of the Church.

came to us at Baptism. He helps us to pray and to love. He gives us the grace to win the fight against sin. He helps us understand the things we learn about God.

The day the Holy Spirit came to the Apostles is called **Pentecost** Sunday. We celebrate this day in church each year. We also call Pentecost Sunday the "Birthday of the Church." Those who were baptized on Pentecost were the first members.

We have talked a lot this year about the Sacraments of Baptism, Penance, and the Holy Eucharist. A sacrament is a special gift from Jesus that gives us grace. Whenever a sacrament is received, special words and things are used as signs of the grace God gives us. There are seven sacraments in all:

1. **Baptism:** When Original Sin is washed away. We receive the new life of grace and become children of God.

2. **Penance:** When our sins are forgiven by Jesus through the priest.

3. **Holy Eucharist:** When we receive the Body and Blood of Jesus under the appearance of bread and wine.

145

Develop

1. Read the rest of p. 143 and the first two paragraphs on p. 145 with the students.

2. Review the Holy Trinity. When do we hear the names of the Persons of the Trinity? Did we hear them when reviewing the Sacrament of Baptism? Yes, because we are baptized in the Name of the Father, and of the Son, and of the Holy Spirit.

3. We believe in one God in three Persons. The Father is the First Person. The Son is the Second Person, and the Holy Spirit is the Third Person. The Father is not the Son or the Holy Spirit. The Son is not the Father or the Holy Spirit. And the Holy Spirit is not the Father or the Son. But all three Persons are God. All three Person have always existed.

4. The Holy Spirit is the love between the Father and the Son, so real that He is another Person! You may tell the students that "Your mother and father love each other so much that they had you!" You are not your mother, nor your father, but together you are one family.

5. The Father is often known as the Creator (He created Heaven and earth). The Son, Who became man in the Divine Person of Jesus, is often known as the Savior (He saved us from our sins, for Himself). The Holy Spirit is often known as the Sanctifier (He makes us holy or "sanctified"). From Jesus, we know about the Trinity and the work that each Person does. We must believe all of this by faith because it is a mystery.

6. We celebrate Pentecost in the Church year 50 days after Easter. The priest wears red (like the fire of the Holy Spirit). Pentecost is called the Church's birthday because by the Holy Spirit coming into the world, He brought God's life to the Church. Celebrate Pentecost with a birthday party.

Name:____________________

Holy Spirit

The Holy Spirit, Who came to the Apostles, is the Third Person of the Trinity. The Holy Spirit came to us at Baptism. He helps us to pray and to love. He gives us the grace to win the fight against sin. He helps us to understand the things we learn about God. He will come to us in a special way when we are confirmed.

Color the picture.

Faith and Life Series • Grade 2 • Chapter 30 • Lesson 3 115

Reinforce

1. Have the students complete *Activity Book*, p. 115.

2. They should memorize their question(s) in the textbook and the Words to Know.

3. The students may have a Pentecost/Church birthday party.

4. If you have not already done so, you may show "The Acts of the Apostles," video from the series Jesus: A Kingdom Without Frontiers, available through Ignatius Press; 30 minutes.

Conclude

1. Lead the children in praying the novena prayer and/or the prayer to the Holy Spirit on p. 147 of the text.

2. Sing "Come, Holy Ghost, Creator blest," *Adoremus Hymnal*, #443.

3. Have the class assist in cleaning up after your Pentecost/Church birthday party.

Preview

In the next lesson, we will learn an overview of the seven sacraments.

CHALK TALK: THE TRINITY

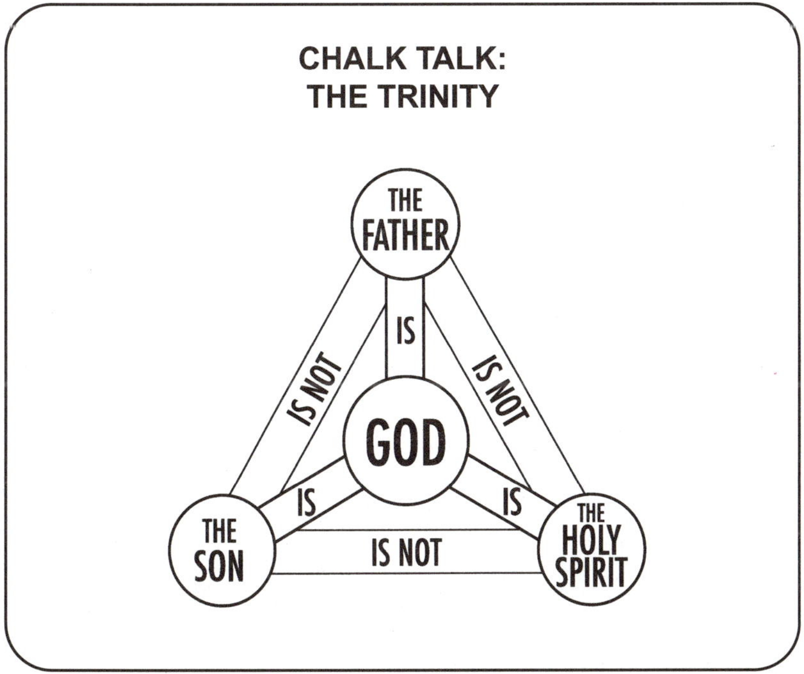

NOTES

LESSON FOUR: THE SACRAMENTS

Aims

The children will learn that God gives us His life in the sacraments, which are special gifts from Jesus.

There are seven sacraments: Baptism, Penance, Eucharist, Confirmation, Marriage, Holy Orders, and Anointing of the Sick.

Materials

- Cards or posters with symbols of the seven sacraments
- Drawing paper and pencils/crayons
- *Activity Book*, p. 116

Optional:
- "Come, Holy Ghost, Creator blest," *Adoremus Hymnal*, #443

Begin

Ask the students if they know what a sacrament is. It is a gift from Jesus that gives us grace. Jesus gave us seven sacraments. Can the children name any of them? They have received three of them already:
Baptism, Penance and the Eucharist. The others are Confirmation, Matrimony, Holy Orders, and Anointing of the Sick.
You may show the children the symbols representing each sacrament as you name them.

4. Confirmation: When the Holy Spirit comes to us with His gifts, just as He did to the Apostles at Pentecost. Grownups and older boys and girls receive this sacrament.

5. Marriage: When a man and a woman marry each other they stand before the Church and make promises to live together according to God's Laws, and to help each other grow holy.

6. Holy Orders: When a man receives this sacrament he becomes a priest. A bishop lays hands on the man's head and confers on him the Sacrament of Holy Orders. This man then has the power from God to forgive sins and say Mass.

7. Anointing of the Sick: When someone is very sick or in danger of death, a priest can anoint him with holy oil. This will give him the grace to die in God's friendship, or it may even heal him of the sickness.

Words to Know:

Pentecost

146

Develop

1. Read pp. 145 and 146 of the text.

2. Using the material in the textbook, explain each of the seven sacraments. The students should know the name and effect of each of the sacraments from this reading. Ask the children about the sacraments they have received: Do they know the minister, the matter and form, too? Teach them these for every sacrament. Then quiz the children on the sacraments. You may make this into a game.

3. You may want to teach them that there are three groups of sacraments: initiation, healing and service/ministry. The sacraments of initiation are Baptism, Confirmation, and Eucharist. These bring us into union with the Church.
The sacraments of healing are Penance and Anointing of the Sick. They heal our souls (and sometimes our bodies, too).
The sacraments of ministry or service are Matrimony (marriage) and Holy Orders. Through these sacraments, we help each other to get to Heaven.

4. Distribute drawing paper. Have the students turn the paper sideways and fold it in half lengthwise. Using the straight edge, they should then divide the top half into three sections and the bottom half into four sections. In each of the seven sections the students should draw a symbol for each of the seven sacraments.
- *Baptism: water, Baptism font, shell, candle, white gown*
- *Confirmation: flask of oil, bishop's mitre, flames, dove*
- *Eucharist: chalice and host, wheat and grapes*
- *Penance: purple stole, hands raised in blessing*
- *Marriage: wedding rings*
- *Holy Orders: hands on head, folded hands*
- *Anointing of the Sick: flask of oil, candles*

5. Play a review game.

Q. 59 *Who is the Holy Spirit?*
The Holy Spirit is God, the Third Person of the Holy Trinity (CCC 685).

We Pray:

Come Holy Spirit,
fill the hearts of your faithful
and enkindle in us the fire of Your Love.

147

Reinforce

1. Have the students complete *Activity Book*, p. 116.

2. Have them complete their posters of the symbols for the seven sacraments.

3. Have them work on their memorization questions and Word to Know.

Conclude

1. Pray the prayer to the Holy Spirit, p. 147 of the text.

2. "Come, Holy Ghost, Creator blest," *Adoremus Hymnal*, #443.

Preview

In the next lesson, we will review the material covered in this chapter.

SACRAMENT	MATTER	FORM	MINISTER
Baptism	Water	I baptize you in the Name of the Father and of the Son and of the Holy Spirit	Usually a priest, but anyone in emergency
Penance	forgiveness	I absolve you from your sins in the Name of the Father and of the Son and of the Holy Spirit	The priest
Eucharist	Bread and Wine	This is My Body. This is the cup of My Blood.	The priest
Anointing of the Sick	Holy Oils	Through this holy anointing may the Lord in his love and mercy help you with the grace of the Holy Spirit. May the Lord who frees you from sin save you and raise you up.	The priest

CHAPTER THIRTY:
REVIEW AND ASSESSMENT

Aims

The students' understanding of the material covered this week will be reviewed and assessed.

Materials

- Quiz 30 (Appendix, p. A-44)
- "Come, Holy Ghost, Creator blest," *Adoremus Hymnal*, #443

Review

1. The students should know the events of Pentecost.

2. Review why wind, flames, and the dove are symbols of the Holy Spirit.

3. Review the effects of the Holy Spirit in the lives of the Apostles.

4. Review Who the Holy Spirit is and be able to explain the Holy Trinity. (One God, Three Persons)

5. The children should know that Pentecost is the birthday of the Church and that in the Liturgical year, it is celebrated 50 days after Easter and that the priest wears red.

6. Review the seven sacraments, their correct names, and their effects. Have them identify the minister, matter, and form from a list.
They should also know the symbols used to represent each of the sacraments.

Name:

God Is Our Father **Quiz 30**

Circle the correct answer:

1. The Holy Spirit is:
   a) The Second Person of the Holy Trinity b) The Father and the Son
   (c) God

2. The Trinity is:
   (a) One God in Three Persons b) Three Gods in One Person
   c) Three Gods in Three Persons

3. The Holy Spirit came:
   (a) at Pentecost b) nine days after the Resurrection
   c) nine days after Christmas

Fill in the chart using the words from the word bank:

SACRAMENT	MATTER	FORM	EFFECTS
Baptism	water	I baptize you in the name of the Father and the Son and of the Holy Spirit	Sin is washed away and grace is received in the soul
Penance	Confessing our sins to a priest	I absolve you from your sins in the name of the Father and of the Son and of the Holy Spirit	sins are forgiven
Eucharist	bread & wine	This is My Body and This is My Blood	We receive the Body and Blood of Jesus
Confirmation	Holy Chrism and the laying on of hands	Be sealed with the gift of the Holy Spirit	Holy Spirit comes
Matrimony Marriage	The vows of the man and woman	The consent to the vows	husband & wife grow holy
Holy Orders	Bishop lays hands on head of the man	The words of the bishop to the one to be ordained upon the laying of hands	man becomes a priest
Anointing of the Sick	oil	By this holy anointing and His most loving mercy, may the Lord forgive you whatever wrong you have done…	Receive the grace to die in God's friendship.

sins are forgiven	this is My Blood	water	oil	Man becomes a priest
bread and wine	Husband and wife grow holy	this is My Body	Holy Spirit comes	

A - 44 *Faith and Life • Grade 2 • Appendix A*

Assess

1. Distribute Quiz 30 and answer any questions that the children may have. When they turn in their quizzes, individually test them on the Memorization Questions and Words to Know from the week.

2. When all quizzes have been turned in, review the correct answers with the class.

Conclude

1. Sing "Come, Holy Ghost, Creator blest," *Adoremus Hymnal*, #443.

2. Pray for the intention of the students.

CHAPTER THIRTY-ONE
GOD'S FAMILY: THE CHURCH

Catechism of the Catholic Church References

Christian Holiness: 2012–16, 2028–29
Christ as Head of Church: 669
Church, Marks of:
- Apostolic: 857–65, 869
- Catholic: 830–35, 838, 868
- Holy: 823–29, 867
- One: 813–22, 866

Church Hierarchical Structure: 871–96, 934–39
- Ecclesial Ministry: 874–79
- Episcopal College and Its Head, the Pope: 880–87
- Task of Teaching: 888–92
- Task of Sanctifying: 893
- Task of Governing: 894–96

Church's Origin, Foundation, and Mission: 758–69, 778

Scripture References

Peter as the Foundation of the Church: Mt 16:18–19

Mystical Body: 1 Cor 12:12

Background Reading: *The Fundamentals of Catholicism* by Fr. Kenneth Baker, S.J.

Volume 3:
"Bishops Are Successors of the Apostles," pp. 104–7

Summary of Lesson Content

Lesson 1

Today there are Christians in every part of the world.

Jesus made Peter the head of the Church. Today, the Pope has Peter's job.

Bishops carry out the work of the Apostles. They are shepherds of a diocese and act in the place of Jesus.

Lesson 2

The Pope and the bishops teach in Jesus' name.

The bishop also makes rules about the sacraments and the Mass.

Priests receive powers from the bishop and are his helpers. They can forgive sins and consecrate the Eucharist.

Lesson 3

Religious sisters and brothers promise to spend their lives doing God's work.

Their apostolates include: teaching, hospital work, serving the poor, and prayer.

Lesson 4

The laity also have an important role in the Church.

The laity together with the Pope, bishops, priests, and religious form the Church—like a body with many parts.

Each person is called to serve the Church in a unique way.

LESSON ONE: THE UNIVERSAL CHURCH

Aims

The students will learn that now there are Christians in every part of the world.

They will review that Jesus made Peter the head of the Church. Today, the Pope has Peter's job.

They will learn that bishops carry out the work of the Apostles. They are shepherds of a diocese, who act in the place of Jesus.

Materials

- World map or globe
- Pictures of Pope and bishops
- *Activity Book*, p. 117

Optional:
- "The Church's one foundation," *Adoremus Hymnal*, #560

Begin

Hold up a picture of the current Pope. Play 20 Questions with the children. Let them ask 20 questions that can be answered as "yes" or "no." Once they identify the Pope, or if they are unable to do so, write the word "Pope" on the board and explain that this man is the Pope, and he takes Jesus' place as head of the Church. Jesus founded the Church but knew that we needed an earthly leader, so He appointed Peter to take His place (p. 141). Since Jesus returned to Heaven, we have had a Pope, or "Holy Father," to take care of Jesus' Church.

Develop

1. Read the first two paragraphs with the students.

2. If you have a map of the world, show the students where the Holy Land is, and explain that Jesus and the Apostles all lived in the Holy Land. Tell them that after Jesus died, the Apostles traveled to many lands, such as Greece, Egypt, Turkey, and India, to spread the Good News. You may point to the surrounding areas and seaports around the Holy Land on the map. The followers of the Apostles then were sent all over the world, bringing the Good News to all people in every country. These people were "missionaries." They are still sent to spread the Good News today. This is how we came to know about Jesus here where we live. Many people have passed down the faith through time and travel. This way, the Church grew throughout the world.

3. Explain to them that the Church has a structure. You may use the model of the school for them to understand. The students are the faithful children. They come to a class (like a parish). They have a leader, the teacher (like a parish priest or pastor). The teachers of the school have to answer to the principal bishops of the diocese), and the the principals have to answer to the superintendent of schools (Pope). There are many people who help a school run, like volunteers and PTA (religious communities). The students may understand this model.

4. Explain the role of the Pope. He is the Vicar of Christ. He is the visible head of the Church who works with the bishops (who represent Christ in their geographic regions, called dioceses) to teach the faith and worship God. The Pope, and the bishops united with him, are called the Magisterium. They are like the Apostles. We are all united through the faith they teach and what we all believe. This faith is summarized in something called the "Creed." Have the students read it on p. 152 in the text.

Name:________________________

Apostles' Creed

Can you fill in the blanks?

I believe in God, the Father Almighty, Creator of Heaven and earth. I believe in Jesus Christ, His only Son, our Lord. He was conceived by the power of the Holy Spirit and born of the Virgin Mary.
He suffered under Pontius Pilate, was crucified, died, and was buried. He descended into hell.
On the third day, He rose again.
He ascended into Heaven and sits at the right hand of the Father. He will come again to judge the living and the dead. I believe in the Holy Spirit, the Holy catholic Church, the communion of Saints, the forgiveness of sins, the resurrection of the body, and life everlasting. *Amen.*

Faith and Life Series • Grade 2 • Chapter 31 • Lesson 1 117

Reinforce

1. Have the students work on *Activity Book*, p. 117. They may use p. 152 of their text to help them.

2. Teach them to sing "The Church's one foundation," *Adoremus Hymnal*, #560.

Conclude

1. Say the Apostles' Creed (on p. 152 of the text).

2. Ask the students to research the name of their bishop and the name of their diocese.

3. Pray for their bishop and parish priests.

Preview

In the next lesson, we will learn more about bishops and priests and their roles in the Church.

IF THE CHURCH WERE A UNIFIED SCHOOL DISTRICT

Church:	School:
Pope	Superintendent
Bishops of dioceses	Principals of schools
Pastors (priests)	Teachers
Religious	Volunteers
Laity	Students

NOTES

LESSON TWO: THE DIOCESE

Aims

The students will review that the Pope and the bishops teach in Jesus' name.

They will learn that bishops are the heads of their diocese. The bishops make rules about the sacraments and the Mass.

They will learn that the priests receive powers from the bishops and are their helpers.

Materials

- *Activity Book*, p. 118

Optional:
- "The Church's one foundation," *Adoremus Hymnal*, #560

- Arrange for a priest or deacon's visit to answer students' questions about Holy Orders

Begin

Review the role of the Pope in the Church. Ask the children how the Church got to be everywhere around the world. What unites us? We have one Pope who represents Jesus. We have the same sacraments. We are united in charity. We share the same faith. This faith is summarized in the Apostles' Creed. Note: this creed was not written by the Apostles, but is a summary of the beliefs going back to the time of Jesus and the Apostles. Have the children take turns saying the Apostles' Creed. Have them work on memorizing it.

31 God's Family—The Church

"And I tell you, you are Peter, and on this rock I will build my church, and the powers of death shall not prevail against it."

Matthew 16:18–19

The Apostles preached and baptized in many lands. The Church grew and grew. Today there are Christians in every part of the world.

Jesus made Peter the head of His Church on earth. Today the **Pope** has Peter's job. He is the leader of Catholics everywhere. **Bishops** carry on the work of the Apostles. There are thousands of bishops in different parts of the world. They look after us as good shepherds taking care of their sheep. The bishops take the place of Jesus on earth.

The Pope and bishops with him teach us in Jesus' name. They explain the Bible to us and tell us how to lead good lives. They also make rules about the Mass and the sacraments. Everything Jesus wants us to know is taught by the Catholic **Church**.

Each bishop has many helpers called priests. Priests receive special powers from the bishop.

149

Develop

1. Read paragraphs 3 and 4 with the students.

2. Using the Chalk Talk at right, write and fill in the chart on the board with names. Our Pope's name is __________.

3. Ask the students the name of our bishop. Write on the board, "our bishop's name is ____________. He is bishop of the Diocese of ____________." Ask them the name of their diocese. Explain to them that a diocese is a geographic region. It has many churches in it and a cathedral where the bishop says Mass. The bishop governs all the Catholics in this diocese.

4. Ask them who the pastor or parish priest(s) is/are. The pastor or priests receive their power to say Mass and hear confessions from the bishop. They must be obedient to him. They are his helpers. The priest represents the bishop and acts in his place because the bishop cannot be at every parish in his diocese every day.

5. You may choose to explain deacons to the students. There are three levels of Holy Orders. The bishop has the fullness of Holy Orders. He can celebrate all seven sacraments. A priest is a bishop's helper. He receives his powers from the bishop. He can baptize, say Mass, hear confessions, witness marriages, anoint the sick, and, in special circumstances, he can confirm people. The deacon is ordained for ministry. He does not have the powers of the priesthood, but he can perform Baptisms, marriages, and funerals. He is dedicated to serving the poor and helping in parishes as needed.

6. If possible, have a priest and/or deacon visit to answer the students' questions.

Name:____________________

QUESTIONS

1. Who did Jesus make as head of His Church?

Peter

2. Who has Peter's job now? What is His name?

Pope John Paul II

3. What do bishops do?

Carry on the work of the Apostles

4. What do the Pope and the bishops together do?

Teach in Jesus' name

5. What do priests do?

They forgive sins in the Sacrament of Penance and change bread and wine into the Body and Blood of Jesus.

6 What do deacons do?

They help both bishops and priests cele-brate the Eucharist

7. What do religious brothers and sisters do?

They teach, work in hospitals, help the poor, and spend time in prayer

8. The rest of us are called laity. What do we do?

We can help the Church in a way that no one else can

118 *Faith and Life Series • Grade 2 • Chapter 31 • Lesson 2*

CHALK TALK:
GOD'S FAMILY

Chalk Talk

"God's Family"

Pope – leads all the Catholics around the world
↓
Bishop – teaches and rules us
↓
Pastor – helps the bishop
↓
Religious – pray, care for the sick, teach in schools
Parents – raise children to follow God's commandments
↓
Children – can help spread God's message to others

Reinforce

1. Have the students work on *Activity Book*, p. 118.

2. Have them practice memorizing the Apostles' Creed, the memorization questions, and the Words to Know. They will need ample time to do this.

Conclude

1. Say the Apostles' Creed together.

2. Sing: "The Church's one foundation," *Adoremus Hymnal*, #560.

Preview

In the next lesson, we will learn about the laity of the Church, as well as the Religious.

NOTES

LESSON THREE: GOD'S FAMILY

Aims

The students will learn that religious sisters and brothers promise to spend their lives doing God's work.

The students will also learn the roles of families and single persons in the Church.

Materials

- *Activity Book*, p. 119

Optional:
- "The Church's one foundation," *Adoremus Hymnal*, #560
- If possible, have a religious sister or brother and a husband and wife come into the class to answer questions
- "Mother Teresa: Seeing the Face of Jesus," video

Begin

Review the roles of the Pope, bishops, and priests. You may do a general review of Holy Orders, too. You may play a review game, such as Bible Baseball or Tic Tac Toe.

Have them draw the chart of "God's Family" on the board (see Chalk Talk on the previous page). Have them give the names for the Pope, local bishop, parish priests, and the diocese.

They can forgive sins in the Sacrament of Penance. They can change bread and wine into the Body and Blood of Christ.

There are other helpers in the Church called Deacons. Deacons help both bishops and priests to celebrate the Eucharist, spread the Good News of Jesus, and minister to the poor.

Some members of God's family live a special kind of life. They promise to spend all their time doing God's work. We call them Religious Sisters and Brothers. They teach, work in hospitals, help the poor, and spend the whole day praying for us all.

Most members of God's family are not bishops, priests, or sisters. They are men, women, boys, and girls like those you see each Sunday in church. Each of us has an important part to play in the Church.

The Church is like a body. A body has many parts. If even one small part is hurt or missing, the whole body suffers. Each small part does something that the others cannot do. That is how the Church is. You can help the Church in a way that no one else can. The prayers and actions of many others help you.

The Church makes us holy. It brings the grace of God to everyone. Each of us can receive that grace and become holy. We can also bring God's grace and love to others.

150

Develop

1. Read paragraphs 5 and 6 with the students.

2. Explain that parents, children, and religious brothers and sisters are called laity. Explain that we are part of the laity, and we have a very important role as well.

3. Explain that there are many different orders of religious brothers and sisters. Many are named after different saints or devotions upon which the order was founded. There are two kinds of religious communities: contemplative and apostolic. Contemplative communities usually do not go out into the world, and their work for the Church is in prayer. Apostolic communities go out into the world, and their works vary from helping in hospitals, schools, orphanages, missions, parish churches, etc.

4. Explain that husbands, wives, and their children are laity. They help each other to become holy. They serve the Church by worship and alms. They offer themselves to God through the Mass and support the church in various ways, such as singing in the choir, or teaching CCD. Sometimes lay people work for the church as a full time ministry, such as a Director of Religious Education. Does your parish have any lay ministers?

5. Ask the students how parents and children help each other to grow in holiness. Parents raise their children to follow God's Commandments and to know the Church's teachings. They take them to Church for worship and they are examples of what it is to be a good Catholic. Children can help spread God's message to others, and they are witnesses to their parents, too. Children can teach their parents what they learn in religion class and be good Catholic examples in the world. They should also pray for their parents, that they will be faithful to God and their sacred work of parenthood.

Name:____________________

God's Family

Can you label each of these pictures?

Priest Pope Bishop Laity

Reinforce

1. Have a panel of guest speakers: someone from a religious community and a married couple. They should be available to answer any questions that the children may have.

2. Have them complete *Activity Book*, p. 119.

3. Have them continue to work on memorizing the Apostles' Creed, the memorization questions, and the Words to Know.

4. If guest speakers cannot come in, show "Mother Teresa: Seeing the Face of Jesus," video, available through Ignatius Press; 30 minutes.

Conclude

1. Lead the class in saying the Apostles' Creed.

2. Sing "The Church's one foundation," *Adoremus Hymnal*, #560.

Preview

In the next lesson, we will learn about the Church as the image of the Body of Christ.

VATICAN COUNCIL II

The most recent Ecumenical Council of the Church, Vatican II was called by John XXIII in 1959 and was convened in 1962.

After the death of John XXIII, Paul VI reconvened the Council in 1963 and its last session ended in 1965. Sixteen documents were formulated and promulgated at this Council: two dogmatic and two pastoral constitutions, nine decrees, and three declarations.

NOTES

LESSON FOUR: BODY OF CHRIST

Aims

The students will learn that the laity, together with the Pope, bishops, priests, and religious form the Church—like a body with many parts.

They will learn that each person is called to serve the Church in a unique way.

Materials

- Children's Bible
- *Activity Book*, p. 120

Optional:
- "The Church's one foundation," *Adoremus Hymnal*, #560

Begin

Have the students review the various roles in the Church by playing a review game, such as Tic Tac Toe.

Have the students establish their own Church hierarchy among themselves. Have them elect a Pope, have one be a bishop, two be priests and others be laity. Then, as a group, have them decide how they should celebrate their First Communion (or a May Crowning, etc.) Remind them that they must act their roles. Help them to see how they must work together.

Words to Know:

Pope bishop Church

Q. 60 *What is the Church?*
The Church is the family of all baptized people (CCC 782).

Q. 61 *Who founded the Church?*
Jesus Christ founded the Church (CCC 763, 771).

Q. 62 *Who is the Pope?*
The Pope is the pastor of the entire Church, who takes the place of Jesus on earth (CCC 880–82).

We Pray:

Everything we believe is in a prayer called the *Apostles' Creed*. The word "creed" means what we believe.

151

Develop

1. Read the rest of the chapter with the students.

2. Have them read from the children's Bible, 1 Corinthians 12:12, about the Body of Christ having many parts.

3. Have them think of what part of the "Body" they would like to be. Would they like to be feet, to carry the message of Jesus to other parts of the world? Would they like to be the mouth, so they could speak or sing about Jesus? Would they like to be the ears, so they can hear about the Good News?

4. Explain to the children that the members of the Body of Christ must work together because we all affect each other. If a body did not have feet, it would be hard to get around. If a body did not have hands, it would be hard to work. If a body had hands, but the hands did not work with the rest of the body, that could be a disaster! Imagine everything that would be dropped, or spilled, or broken! Each and every person is important to the Body of Christ.

5. *God has a special job for every person. Sometimes we do that job when we grow up. Some people become priests, some become nurses or doctors, some become teachers. God calls everyone to somehow help others. To what do the children think God is calling them? You may explain vocations to the children. God calls some men to the priesthood. God calls some men and women to religious life. God calls many men and women to marriage, and some people He calls to the single life so they can serve the Church in the world.*

6. Individually quiz the children on their memorization of the Apostles' Creed.

APOSTLES' CREED

I believe in God,
the Father almighty,
creator of heaven and earth.
I believe in Jesus Christ,
his only Son, our Lord.
He was conceived by the
power of the Holy Spirit
and born of the Virgin Mary.
He suffered under Pontius Pilate,
was crucified, died, and was
buried.
He descended into hell.
On the third day he rose again.
He ascended into heaven
and is seated at the right
hand of the Father.
He will come again to judge
the living and the dead.
I believe in the Holy Spirit,
the holy catholic Church,
the communion of saints,
the forgiveness of sins,
the resurrection of the body,
and the life everlasting.
Amen.

152

Reinforce

1. Have the students work on *Activity Book*, p. 120.

2. Have the students work on their memorization material.

Conclude

1. Together, pray the Apostles' Creed.

2. Sing "The Church's one foundation," *Adoremus Hymnal*, #560.

Preview

In the next lesson, we will review the material covered in this chapter.

"OUTSIDE THE CHURCH THERE IS NO SALVATION"

"Basing itself on Scripture and Tradition, the Council teaches that the Church... is necessary for salvation: the one Christ is the mediator and the way for salvation; he is present to us in his body which is the Church. He himself explicitly asserted the necessity of faith and Baptism, and thereby affirmed... the necessity of the Church which men enter through Baptism as through a door. Hence they could not be saved who, knowing that the Catholic Church was founded as necessary by God through Christ, would refuse either to enter it or remain in it."

—Vatican II, *Lumen Gentium* 14;
cf. Mk 16:16; Jn 3:5, quoted inCCC, #846

NOTES

CHAPTER THIRTY-ONE:
REVIEW AND ASSESSMENT

Aims

The students' understanding of the material covered this week will be reviewed and assessed.

Materials

- Quiz 31 (Appendix, p. A-45)
- "The Church's one foundation," *Adoremus Hymnal*, #560

Review

1. Review how the Church has grown through the teaching of the Apostles and the disciples who brought the Good News to different parts of the world.

2. They should have a general understanding of the hierarchy of the Church. They will know the roles of the Pope, bishops, priests, laity, and religious, as well as the name of the current Pope, local ordinary (bishop), and parish clergy.

3. Review that the Church is like the Body of Christ with many parts, which work together for the Kingdom of God. All parts are necessary and complement one another. Every person has a unique role in the Church.

4. Review that our beliefs unite us as a Church. They should know the Apostles' Creed.

Name:

God's Family — The Church **Quiz 31**

Explain the roles of each of these members of the Church:

1. Pope. He is the Vicar of Christ and visible head of the Church.

2. Bishop. They represent Christ in their geographic regions called dioceses. Together with the Pope, they teach the faith.

3. Priest. The priest represents the bishop and acts in his place. He receives power to say Mass and hear confessions from the bishop. He administers the sacraments.

4. Religious. Religious are either contemplative or apostolic communities.

5. Laity. Husbands, wives, and their children are laity. They serve the Church by worship and help each other become holy.

Please answer in complete sentences:

1.Who is your bishop and what is your diocese?
Answers will vary.

2. What powers do the priests receive from the bishop?
The priests receive the power to say Mass and hear confessions from the bishop.

3. What kinds of work do religious sisters and brothers do (name three)?
Religious sisters and brothers may help in hospitals, schools, orphanages, missions, parish churches, etc. Or, they may devote their lives to prayer.

4. Explain how the Church is the Body of Christ.
Members of the Church make up the Mystical Body of Christ, and each members works together.

Faith and Life • Grade 2 • Appendix A *A - 45*

Assess

1. Distribute Quiz 31. Answer any questions that the children may have. As they hand in their quizzes, individually test them on the Memorization Questions and Words to Know from the chapter.

2. When all quizzes have been turned in, review the correct answers with the class.

Conclude

1. Sing "The Church's one foundation," *Adoremus Hymnal*, #560.

2. End by praying the Apostles' Creed.

CHAPTER THIRTY-TWO
MARY, OUR MOTHER

Catechism of the Catholic Church References

Annunciation and Motherhood of Christ: 485, 509, 723
Assumption: 966, 974
Devotion to the Blessed Virgin: 971
Mary and the Church: 829, 963–72
Mary as Eschatological Icon of the Church: 972, 975
Mary in God's Plan: 488–93, 508
Mary as Mother of the Church and Our Mother: 963–70, 973–74
Mary's Divine Motherhood: 495, 509
Obedience and Faith of Mary: 144, 494, 511
Prayer in Union with Mary: 2673–79, 2682
Prayer of Mary: 2617–19, 2622

Scripture References

Jesus Gives Us Mary to Be Our Mother: Jn 19:26–27
Wedding at Cana: Jn 2:1–11

Background Reading: *The Fundamentals of Catholicism* by Fr. Kenneth Baker, S.J.

Volume 2:
"Hail, Holy Queen," pp. 375–78

Volume 2:
"Mary, Mother of the Church," pp. 385–87

Summary of Lesson Content

Lesson 1

Mary was with the Apostles at Pentecost.

At the end of Mary's Life, she was assumed (body and soul) into Heaven.

Mary is the Queen of Heaven and earth.

Lesson 2

Jesus gave Mary to us to be our Mother when He was dying on the Cross.

Mary is the Mother of the Church.

Mary is an example for all Catholics, and she intercedes on our behalf.

Lesson 3

Mary has a special love for children.

Mary appeared at Fatima, Portugal.

Mary asks for sacrifices for sinners and that men pray the Rosary.

Lesson 4

Today, millions of people have a devotion to Mary and pray the Rosary.

The fourth lesson will teach the children how to pray the Rosary and the twenty Mysteries.

LESSON ONE: MARY'S SPECIAL GIFT

Aims

The students will learn about the role of Mary in the early Church.

They will also learn that Mary was taken to Heaven, body and soul. She is Queen of Heaven and earth.

Materials

- Pictures of the Assumption and Coronation of Mary (see *Activity Book*, pp. 121 and 154)
- Rosaries
- *Activity Book*, p. 121

Optional:
- "Immaculate Mary," *Adoremus Hymnal*, #532

Begin

Review with the children who the Blessed Virgin Mary is:
- Mary is the Mother of Jesus by the power of the Holy Spirit
- She is the wife of Joseph
- We remember Mary from the Christmas story
- Mary was at the Wedding of Cana (Jn 2:1–11)
- Mary was with Jesus under the Cross
- Mary was in the upper room at Pentecost
- We ask Mary to pray with and for us with the Hail Mary Prayer
- Mary is our Mother
- Mary is the Mother of God

32 Mary Our Mother

> When Jesus saw his mother, and the disciple whom he loved standing near, he said to his mother, "Woman, behold your son!" Then he said to the disciple, "Behold, your mother!" And from that hour the disciple took her to his own home.
>
> John 19:26–27

Mary was with the Apostles at Pentecost. During the days after Pentecost Mary did everything she could to help the new Church grow. She wanted everyone to know about what her Son had done for all men.

When it was time for Mary's life on earth to end, God did something very special for her. He took her, body and soul, into Heaven. How happy Mary was to see her Son again! Jesus made His Mother the Queen of Heaven and earth.

Do you remember how Jesus gave His Mother to us when He was dying on the Cross? Mary is Mother of the Church and the Mother of each of us. We can turn to Mary and tell her about our problems. She

153

Develop

1. Read the first two paragraphs with the children. Discuss the reading.

2. Review the role of the Blessed Virgin Mary at Pentecost. She was with the Apostles in the upper room, praying with them for the coming of the Holy Spirit. Mary would have already known the Holy Spirit, as she conceived by the Holy Spirit.

3. Mary would have done all she could to help the early Church. It is known that she was taken in by the Apostle John. We can imagine that she would have told him about her time with Jesus and all He had taught her. John would have written about these things in the Gospel of John found in the Bible.

4. At the end of Mary's earthly life, she was taken body and soul to Heaven, which is called the "Assumption." You may write this word on the board. The Assumption is also one of the Glorious Mysteries of the Rosary. The Assumption may have been much like the Ascension of Our Lord. Jesus and Mary are the only two people in Heaven with their bodies.

5. Jesus made Mary Queen of Heaven and earth. In the Old Testament, the mother of the king was always made queen. Mary is our Queen, Jesus is the King. We are heirs to the Kingdom. This means that Mary is our Mother, and Jesus is our brother through Baptism (when God the Father adopts us).

6. Have the children look at pictures of the Assumption and the Coronation, and pray the last two Glorious Mysteries of the Rosary as a class. If possible, do this in front of a Mary statue. There are instructions for the Rosary found on p. 156 of the text. You may need to provide rosaries.

Name:____________________

Assumption

Color the picture.

Mary was taken to Heaven with her body and soul.

Faith and Life Series • Grade 2 • Chapter 32 • Lesson 1 121

Reinforce

1. Have the students work on *Activity Book*, p. 121.

2. Teach them to pray the Rosary.

3. You may make rosaries as a class. (Note: If rosaries are made with beads and spacers, their construction will take about 1/2 hour. If made with cords and knots, it will take longer.)

4. Teach the children to sing "Immaculate Mary," *Adoremus Hymnal*, #532.

Conclude

End by praying the last two Glorious Mysteries of the Rosary.

Preview

In the next lesson, we will learn about the Blessed Virgin Mary as our Mother.

THE ASSUMPTION = THE DORMITION

This dogma was declared "ex cathedra" in 1950 by Pope Pius XII in his encyclical *Munificentissimus Deus*:

"Finally the Immaculate Virgin, preserved free from all stain of original sin, when the course of her earthly life was finished, was taken up body and soul into heavenly glory, and exalted by the Lord as Queen over all things, so that she might be the more fully conformed to her Son, the Lord of lords and conqueror of sin and death." (quoted in the *Catechism of the Catholic Church*, #966).

Since there is no declaration regarding her death, the Eastern Church calls this the Dormition, for they believe Mary merely fell asleep before being assumed into Heaven.

NOTES

____

____

____

____

____

____

____

____

____

____

LESSON TWO: MARY OUR MOTHER

Aims

The students will learn that Jesus gave Mary to us to be our Mother when He was dying on the Cross. Mary is the Mother of the Church.

They will learn that Mary is a good example for us and that she prays for us.

Materials

- Children's Bible
- Prayer cards of the Hail Mary
- *Activity Book*, p. 122

Optional:
- "Immaculate Mary," *Adoremus Hymnal*, #532

Begin

Have them pray the Hail Mary. If they do not already have it memorized, give them prayer cards with the Hail Mary on them. The second half of this prayer reads: Holy Mary, Mother of God, pray for us sinners...
There are two things the children need to know here:
1) Mary is the Mother of God (Jesus is God the Son).
2) Mary can pray for us to God her Son.

Develop

1. Read the third paragraph of this chapter with the children.

2. From a children's Bible, read the crucifixion account from the Gospel of John: Jn 19:25–27. Emphasize that Jesus gave us Mary to be the Mother of us all. By our Baptism, we are adopted children of God the Father; Jesus becomes our brother, and Mary becomes our Mother through grace. As well, the disciple represents the Church in this reading. Mary is the Mother of all by the order of grace. She is Mother of the Church.

3. Ask the children what things they do with their mothers:
   - Obey them
   - Help them
   - Love them
   - Receive their love
   - Tell them about their days and problems, etc.

Stress that the children should turn to Mary as their Mother, too. She wants them to share their day with her, their faith with her, their love for her Son with her. We can also turn to Mary with our problems. She will always understand. Mary can then help them.

4. Mary is a good example for us. If we do not know what we must do, we can think about what Mary would have done, and do the same thing. She is a model of virtue.

5. We can ask Mary to help us, and to pray with and for us. Jesus told us that where two or three are gathered in His name, He is there in their midst (Mt 18:20). Mary can pray with us so that we do not have to pray alone. Further, Mary can pray for us—she can take our prayers to God and add her own, too. Just as you would pray for a friend who asked you to pray for him or his needs, Mary will do this for you.

Name:____________________

Color the picture.

Just as the Child Jesus could go to Mary, so can we go to our Mother. We can ask her to pray for us, to help us, and to bring us closer to her Son Jesus. Mary loves us all.

122 *Faith and Life Series • Grade 2 • Chapter 32 • Lesson 2*

Reinforce

1. Have the students complete *Activity Book*, p. 122.

2. Have the children memorize the twenty Mysteries of the Rosary. Quiz them with a game. Ask the children the names of the Mysteries, what they mean, and their proper order.

Conclude

1. Pray a Mystery of the Rosary (e.g., The Crucifixion) and end with the litany on p. 157.

2. Sing "Immaculate Mary," *Adoremus Hymnal*, #532.

Preview

In the next lesson, we will learn about the apparitions in Fatima, Portugal.

DEVOTION TO OUR LADY OF SORROWS

Our Lady, as the first and greatest disciple of Christ, participated in His redemptive suffering in a profound way. Devotion to the Sorrowful Mother can be traced back to apostolic times, beginning with John's account of Mary's grief while standing at the foot of the Cross (Jn 19:25). Luke records the prophecy of Simeon at the Presentation at the Temple: "and a sword will pierce through your own soul also" (Lk 2:35). During the Middle Ages, this devotion became popular, thus the well-known medieval hymn "Stabat Mater." In art, Our Lady of Sorrows is traditionally depicted in black with seven swords piercing her heart. Her feast day is September 15.

NOTES

LESSON THREE: BEAUTIFUL MARY

Aims

The students will learn about the apparitions in Fatima, Portugal, and Mary's special love for children.

Materials

- Various images of Mary, including Our Lady of Fatima
- *Activity Book*, p. 123
- World map
- Drawing paper, pencil, crayons

Optional:

- "Immaculate Mary," *Adoremus Hymnal*, #532
- "Fatima: The Day the Sun Danced," video

Begin

Show the students various images of Mary. Explain to them that Mary has many titles. For example, sometimes she is called by the place she is associated with, sometimes she is called by the way she helps us, sometimes she is called by who she is. For example, there is only one of me (teacher). You may call me Miss/Mr./Mrs. ________, or by my first name. You may call me daughter of (parents' names) or by where you saw me (name a church name), or by what I do (name, teacher of CCD). So it is also with Mary. Give many examples.

will understand. We can learn from Mary how to be good. She always did what God wanted her to do and she never sinned. If you are ever tempted to do something wrong, ask Mary to help you, and to pray with and for you. She will pray with you. She will pray for you.

Mary has a special love for little children. Sometimes she lets them see her. About one hundred years ago she came down from Heaven to visit two girls and a boy who lived in Fatima, Portugal. She asked them to make sacrifices for sinners and to say the **rosary** every day. The children thought Mary was the most beautiful, wonderful person they had ever seen. They were happy to do what she said.

Today millions of people say the rosary each day for world peace, because of what Mary told those three children. She told them that we would only have peace if we were good and pleasing to God.

Words to Know:

rosary

155

Develop

1. Read paragraph 4 with the students.

2. Show them where Fatima, Portugal, is on a map and where it is in relation to where you are.

3. Show "Fatima: The Day the Sun Danced," video, available through Ignatius Press; 30 minutes.

4. Discuss the video and apparitions with them:
   - What did Mary look like?
   - Where did she appear?
   - Why did she talk with children?
   - What did Mary ask the children to do?
   - Who is Saint Michael and what did he do?
   - What kinds of sacrifices did the children make?
   - Did the children know how to pray the Rosary? How did they learn?
   - Did the children obey Mary?
   - Were the children happy because of the apparitions?

5. You may tell them that two of the children of Fatima (Jacincta and Francisco) were both beatified in 2000. This means that they have been recognized as good examples and they may be made saints soon. The children can pray to them, asking them to help them love Mary as they did. You may also tell the children that Lucia is still alive (2002) and that she is a religious sister.

6. You may ask the children to draw pictures of Our Lady of Fatima.

7. You may ask the children what sacrifices they can make to show God how much they love Him. They should make sacrifices for sinners. Give them some examples.

Name:____________________

Color the picture.

Mary is the most beautiful and wonderful person.

Faith and Life Series • Grade 2 • Chapter 32 • Lesson 3 123

Reinforce

1. Have the students complete *Activity Book*, p. 123.

2. Have them draw pictures of the Fatima apparitions.

3. Have them work on memorizing the twenty Mysteries of the Rosary.

Conclude

1. End with praying a Mystery of the Rosary and the litany on p. 157 of the text.

2. Together sing "Immaculate Mary," *Adoremus Hymnal*, #532.

Preview

In the next lesson, we will continue to focus on the Rosary.

THE SEVEN SORROWS OF MARY

1. *The prophecy of Simeon*
2. *The Flight into Egypt*
3. *The loss of the Child Jesus for three days*
4. *Meeting Jesus on the Way to Calvary*
5. *The Crucifixion and death of Jesus*
6. *Jesus taken down from the Cross*
7. *Jesus laid in the tomb*

NOTES

LESSON FOUR: THE ROSARY

Aims

The studens will learn more about the Rosary, and they will make rosaries of their own.

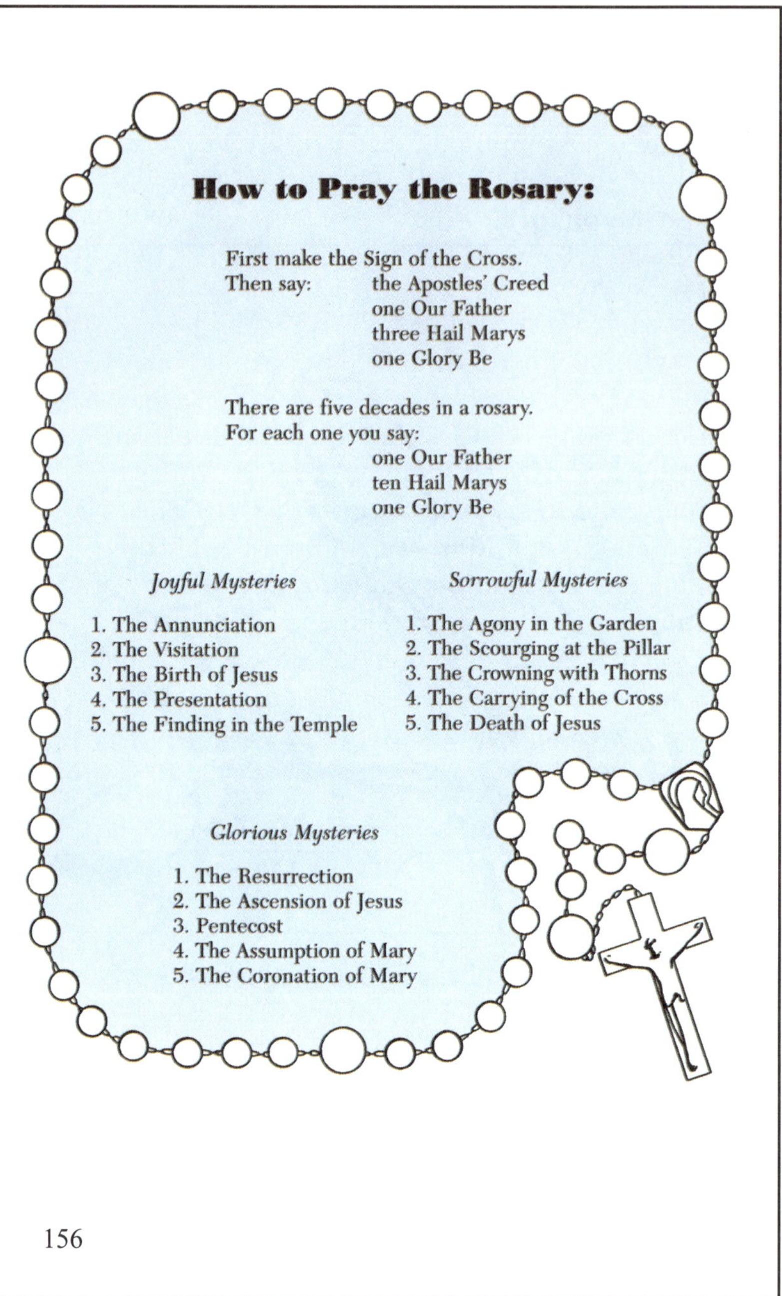

Materials

- *Activity Book*, p. 124
- Pictures of the Mysteries of the Rosary
- Rosary-making kits

Optional:
- "Immaculate Mary," *Adoremus Hymnal*, #532
- Arrange for a priest to visit to bless the rosaries

Begin

Have the students recount the story of Our Lady of Fatima. What special prayer did Mary ask that we say? What is the Rosary? Have the children now memorized the twenty Mysteries of the Rosary?

Display pictures of each of the 20 Mysteries. Point to them asking the children to identify them by name, then ask them to describe what is happening in each of the pictures.

Develop

1. Finish reading the chapter in the text with the students.

2. Have them make rosaries. Numerous companies provide rosary-making kits. Some are string rosaries with beads and plastic spacers, others are cord rosaries to be made with knots. It will take the children about 30–45 minutes to make a bead rosary and a little longer to make a knot rosary. Bead rosaries are easier for the children and can be made in different colors. Rosary kits will come with instructions on how to assemble the rosaries.

Note: You may want to get some parent volunteers in for this class because the children may have hard times with the knots or counting beads for the decades (quality control). Assistants can ensure that the beads do not get away from the children. Set up and clean up help is great, from cutting string, to sorting beads, helpers are greatly appreciated.

3. Once the rosaries are made, take time to teach the children how to pray with them. You may want to walk through the motions of "on this bead, we will pray . . . , then on the next ten beads, we will pray . . ."
As you approach each Mystery, point to the picture and ask the children the name of the Mystery to be meditated upon.

4. Having taught the children how to pray the Rosary, you may pray a decade.

5. If possible, have a priest visit the classroom and bless the rosaries.

6. Allow time for clean-up (looking for beads on the floor, etc.)

Queen of Angels . . .
Queen of Apostles . . .
Queen of all Saints . . .
Queen of the most holy Rosary . . .
Queen of Peace . . .

Pray for us.

Q. 63 *What special thing did God do for Mary at the end of her life on earth?* At the end of Mary's life on earth, God took her into Heaven, body and soul. This is called the Assumption (CCC 966).

157

Reinforce

1. Have the students complete *Activity Book*, p. 124.

2. Have them explain how to pray the Rosary.

3. They may continue memorizing the Mysteries of the Rosary.

Conclude

1. Lead them in praying a decade of the rosary, and end with the litany on p. 157 of the text.

2. Sing "Immaculate Mary," *Adoremus Hymnal*, #532.

Preview

In the next lesson, we will review the material covered in this chapter.

SCRIPTURE AND TRADITION

The Catholic Church differs from Protestant denominations because it gives equal reverence and acceptance to Scripture and Tradition, the two pillars of the Church. Tradition refers to those things which are unwritten and which have been passed on from Christ to His Apostles. Catholics believe that Christ instituted the Church with the authority to interpret Scripture and to defend and transmit revealed truth.

NOTES

CHAPTER THIRTY-TWO: REVIEW AND ASSESSMENT

Aims

The students' understanding of the material covered this week will be reviewed and assessed.

Materials

- Quiz 32 (Appendix, p. A-46)
- Unit 8 Test (Appendix, pp. A-49 and A-50)
- "Immaculate Mary," *Adoremus Hymnal*, #532
- Mary statue with a crown, flowers, rosaries

Review

1. Review the various biblical events when the Blessed Virgin Mary was present:
   - the Annunciation
   - the Nativity
   - the wedding at Cana
   - the Crucifixion
   - Pentecost

2. They should know that the Blessed Virgin Mary was taken to Heaven body and soul. This event is called the Assumption. We recognize the Blessed Virgin Mary as Queen of Heaven and earth.

3. They should know that Jesus gave the Blessed Virgin Mary to us to be our Mother. She is the Mother of the Church.

4. The Blessed Virgin Mary can be a good example for us, help us, and pray for us.

5. The Blessed Virgin Mary appeared to three children in Fatima, Portugal. The students should be able to recount the story of these apparitions.

6. They should know how to pray the Rosary, and the Mysteries of the Rosary.

Name:

Mary Our Mother **Quiz 32**

Circle the Correct answer:

1. Which of these events was Mary not present for:
   a) Pentecost
   (b) Baptism of Jesus
   c) Crucifixion

2. When did Jesus give Mary to us for our Mother?
   a) Annunciation
   b) Nativity
   (c) Crucifixion

3. Mary can help us by:
   a) praying for us
   b) being a good example
   (c) both a and b

4. The rosary has how many decades?
   a) three
   (b) five
   c) seven

5. Mary asked the children of Fatima for:
   a) prayer
   b) sacrifice
   (c) both a and b

Place the mysteries of the rosary in the correct order:

JOYFUL (1-5)	SORROWFUL (1-5)	GLORIOUS (1-5)
5 Finding in the Temple	2 Scourging at the Pillar	3 Pentecost
1 Annunciation	4 Carrying the Cross	5 Coronation of Mary
3 Birth of Jesus	5 Death of Jesus	1 Resurrection
4 Presentation	3 Crowning with Thorns	4 Assumption of Mary
2 Visitation	1 Agony in the Garden	2 Ascension of Jesus

A - 46 *Faith and Life • Grade 2 • Appendix A*

Assess

1. Distribute the Quiz 32 and answer any questions that they may have.

2. As the students hand in their quizzes, individually quiz them on the Memorization Questions and Words to Know.

3. When all quizzes have been turned in, review the correct answers.

4. Repeat steps 1 and 3 for the unit test.

Conclude

1. Sing "Immaculate Mary," *Adoremus Hymnal*, #532.

2. Have a Crowning of Mary ceremony.

3. Pray a Hail Mary.

CHAPTER THIRTY-THREE
JESUS IS ALWAYS PRESENT

Catechism of the Catholic Church References

Adoration of Jesus in the Eucharist: 1378–79, 1418
Christian Holiness: 2012–16, 2028–29
Christ's Presence in the Church: 1380–81
Christ's Presence in the Eucharist: 1088, 1373–77, 1413
Consecration of the Mass: 1352–54, 1413
Fruits of Communion: 1391–401, 1416
Holy Communion: 1355, 1382–90, 1415, 1417
Holy Spirit and the Church in the Liturgy: 1091–109, 1112
Holy Spirit and the Church: 737–41, 746–47, 767–68
Holy Spirit: Gift of God: 733–36
Prayer in Church: 2691, 2696
Prayer to Jesus: 2665–69, 2680
Work and Presence of Christ in the Liturgy: 1084–90, 1111
Worship: 2096–97, 2135–36

Scripture References

The Bread of Life: Jn 6
Jesus with Us: Mt 18:20
Ascension: Mt 28:16–20; Acts 1:1–12
Jesus Blesses the Children: Mt 19:13–15; Mk 10:14–16; Lk 18:16
Invitation to Pray (Adoration): Mt 26:36–40; Mt 14:32–37

Background Reading: *The Fundamentals of Catholicism* by Fr. Kenneth Baker, S.J.

Volume 3:
"The Catholic Doctrine of the Real Presence," pp. 229–31

Summary of Lesson Content

Lesson 1

Jesus promised to be with the Church always.

He is with the Church through the Holy Spirit, Whom He sent with the Father. He is with the Church in the sacraments, and most especially in the Eucharist.

The Eucharist is reserved in Catholic churches throughout the world. Jesus is present sacramentally in the tabernacles of the Church.

Lesson 2

To receive Jesus in Communion is a tremendous gift. Man should make every effort to receive Him as frequently as possible.

Jesus waits for man to visit Him in the Blessed Sacrament; graces can be received by such visits.

Lesson 3

Because Jesus is in the Blessed Sacrament, it is right to worship the Lord in the Eucharist.

The Catholic Church offers times of Eucharistic worship, called Adoration and Benediction.

Lesson 4

Man is called to be reverent in the presence of the Lord. Reverence includes church etiquette, such as genuflecting, silence in church, and devotion and attention at Mass.

LESSON ONE:
JESUS IS WITH US

Aims

The students will review that Jesus promised to be with the Church always.

They will learn that Jesus is with the Church through the Holy Spirit, in the sacraments and liturgy, and most especially in the Eucharist.

They will review that Jesus is present, Body, Soul, and Divinity in the tabernacle of the Church.

Materials

- Children's Bible
- Visit to tabernacle
- *Activity Book*, p. 125

Optional:
- "Tantum ergo," *Adoremus Hymnal*, #393

Begin

Review the Ascension and Jesus' promise to remain with us. You may read this out of the children's Bible (Mt 28:16–20; Acts 1:1–12).

You may ask them how Jesus remains with us. They should already know that Jesus is with us in the tabernacle. Today they will learn the many ways Jesus remains with us until the end of time.

Develop

1. Read paragraphs 1–3 with the students

2. Teach them the many ways that Jesus remains with us:
- *"Where two or three are gathered in my name" (Mt 18:20) When we come together as a group to pray or worship, or even to teach the faith in Jesus' name, He is there in our midst.*
- *In the Liturgy, Jesus is present in our midst because we are gathered in His name. He is also present as the word of God in the Holy Scripture. It is His words, His teachings, that come to us when the Bible is read.*
- *Jesus is with us through the teachings of the Church, for they are what He teaches through word and Tradition; safeguarded by the Holy Spirit sent by Jesus and the Father.*
- *Jesus is present in the seven sacraments, which bring us God's life of grace (you may go through each sacrament, showing how Jesus is present in each).*

*Baptism: *We are baptized in the three Persons of the Trinity. We are adopted into God's family, and Jesus is now our brother. It is Jesus who shares His life with us, won on the Cross.*

*Penance: *Jesus forgives our sins through the priest*

**Confirmation: Jesus gives us a greater share in His life and ministry in the Church through the outpouring of the Holy Spirit.*

*Marriage/Matrimony: *Jesus unites a husband and wife so they can live in love (like the love Jesus has for His Church) and make each other holy.*

*Holy Orders: *Jesus makes men His ministers and instruments, and works through them for the life of the Church.*

*Anointing of the Sick: *Jesus heals and helps those who are sick and suffering.*

*Eucharist: *Jesus is most especially present in the Eucharist, Body, Blood, Soul, and Divinity.*

Name:__________________

1. How is Jesus with us?
He is with us in the Church, Holy Eucharist, and many other ways
2. Jesus is with us in a special way too, what is that?
In the Holy Eucharist
3. What is in the tabernacle?
The Consecrated Hosts
4. How can you tell Jesus is present in the Church?
A sanctuary lamp is lit
5. Is Jesus really in the Church?
Yes!

Draw a beautiful tabernacle for Jesus.

Faith and Life Series • Grade 2 • Chapter 33 • Lesson 1 125

Reinforce

1. Take the students into the church and reread paragraph 3 from the text. Show the children the tabernacle, the sanctuary lamp, and remind the children to genuflect. Give them time to pray there.

2. Have the children complete *Activity Book*, p. 125.

3. Teach the children to sing "Tantum ergo," *Adoremus Hymnal*, #393.

Conclude

1. Because the children learned today that Jesus is present through the reading of Scriptures, end the class with a Scripture reading, such as Phil 2:1–11.

2. End with a Hail Mary and a Glory Be.

Preview

In the next lesson, the children will review the gift of receiving Jesus in Holy Communion.

SAINT MARIA GORETTI

Saint Maria Goretti was born on October 16, 1890, in Corinaldo, Italy, the daughter of humble sharecroppers. Always cheerful in her daily duties even after her father's death, she was soon propositioned by her neighbor, 20-year-old Alessandro Serenelli. On July 5, 1902, after she refused him again, he stabbed her fourteen times. After forgiving her killer, Maria died the next day at the age of eleven. Pius XII canonized her on June 24, 1950. The youngest officially recognized saint, she is the patroness of modern youth; her feast day is July 6. Serenelli converted after Maria appeared to him in prison. He was present at her canonization.

NOTES

____
____
____
____
____
____
____
____
____
____

LESSON TWO: BEING WITH JESUS

Aims

The students will learn what a great blessing it is to receive Jesus in Communion.

They will also review that Jesus waits for man to visit Him in the Blessed Sacrament.

They will learn that they may receive graces by visiting Our Lord in the church.

Materials

- Box of candies
- Children's Bible
- *Activity Book*, p. 126

Optional:
- "Tantum ergo," *Adoremus Hymnal*, #393

Begin

Show the students a box of candies. Tell them that they can come and receive as many of them as they wish. They can have all of them if they wish. Have them actually come forward and all receive some candies. Ask them if you have candies tomorrow, if they would want to come and get some then, too. The answer will probably be yes.

Explain to them that they can receive the greatest treasure of all every day. They simply need to come and receive it.

33 Jesus Is Always Present

"Amen! Blessing and glory and wisdom and thanksgiving and honor and power and might be to our God for ever and ever! Amen!"

Revelation 7:12

Before He ascended into Heaven, Jesus said, "I am with you always, even to the end of time."

Jesus is with us in many ways. He sent us His Spirit to lead and guide us. He is with His Church. He teaches us through our Holy Father, the Pope.

But Jesus is with us in a special way through the Holy Eucharist. At the Consecration, during Mass, Jesus comes to us under the appearance of bread and wine. After Mass, some of the Consecrated Hosts are put in the tabernacle. You can tell that Jesus is present in the tabernacle when a special lamp, called the sanctuary lamp, is lit. So Jesus lives in every Catholic church in the world. He is there as really and truly as He was in Bethlehem.

Since Jesus gave us so great a gift, we should receive Him whenever we can in Holy Communion.

159

Develop

1. Read paragraphs 4 and 5 with the students.

2. Ask them what great treasure they may receive every day. Jesus in the Eucharist. Do the children know that there is daily Mass offered in the church? At what times? What times are Masses on Sunday? Let the children know that they can come to Mass daily and at every Mass, if they are prepared (review: healthy soul, Eucharistic fast, know Whom they will receive, reverent reception, and thanksgiving), they may receive Our Lord , the greatest treasure of all, every day.

3. Ask them why they should want to receive Jesus every day in the Eucharist. Review food for the soul. Also, stress the union of love we share with Jesus in the Eucharist.

4. Read with the children the blessing of the children who came to Jesus: Mt 19:13–15; Mk 10:14–16; Lk 18:16. Jesus wants children to come to Him and He blesses them. Just as the children went to Jesus in the Bible story, so, too, the children now can come to Jesus. He is present in the tabernacle. He is waiting there for us to come to Him. He loves it when we go and visit Him. We can tell Him anything. When we visit Jesus in the tabernacle, we show Jesus how much we love Him and that we believe He is truly present. He will give us grace for visiting Him, and He will bless us, like He did the children in the Bible story.

5. Review with the students the hours your church is open for prayer. Often, because of the times we live in, churches are locked for safety reasons. Let the children know that even if the church is locked, they can say hello to Jesus, and a short prayer before they leave. Jesus knows that they have come to visit with Him. Their visits please Him very much.

Name:____________________

List some times you can stop into the church to visit Jesus.

Answers will vary

Write a poem about Jesus in the Blessed Sacrament.

126 *Faith and Life Series • Grade 2 • Chapter 33 • Lesson 2*

Reinforce

1. Have the students complete *Activity Book*, p. 126.

2. Take the class before the tabernacle for some prayer time with Jesus in the Blessed Sacrament. They may sing "Tantum Ergo", or "O Lord I am not Worthy", or another song such as "Holy God, We Praise Thy Name"—a song of love and devotion to Jesus in the Blessed Sacrament.

3. Have them start memorizing the Words to Know for this chapter: Sanctuary Lamp, Tabernacle (they will learn monstrance next).

Conclude

1. End with prayer.

2. Sing as a class "Tantum ergo," *Adoremus Hymnal*, #393.

Preview

In the next lesson, we will learn about Eucharistic Adoration and Benediction.

PATRON SAINTS

- Thieves: Saint Nicholas (December 6)
- Television: Clare of Assisi (August 11)
- Heirs (male): Saint Felicity (July 10)

SAINTS TO INVOKE FOR:

- Toothache: Saint Apollonia (February 7)
- Thunder and Lightning: Saint Barbara (December 4)

NOTES

LESSON THREE: O COME LET US ADORE HIM

Aims

The students will review that it is right to worship the Lord in the Eucharist.

They will learn that the Catholic Church offers times of Eucharistic worship, called Adoration and Benediction.

Materials

- Children's Bible
- *Activity Book*, p. 127
- Pictures of images in the Divine Praises

Optional:

- If possible, arrange for a priest to come in and explain Adoration and Benediction, then have 15 minutes of Eucharistic Adoration and Benediction and a demonstration of all things used in Adoration/ Benediction
- "Tantum ergo," *Adoremus Hymnal*, #393

Begin

Begin with a demonstration of all the things used in Adoration/Benediction (see opposite page for details). Handle these items with great care and reverence. If possible, have a priest make this presentation. Allow them to come close to see (but not touch) the monstrance. They can smell the incense. They may be allowed to touch the humeral veil. Have them practice singing the songs for Adoration and Benediction—they have learned them all this year.

Most churches offer Mass every day of the week. Maybe you can find a way to go more often.

We can visit the church during the week. Jesus is there in the tabernacle. He would love to have you come and talk to Him for a little while. Visiting Jesus in the tabernacle is one way to receive much grace. You will be happier and holier after you make these visits. If the church door is locked, say hello to Jesus, and a short prayer, before you go. He will hear you and be very pleased.

Sometimes your church may have a special time of worship that is not the Mass. It may be a holy hour or a time of adoration and benediction. The priest takes our Lord from the tabernacle. He places Him in a monstrance. Then everyone can see and adore Jesus in the Holy Eucharist. The priest blesses the people and they sing a special song or say special prayers.

We know that Jesus is present in the church. We must be serious and remember His presence. Babies make noise and run in church because they do not know about Jesus. But those who know and love Him do not talk in church. We walk quietly to our seats. We genuflect with respect. We do not turn around and stare at others. We spend our time in loving prayer with Jesus.

160

Develop

1. Read paragraph 6 from the text with the students.

2. Explain to the students that a Holy Hour is when one comes to pray before the Blessed Sacrament for one hour. Many people do this in front of Jesus exposed in a monstrance, however, this may be done with Jesus in the tabernacle, too. You may read from a Bible of Jesus' invitation to the Apostles to watch and pray for one hour with Him in the Garden of Gethsemane (Mt 26:36–40; Mk 14:32–37).

3. If possible, take the children to the church for some time of Adoration and Benediction. If this is not possible, take them to visit Jesus in the tabernacle. Remind the children to be reverent in church. Tell them that when Jesus is exposed in the monstrance, if someone needs to get out of his seat, he does a special genuflection: he goes down on both knees and makes the Sign of the Cross.

4. Have the students take their textbooks with them. On p. 162, can be found the Divine Praises. Whether in adoration or prayer before the tabernacle, lead the children in saying this prayer.

5. Ask the children about their time in adoration. Did they enjoy this? Did they feel close to Jesus? How did they feel when they were blessed by Jesus? What did they like about this experience?

6. Review the prayer of the Divine Praises with the children. Explain any words they do not know. You may need to review the Immaculate Conception: when Mary was conceived in her mother's womb without Original Sin. A Paraclete is like an advocate or defense lawyer, someone on your side to help you. You may have pictures of the various devotions to show the children, such as the Sacred Heart, etc.

Name:____________________

Draw a monstrance on the altar on the next page. Put a candle on each side to show that Christ is present.

Faith and Life Series • Grade 2 • Chapter 33 • Lesson 3 127

Reinforce

1. Have the students complete *Activity Book*, p. 127.

2. Have them work on the Words to Know for this chapter, including Sanctuary Lamp, Tabernacle, and Monstrance.

3. You may have the children review the difference between genuflecting when Jesus is in the tabernacle and genuflecting (double) when Jesus is exposed in the monstrance.

Conclude

1. Together, pray the Divine Praises.

2. Together sing "Tantum ergo," *Adoremus Hymnal*, #393.

Preview

In the next lesson, we will learn more about proper church etiquette.

THINGS USED IN BENEDICTION/ADORATION

- Monstrance
- Incense
- Thurible
- Cope
- Humeral veil
- Songs: "O Saving Victim," "Tantum Ergo," "Holy God We Praise Thy Name," others as used by your parish

See Appendix p. C-4.

NOTES

LESSON FOUR: REVERENCE

Aims

The students will learn that they should behave with reverence in the presence of the Lord.

They will learn church etiquette, such as genuflecting, silence in church, and devotion and attention at Mass.

Materials

- *Activity Book*, p. 128
- Poster paper, markers

Optional:
- "Tantum ergo," *Adoremus Hymnal*, #393

Begin

Begin the class by asking the students how they should behave in church:
- They should listen
- They should respond to the parts of the Mass
- They should not look around
- They should receive Holy Communion reverently
- They should sit still and be quiet
- They should pray
- They should remember that Jesus is present

Monstrance: A beautiful holder for the Host. It is used at adoration and benediction services.

Sanctuary Lamp: A special light that burns by the tabernacle to let us know that Jesus is there.

Tabernacle: A box-like container in our churches where the Holy Eucharist is kept.

Q. 64 *Does Jesus remain in the Blessed Sacrament after the Mass?*
Yes, Jesus remains in the Blessed Sacrament after the Mass. Jesus is reserved in the tabernacle (CCC 1379–80).

161

Develop

1. Read the rest of the chapter with the students.

2. Review church etiquette with the students:
   - Ask them what they should do when they first enter the church. They should bless themselves with Holy Water to remind them of their Baptisms.
   - Ask them how they should walk to their pews. Quietly.
   - Ask them what they should do before they enter their pews.They should genuflect to Jesus in the tabernacle. If Jesus is not reserved in the main body of the church, they should bow toward the altar. Review these two gestures with the children.
   - Ask them what they should do before Mass begins. They should spend time praying quietly in their pews.
   - You may review the order of the Mass and the proper responses.
   - Ask them what they should do when they get up to leave after Mass. They should finish their prayers, then quietly get up and genuflect (or bow) as they leave their pews. They should leave the church quietly so they do not disturb others who may be praying, and be reverent in Jesus' presence.
   - Ask them what they should wear to Mass. Their best clothes, to honor Jesus their King.

3. Ask them if they are only in Jesus' presence in the church. God is always with them, He is everywhere and they should be aware (this is a fruit of the Holy Spirit: Fear of the Lord). Remind them that just because they are not in church, does not mean that they should behave badly. They should speak to others and behave with others knowing that Jesus is in their midst; this is one way that they may learn to avoid sin.

4. You may go to the church to review church etiquette in practice, and take time to pray before Jesus in the tabernacle.

We Pray:

THE DIVINE PRAISES

Blessed be God.
Blessed be His Holy Name.
Blessed be Jesus Christ, true God and true Man.
Blessed be the Name of Jesus.
Blessed be His Most Sacred Heart.
Blessed be His Most Precious Blood.
Blessed be Jesus in the Most Holy Sacrament of the Altar.
Blessed be the Holy Spirit, the Paraclete.
Blessed be the great Mother of God, Mary most holy.
Blessed be her holy and Immaculate Conception.
Blessed be her glorious Assumption.
Blessed be the name of Mary, Virgin and Mother.
Blessed be Saint Joseph, her most chaste spouse.
Blessed be God in His angels and in His saints.

162

Reinforce

1. Have the students work on *Activity Book*, p. 128.

2. Have the children make posters about church etiquette. You may assign different groups for different rules of church etiquette, e.g., wear your best clothes, be quiet in church, remember to genuflect, etc. Their posters may then be displayed in the classroom.

Conclude

1. Have the children pray the Divine Praises, p. 162 of the text.

2. Sing "Tantum ergo," *Adoremus Hymnal*, #393.

Preview

In the next lesson, we will review the material covered in this chapter.

THE ALTAR

The Holy Sacrifice of the Mass is offered on an altar (from the Latin *altaria*), which is the center and focal point of the church, and upon which Christ is made sacramentally present during the Consecration. In the early days of Christianity, Mass was celebrated on the tombs of martyrs in the catacombs of Rome. Because of this, modern altars have the relics of saints, called the altar stone, upon their surface. Altars are usually made of stone, but can also be made of wood. They represent two aspects of the Christian mystery: the sacrificial altar where Christ offers Himself for our sins, and the table of our Lord, upon which Christ gives Himself for our food.

NOTES

CHAPTER THIRTY-THREE: REVIEW AND ASSESSMENT

Aims

The students' understanding of the material covered this week will be reviewed and assessed.

Materials

- Quiz 33 (Appendix, p. A-47)
- "Tantum ergo," *Adoremus Hymnal*, #393

Review

1. Review that Jesus said that He will remain with us always. They should know that He is always with us:
   - When two or three are gathered in His name
   - When the Bible is read
   - During the liturgy
   - In the seven sacraments
   - Especially in the Holy Eucharist

2. Review that Jesus is reserved in the tabernacle. His presence is signified by the sanctuary lamp.

3. Review that we are invited to worship Jesus in the Blessed Sacrament. We can do this through a Holy Hour, or by attending Adoration and Benediction. They may also visit Jesus in the church—this pleases Jesus.

4. They should be aware of church etiquette, including:
   - Reverence in church
   - Genuflection to Jesus in the tabernacle/bowing to the altar (versus a two-knee genuflection when Jesus is exposed in the monstrance)
   - Blessing ourselves with Holy Water
   - Being quiet
   - Being aware of Jesus' presence

Name:

Jesus Is Always Present **Quiz 33**

Circle the correct answer.

1. Jesus is with us always, but most especially:
   a) where two or three are gathered in His name
   b) when we read the Bible
   (c)) in the Blessed Sacrament

2. We know Jesus is present in the tabernacle by:
   (a)) the Sanctuary Lamp
   b) people praying there
   c) our teaching telling us so

3. The greatest gift we can receive is:
   a) a great birthday gift
   b) a present at Christmas
   (c)) Jesus Himself in Holy Communion

4. Why should we visit the church?
   a) because it is a fun building to play in
   (b)) to visit Jesus in the tabernacle
   c) to show others we are Catholic

5. During Adoration and Benediction, Jesus is:
   a) in the tabernacle
   (b)) in a monstrance
   c) beside the Sanctuary Lamp

Complete the chart below:

WHEN	WHAT YOU SHOULD DO
At the entrance of the Church by the Holy Water font	We should bless ourselves with Holy Water
Before you enter your pew During the Mass	We should genuflect to Jesus in the tabernacle
As you walk to and from your pew	Walk quietly
When Jesus is exposed in the monstrance (before you enter your pew, or as you leave it)	Make a special genuflection by kneeling on both knees and making the Sign of the Cross

Faith and Life • Grade 2 • Appendix A *A - 47*

Assess

1. Distribute Quiz 33 and answer any questions they have. As the students turn in their quizzes, individually quiz them on the Memorization Questions and Words to Know.

2. When all quizzes have been turned in, review the correct answers.

Conclude

1. Sing "Tantum ergo," *Adoremus Hymnal*, #393.

2. Pray the Divine Praises.

CHAPTER THIRTY-FOUR
HEAVEN, OUR HOME

Catechism of the Catholic Church References

Christ's Resurrection and Ours: 992–1004, 1015–17
Christian Beatitude: 1720–24, 1728–29
Christian Holiness: 2012–16, 2028–29
Communion of Saints: 946–59, 960–62
Heaven: 1023–29, 1053
  Place of God: 326
  Place of Deceased: 1023–29
Hell: 1033–37, 1056–57
  Consequence of Mortal Sin: 1861
  Location of the Damned: 633
  In Church Teaching: 1035
Individual Judgment: 1038–41, 1059
Last Judgment: 677–78, 681–82, 1038–41, 1051–52
Prayer for the Dead: 1032, 1055
Purgatory: 1030–32, 1054
Resurrection of the Body: 988–91
Resurrection of the Dead: 988
To Die in Christ Jesus: 1005–14, 1018–19, 1020, 1052

Scripture References

Angels Bless the Lord: Rev 7:12
Faith and Works: James 2:24
Great Commandment: Mt 22:37–40; Mk 12:30–33; Lk 10:27 (see also 1 Cor 2:9)

Background Reading: *The Fundamentals of Catholicism* by Fr. Kenneth Baker, S.J.

Volume 3:
"The Law of Death," pp. 361–63

Volume 3:
"The Resurrection of of the Body," pp. 379–82

Summary of Lesson Content

Lesson 1

Death is a consequence of Original Sin. At death, our bodies and souls are separated. Our soul will live forever because it is a spiritual being.

Heaven is the eternal reward of the just.
Purgatory is a transitional state of purification for those who have died in the friendship of God but are not yet ready for Heaven (either they have venial sins or have not done sufficient penance in this life).
Hell is for those who choose to reject God and do not have His life in their soul (i.e., by mortal or Original Sin).

Lesson 2

At the end of the world, man's body will be reunited with his soul. This is called the Resurrection of the body.

The body will resurrected with different qualities:
- It will be the same body we have now, but glorified
- It will not be limited by space and time
- It will not suffer or die again
- It is beautiful and glorious
- It will have a spiritual nature

Lesson 3

Man's life on earth determines his eternal state, and therefore, he should love God and abide by His Laws.

Lesson 4

Heaven is our eternal home, and if man lives according to God's love and Laws, man will be happy in this life and the next.

In Heaven, we will be in the presence of God, Mary, and the saints, as well as our loved ones who have gone before us who are in Heaven.

LESSON ONE: HEAVEN, OUR HOPE

Aims

The students will review that death is a consequence of Original Sin.

They will learn that at death, our bodies and souls are separated. Our souls will live forever.

They will be introduced to the concepts of Heaven, Purgatory, and hell.

Materials

- *Activity Book*, p. 128
- Writing paper, pencils

Optional:

- "May flights of angels lead you on your way," *Adoremus Hymnal*, #573

Begin

You may want to invite in families for this lesson because some children do not yet really understand death, while others understand it too well. You may begin the class by asking the children if they know what death is. Everyone will die someday because of Original Sin. It is when a person leaves this world. His body and his soul are separated. His soul lives forever. The body is buried and returned to the earth—this is called a funeral. Let the children share their experiences with death and funerals (pets and family members).

34 Heaven, Our Home

"In my Father's house are many rooms; if it were not so, would I have told you that I go to prepare a place for you?"

John 14:2

We all die someday. Our souls and our bodies will be separated. If we have loved God in this life, we will be ready to love God forever. God will welcome us into Heaven. We will be happy there forever. We will see Jesus and Mary and people in our family who have died. The souls in Heaven are called **saints**.

Some will die with their souls almost ready for God, but not quite. Maybe they have committed venial sins, or they have not made up for their sins with penance. Before these souls go to Heaven, they go for a while to **Purgatory** to be made clean of all sin and its punishment. Souls in Purgatory are sad because they do not see God, but happy because they know that they will see Him soon.

If a person has not loved God in this life and dies with a mortal sin on his soul, he will not be able to love God or want to be with Him. A soul that hates God will be in a place called **Hell**.

163

Develop

Note: Because this chapter covers the topics of death, Heaven, Purgatory, and hell, I encourage the teacher to read through the entire chapter on the first day to provide context.

1. Read the entire chapter from beginning to end. Have the children take turns reading paragraphs aloud. Today's lesson will focus on paragraphs 1–3.

2. Explain to the children that we determine, by our response to God's love, where our soul will go at the end of this life. If we love God and obey His Laws, God will invite us to be happy with Him forever in Heaven, with Mary, the angels, and the saints. This is our greatest hope. We were created to be with God forever in Heaven. If we live this life preparing for Heaven, we will be happy in this life, too.

3. Explain to them that a person does not go to Purgatory forever. If we go to Purgatory, we will also go to Heaven. Souls that have venial sins, or that have not done enough penance in this life, go to Purgatory, where their souls are cleaned and made ready for Heaven. The soul is happy because it knows it will go to Heaven. The soul is also sad because it is not yet with God in Heaven and because it must make up for its sins. We can pray for souls in Purgatory, to help them to get to Heaven and to relieve their suffering.

4. Explain to the children that hell is a place of eternal suffering: it lasts forever. We choose to go to hell by rejecting God and His love, and removing His life in us. We do this through mortal sin: we know something is seriously wrong, and we freely intend and choose to do it anyway.

5. You may teach about the sacrament of the Anointing of the Sick.

Name:____________________

Draw people, angels, and saints worshiping our Lord in the Eucharist

128 *Faith and Life Series • Grade 2 • Chapter 34 • Lesson 1*

Reinforce

1. Have the students complete *Activity Book*, p. 128.

2. If time permits, teach them how the Anointing of the Sick prepares man's soul for a happy death.

3. Teach them to sing "May flights of angels lead you on your way," *Adoremus Hymnal*, #573.

Conclude

1. Have them write prayers, asking God to help them get to Heaven.

2. Pray a decade of the Rosary for the souls in Purgatory.

Preview

In the next lesson, we will learn about the resurrected body.

ANOINTING OF THE SICK

Christ instituted this sacrament (see Mk 6:13 and Jas 5:14, 15) to give spiritual health, including the remission of sins, to Christians who are seriously ill. It may also restore bodily health. The sacrament consists of a priest anointing the sick person, accompanied by certain special prayers. The priest uses oil made from olives and blessed by the bishop to anoint the forehead and hands (in the Roman rite) or other parts of the body (Eastern rite). It may only be administered to baptized Catholics who retain the use of reason and who are in danger of death due to illness (i.e., not a condemned criminal, nor a martyr). All sin, including mortal, is forgiven.

NOTES

LESSON TWO: THE RESURRECTED BODY

Aims

The students will learn that at the end of the world, man's body will be reunited with his soul. This reunion is called the Resurrection of the body.

They will learn that the body will be a resurrected body with different qualities.

Materials

- Children's Bible
- *Activity Book*, p. 129

Optional:
- "May flights of angels lead you on your way," *Adoremus Hymnal*, #573

Begin

Review the Resurrection of Jesus (Chapter 24) and the qualities of His Body.
- Jesus was really risen, body and soul
- Jesus ate
- Jesus was not always recognized in his risen body
- Jesus would appear and disappear and be wherever He wished to be

Review the Ascension of Jesus (Chapter 29) and the Assumption of Mary (Chapter 32)
- Jesus and Mary are in Heaven, body and soul

Develop

1. Reread as a class paragraph 4.

2. *Explain to the students the qualities of a resurrected body:*
   - *It will be the same body we have now, but glorified:* *God does not give us a new body, but raises up the one we have now and glorifies it. This is why it is so important to care for our bodies and to bury the dead. We are not sure how God will do this, but we know from the Resurrection of Jesus that the same body of the deceased is raised up and glorified (Mary's body, too, was assumed).*
   - *It will not be limited by space and time:* *Just as Jesus was able to be in many places without time passing, enter a locked room, and disappear after breaking bread in Emmaus, we know that the resurrected body will be able to travel through space without the bounds of time. Our bodies will obey our souls and will respond perfectly.*
   - *It will not die again:* *Our bodies will not die again. They will be with the soul forever. If our soul is in hell, our body will also go to hell and will suffer for all eternity with the soul. If our soul is in Heaven, our body will also go to Heaven and will rejoice and be happy forever with God and the angels and the saints.*
   - *It is beautiful and glorious:* *Jesus was not immediately recognized, even though he still bore the wounds of the crucifixion (remember, Saint Thomas put his hands in the wounds). Jesus' body was made beautiful and illuminated with radiance. We also saw this with the transfiguration of Christ. Our bodies, too, will be made beautiful and radiant for all of eternity.*
   - *It will have a spiritual nature:* *The resurrected body of Jesus was a real body, but it had a spiritual nature. It knew the glory of Heaven and ascended there. So, too, with the Resurrection of the body, will our bodies be made spiritual and subject to our souls.*

Name:__________________

Word Find

BODIES	REUNITED	GOD	MARY
HEAVEN	DIE	VENIAL SIN	SOULS
MORTAL SIN	HELL	HOME	PURGATORY

```
M O R T A L S I N D I E
R G O D E R E D W D S H
E B P U R G A T O R Y E
U L H O M E S T N S A L
N F O R A V E R E C R L
I O B R R A D M E I E E
T D C H Y R C H R P F A
E S T R I N I Y E L U S
D E L E B R A T E E L T
E I B V E N I A L S I N
S O U L S Y H E A V E N
D E R B O D I E S I T Y
```

Faith and Life Series • Grade 2 • Chapter 34 • Lesson 2 129

THE STATE OF RESURRECTED BODIES

Impassibility: The body will no longer suffer pain or death; it will not corrupt

Brightness: The body will be beautiful and brilliant

Agility: The body will be able to pass through matter and go to all parts of the universe with great speed

Subtility: The body will be a spiritual rather than a corporeal body

Reinforce

1. Have the students complete *Activity Book*, p. 129.

2. The students may discuss their thoughts on what the resurrected body may be like and what Heaven may be like. You may lead with sentence starters such as: Heaven is more fun than_____, Heaven is more beautiful than_____, Heaven is better than_____, in Heaven I will see_____, I want to_____in Heaven, I want to go to Heaven because_____, I want my resurrected body to be like_____, etc.

Conclude

1. Pray a decade of the Rosary for the souls in Purgatory.

2. Sing with the children "May flights of angels lead you on your way," *Adoremus Hymnal*, #573.

Preview

In the next lesson we will learn more about the importance of the way we live and respond to God's love (and that this will determine our eternal state).

NOTES

____

____

____

____

____

____

____

____

____

____

____

LESSON THREE: I CHOOSE HEAVEN

Aims

The students will review that Jesus died on the Cross for all of our sins. He wants all of us to go to Heaven.

They will learn that we must respond to God's love with faith and obedience to His Laws to go to Heaven.

Materials

- Children's Bible
- *Activity Book*, p. 130

Optional:
- "May flights of angels lead you on your way," *Adoremus Hymnal*, #573

Begin

Review that we choose whether we go to Heaven or hell. God wants all of us to go to Heaven, but we can choose. He made us free to choose because He loves us so much. God wants all people to respond to His love by faith in Him and by obeying His Laws. Review the Great Commandment (found in children's Bible: Mt 22:37–40; Mk 12:30–33; Lk 10:27). We are promised the wonder of Heaven if we obey this Law of love in response to God (1 Cor 2:9).

At the end of the world our souls will be reunited with our bodies. We will be able to enjoy Heaven with both our bodies and souls.

That is why it is important to live according to God's Laws. Each good thing we do makes us pleasing to God and ready for Heaven. Even little things like saying our prayers and cheerfully helping others help to get us ready.

Heaven is our real home. Earth is only a place where we stay for a while and learn to love God. Jesus told us to spend our life "storing up treasure in Heaven." We can begin right now. The sight of the Blessed Trinity and the Mother of God will be more beautiful than anything we know. Let's pray every day for God to make us saints!

Words to Know:

saints Purgatory Hell

Q. 65 *What will happen at the end of the world?*
At the end of the world, the dead will be resurrected and their bodies will be reunited with their souls (CCC 988, 997).

165

Develop

1. Read paragraph 5 with the students.

2. Read from the children's Bible James 2:24 (not by faith alone, but also by works). Ask them how they will act if they believe in God:
   - They will pray
   - They will obey His Laws
   - They will love their neighbors
   - They will want to share the Good News with others
   - They will be faithful to God in all things, and show Him as much as possible how much they love Him

3. Ask them why we must keep the Commandments:
   - Because it is the right thing to do
   - Because we love God

4. Ask the children if they can reject God's love. How?
   - By sinning

5. Ask them if they can return to God's love and try to respond in love again if they sin. Yes. What must they do? Receive the Sacrament of Penance.

6. Ask the children how they can be strengthened in God's love and get help to overcome sin and temptation. Through the sacraments, especially in the Sacraments of Penance and the Eucharist and by praying in front of Jesus in the Blessed Sacrament.

7. *Ask the children if our actions have consequences. If they are mean to their brother or sister, what happens? If they give their mother a gift, what happens? If they disobey their father, what happens? If they pray to grow in holiness, what happens? If they die in mortal sin, what happens? If they die with God's grace, what happens? If they die with God's grace but need purification, what happens? How can we go to Heaven? By choosing to love God faithfully.*

Name:____________________

Draw a picture of you in your true home, Heaven.

130 *Faith and Life Series • Grade 2 • Chapter 34 • Lesson 3*

Reinforce

1. Have the students work on *Activity Book*, p. 130.

2. Have them begin memorizing the Words to Know for this chapter.

Conclude

1. Lead them in praying a decade of the Rosary for the souls in Purgatory.

2. End with singing "May flights of angels lead you on your way," *Adoremus Hymnal*, #573.

Preview

In the next lesson, we will learn how living this life to prepare for Heaven will make us happy in this life and the next.

THE HOLY SOULS

The prayers and penances of the faithful on earth can alleviate the sufferings of the holy souls in Purgatory. So, too, can Masses be offered in their honor. Upon reaching Heaven, it is believed that the just souls thus aided will respond by praying for the faithful on earth who prayed for them.

NOTES

LESSON FOUR: TRUE HAPPINESS

Aims

The students will learn that if they live this life preparing for Heaven, they will be happy in this life and the next.

They will learn that in Heaven, they will be happy forever with the Trinity, Mary, the angels and the saints, as well as loved ones.

Materials

- *Activity Book*, pp. 131 and 132

Optional:

- "May flights of angels lead you on your way," *Adoremus Hymnal*, #573

Begin

Ask them what they want to be when they grow up. Ask them what they must do to become what they want to be. (For some this means school, practicing sports or music, etc.) Ask them where they want to be for all of eternity. Ask them what they must do to get there. Review with the children that they choose Heaven by how they respond to God in love.

Name:__________________

Color the squares that will help you get to Heaven in red. Color the squares that will not help you get to Heaven in blue.

Hide a letter to your parents	Hit your brother or sister	Not include a friend in your games
Play with your brother or sister	Visit Jesus at church	Pick on a student at school
Talk back to your father	Say God's name in vain	Watch TV during prayer
Disobey your mother	Decide to play and not pray	Visit your grand-mother
Help your mom at home	Pray for your sick friend	Do not learn your answers for school
Learn your prayers	Be nice to everyone	Say bad words
Study for your test	Say something mean	Feed the dog
Tell a lie	Do your homework	Play rough at recess
Talk during Mass	Pick up your toys	Tell the truth

Faith and Life Series • Grade 2 • Chapter 34 • Lesson 4 131

Develop

1. Read the last paragraph of the text with the students.

2. Ask the children if they are happy when they sin. No. Why do people sin then? Because people think that is what will make them happy, even though it will not. Tell the children that we will always be happiest if we do what God wants us to do because He made us that way. We were made to be happy when we are faithful to God, and unhappy when we are not.

3. If we must prepare for Heaven by obeying God, keeping His Commandments, and loving Him—and these things make us happy here on earth, as well as in Heaven—then shouldn't we always try to please God?

4. Ask the children what are some ways they can follow God and please Him?

5. *Explain to the students that although we know that we will die, we never know when, so it is important to always live in a way that is pleasing to God. What should we do to be sure we are always ready to meet God in Heaven?*
   - *Receive the Sacrament of Penance regularly*
   - *Go to Holy Communion frequently*
   - *Say our prayers*
   - *Not sin, obey God*
   - *Show God and others how much we love them*

6. You may explain the Communion of saints to the children. Explain to the children that in Heaven, they will be with God forever, but also with the Blessed Virgin Mary, the angels, the saints, and the souls of friends and family who are in Heaven. We will also meet the souls from Purgatory, for whom we have prayed, and all the souls that are pleasing to God. We will be so happy in Heaven with the Church Triumphant.

Name:__________________

QUESTIONS

1. Who is in Heaven?
All who have loved God in this life

2. How can we get to Heaven?
By loving God in this life

3. Do all people go to Heaven? Where might they go?
No. Some might go to Purgatory and others to hell

4. Who goes to Purgatory? What happens there?
Those who are almost ready for God. They will be made clean of all sin and punishment

5. Who goes to hell? What happens there?
Those who have not loved God in this life and died with mortal sins on their souls

6. What will happen at the end of the world?
Our souls will be reunited with our bodies

7. Why are we on earth?
To learn to love God

8. Where is our true home?
Heaven

9. What is the most beautiful sight?
The sight of the Blessed Trinity and the Mother of God

132 *Faith and Life Series • Grade 2 • Chapter 34 • Lesson 4*

CHALK TALK:
THE THREE STATES OF THE CHURCH

Triumphant: These are the angels and saints who are happy with God in Heaven for all eternity

Militant: These are the faithful on earth who are soldiers for Christ in this world; they struggle to avoid sin, to love God, and to help each other die in the state of grace

Suffering: These are the holy souls in Purgatory who are suffering for the sins they committed on earth in order to be purified to reach Heaven and eternal happiness

Reinforce

1. Have the students work on *Activity Book*, p. 131, and the questions on *Activity Book*, p. 132.

2. Have the students pray for their deceased family members and the souls in Purgatory, with the intercession of the angels and saints.

Conclude

1. Lead them in praying a decade of the Rosary for the souls in Purgatory.

2. End with singing "May flights of angels lead you on your way," *Adoremus Hymnal*, #573.

Preview

In the next lesson, we will review the material covered in this chapter.

NOTES

CHAPTER THIRTY-FOUR:
REVIEW AND ASSESSMENT

Aims

The students' understanding of the material covered this week will be reviewed and assessed.

Materials

- Quiz 34 (Appendix, p. A-48)
- Unit 8 Test (Appendix, pp. A-49 and A-50)
- "May flights of angels lead you on your way," *Adoremus Hymnal*, #573

Review

1. Review that all people must die because of Original Sin. Bodily death occurs when the body and soul are separated. The soul will live forever. The body will be returned to the earth, usually through a ceremony called a funeral.

2.Review the following:
Heaven: An eternal happiness for people who have responded to God in love and faithfulness
Purgatory: A temporary purification for people who have died in the friendship of God, but with venial sins (or they have not done enough penance in this life)
Hell: An eternal suffering for people who have chosen to reject God and have died without His life of grace (have mortal sin on their souls)

3. Review that bodies will be reunited with souls at the end of time. This is called the resurrection of the body.

4. Review that we choose where our soul will go for all eternity by our faith and actions. To go to Heaven, we must love God and show Him this by obeying His Laws and loving our neighbors.

5. They should be able to explain the Communion of saints.

Name:

Heaven, Our Home **Quiz 34**

True or False:

T 1. We will all die someday because of original sin.
T 2. When we die, our soul lives forever.
F 3. All people go to Heaven.
F 4. A soul that goes to Purgatory will go to hell.
T 5. A saint is someone in Heaven.
T 6. Our bodies will be reunited to our souls.
T 7. We choose by our actions in this life, where our soul will go.
T 8. Heaven is our real home.
T 9. By preparing for Heaven in this life, we will be happy now and forever.
T 10. We can pray for the souls in Purgatory.

Please answer in complete sentences:

1. What must a person do to go to Heaven?
We must love God in this life in order to go to Heaven.

2. What must a person do to go to Hell?
If a person does not love God in this life, he will go to Hell.

3. What is the Communion of Saints?
The Communion of Saints refers to all the members of Christ's Church on earth as well as the saints in heaven and the souls in Purgatory.

4. Who do we know is in Heaven?
All those who were faithful to God while on earth.

A - 48 *Faith and Life • Grade 2 • Appendix A*

Assess

1. Distribute Quiz 34 and answer any questions that they may have.

2. When they turn in their quizzes, individually quiz them on the Words to Know.

3. When all quizzes have been turned in, review the correct answers with the class.

4. Repeat steps 1 and 3 for the unit test.

Conclude

1. Have an end of the year party. Be sure the children take home their books and assignments from the year.

2. Sing "May flights of angels lead you on your way," *Adoremus Hymnal*, #573.

3. End with prayer, asking God to watch over the children until the next year of class and to bring them back safely.

Faith and Life series: Jesus Our Life Appendices

APPENDIX A: QUIZZES AND UNIT TESTS

APPENDIX B: GAMES, CRAFTS, AND SCRIPTS

APPENDIX C: WE GO TO MASS

Name:

Our Heavenly Father — Quiz 1

Matching

God	The part of the Bible that tells us about Jesus and the Church.
Bible	The Creator of Heaven and earth, our Father.
Soul	The part of the Bible that tells us how people prepared for Jesus.
Heaven	The part of you that makes you live—it will live forever.
Old Testament	The Word of God.
New Testament	A place of perfect happiness where we will someday be with God.

Fill in the blanks *Use the words below to help you.*

Heaven	special	Father	forever	soul
Bible	New	Old	Sunday	Mass

1. God is our ________________. He watches over us and takes care of all our needs. He wants you to be with Him forever in ________________.

2. God made you different from everyone else, because you are _________.

3. God's special gift to you is a ____________. It allows you to live, to think, and to live ________________.

4. God wanted us to know about Him and how to get to be with Him in Heaven. He gave us His Word in the ________________, which has two parts: the ________ Testament and the __________ Testament.

5. At ______________ we hear readings from the Bible. On _____________ we hear three readings.

Name:

The Blessed Trinity — Quiz 2

For each question, write the Person of the Trinity which best suits the description: Father, Son or Holy Spirit.

1. ____________________ Died for our sins on a Cross and rose from the dead.
2. ____________________ Created the whole world out of nothing.
3. ____________________ Helps us to pray.
4. ____________________ Came down from Heaven and became man.
5. ____________________ Comes to live in you at Baptism.
6. ____________________ Jesus Christ.
7. ____________________ Is the First Person.
8. ____________________ Is the Second Person.
9. ____________________ Is the Third Person.
10. ____________________ Is not the Father or the Son.
11. ____________________ Is not the Son or the Holy Spirit.
12. ____________________ Is God and Man.

Part Two:

Draw your own picture of the Trinity. (You may use the back of this quiz if you need more space.)

Name:

God Made Us Quiz 3

Please answer in complete sentences.

1. Why did God create the world and people?

2. How can we help God take care of His creation?

3. How can we give thanks and praise to God?

Multiple Choice *Circle the correct answer.*

1. We know God is wise because:
a. All creation works together.
b. Rocks cannot think.
c. Plants do not talk to us.

2. We know God is powerful because:
a. Flowers are delicate.
b. He made mountains, rivers, and the stars.
c. Monkeys make us laugh.

3. We know God is good because:
a. Some animals bite.
b. We sometimes make mistakes.
c. God gives us all we need.

4. We know God is beautiful because:
a. Rocks are very hard.
b. We can see beauty in creation.
c. We cannot see beauty in creation.

Name:

God Made Us — Quiz 4

Fill in the blanks

GUARDIAN ANGEL GRACE IMAGE OF GOD GARDEN OF EDEN

1. God made Adam and Eve, and they lived in the ______ ______ ______.

2. Adam and Eve had a gift called ______________.

3. We are all made in the __________ ______ __________.

4. God gave us a special friend to help us to know, love and serve God.

This friend is our ______________ __________.

Write three ways you can know God.

1.

2.

3.

Write three ways you can love God.

1.

2.

3.

Write three ways you can serve God.

1.

2.

3.

Name:

Unit 1 Test — Chapters 1-4

True or False *Circle the correct answer.*

T F God is our Father. He is everywhere.

T F Your soul is what give you life. It lives forever.

T F The Bible has three parts to it: The Old Testament, The New Testament and the Renewed Testament.

T F The Old Testament tells us about people who lived before the coming of the Savior.

T F The New Testament tells us about Jesus and His Church.

Multiple Choice *Circle the correct answer.*

1. God is:
   a. One God in three Persons.
   b. Three Gods in one Person.
   c. Three Gods in three Persons.

2. God is not:
   a. all holy
   b. all powerful
   c. almost perfect

3. Which is not true:
   a. God the Father is the First Person of the Trinity.
   b. God the Son is the Third Person of the Trinity.
   c. God the Holy Spirit is the Third Person of the Trinity.

4. Which is true:
   a. God the Father became Man as Jesus Christ, our Savior.
   b. God the Son became Man as Jesus Christ, our Savior.
   c. God the Holy Spirit became Man as Jesus Christ, our Savior.

5. Which prayer reminds us of the Trinity:
   a. The Our Father
   b. The Glory Be
   c. The Guardian Angel Prayer

Fill in the blanks *Circle the correct answer.*

1. God was______________by Himself, but He made the world and all the creatures, including man (sad, happy).

2. We can know that God is ______________ because of the way everything in the world works together (beautiful, wise).

3. God _____________ take care of everything He created (does, does not).

4. We are all called to ______________ creation (hurt, take care of).

Draw a picture of what it would have been like in the Garden of Eden. Under the picture, describe what you have drawn.

Name:

God Is Offended **Quiz 5**

Matching

Angels	God made him and called him Adam.
Man	Creatures that are pure spirits, which serve God.
Woman	God made her to love and help Adam.
Devils	Creator of Heaven and earth.
God	Creatures that did not obey God and were sent to hell.

Place these events in the right order. Put a 1 beside what happened first, a 2 beside what happened next, and a 3 by what happened last.

____ A snake told Eve to eat the forbidden fruit.

____ Some angels did not obey God and were sent to hell.

____ God told Adam and Eve not to eat of a tree in the garden.

Put a 4 by what happened next, a 5 by what happened after, and a 6 by what happened last.

____ Adam and Eve had to leave the Garden of Eden.

____ Eve ate the fruit and gave it to Adam to eat.

____ God promised to send a Savior.

True or False:

T F Adam and Eve knew it was wrong to disobey God.

T F Adam and Eve chose to disobey God.

Name:

Becoming a Child of God **Quiz 6**

Fill in the blanks *Use the words below to help you.*

Heaven	grace	Sin		
family	Original	sacrament	children	Baptism

At ____________, we become members of God's ____________. Baptism is a ______________. It washes away ____________ ______, and fills our soul with __________. It makes us ______________ of God, and allows us to go to ______________.

List two ways you should try to keep your soul free from sin and filled with grace.

1. ____

2. ____

Write a little about your patron saint, or another saint.

Name:

Obeying God Our Father — Quiz 7

Matching *Write the letter for the person next to the sentence that best describes him.*

a. Adam	___ He was a shepherd made king.
b. Noah	___ He was the first man and ate the forbidden fruit.
c. Isaac	___ A child of God.
d. Eve	___ She was the wife of Adam.
e. Abraham	___ He was asked to sacrifice his son.
f. David	___ The son of really old parents.
g. You	___ He was asked to build a big boat.

Circle T for True, and F for False.

T F Eve gave the forbidden fruit to Adam to eat.

T F Abel killed Cain.

T F Noah built an ark.

T F Abraham sacrificed his son.

T F David killed Goliath with a slingshot.

Name:

God Gives Us His Laws — Quiz 8

Please answer in complete sentences.

1. What bad thing happened to the descendants of Abraham?

2. Whom did God send to help His people?

3. What did God give to His people so they could be happy?

Put the Ten Commandments in order:

____ You shall not kill

____ You shall not use God's name in vain.

____ You shall not lie.

____ Remember to keep God's day holy.

____ Honor your father and mother.

____ You shall not have other gods beside Me.

____ You shall not covet your neighbor's goods.

____ You shall not commit adultery.

____ You shall not steal.

____ You shall not covet your neighbor's wife.

Name:

Unit 2 Test — Chapters 5-8

Circle the correct answer.

1. The angels
   a) are stronger and smarter than God.
   b) all became devils and were sent to hell.
   c) are God's faithful spirits that serve Him in Heaven.

2. God tested Adam and Eve by
   a) telling them to obey the snake or they would die.
   b) forbidding them from eating of only one tree in the garden.
   c) having them leave the Garden of Eden.

3. Sin is
   a) doing something we didn't know was wrong.
   b) an accident.
   c) choosing to offend God.

4. Adam and Eve gave us
   a) original justice.
   b) grace.
   c) Original Sin.

5. God promised
   a) to help Adam and Eve become better people.
   b) to send a Savior.
   c) never to test people again.

Circle T for True, and F for False

T F Baptism takes away Original Sin and gives us grace.

T F Baptism does not help us to go to Heaven.

T F Baptism is not a sacrament.

T F Many Catholic children have a patron saint.

Matching *Draw lines from the people to the sentences that best describe them.*

Adam and Eve	The story of a man, his boat, and a flood.
Noah	The story of a boy and a giant.
Abraham and Isaac	The story of Creation and the fall of man.
David and Goliath	The story of a father loving God so much he would give up his son.

Fill in the chart below.

For each of the Commandments below, write something that you can do to keep it.

1. The First Commandment.

2. The Second Commandment

3. The Fourth Commandment

4. The Seventh Commandment

5. The Eighth Commandment

Name:

I Choose to Love God Quiz 9

Read each example listed below. On the space provided, write an "A" for accident or "S" for sin.

1. _______ Cathy bumps her elbow and spills her milk.
2. _______ Paul does not come when his father calls him.
3. _______ Jessica refuses to share with her little brother.
4. _______ Andy tells his mother he finished his homework when he really didn't.
5. _______ Nancy pretends she is sick so she can miss school.
6. _______ Roger leaves his homework at home by mistake.
7. _______ Edward uses God's name in a disrespectful way.
8. _______ Anna hits her sister when she doesn't get what she wants.
9. _______ Janet doesn't see the vase on the floor and trips on it.
10. ______ Adam forgets to feed the cat.

Fill in the missing parts of the Great Commandments below:

1. Love God with all your ______________________ .

2. Love your neighbor as ____________________________ .

Write what these words mean:

Sin:

Mortal Sin:

Venial Sin:

Name:

Preparing for Our Saviour Quiz 10

Circle the correct answer.

1. God wanted all people to:
   a) make lots of money
   b) go to school
   c) be happy forever with Him in Heaven

2. God promised to send:
   a) a Savior
   b) a ladder to Heaven
   c) a serpent

3. God chose Mary to be:
   a) the sister to the Son
   b) the aunt to the Holy Spirit
   c) the mother of the Son

4. Mary was free from:
   a) original justice
   b) Original Sin
   c) grace

5. Who came to tell Mary the good news?
   a) Joseph
   b) God
   c) Gabriel

Name:

The Savior Is Born Quiz 11

Write what happened in the Christmas Story using these words.

Bethlehem	shepherds	star	poor
manger	Joseph	gifts	
angel	Jesus	Herod	

1. Jesus was born in a city called ______________________ .

2. Jesus was placed in a ______________ filled with straw.

3. The first people to learn about the newborn Savior were __________ .

4. God did not wish to share His life with the rich first, but with the ______ .

5. An ______________ came to the shepherds to tell about the birth of Jesus.

6. Three wise men followed a big, bright __________ moving across the sky.

7. The wise men brought ______ of gold, frankincense, and myrrh to Jesus.

8. A wicked man named ________ ruled over the land where Jesus was born.

9. God warned __________ to take Jesus and Mary away from Bethlehem.

Name:

The Holy Family Quiz 12

Fill in the blanks *Use the words below to help you.*

Mary	God	Holy Family	sister
Joseph	Nazareth	brother	heavenly
foster-father	obedient	home	carpenter

1. After Herod died, the Holy Family went to live in ___________.
2. Joseph was Jesus' ____________________________.
3. For a job, Joseph was a ________________.
4. ___________ was the wife of Joseph and mother of Jesus.
5. Mary kept the _________ for the Holy Family.
6. Jesus was ____________ to Mary and Joseph.
7. The Father of Jesus is ______________.
8. Jesus, Mary, and Joseph are the _________________.
9. Through Baptism, Jesus is our _____________.
10. Jesus always did what was pleasing to His ______________ Father.

Write five ways you can follow Jesus' example in your family.

1. ____

____

2. ____

____

3. ____

____

4. ____

____

5. ____

____

Name: ____________________

Unit 3 Test — Chapters 9-12

PART I: Please write the Two Great Commandments:

1. ____

2. ____

Please put the Ten Commandments in the right order.

___ Honor your father and mother.
___ You shall not steal.
___ Remember to keep God's day holy.
___ You shall not commit adultery.
___ You shall have no other gods besides me.
___ You shall not covet your neighbor's wife.
___ You shall not lie.
___ You shall not use God's name in vain.
___ You shall not covet your neighbor's goods.
___ You shall not kill.

Please answer in complete sentences.

1. What is a sin?

2. What is a mortal sin?

3. What is a venial sin?

PART II: Please circle the correct answers.

1. Whom did God send to help His people prepare for the Savior?
   a) priests b) prophets c) kings

2. Mary was special because she was free from:
   a) grace b)original justice c) Original Sin

3. Whom did God send to Mary to ask her to be Jesus' mother?
   a) Moses b) Joseph c) Gabriel

4. Who is Jesus' Father?
a) Joseph b) David c) God

5. What season do we celebrate to prepare for Jesus' coming?
a) Advent b) Lent c) Easter

PART III: Answer T for True, and F for False.

____ Jesus was born in Nazareth.
____ Jesus was first visited by shepherds.
____ Wise men followed a star.
____ Jesus was laid in a manger.
____ Herod wanted to honor Jesus.

PART IV: Use the following words in sentences that tell us about the Holy Family. Answer 5 of the 7 listed below.

Nazareth: ____
____

Carpenter: ____
____

Mary: ____
____

Foster-father:____
____

Obey: ____
____

Jesus: ____
____

Joseph: ____
____

Name:

The Good News Quiz 13

Circle the correct answer.

1. Jesus was baptized by:
   a) Saint Joseph b) Mary, His mother c) John the Baptist

2. Jesus went into the desert for:
   a) one month b) forty days c) three months

3. Jesus went from town to town to:
   a) preach the Good News b) purchase goods for the Kingdom
   c) bury people

4. Jesus chose ____________ Apostles.
   a) ten b) eleven c) twelve

5. What two parables did you study?
   a) The Pearl and Fisher's Net b) Flour and Leaven and Good Seed
   c) The Mustard Seed and Buried Treasure

Circle the names of the Twelve Apostles:

Bartholomew Biff Andrew Peter Philip Tim Simon
John James James Judas Thaddeus Thomas Matthew
Bob Sam

Name: ____

Jesus Our Teacher — Quiz 14

Answer these questions.

1. Jesus told a story of a good man who helped a stranger in need. Who was this good man? ____________________
2. By helping the poor, the needy, and those wanting help, we are helping our ____________________.
3. In loving our neighbor, we are really loving ______________.

Write how you can live each of the Corporal Works of Mercy:

1. Feed the Hungry:

2. Give Drink to the Thirsty:

3. Clothe the Naked:

4. Shelter the Homeless:

5. Visit the Sick:

6. Visit the Imprisoned:

7. Bury the Dead:

Name:

Let Us Pray — Quiz 15

Matching *Place the letter from column 2 in the correct space of column 1.*

Column 1	Column 2
____ Our Father Who art in Heaven	a. May what God wants be done so everyone will be happy.
____ Hallowed be Thy Name	b. As His children, we can say this.
____ Thy Kingdom come	c. May God provide all we need.
____ Thy will be done on earth as it is in Heaven.	d. May everyone be united with Him.
____ Give us this day our daily bread	e. May we use God's name with respect and honor.
____ And forgive us our trespasses as we forgive those who trespass against us	f. Let us not give in to sin, and may God protect us.
____ Lead us not into temptation but deliver us from evil.	g. May our sins be washed away, and may we love one another.

1. Circle how often God hears our prayers:

sometimes usually always often never

2. Circle why we can trust God to answer our prayers in the best way:

His love we work hard we bother Him He has to

Name:

We Believe **Quiz 16**

Place an M beside the miracles, and an X beside the events which are not miracles.

____ 1. Mom buys your favorite cookies without being asked.

____ 2. A person is raised from the dead.

____ 3. A person walks on water.

____ 4. A rabbit is pulled from a hat.

____ 5. The sun sets.

____ 6. A lost pet is returned home.

____ 7. After prayers to God, a person is healed.

____ 8. A pizza arrives at your door, but you did not order it!

____ 9. A man escapes from an accident unharmed.

____10. A person skates on ice.

Answer the following questions in complete sentences.

1. Why did Jesus perform miracles?

2. How could Jesus perform miracles? By what power?

3. Name three miracles Jesus did.

   i)

   ii)

   iii)

Name:

Unit 4 Test — Chapter 13–16

PART I: Circle the correct answer.

1. At the beginning of Jesus' public ministry, what did He first do?
   a) went into the desert b) went from town to town
   c) went to the Jordan to be baptized

2. After how many days did Jesus leave the dessert?
   a) 30 b) 40 c) 50

3. What is the Good News?
   a) God wants us to be with Him forever in Heaven.
   b) Jesus was baptized. c) Jesus was a good story-teller.

4. Jesus chose twelve:
   a) followers b) disciples c) parables

PART II: Fill in the blanks.

Our ______________, who art in __________, hallowed be Thy

____________. Thy _____________ come, Thy ________ be done on

____________ as it is in ___________. Give us this _______ our daily

____________, and _______________ us our _______________ as we

_____________ those who trespass against _____, and lead us not into

_________________ but deliver us from _________. Amen.

PART III: Answer in complete sentences:

1. What is prayer?

2. How should we pray?

3. Who taught us the Our Father prayer?

PART IV: Matching

Cana	made to see
Jairus' daughter	calmed
5000	changed water to wine
blind	raised from the dead
storm	fed with bread and fish

PART V: Answer in complete sentences

1. Why did Jesus perform miracles?

2. How are miracles different from magic?

3. By what power did Jesus perform miracles?

4. What was Jesus' first miracle?

5. How do we know that Jesus' power is even stronger than death?

Name:

Asking Forgiveness Quiz 17

Matching

Heartily	hate, am ashamed of
Offended	ought to have
Detest	a share in God's own life
Just	strongly
Punishments	very, with all my heart
Deserving	tell all
Firmly	to make up for a sin by doing something good
Resolve	hurt, saddened
Grace	to do better
Confess	fair
Penance	determine, promise
Amend	penalties

Answer the following questions.

1. Is God like the father in the story of the prodigal son?

2. Why is sin such a sad thing?

3. Does God always forgive us if we are sorry?

Name:

Jesus Forgives Quiz 18

Answer the following questions.

1. How can Jesus heal your soul?

2. Who gave priests the power to forgive sins?

3. What is the sacrament called, in which Jesus hears our sins and forgives them through a priest? (Three names)

   a.

   b.

   c.

4. What is the Sacrament of Penance?

5. What are the five steps to a good confession?

Step 1:

Step 2:

Step 3:

Step 4:

Step 5:

6. What are three effects of the Sacrament of Reconciliation?

   a.

   b.

   c.

Name:

The Sacrament of Penance — Quiz 19

Part 1. Place the steps to a good confession in the correct order.

____ Tell your sins to a priest.
____ Know your sins.
____ Do the penance the priest gives you.
____ Be sorry for your sins.
____ Make up your mind not to sin again.

Part 2. Fill in the blanks.

Cross	sorry	Amen
sins	Bible	confession
kneel	penance	Contrition

Go in and sit in the chair or _______ behind the screen.
Make the Sign of the _______.
Tell the priest how long it has been since your last __________.
Tell your _______ to the priest.
Say: "For these and all my sins, I am _______."
The priest will talk to you and give you a _________.
The priest may read from the _______.
Make an Act of _________.
Receive absolution, and say "_______."

Name:

Making up for Our Offenses Quiz 20

Multiple Choice *Circle the correct answer.*

1. Zacchaeus make up for his sins by repaying people how many times the money he had taken from them?
   a) three
   b) four
   c) five

2. Who can make up for our sins?
   a) Jesus
   b) We can
   c) a and b

3. Penance is:
   a) when we are sorry for our sins
   b) when we make up for our sins
   c) when we repair our relationship with another

4. A habit of doing bad is overcome by:
   a) work, confession, penance, and prayer
   b) time and growing up
   c) pretending we do not have a bad habit

5. You should want to make up for your sins to:
   a) be happy
   b) please Jesus
   c) a and b

List five penances you can do:

1.
2.
3.
4.
5.

Name: ____________________

Unit 5 Test — Chapters 17-20

PART I: Answer the following questions in complete sentences.

1. Why did Jesus work miracles?

2. How do we know that Jesus is God?

3. What are three miracles that Jesus did?
   1.
   2.
   3.

Part II. Write a "T" beside the sentences which are true, and an "F" beside the sentences which are false.

____ Sin is when we choose to break God's laws.
____ God the Father is waiting for us to sin.
____ Sin offends God.
____ God wants us to come back to Him when we sin.
____ For God to forgive us, we must be sorry and admit that what we have done is wrong.
____ God will not always forgive us.
____ There is nothing we can do that is so bad that God won't forgive us if we are truly sorry.
____ By telling God we are sorry, we show God how much we love Him.
____ Sorrow for sin means that we are sorry for our sins, and we do not want to do them again.
____ Only God can forgive sins.

Fill in the blanks:

O my _______, I am heartily __________ for having ____________ you. I detest all my _______ because of your ________ punishments, but __________of all because they offend ________, my God, who are all _______ and deserving of all my ___________. I firmly resolve, with the _________ of Your ______________, to ____________ my sins, to do ____________, and to ____________my life. Amen.

Part III: Matching

God	Jesus hears us and forgives us through him.
Priest	He alone can forgive sins.
Sacrament of Penance	When your sins are forgiven.
Absolve	The sins you commit after Baptism are forgiven when you tell them to a priest.
Confess	To tell something.

Write the five steps to a good confession.

1.
2.
3.
4.
5.

Put these things in the correct order:

____ The priest will talk to you and give you a penance
____ Receive absolution, and say "Amen."
____ Tell the priest how long it has been since your last confession
____ Welcome
____ Say: "For these and all my sins, I am sorry."
____ Make the Sign of the Cross
____ The priest may read from the Bible
____ Dismissal
____ Tell your sins to the priest
____ Make an Act of Contrition.

PART IV: Multiple Choice *Circle the correct answer.*

1. You can make up for your sins by:
   a) going to confession b) not doing them again c) doing penance
2. You should make up for your sins to:
   a) show how good you are b) please Jesus c) grow in vice
3. Penance is:
   a) easy b) hard c) silly
4. The Sacrament of Penance does what two things:
   a) forgives sins and gives grace
   b) heals souls and gives peace c) both a & b
5. We should try to grow in: a) vice b) virtue c) sin

Name:

The Good Shepherd Quiz 21

Matching:

Obedient	Say your daily prayers.
Humble	Always do what pleases God.
Forgiving	Be kind to everyone.
Prayerful	Love your enemies.
Merciful	Tell the truth.

Answer the following questions in complete sentences.

As the Good Shepherd, how does Jesus…

1. … lead His sheep?

2. … feed His sheep?

3. … protect His sheep?

4. …know His sheep?

5. …lay down His life for His sheep?

Name:

The Last Supper Quiz 22

Circle the correct answer.

1. Jesus celebrated the Last Supper
   a. with all of His friends
   b. during the feast called Passover
   c. every time He had dinner

2. When the words of Jesus are said over the bread and wine by a priest
   a. they are no longer bread and wine
   b. they become the Body, Blood, Soul, and Divinity of Jesus really and truly present
   c. both a and b

3. The sacrament of Christ's Body and Blood is called
   a. the Eucharist
   b. the Passover
   c. the Last Supper

4. The priest at Mass says the words of Jesus in the prayer of
   a. tabernacle
   b. communion
   c. Consecration

5. What is transubstantiation?
   a. When the bread and wine are changed into Jesus' Body and Blood.
   b. The place where the Eucharist is stored in the church.
   c. The first time the Apostles received Holy Communion.

What words must be said by a priest over the bread and wine for them to change into Jesus' Body and Blood?

Name:

Jesus Dies for Us — Quiz 23

1. Place the Stations of the Cross in the correct order:

___ Jesus is helped by Simon.
___ Jesus is stripped of His clothes.
___ Jesus is placed in the tomb.
___ Jesus carries His Cross.
___ Jesus speaks to the women.
___ Jesus falls the first time.
___ Jesus is taken down from the Cross.
___ Jesus meets His Mother.
___ Jesus falls a second time.
___ Jesus is condemned to death.
___ Jesus dies on the Cross.
___Veronica wipes the face of Jesus.
___ Jesus falls a third time.
___ Jesus is nailed to the Cross.

2. Please answer in complete sentences:

1. Why did Jesus want to suffer and die on the Cross?

2. How are the Last Supper and the crucifixion connected to the Mass?

3. Why can we say that Mary is our Mother?

4. What did Jesus win for us by dying on the Cross?

5. Jesus asks us to pray with Him. How can we do this?

Name:

He Is Risen, Alleluia! Quiz 24

Circle the correct answer:

1. The women went to the tomb of Jesus on:
   a) Good Friday
   b) Holy Saturday
   c) Easter Sunday

2. Whom did the women see at the tomb?
   a) soldiers
   b) angel
   c) Jesus

3. After His death, what did Jesus Christ do?
   a) rose from the dead
   b) appeared as a ghost
   c) gave up His body

4. What did Jesus give to the Apostles in the upper room?
   a) money
   b) peace
   c) gifts

5. Easter reminds us of Jesus':
   a) death
   b) suffering
   c) Resurrection

Please answer in complete sentences:

What was Jesus like after the Resurrection? Was He a ghost?

To whom did Jesus appear after the Resurrection?

Name:

Unit 6 Test

Chapter 21-24

Part I:

Draw a picture of, and write what happened on the first Palm Sunday.

Using these examples, explain how Jesus is the Good Shepherd.

A shepherd knows his sheep.

A shepherd feeds his sheep.

A shepherd protects his sheep.

A shepherd leads his sheep.

A shepherd should lay down his life for his sheep.

Matching:

Obedient	Forgive those who hurt you.
Humble	Always do what pleases God.
Forgiving	Be kind to everyone.
Prayerful	Be honest and thankful.
Merciful	Say your daily prayers.

PART II: Answer in complete sentences *(use the back of this sheet)*:

1. When was the first Holy Communion?
2. What does Passover celebrate?
3. What happened to the bread and wine when Jesus said the words of Consecration?
4. What is the Sacrament of the Body and Blood of Christ called?
5. What did Jesus do when He said, "Do this in memory of me."

Fill in the blanks: (Blood, Body, bread, cup, forgiven, given up, Jesus, priest, shed, sins, wine)

The minister of the Eucharist is the ____________. He says the words of ____________ (who?). The _________ and __________ become the Body and Blood of Jesus. What are the words Jesus said at the Last Supper? This is my ____________ which is being ________ ____ for you. This is the ________ of my _________ ... It will be _______ for you so that _________ may be _________.

Part III: Write what happened after the Last Supper
(use the back of this sheet)

Place these in the correct order.

___ Jesus carries His Cross.
___Veronica wipes the face of Jesus.
___ Jesus falls a second time.
___ Jesus is placed in the tomb.
___ Jesus speaks to the women.
___ Jesus is nailed to the Cross.
___ Jesus is condemned to death.
___ Jesus meets His Mother.
___ Jesus is taken down from the Cross.
___ Jesus falls a third time.
___ Jesus is helped by Simon.
___ Jesus is stripped of His clothes.
___ Jesus falls the first time.
___ Jesus dies on the Cross.

Part IV: True or False:

___ Jesus first appeared to the disciples.
___ Everyone recognized Jesus when He first appeared to them.
___ Jesus was a ghost.
___ The tomb was empty.
___ An angel said Jesus had risen from the dead.
___ Jesus said to His Apostles, "Peace be with you."
___ Jesus did not say He would die and rise again.
___ The disciples were sad Jesus had risen.
___ Jesus ate with the disciples.
___ Easter is the biggest feast of the Church year.

Decorate Paschal Candle:

Name:

The Holy Mass Quiz 25

Circle the correct answer:

1. At the Last Supper, Jesus gave the Church
   a) The Eucharist b) The Priesthood
   c) The Eucharist and the Priesthood

2. The Sacrifice of the Mass is
   a) The same sacrifice of Jesus on the Cross offered to the Father for our sins.
   b) The sacrifice of Jesus offered over and over again.
   c) A new sacrifice of ourselves, instead of Jesus, for the forgiveness of our sins.

3. We go to Mass on Sunday because
   a) It is the day the Jewish people celebrate.
   b) It is the day chosen by the early Christians.
   c) It is the day Jesus rose from the dead.

4. The perfect prayer is
   a) The Our Father, as taught to us by Jesus Himself.
   b) The Rosary. c) The Mass.

5. By going to Mass, we honor which of the Ten Commandments?
   a) The Third Commandment b) The Fifth Commandment
   c) The Eighth Commandment

Place a red "X" beside things we should not do on Sunday, and a green "O" beside things we should do on Sunday, in order to honor God's Law.

____ Go to Mass
____ Go shopping
____ Spend time with family
____ Do homework
____ Fight with brothers and sisters
____ Read the Bible
____ Pray
____ Misbehave at church
____ Help our neighbor
____ Sing songs praising God

Name:

What We Do at Mass — Quiz 26

Fill in the chart below.

Parts of the Mass	What the Priest Does	What We Do
Entrance:	Goes to the Altar Gives the greeting	
		Listen to the word of God
	Offers the bread and wine to God	
Consecration:		Offer Jesus as sacrifice to the Father
	Gives the people the Body and Blood of Jesus	
Blessing:		

Matching:

a. Altar	__	The bottles that hold the water and wine.
b. Chalice	__	The plate of precious material that holds the bread which becomes the Body of Jesus at Mass.
c. Ciborium	__	The table Mass is offered on.
d. Cruets	__	The book with the prayers of the Mass.
e. Missal	__	The cup of precious material that holds the Body of Christ which people receive at Communion.
f. Paten	__	The cup of precious material that holds the wine which becomes the Blood of Jesus at Mass.

Name:

Jesus Comes to Us Quiz 27

Please answer with complete sentences.

1. What is the part of the Mass called when the priest changes bread and wine into the Body and Blood of Jesus?

2. What is this change called?

3. What are the words that change the bread and wine?

4. How is the Eucharist food for our souls?

5. Who is the minister of the Sacrament of the Eucharist?

6. Jesus wants us to come to Him. How can we do this (two ways)?

7. What are two ways we can receive Jesus in Holy Communion?

Name:

Jesus, My Lord and My God Quiz 28

Write in complete sentences the five steps to a good Holy Communion.

1.

2.

3.

4.

5.

Write T for True and F for False

____ 1. If we are in mortal sin, we must go to confession before we receive Holy Communion.

____ 2. Eucharistic fast means not eating or drinking for 10 hours before receiving Holy Communion.

____ 3. We must say only memorized prayers to Jesus.

____ 4. We should not look around or talk to others when receiving Communion (or before or after).

____ 5. We can offer ourselves to God in union with Jesus in Holy Communion.

____ 6. We need to follow the steps to a worthy communion for our First Communion only.

____ 7. We receive God in Holy Communion.

____ 8. Jesus' Body and Blood are present in the Consecrated Host.

____ 9. Jesus stays with us after Holy Communion.

____10. Receiving Jesus in Holy Communion is the greatest thing you can do in this life.

Name:

Unit 7 Test — Chapters 25-28

PART I: Write a T for True, and an F for False:

1. ____ Jesus gave us the Eucharist at the Last Supper.
2. ____ Jesus gave us the priesthood at the Last Supper.
3. ____ Going to Mass on Wednesday fulfills the 3rd Commandment.
4. ____ All Catholic priests have the power to change bread and wine into Jesus.
5. ____ A sacrifice is giving up something completely for God.
6. ____ The Mass is a sacrifice.
7. ____ Mass is celebrated on Sunday because it is the day of the Resurrection.
8. ____ Mass is the perfect prayer.
9. ____ The sacrifice of Jesus on the Cross has nothing to do with the Mass.
10. ___ The sacrifice of Jesus is offered to the Father for our sins.

PART II: Fill in the boxes.

Parts of the Mass	What the Priest Does	What We Do
Entrance:	Goes to the altar Gives greeting	
Readings:	Reads from the Bible	Listen to the word of God
	Offers the bread and wine to God	Offer ourselves to God
	Changes the bread and wine into the Body and Blood of Jesus	Offer Jesus as sacrifice to the Father
Communion:	Gives the people the Body and Blood of Jesus	
Blessing:	Blesses and dismisses the people	Receive God's Blessing

Write the correct Mass responses:

1. The Lord be with you.

2. In the Name of the Father, and of the Son, and of the Holy Spirit.

3. Lord have mercy.

Matching:

Altar	The plate of precious material that holds the bread which becomes the Body of Jesus at Mass.
Chalice	The cup of precious material that holds the Body of Jesus which people receive at Communion.
Ciborium	The table the Mass is offered on.
Cruets	The cup of precious material that holds the wine which becomes the Blood of Jesus at Mass.
Paten	The bottles that hold the water and wine.

PART III: Answer in complete sentences

1. Who is the minister of the Sacrament of the Eucharist?
2. What is the matter of the Sacrament of the Eucharist?
3. What is the form of the Sacrament of the Eucharist?

PART IV: Place the steps to a worthy Holy Communion in the correct order by numbering them.

____ Know Whom you are about to receive.
____ Thank Jesus for coming to you.
____ Do not eat or drink for one hour.
____ Receive Jesus reverently.
____ Have a healthy soul.

Write three things you can tell Jesus before you receive Him in Communion:

1.

2.

3.

Write three things you can tell Jesus after you receive Him in Communion:

1.

2.

3.

Name:

Jesus Returns to the Father Quiz 29

Circle the correct answer.

1. After the Resurrection, Jesus stayed on earth for how long?
   a) 40 days b) 4 months c) 4 years

2. After the Resurrection, Jesus gave the Apostles the power to:
   a) Consecrate the Eucharist b) forgive sins c) ascend into Heaven

3. How many times did Jesus ask Peter if he loved Him?
   a) one time b) two times c) three times

4. Jesus had to go:
   a) to Galilee b) to be with Mary c) back to the Father

5. Jesus promised to send:
   a) many followers b) the Holy Spirit c) angels

6. On the mountain, Jesus told His Apostles to:
   a) teach and heal b) teach and baptize c) fish and baptize

7. How long will Jesus be with us?
   a) for many years b) until the Holy Spirit comes c) always

8. We call Jesus' rising into the sky:
   a) the Resurrection b) the Ascension c) the Assumption

9. In Heaven, Jesus is:
   a) having a well-deserved holiday
   b) preparing a place for those who love Him
   c) all alone

10. When will Jesus come again?
    a) only the Apostles know the time b) never
    c) at the end of time

Name:

God Is Our Father — Quiz 30

Circle the correct answer:

1. The Holy Spirit is:
   a) The Second Person of the Holy Trinity b) The Father and the Son
   c) God

2. The Trinity is:
   a) One God in Three Persons b) Three Gods in one Person
   c) Three Gods in Three Persons

3. The Holy Spirit came:
   a) at Pentecost b) nine days after the Resurrection
   c) nine days after Christmas

Fill in the chart using the words from the word bank:

SACRAMENT	MATTER	FORM	EFFECTS
Baptism		I baptize you in the Name of the Father and the Son and of the Holy Spirit	Sin is washed away and grace is received in the soul
Penance	Confessing our sins to a priest	I absolve you from your sins in the Name of the Father and of the Son and of the Holy Spirit	
Eucharist			We receive the Body and Blood of Jesus
Confirmation	Holy Chrism and the laying on of hands	Be sealed with the gift of the Holy Spirit	
Matrimony Marriage	The vows of the man and woman	The consent to the vows	
Holy Orders	Bishop lays hands on head of the man	The words of the bishop to the one to be ordained upon the laying of hands	
Anointing of the Sick		By this holy anointing and His most loving mercy, may the Lord forgive you whatever wrong you have done...	Receive the grace to die in God's friendship

sins are forgiven	this is My Blood	water	oil	Man becomes a priest
bread and wine	Husband and wife grow holy	this is My Body	Holy Spirit comes	

Name:

God's Family — The Church Quiz 31

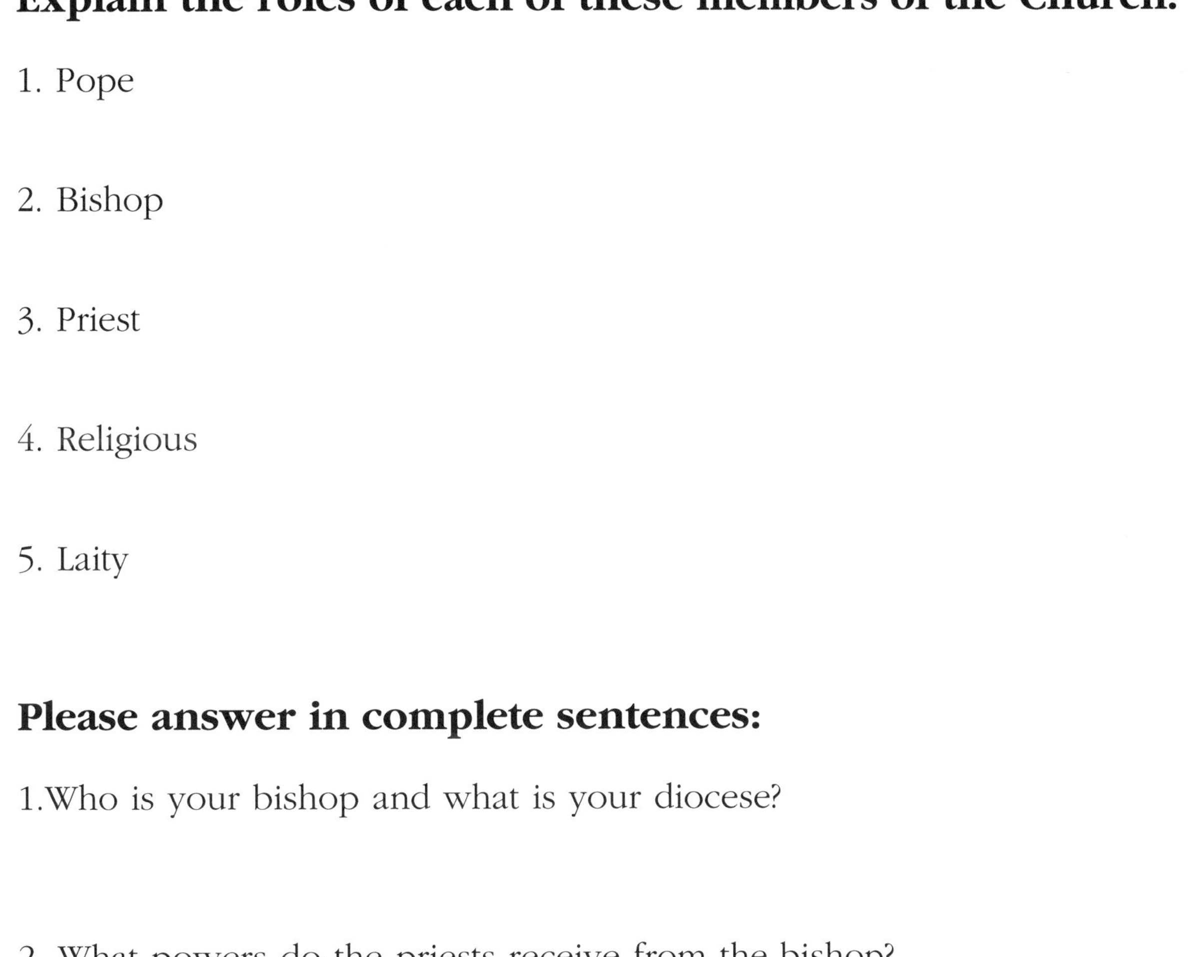

Explain the roles of each of these members of the Church:

1. Pope

2. Bishop

3. Priest

4. Religious

5. Laity

Please answer in complete sentences:

1.Who is your bishop and what is your diocese?

2. What powers do the priests receive from the bishop?

3. What kinds of work do religious sisters and brothers do (name three)?

4. Explain how the Church is the Body of Christ.

Name:

Mary Our Mother Quiz 32

Circle the correct answer:

1. Which of these events was Mary not present for:
   a) Pentecost
   b) Baptism of Jesus
   c) Crucifixion

2. When did Jesus give Mary to us for our Mother?
   a) Annunciation
   b) Nativity
   c) Crucifixion

3. Mary can help us by:
   a) praying for us
   b) being a good example
   c) both a and b

4. The Rosary has how many decades?
   a) three
   b) five
   c) seven

5. Mary asked the children of Fatima for:
   a) prayer
   b) sacrifice
   c) both a and b

Place the Mysteries of the Rosary in the correct order:

JOYFUL (1-5)

___ Finding in the Temple
___ Annunciation
___ Birth of Jesus
___ Presentation
___ Visitation

SORROWFUL (1-5)

___ Scourging at the Pillar
___ Carrying the Cross
___ Death of Jesus
___ Crowning with Thorns
___ Agony in the Garden

GLORIOUS (1-5)

___ Pentecost
___ Coronation of Mary
___ Resurrection
___ Assumption of Mary
___ Ascension of Jesus

Name:

Jesus Is Always Present — Quiz 33

Circle the correct answer.

1. Jesus is with us always, but most especially:
   a) where two or three are gathered in His name
   b) when we read the Bible
   c) in the Blessed Sacrament

2. We know Jesus is present in the tabernacle by:
   a) the Sanctuary Lamp
   b) people praying there
   c) our teaching telling us so

3. The greatest gift we can receive is:
   a) a great birthday gift
   b) a present at Christmas
   c) Jesus Himself in Holy Communion

4. Why should we visit the church?
   a) because it is a fun building to play in
   b) to visit Jesus in the tabernacle
   c) to show others we are Catholic

5. During Adoration and Benediction, Jesus is:
   a) in the tabernacle
   b) in a monstrance
   c) beside the Sanctuary Lamp

Complete the chart below:

When	What you should do
At the entrance of the church by the Holy Water font	
During the Mass	
As you walk to and from your pew	
When Jesus is exposed in the monstrance (before you enter your pew, or as you leave it)	

Name: ___

Heaven, Our Home — Quiz 34

True or False:

___ 1. We will all die someday because of Original Sin.
___ 2. When we die, our soul lives forever.
___ 3. All people go to Heaven.
___ 4. A soul that goes to Purgatory will go to hell.
___ 5. A saint is someone in Heaven.
___ 6. Our bodies will be reunited to our souls.
___ 7. We choose by our actions in this life where our soul will go.
___ 8. Heaven is our real home.
___ 9. By preparing for Heaven in this life, we will be happy now and forever.
___10. We can pray for the souls in Purgatory.

Please answer in complete sentences:

1. What must a person do to go to Heaven?

2. What must a person do to go to hell?

3. What is the Communion of saints?

4. Who do we know is in Heaven?

Name:

Unit 8 Test — Chapters 29-34

PART I: Write a T for True and an F for False

1. ____ After the Resurrection, Jesus stayed on earth for 50 days.
2. ____ Jesus gave the Apostles the power to forgive sins.
3. ____ Apostle means "one who is sent".
4. ____ Jesus made Peter the leader of His Church.
5. ____ Peter was the second Pope.
6. ____ Jesus promised to send the Holy Spirit.
7. ____ Jesus told his Apostles to teach and baptize.
8. ____ Jesus' going to Heaven is called the Assumption.
9. ____ Jesus is King.
10. ___ Jesus will come again.

PART II: Circle the correct answer:

1. The Holy Spirit is:
a) a dove
b) God
c) flames of fire

2. The Holy Spirit is the ______ Person of the Holy Trinity:
a) First
b) Second
c) Third

3. The Holy Spirit came to the Apostles at:
a) Annunciation
b) Baptism of Jesus
c) Pentecost

4. The Holy Spirit is the:
a) Sanctifier
b) Creator
c) Savior

5. The Holy Spirit is:
a) the Father
b) the Son
c) neither a nor b

PART III: Write the roles of:

1. The Pope

2. The Bishop

3. The Priest

4. Religious Sisters and Brothers

5. The Laity

PART IV: Fill in the blanks:

Apostles' Creed

I believe in ________, the ______________ almighty, _____________ of Heaven and earth. I believe in ___________ Christ, his only __________, our ___________. He was conceived by the _____________ of the Holy _________, and born of the Virgin _________. He suffered under Pontius Pilate, was crucified, _________, and was buried. He descended into ________. On the ________ day He rose again. He _________________ into Heaven and is seated at the _________ hand of the Father. He will come again to ___________ the living and the dead. I believe in the Holy ___________, the Holy _____________ Church, the Communion of _________, the forgiveness of ___________, the Resurrection of the _________ and __________ everlasting. *Amen.*

Telephone

Have the children sit in a circle on the floor. The teacher begins the game by whispering a sentence to one of the students. This sentence is taken from the lesson of the day. For example, to reinforce the promise of the Savior, the sentence could be, "God promised Adam and Eve that he would send a Savior." The child, after receiving the message, whispers it to the child next to him. The message continues around the circle in this way until the last person receives it. The last person then stands and repeats it for the entire class. If any child has difficulty understanding the message that is whispered to him, he may say "Operator," which means that he needs to have the message repeated to him again before he can pass it to the next person.

Bible Baseball

1. Set up bases around the room.
2. Choose teams.
3. Ask a question of a student on one of the teams. If he gets the answer, the student goes to first base and the next student is up for a question. If he misses the answer, that student is out. In this case, the next teammate must answer the same question. If three students on the same team cannot answer the question or if three questions are misssed, their team is out and the other team is up.
4. Points are received for "home runs," that is, when a student has passed through all three bases and reached home base.

Tic Tac Toe

1. Draw Tic Tac Toe grid on the chalkboard.
2. Choose sides. "X" goes first
3. Ask a student on the first team a question. If he answers it correctly, his team chooses where to put the "X". If he answers incorrectly, the other team has a chance to answer the question. If the "O" team answers, they can choose where to put the "O", and then they get their turn, that is, one student is asked a question. If they answer incorrectly, they merely get their normal turn.
4. The team that has three "X's" or three "O's" in a row wins the round. Losers start the next round.

Staircase of Creation

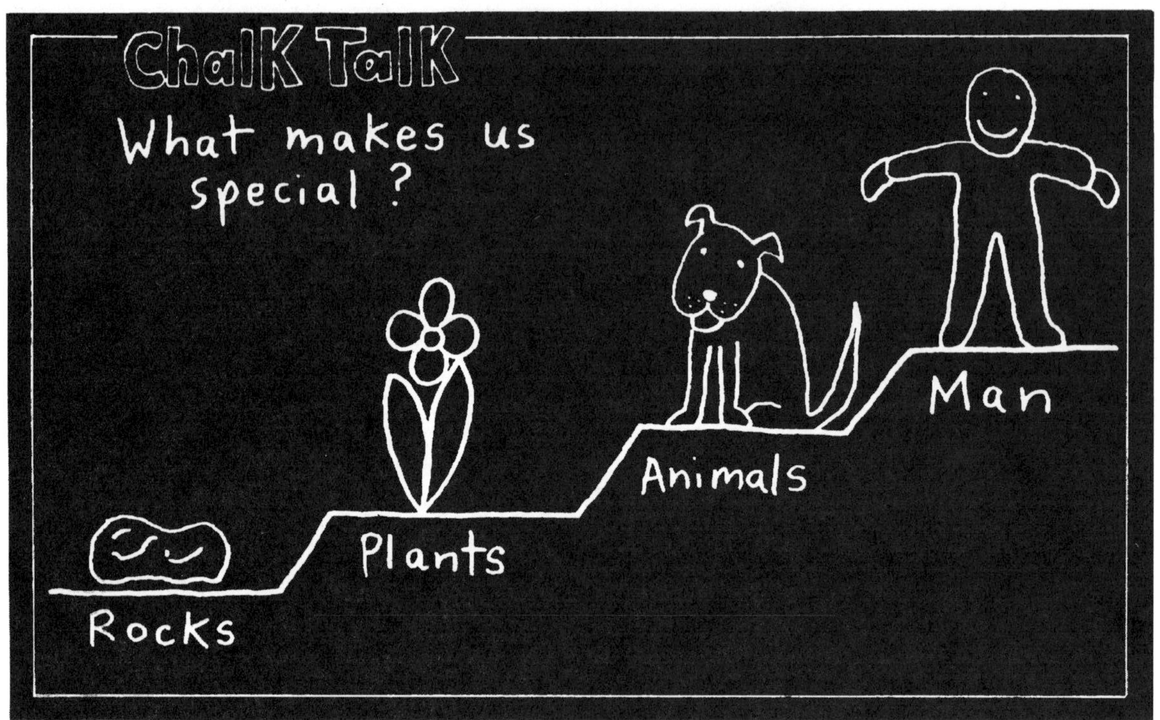

The Seder Meal

On Holy Thursday evening many Catholic families hold a Seder dinner ceremony in memory of the Jewish Passover. The traditional Passover meal, with roast lamb, bitter herbs, matzo, and wine, is served. An empty place is left at the table for the prophet Elijah.

Jesus and His Apostles would have celebrated a dinner much like this one on the night of the Last Supper.

Chapter 8

The Seder: Introduction

The Seder is the ritual meal that takes place in Jewish homes on the first night of Passover. The service, which commemorates the night God delivered the Hebrews from slavery in Egypt, involves the recitation of special prayers and the consumption of symbolic foods.

The Last Supper of Jesus with his disciples was a Passover Seder. During the meal, Jesus taught that he is the Lamb of God, the perfect sacrifice to the Father, which frees us from the slavery of sin and death. During each Mass, parts of the Last Supper are reenacted; some of the gestures and prayers of the Mass, therefore, come from the Seder service.

Materials:

large serving platter for Seder tray

matzah—three whole matzahs for under the Seder tray; additional matzahs for table

horseradish—mild creamed horseradish is easiest to use

celery—two sticks for each participant

ground apple—about a tablespoon per person

ground walnuts—about a tablespoon per person

cinnamon—mix with apples and walnuts to taste

"wine"—grape juice, about two ounces per person, plus enough to moisten apple-nut mixture

shank bone—turkey thigh bone, chicken leg or neck bone, or whatever you can get from the butcher; boil to clean and roast till brown

hard-boiled eggs—1/4 egg per person, plus one whole egg, roasted till brown, for Seder tray

large cloth napkin—folded in four and stitched closely along the folded sides to form three pockets for holding the matzah that is placed under the Seder tray

"wine" glasses—one per person

bowls for salt-water—paper nut cups will do; one per person

bowls for fresh-water—short paper cups will do; one per person

napkins, paper plates, spoons

two candles, matches

necktie, yarmulke (skull cap), necklace, shawl

Bibles or photocopies of Psalms to be recited

The Seder: Preparation

Before class, arrange the tables or desks in a U-shape or a rectangle, with the leader's chair at the head, facing the students. Decorate the tables with cloths, plates, and candles of dark blue and white (the colors of the Israeli flag) or white and violet (the color for Lent). A floral arrangement or a ceramic or toy lamb with a ribbon around its neck makes a nice centerpiece. At the head of the table, place a Seder tray, which is a platter with samples of the following symbolic foods:

Maror—Ground horseradish, representing the bitter suffering the Hebrew slaves endured at the hands of their Egyptian taskmasters.

Karpas—Cut celery or other green vegetable representing spring. It is dipped in salt water, which symbolizes the tears shed by the Hebrews during their slavery.

Haroses—Ground apples and walnuts, symbolizing the mortar the Hebrews were forced to make for the Pharaoh's buildings.

Zeroah—The bone representing the lamb that was sacrificed and eaten on the first Passover. Those who painted their doorways with its blood were "passed over" by the tenth plague of death, which afflicted the first-born of the Egyptians. *Zeroah* means "arm", for it was the mighty arm of God that compelled Pharaoh to free the Hebrew slaves.

Baytza—A hard-boiled egg, symbolizing the animal sacrifices the Israelites brought to the temple in Jerusalem during holidays such as Passover. The eggs are dipped into salt water, signifying the mourning of the Jews over the destruction of the temple.

Underneath the Seder tray are placed three matzahs (unleavened bread) in a matzah holder or wrapped in layers in a cloth napkin. More matzah is on the table. The matzah represents the bread the Hebrews made in haste before their departure from Egypt.

Set each place with a glass of grape juice, a napkin, a dish of salt water, a spoon, a dish of fresh water, and a plate. On each plate, place two pieces of celery, a spoonful each of horseradish and apple-nut mixture, and a slice of hard-boiled egg.

The Seder is a family meal. Choose a boy to be the father and give him a necktie and yarmulke (skull cap) to wear. Choose a girl to be the mother, wearing a necklace and shawl. Choose a third student to act the part of the youngest child.

Candle-Lighting Ceremony

Usually, the mother of the family leads the candle-lighting ceremony, using two tapers or a special Passover candelabra. She lights the candles and says:

> Blessed are you, O Lord our God, King of the universe, who sanctified us with his commandments and commanded us to kindle the festival lights.
>
> Blessed are you, O lord our God, King of the universe, who gave us life and sustained us and brought us to this joyful season.

Opening

The father usually leads the rest of the Seder. He sits at the head of the table and begins the service:

> We have gathered to observe the Passover, the night God delivered Israel from bondage and brought them out of Egypt. Let us proclaim the power, the goodness, and the faithfulness of God.

The First Cup

The father leads the blessing. All raise their cups and say:

> Blessed are you, O Lord our God, King of the universe, who has created the fruit of the vine.

All take a sip.

The First Washing

All participants wash their hands with the water provided. In ancient times, a household servant washed the dusty feet of the dinner guests. At the Last Supper, Jesus himself performed this service and washed the disciples' feet. In modern Jewish households, each person has his own water and towel, or a bowl and towel are carried from person to person by the mistress of the house.

Appetizer: Karpas

The father asks everyone to take some celery, dip it in the salt water, and say:

> Blessed are you, O Lord our God, King of the universe, who has created the fruit of the earth.

All eat the celery. At the Last Supper, Judas' betrayal was revealed by Jesus during the dipping.

Yahatz: Breaking the Middle Matzah

The father takes the middle piece of matzah and breaks it into two parts. One part is wrapped up and saved for the end of the meal. The teacher might select some students to "steal" this piece and hide it, a tradition in many Jewish families today. The remaining part is lifted by the father, who says:

A SEDER OUTLINE

> This is the bread of affliction, which God's people ate in the land of Egypt. Let all who are hungry come and eat.

He then places the matzah on top of the others.

The Four Questions and the Hagadah

The youngest child asks four questions about why this night is different from all the others:

> Why do we eat only unleavened bread?
> Why do we eat bitter herbs?
> Why do we dip the herbs twice?
> Why do we dine with special ceremony?

The father answers the questions by telling the Hagadah, the story of the Hebrew people from Abraham to Moses. The father, the teacher, or another student reads this narrative:

> In the beginning, our people worshiped idols, but God revealed himself to them and made a covenant with our father Abraham, in which he promised to make him a great nation. Abraham and Sarah had a son, Isaac, in their old age. Isaac's younger son, Jacob, inherited his father's promise. Jacob became the father of Joseph, who was sold into slavery by his jealous brothers. Joseph became great in Pharaoh's service by saving Egypt from famine. His own family came to him for food and settled in Egypt. Many years later, another Pharaoh enslaved the Hebrews. But the people of Israel cried out to God, who heard their cry and sent Moses to lead them to freedom. Moses asked Pharaoh to let his people go. When he refused, God sent ten plagues that compelled Pharaoh to free the Hebrew slaves.

The Showing of the Foods

To make the connection between the story and the foods, the teacher points to each item on the Seder tray and explains its significance.

The First Part of the Hallel

To show thanks for the mighty works of God, the Hallel, or Psalms, are recited. The Hallel includes Psalms 112, 113, and 114. The teacher chooses one to be recited by the class.

The Second Cup

The father leads in taking a second sip of the grape juice. All say:

> Blessed are you, O Lord our God, King of the universe, who has created the fruit of the vine.

The Second Washing

All wash their hands again.

A SEDER OUTLINE

Eating the Matzah, Maror, and Haroses

The father breaks the original top matzah and the broken half of the middle matzah into enough pieces for all and distributes them. This is the point at which Jesus said, "This is my body." Each person holds a piece of matzah while the father says:

> Blessed are you, O Lord our God, King of the universe, who brings forth bread from the earth.

All eat the matzah. Each person takes another piece of matzah from the table, dips it into the maror and the haroses, and eats it. (A spoon may be used for dipping and spreading.) Each person takes a piece of hard-boiled egg, dips it into salt water, and eats it. At this point in the Seder, the table is cleared of the symbolic foods, and the rest of the meal is served.

Grace after Meals

After the meal is finished, Psalm 126 is recited. The father then looks for the hidden matzah or asks the children who hid it to bring it back. He divides it among all the participants, and all eat.

The Third Cup

The father asks the others to raise their cups and say:

> Blessed are you, O Lord our God, King of the universe, who has created the fruit of the vine.

This is the point at which Jesus said, "This is my blood."

All sip from their glasses, which are refilled if necessary.

The Second Part of the Hallel

More Psalms are then recited, including Psalm 115 and 135. The teacher chooses one for the class to recite.

The Fourth Cup

The Father concludes by asking all to raise their cups one last time and say:

> Blessed are you, O Lord our God, King of the universe, who has created the fruit of the vine.

All drink. The father says:

> Our Seder has ended. Let us go in joy.

Sources

Kolatch, Alfred J., *The Concise Family Seder* (New York: Jonathan David Publisher, Inc., 1989).

Rosen, Ceil and Moishe, *Christ in the Passover: Why Is This Night Different?* (Chicago: Moody Press, 1980).

Stained Glass Angel

Popsicle Stick Puppets and Shoe Box Theater

The puppets are easily made from popsicle sticks and either felt, construction paper, or cut out pictures. For example:

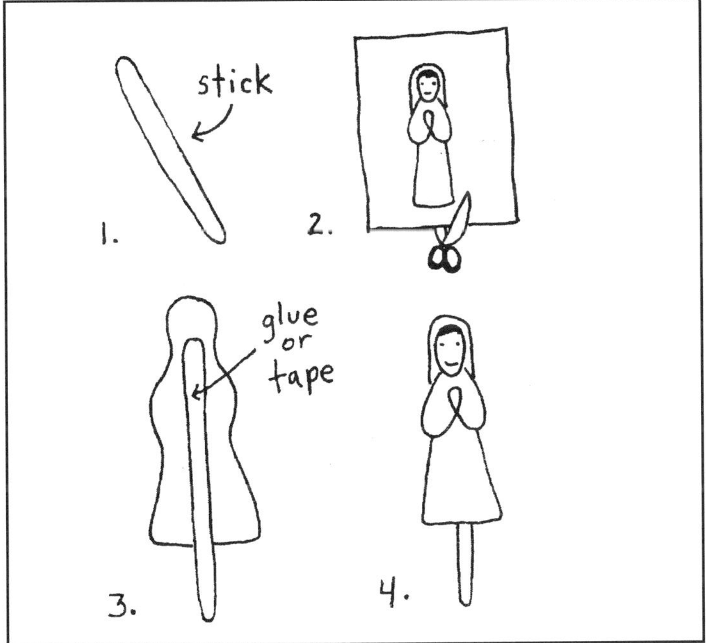

For the theater, take a large shoe box and cut two slots, one toward the top of the box on one of the long sides, and the other toward the bottom of the box on the opposite long side (the slot toward the top will be where you insert the puppets; the slot toward the bottom will be for inserting the backdrop or scenery).

Masks

To identify the different characters in a play without having to make elaborate costumes, it is quite easy to make masks. For example, if you wished to dramatize the temptation and fall of man, you could make the following masks out of paper and have the students color them; alternatively, the students could make the masks out of construction paper.

To show the change from perfect happiness to the fallen state of Adam and Eve, make the masks reversible. They may be handheld and flipped:

Baptism

Baptism

Materials

Bible
necktie, suit jacket, shawl, woman's hat, matches, white candle
priest's stole (violet on one side, white on the other)
surplice (optional)
Photocopy (double-sided if possible) of the Baptism Ceremony for each student
desk or table covered with white cloth
baby doll dressed in white gown
small container (for chrism)
shell (for pouring water); large bowl (font) for water

Note: The practice of having the priest or deacon begin the rite with the violet side of the stole visible, then turning it to the white side after pouring the water, is not currently part of the rite, but it is still good symbolism and a nice detail for the students to practice.

Characters

mother	godfather	lector
father	godmother	congregation
priest		

Direct Aims

- to become familiar with the basic elements of the baptismal rite
- to appreciate the relationship between the effects of original sin and those of Baptism

Preparation

Set up a table at the front of the room with the items needed to perform a pretend baptism (see list of materials needed, above).

What to Do and Say

Read or review chapter 6 with the students. Say:

We just read that Adam and Eve are called our "first parents". We call them that, because the entire human race descended from them. They are the parents of the whole human family. And because they are the first parents of all of us, we all inherit the effects of their disobedience.

What were the effects?—Let's list them on the board.

EFFECTS OF ORIGINAL SIN
lost God's life in their souls (grace)
could not go to heaven
were driven from the garden
brought spiritual death to descendants

Baptism

Point to each item on the list and read aloud. Say:

None of us asked for or committed original sin, but all of us receive the effects of it.—That's the bad news!

Now for some good news!—The parents that you have here and now have given you something you didn't ask for either.

You may not remember it, but your parents requested baptism for you, and together with your godparents they promised to raise you up in the Catholic Faith. You received the priceless gift of baptism without even knowing that it happened. In a way, baptism undoes all the damage caused by original sin.

EFFECTS OF BAPTISM

receive God's life in your soul (grace)
can go to heaven
are welcomed into the Church
gives hope of eternal life

Say:

Adam and Eve's big mistake was to listen to the devil instead of to God. In baptism, your parents promised to teach you to reject the lies of the devil and to live always as a child of the light.

Take out the materials for acting out a baptism. Show them to the students. Hold up each item as it is mentioned. Say:

I have everything we need to perform a pretend baptism. Here is a tie and jacket for the dad, a shawl and hat for the mom, a stole and surplice for the priest, a bowl and shell for baptizing, and a container of holy oil for anointing. I even have a baby doll dressed in a baptismal gown. But I don't have all the people. Who would like to volunteer?

Choose well-established readers for the roles of mother, father, lector, priest, godfather, and godmother. Assign all the other students to play the part of the congregation. Have the main actors stand up in front of the class next to the table you have prepared. Distribute copies of the adapted Rite of Baptism .

Have the student playing the part of the priest begin. Those playing the parts of parents and godparents give the responses according to the adapted Rite.

Baptism

A BAPTISM CEREMONY

Priest: What is the baby's name?

Mother and Father: (Say baby's name.)

Priest: What do want from the Church for (baby's name)?

Mother and Father: Baptism.

Priest: You have asked me to baptize your baby. You must teach him (her) to love God, to keep the commandments, and to love his (her) neighbor. Are you ready to do this?

Mother and Father: Yes!

Priest: Godparents, are you ready to help them?

Godparents: Yes!

Priest: (baby's name), the Church welcomes you with great joy! In its name, I claim you for Jesus by tracing the Sign of the Cross on your forehead [*priest does so*]. I ask your parents and godparents to trace the Sign of the Cross on your forehead, too. [*All trace cross on baby's forehead.*]

LITURGY OF THE WORD

Lector: A reading from the holy Gospel according to St. Matthew. [*Read Matthew 28:18–20.*]

This is the Gospel of the Lord.

All: Praise to you, Lord Jesus Christ.

PRAYERS OF PETITION

Priest: Lord, give this child new life and welcome him (her) into your holy Church.

All: Lord, hear our prayer.

Priest: Lead this child to the happiness of heaven.

All: Lord, hear our prayer.

Baptism

Priest: Make his (her) parents and godparents good examples.

All: Lord, hear our prayer.

Priest: Keep this family always in your love.

All: Lord, hear our prayer.

INVOCATION OF THE SAINTS

Priest: Holy Mother of God:

All: Pray for us.

Priest: Saint John the Baptist:

All: Pray for us.

Priest: Saint Joseph:

All: Pray for us.

Priest: (Add additional names, including the child's patron saint and those of family members.)

All: Pray for us.

Priest: All you saints of God:

All: Pray for us.

BLESSING OF THE WATER

Priest: [*turns toward the baptismal water*] Father, you give us grace through signs and symbols that we can see to tell us of your power that we cannot see. In baptism we use your gift of water to bring your grace to this baby. During Noah's time, a flood of water made an end to sin and a new beginning of goodness. Through the waters of the Red Sea you led your chosen people out of slavery into freedom. In the waters of the Jordan River your Son, Jesus, was baptized by John. After his resurrection, Jesus told his disciples to "Go out and teach all nations, baptizing them in the name of the Father and of the Son and of the Holy Spirit."

[*touches the water with his right hand*]

Send the Holy Spirit upon this water. May all who are baptized with Jesus also rise with him to new life. We ask this through Christ our Lord.

All: Amen.

Baptism

REJECTION OF SIN and PROFESSION OF FAITH

[*The priest asks the questions, and the parents and godparents answer for themselves and for the child.*]

Priest: Do you reject the Devil?

Mother and Father, Godparents: Yes.

Priest: And all his works?

Mother and Father, Godparents: Yes.

Priest: And all his lies?

Mother and Father, Godparents: Yes.

Priest: Do you believe in God the Father almighty, maker of heaven and earth?

Mother and Father, Godparents: Yes.

Priest: Do believe in Jesus Christ, his only Son, who died and rose and now lives forever?

Mother and Father, Godparents: Yes.

Priest: Do you believe in the Holy Spirit, the Holy Catholic Church, the communion of saints, the forgiveness of sins, the resurrection of the body, and life everlasting?

Mother and Father, Godparents: Yes.

Priest: This is our faith, we are happy to profess it in Christ Jesus our Lord!

All: Amen!

Priest: Do you want (baby's name) to be baptized in the faith of the Church which we have all professed together?

Mother and Father, Godparents: Yes.

Priest: [*The mother holds the child over the baptismal font while the priest pours water over his (her) forehead, saying*:] (baby's name), I baptize you in the name of the Father, [*pour water*] and of the Son, [*pour water*] and of the Holy Spirit [*pour water*].

Baptism

[*The priest now turns his stole from the violet side to the white.*]

THE WHITE GARMENT

Priest: (baby's name), you have become a new creation in Jesus Christ. [*touch the baptismal gown*] See in this white garment the outward sign of your new life. Let your family and friends help you by word and example to live your new life in Jesus here on earth and someday in heaven.

All: Amen!

[*Priest lights the baptismal candle and hands it to the father.*]

Priest: (baby's name), receive the light of Jesus Christ. Keep the flame of faith alive in your heart. Parents and godparents, you must help keep this light burning brightly.

THE LORD'S PRAYER

Priest: Let us pray together the words Jesus taught us:

[*All pray together the "Our Father".*]

All: Our Father who art in heaven, hallowed be thy name. Thy kingdom come, thy will be done, on earth as it is in heaven. Give us this day our daily bread, and forgive us our trespasses as we forgive those who trespass against us, and lead us not into temptation, but deliver us from evil. Amen.

BLESSING and DISMISSAL

Priest: May almighty God bless you, in the name of the Father, and of the Son, and of the Holy Spirit.

[*All make the Sign of the Cross.*]

All: Amen.

Priest: Go in peace.

All: Thanks be to God.

Examination of Conscience

Chapter 9

Examination of Conscience and Penitential Rite

Materials: one missalette for each child.

Direct Aims

- to learn to examine one's conscience regularly
- to learn to participate in the penitential rite at Mass

Indirect Aim

- to begin preparation for First Penance

What to Do and Say

Read or review Chapter 9 with the students. Say:

On the last page of this chapter is some very good advice. It says that we should take some time each night to remember our sins and to ask God for forgiveness. There is a name for this. We call it "examination of conscience".

Write "examination of conscience" on the board and have the students repeat the words a few times. Say:

Our conscience is the part of us that lets us know the difference between right and wrong. God gave all of us a conscience, and He expects us to use it. Our book also tells us that the chart on page 37 will help us to examine our conscience. Let's turn to page 37 now.

Read or review the chart on page 37 with the students. Tell them to recall silently any sins they have committed. Then say:

God has given us a special way to say we are sorry for any venial sins and to receive forgiveness.

Choose one of the following options based on what the students usually hear at Mass.

Option 1: Very near the beginning of Mass, the priest says, "My brothers and sisters, to prepare ourselves to celebrate these sacred mysteries let us call to mind our sins."

Option 2: Do you remember hearing the prayer at Mass that begins "I confess to almighty God . . ."?

Option 3: Do you remember hearing the prayer at Mass that begins "Lord have mercy . . ."?

Examination of Conscience

Affirm the students' responses. Say:

When we say this prayer and are truly sorry for our sins, God forgives them. He takes away our sins and fills our souls with grace. This makes us ready to pray the rest of the Mass with a pure heart.

Pass out the missalettes. Say:

I will show you exactly where you can find this prayer for forgiveness. Then, whenever you are at Mass, you can say it along with everyone else.

Begin at the beginning of Mass, taking the students step by step to the penitential rite.

Look at page ___. When Mass begins, we stand up and sing a song or say one of the short prayers that are listed here. There is a different one for each Sunday.

Turn the page. Say:

While we are singing or praying, the priest and servers walk in. Father bows to the altar and kisses it. Then he begins Mass with the Sign of the Cross. Father offers everyone a greeting in Christ's name, and then he begins the penitential rite.

Make sure each child is following along in the missalette. Explain that either one, the other, or both forms (Confiteor *or* Kyrie) *may be used. Help each child find the right place on the page, depending on your parish practice. Say:*

Now we will pretend we are at Mass. We will say the penitential rite. Before we begin, take a minute to remember one or two sins for which you are sorry. Think about how sorry you are as we read the prayer.

To build the habit of regular examination of conscience and penitence, spend about ten minutes each week briefly repeating this process. Friday afternoon may be a good time. Remind the students to use the missalette at Sunday Mass and always to participate in this opportunity for forgiveness and renewal.

Ten Commandments Puzzle

Show the students the photocopies of the hearts and the tablets. Say:

> Here is a project for you to complete. When you are finished, you will have a little puzzle of the Ten Commandments. You can use it to tell others about God's law of love.

Show the students your finished puzzle. Say:

> The puzzle pieces fit inside the tablets. Each piece has a number on the back. I keep them stacked in order, with number one on top. When I want to tell someone about the Ten Commandments, I unfold the tablets and put them on the table. Next to them, I put the puzzle pieces, face down.

Set the stack face down on a student's desk next to the open tablets. Say to that student:

> Did you know that the Ten Commandments are really about love? That may be surprising, but it's true. If you don't keep the Ten Commandments, you haven't really learned to love.

Turn the first puzzle piece over. Show it to the class, then set it on the left mid-section of the tablets. Say:

> The first three commandments tell us the three best ways to love God. Read them.

The student reads the first three commandments. Turn over the second puzzle piece. Show the class, then place it on the right mid-section of the tablets. Say:

> The other seven commandments tell us the seven best ways to love our neighbor. Read them.

Have the student read the commandments. Ask him to explain all the commandments. Pause while the student tells you the meaning of each. Give him help if needed.

Turn over the third and fourth puzzle pieces. Show them to the class, then place them above the first two. Say:

> Together, the commandments add up to the ten best ways to love.

Turn over the fifth piece. Show it to the class, then place it at the bottom center of the tablets to form a heart. Say:

> If you would like to read the story of Moses and the Ten Commandments, you can find it in chapters 19 and 20 of the Book of Exodus.

Pass out the photocopies of the hearts and the tablets. Assist the students in cutting, pasting (if necessary), and folding the puzzle. Provide several opportunities for them to practice with the puzzle before sending it home. Assign the students the task of sharing the Ten Commandments with someone at home. This exercise makes a good review for chapters 8 and 9.

DIRECTIONS FOR TEN COMMANDMENTS PUZZLE

1. Cut out the shape of the Tablets from the colored paper. This forms the "base" of the puzzle.
2. Cut out the shape of the Heart, and then cut the Heart-shape into pieces along the dashed lines.
3. Number the *backs* of the Heart pieces as shown in the diagram below.

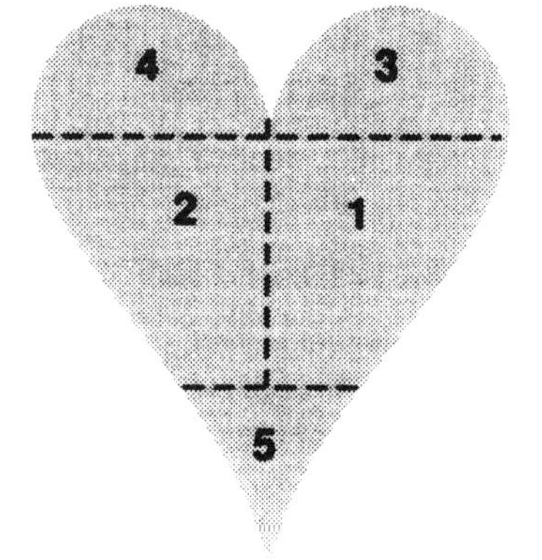

Ten Commandments Puzzle

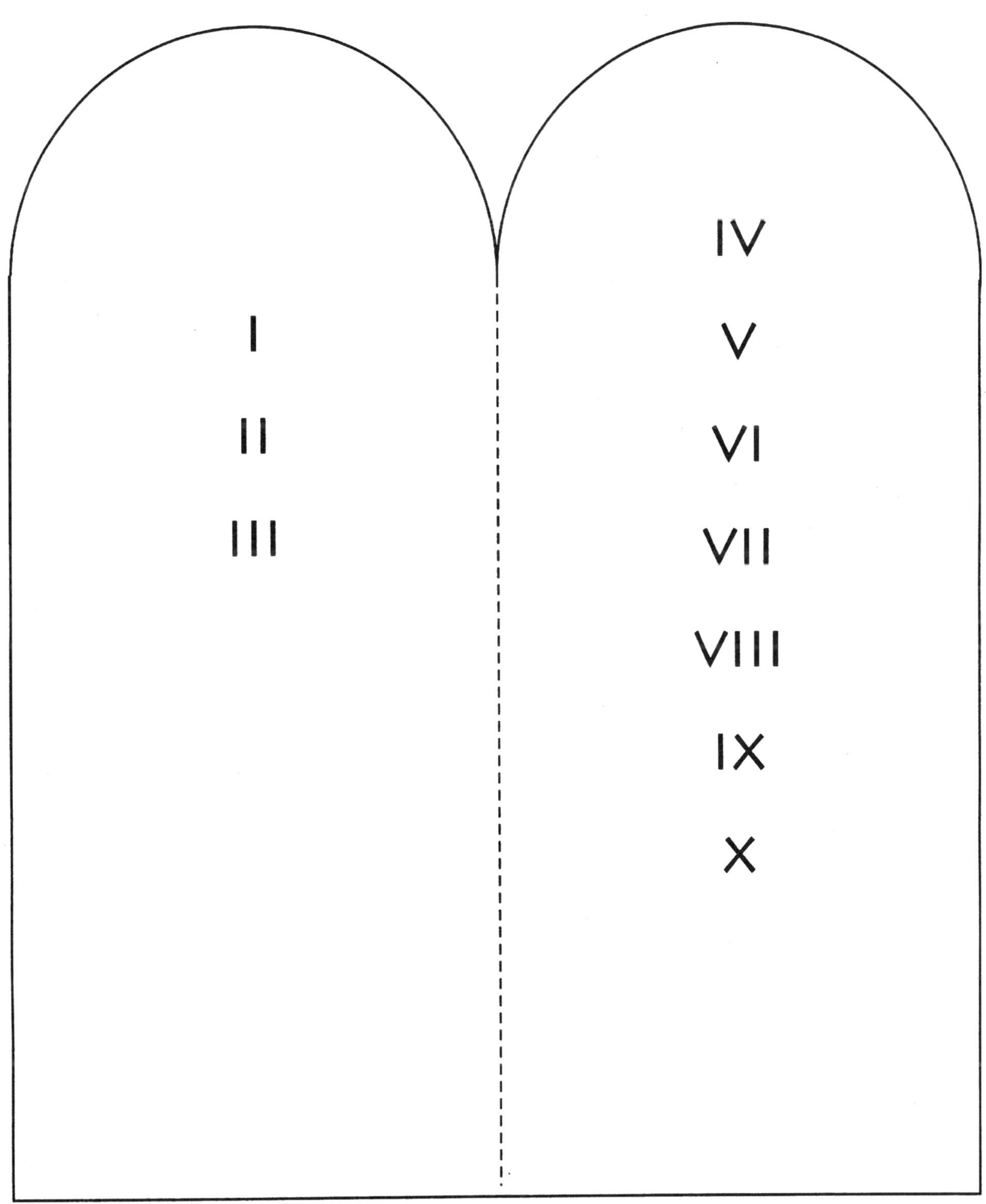

Ten Commandments Puzzle

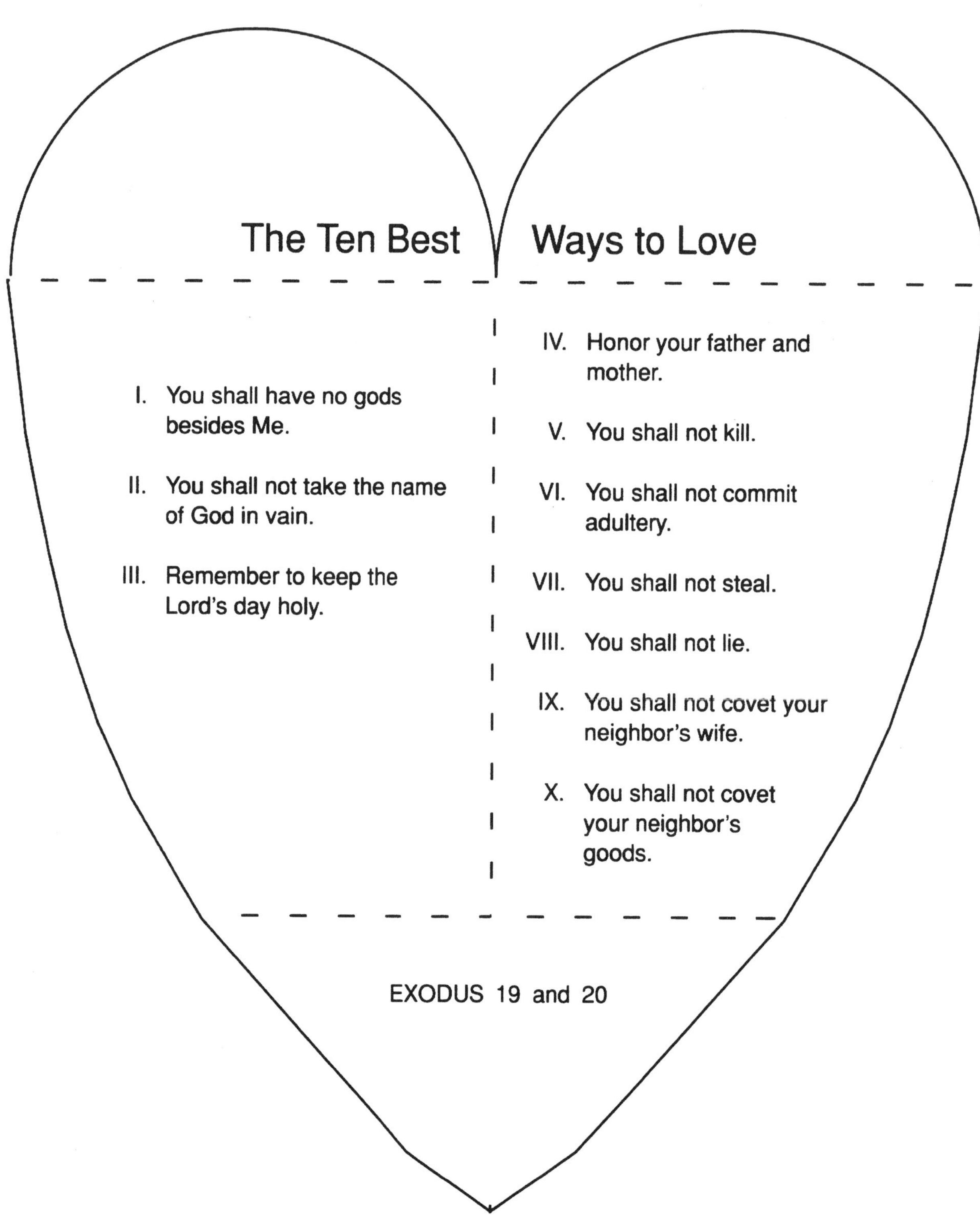

Advent Calendar

Gloria In Excelsis Deo

Diorama of the Crucifixion

Diorama of the Crucifixion

Materials: Bible, shoe boxes, blue and brown construction paper, scissors, crayons, coloring pencils, glue, photocopies of patterns (page C-68) on heavy paper.

Aim: to construct a diorama of the Crucifixion

Preparation: Prepare a diorama of the Crucifixion to show the students as an example. Make photocopies of patterns on heavy paper. Color. Cut out figures along solid lines. Cover inside back and sides of shoe box with blue construction paper. Cover bottom with brown construction paper. Glue cross to back wall of *upright* shoe box (see illustration). Cut tabs apart at center. Bend one tab forward and one tab back. Glue to bottom of shoe box. Make title card for top of box.

What to Do and Say

Read or review Chapter 23 with the students. Say:

> At the Last Supper, Jesus told the apostles that He would pour out His blood for the forgiveness of sins. That very night, He was arrested, and the next day He died on the Cross. Our books tell us that at the moment Jesus died, the gates of heaven were opened and we were brought back to friendship with God.

Show the students your diorama. Say:

> Like the Last Supper, the Crucifixion is something that I want to remember always. I have made this diorama to help me remember. Listen while I read the story of Jesus' death from the Bible.

Put the diorama where the students can see it. Read John 19:16–19 and 25–30. Pick up the diorama again. Say:

> For the title of my diorama I used the last words of Jesus, "It is finished!" He had completed the work the Father sent Him to do—He had purchased our salvation with His own blood. Every time I look at this scene, I will remember that Jesus loved me enough to give His life for me.
>
> Would each of you like to make a diorama like this?

Assist the students in cutting, coloring, and gluing their dioramas.

Diorama of the Crucifixion

Little Lamb

Noah's Ark

Materials Needed: poster board, copy of the following patterns

1. Color and cut out the parts of the ark and the animals.
2. Glue cabin and roof to the poster board.

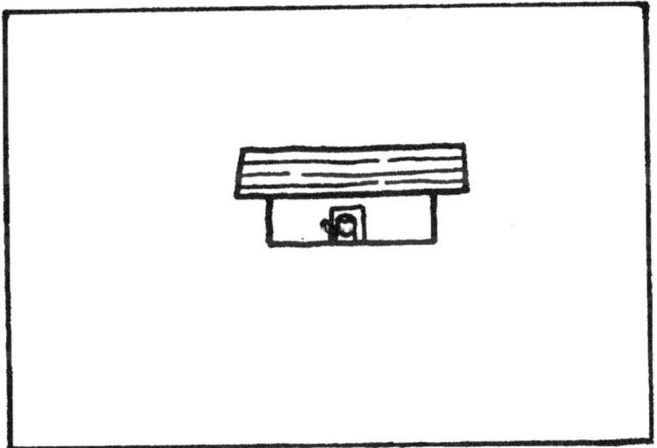

3. Glue sides and bottom of the hull to the poster board, forming a pocket in which to place the animals.

An additional suggestion: Draw a rainbow above the ark and a mountain under the ark. Make an ocean and clouds out of colored paper. Paperclip these items on the poster to cover up the rainbow and the mountain. Remove them at the proper time in the story.

Noah's Ark

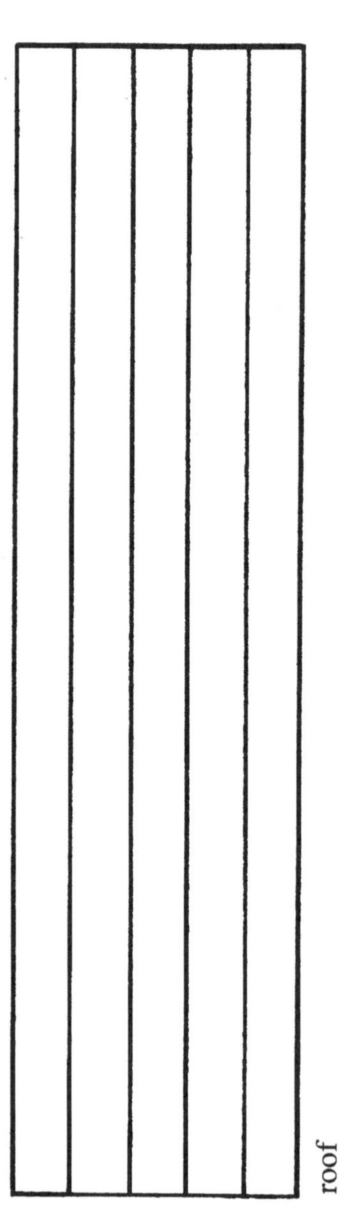

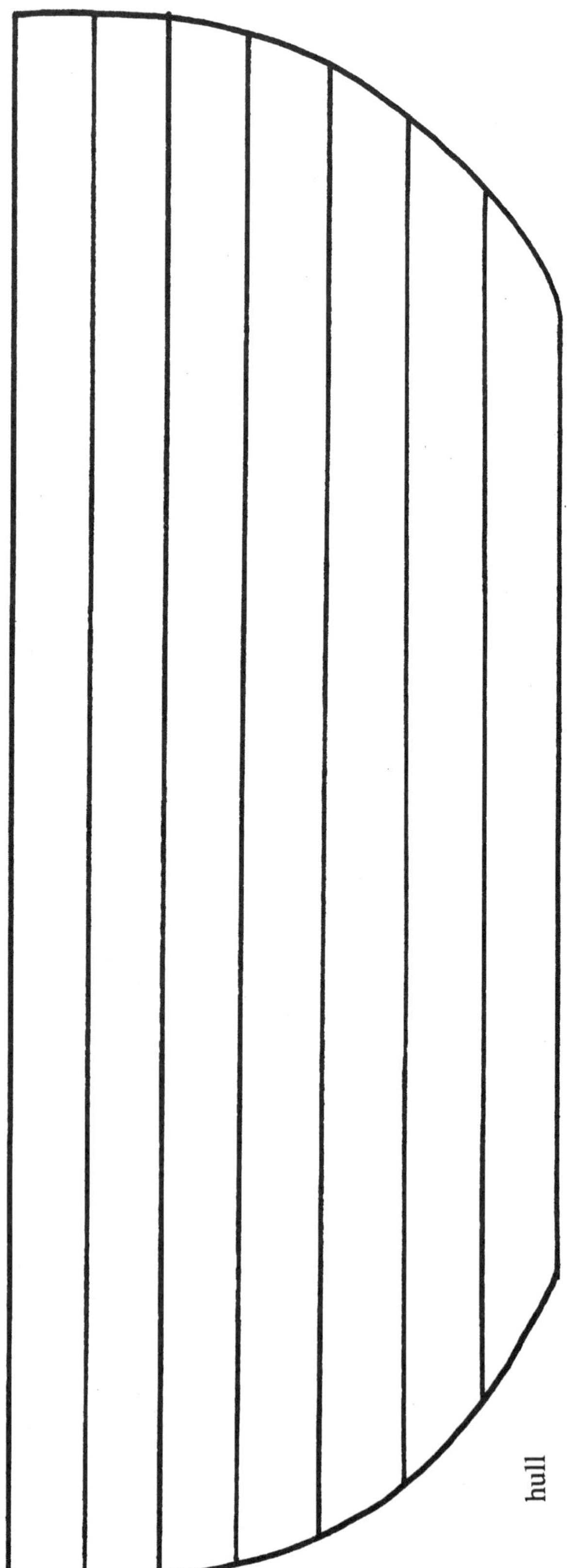

Noah's Ark

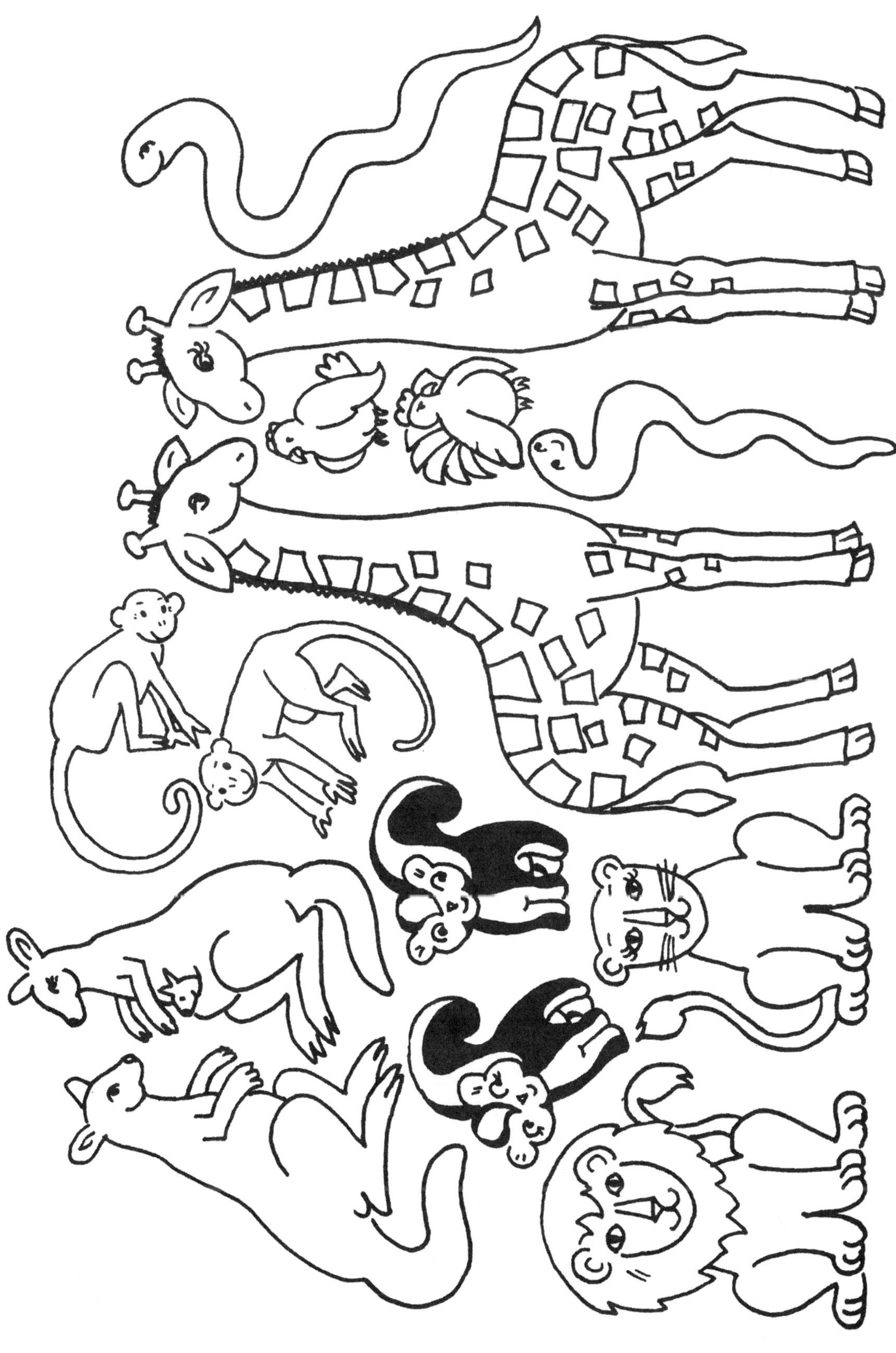

Noah's Ark

We Go to Mass

Introduction

Instead of providing a week's worth of lesson plans, the following is a series of informative pages devoted to brief explanations of various aspects of the church building, the liturgy, and liturgical life. Several of these items were referenced throughout the Teacher's Manual, so you may be familiar with them already. What has been written here is for you, the teacher, to read and pass along to students in a manner that is age-appropriate. The two books referenced below are recommended for personal study as they contain more precise explanatory information than is noted in these pages.

Reference Material

Ceremonies of the Modern Roman Rite: The Eucharist and the Liturgy of the Hours
by Msgr. Peter J. Elliott (San Francisco: Ignatius Press, 1995)

Liturgical Question Box: Answers to Common Questions about the Modern Liturgy
by Msgr. Peter J. Elliott (San Francisco: Ignatius Press, 1998)

Catechism of the Catholic Church References

The Eucharistic Celebration: 1341–44, 1356
Elements in the Mass:
Anaphora: 1352–54
Collection: 1351
Communion: 1355, 1382
Epiclesis: 1105, 1353
Fundamental Structures: 1346
Gathering of Christian Faithful: 1348
Liturgy of the Word: 1349
Presentation of the Gifts: 1350

TABLE OF CONTENTS

We Go to Mass
Church Architecture

APSE — The apse is the semi-circular end of the church, characteristic of the early Christian era, which housed the bishop's chair.

BAPTISTERY — As the name indicates, this is the distinct area, which may be located in a small chapel or seperate building, where the Sacrament of Baptism is performed. The font itself should be stationary and its appearance befitting of its use. Its name derives from the Latin *baptisterium*, which means "a cold plunging-bath."

NAVE — In any church, the area that is designated for the faithful is called the nave. This word comes from the Latin *navis*, meaning "ship," to which the church has been traditionally compared. Among other things, the pews, confessionals, and Stations of the Cross are located in the Nave.

SANCTUARY — Derived from *sanctus*, the Latin word meaning "holy" or "sacred," this is the part of the church immediately surrounding the altar where the ceremonial actions of the Mass take place.

SACRISTY — From the Latin *sacrum*, meaning "holy object." In the sacristy are housed the sacred vessels, vestments, linens, books, and other items needed for the Mass. It is also the vesting room for the priest and altar servers; it is not part of the church proper.

SACRARIUM and PISCINA — The sacrarium is a drain leading directly into the earth for the disposal of water that has been used for some liturgical purpose and is no longer needed. The piscina is the sink-like basin to which the sacrarium is connected. The sacrarium and piscina are most often found in the sacristy.

SIDE ALTAR — In many churches can be found side altars or side chapels dedicated to various saints or which act as shrines to Our Lord or Our Lady.

TRANSEPT — In older churches that were built in the form of a cross, the transepts are the "arms" of the cross.

We Go to Mass
Church Furnishings

Every church is built for the Holy Sacrifice of the Mass, to house an altar, and as a place where God's word is proclaimed to the faithful. Its structure and furnishings should express the hierarchy of ministry within the Mystical Body; the cathedral is the model for all other churches.

ALTAR	The Holy Sacrifice of the Mass is offered on an altar (from the Latin *altaria*), which is the center and focal point of the church, and upon which Christ is made sacramentally present during the Consecration. In the early days of Christianity, Mass was celebrated on the tombs of martyrs in the catacombs of Rome. Because of this, modern altars have the relics of saints, called the altar stone, upon their surface. Altars are usually made of stone, but may also be made of a solid, well-made wood. They represent two aspects of the Christian mystery: the sacrificial altar where Christ offers himself for our sins, and the table of our Lord, upon which Christ gives himself for our food.
ALTAR CLOTH	At least one altar cloth must be used during Mass, the top one of which must be white. To keep it clean outside of Mass, the white of the altar cloth may be covered with a dust cloth.
ANTEPENDIUM	This frontal piece upon the altar, though not obligatory, enhances the altar and usually matches the lectern fall and tabernacle veil. Antependium is from the Latin words *ante*, "before," and *pendere*, "to hang."
TABERNACLE	The tabernacle is a small, box-like receptacle, in which the Blessed Sacrament is reserved in the church; it is usually found on the altar. A tabernacle should be made of solid, nontransparent material and its interior lined with fabric. It is kept locked to prevent desecration of the Eucharist. The word is from the Latin *tabernaculum*, the diminutive of *taberna*, meaning "hut, booth, or tent."
TABERNACLE VEIL	This veil is a sign of the Real Presence of Christ in the tabernacle. It may be white, or the appropriate color for the day, but never black. It represents the holy tent of God; it reveals by concealing.
SANCTUARY LAMP	The sanctuary lamp, which is usually a candle in a red casing, burns day and night whenever the Blessed Sacrament is reserved in the tabernacle to alert the faithful of his presence.
CROSS	A cross should be located near the altar, either atop it, behind it, or suspended above it. In the Roman liturgy this designates a crucifix with a figure of Christ upon it.
CANDLES	Mass normally may not be said unless there is the presence of at least two lighted candles on the altar, though more are allowed for High Mass. They should be good quality, clean burning, and white, in most cases. Pure beeswax candles are not obligatory.
CREDENCE	This is the name of the table at the Epistle side of the altar, which holds the cruets (one with wine, another with water), the basin, and the finger towel. Oftentimes the credence table holds a ciborium, chalice, paten, and the hosts to be consecrated during Mass, at which time it should be covered with a cloth.
PULPIT, or AMBO	The pulpit, lectern, or ambo is where the readings and Gospel are proclaimed during the Liturgy of the Word. They are built into the church's structure and are immovable. The priest will usually give his homily from behind one of these.
LECTERN FALL	The fall is a cloth hanging in front of the pulpit or ambo that matches the color of the day or season.
PRESIDER'S CHAIR	This is the name of the chair in which the main celebrant sits during the readings and at other times during Mass. It should be located behind or near the altar.

We Go to Mass

Sacred Vessels and Other Accoutrements

The chief sacred vessels in the Latin Rite are the chalice and paten (which must be consecrated by a bishop), the ciborium and pyx (blessed by a priest) and the monstrance. Other vessels used during the Divine worship are the cruets, thurible, boat, and aspergillum. Once consecrated, these vessels may not be handled by a layman, i.e., a person who has not taken Holy Orders, unless he has been given charge of the sacristy, or in cases of extreme necessity. Those given charge of caring for sacred vessels should use a small linen cloth when handling them, so as not to actually touch them; all sacred vessels must be handled with reverence.

CHALICE From the latin *calix*, "a cup," the chalice is the most sacred of all the vessels. It is used at Mass to hold the wine, which after the Consecration becomes the Precious Blood of Christ. The chalice is made in the form of a cup with a stem, and may be made of gold, silver, or tin in poorer churches, though the inside should be gilt. The chalice is consecrated with holy chrism by the bishop and is desecrated by profanation. It may be touched only by those clerics and laymen authorized to perform the duties of sacristan.

PATEN The paten, which comes from the Latin *patena*, "a dish," is a thin circular plate of metal, large enough to rest on top of the chalice and upon which the host of the Mass is laid. A bishop should consecrate each paten, its concave surface, at least, must be gilt, and it is usually made of the same material as the chalice.

PYX A pyx is a small round metal container (with a hinged lid that is usually made of gold) used to bring the Blessed Sacrament to the sick and to Catholics who cannot attend Mass. Originally a form of tabernacle, either suspended or standing free, its name comes from the Latin *pyxis* or "box."

CIBORIUM The ciborium resembles the chalice, though it has a lid. Particles of the Blessed Sacrament are kept in the ciborium for distribution of Holy Communion, and to be reserved in the tabernacle. The inside surface, at least, must be gilt, and it is often covered with a veil. Its name is the Latin word for "drinking cup."

MONSTRANCE From the Latin word, *monstare*, "to show," the monstrance is a large vessel used for exposition of the Blessed Sacrament and for processions on feasts, such as Corpus Christi. The monstrance consists of a broad base, a stem, and a receptacle in which the Host is exposed; this hinged glass or crystal cover is called a "lunette" from *luna*, the Latin word for the moon. In many churches, the monstrance is made of gold and decorated with jewels.

CRUETS Cruets are the two small vials made of glass or crystal that contain the water and wine poured into the chalice during Mass. The Cruets sit in the lavabo bowl, a small bowl that is used to receive the water in the ceremony of washing the priest's hands.

THURIBLE Also called a censor, the thurible is a vented vessel in which incense is burned for liturgical purposes, such as Mass and Adoration, to symbolize the zeal of the faithful and their prayers lifted up towards Heaven. It consists of a metal body with a lid to hold the charcoal and incense, three chains attached to the body, and a fourth that lifts the lid. The word thurible comes from the Latin *thuris*, meaning "frankincense."

INCENSE BOAT A boat-like vessel for holding incense before it is placed in the thurible. It derives its name from its shape. The incense is placed in the thurible with a spoon.

ASPERGILLUM This is the instrument used to sprinkle Holy Water onto persons or other items in ceremonies either before or during Mass. The word aspergillum derives from the Latin *aspergere*, which means "to scatter upon."

LAVABO This is the Latin verb "I will wash" said by the priest as he washes and then dries his hands after the Offertory; it is also the name of the washing ceremony, in which the server pours water out of the cruet and onto the priest's fingers.

Other liturgical sacred objects include:

BOOK OF THE GOSPELS Because this book is the visible sign of Christ the Word, it should be handsomely bound or kept in rich covers that change with the season. The book of the Gospels is the central object of the Mass after the chalice and paten and is carried in procession to the altar.

ROMAN MISSAL Also called the "sacramentary" or the "Book of the Sacred Mysteries," it contains the prayers and ceremonies of the Mass used by the priest.

LECTIONARY The lectionary contains the readings and the Gospel for Mass, which are read at the ambo.

We Go to Mass

Vestments

Vestments are the special garments worn by priests and deacons in the exercise of divine worship and during the administering of the sacraments. The Early Church had no special dress requirements; the current vestments in use developed from the everyday clothing of the Roman Empire. When styles changed, the priests continued to wear these clothes so that by the 9th century, Pope Leo IV decided that these garments should be worn during the Holy Sacrifice of the Mass. By the 13th century, vestments became highly decorative, heavy, and recognized as having symbolic religious significance. Today, vestments are lighter and simpler in design, though they should always be beautiful since they are worn during Mass. The sacred vestments include amice, alb, citure, stole, chasuble, and dalmatic.

AMICE From the Latin *amictus* meaning "garment," an amice is a rectangular piece of white linen cloth with two long strings. This vestment covers the priest's neck and shoulders and is worn under the alb, though it is optional if the alb fully covers the neck. The amice is a symbol of the "helmet of salvation," the "discipline of the tongue," and protection from the devil.

ALB The name of this vestment is derived from the Latin *tunica alba*, which means "white tunic." An alb is a full-length white linen garment with long flowing sleeves, which may or may not be worn over a cassock. Modern liturgical albs may have hoods and ornamentation; however, decoration should not detract from its character, since the color of the linen is a symbol for purity of heart.

CINTURE Also called a girdle, the cinture is a long rope made of linen, silk, or cotton with tassled ends. The word cinture comes from the Latin *cintura*. The cinture is worn around the alb as a belt signifying the priest's chastity.

STOLE This vestment derives its name from the Latin *stola* and the Greek *stole*. It consists of a band of fabric, the color of which varies with the season or occassion, has a cross stitched on the center back, and which is worn around the neck by bishops and priests and is allowed to hang loose. The stole is a sign of the priest's teaching authority in the Church as a representative of the bishop, who is a successor of the Apostles. Worn over the alb and under the chasuble, the stole is a symbol of justice and immortality. It is also worn in the administration of sacraments, generally over the alb or surplice. A deacon receives a stole at his ordination; he wears it over his left shoulder, gathered together at the waist on his right side, that is, over the alb and under the dalmatic.

CHASUBLE This vestment derives its name from two Latin words: *casubla*, or "hooded garment," and *casula*, or "little house." The chasuble is the sacrificial garment proper to the celebrant at Mass. It is made of one piece of cloth with open sides and without sleeves; it is worn over the alb, stole, and amice, hanging from the shoulders in front and behind, down to about the knees. Often, the chasuble, stole, and chalice veil are made as a set of vestments, using the same material, color, and design. Chasubles often have a "Y" cross on them; this is a symbol of charity and represents mercy, so that the stole (justice) and the chasuble (mercy) are worn together by the priest or bishop at Mass.

DALMATIC Worn first by the 5th century deacons of Rome, the dalmatic is a distinctive diaconal vestment, the fabric and color of which match those of the celebrating priest. It was originally introduced to Rome from Dalmatia (from whence it received its name) as a secular garment. Today, these tunic-like vestments with open sides and wide sleeves are worn without a cinture and over the alb and stole (even when the acting-deacon is a priest), although cardinals or bishops wear them under their chasubles at a Pontifical Mass. The dalmatic has two bands accross the front and back that vary in color according to the liturgical season or occassion of the Mass.

TUNICLE This garment is smaller than a dalmatic and less decorated. It has full sleeves and only one band, which matches the color of the season, across the front and back.

Other priestly vestments and accoutrements used outside of Mass include:

CLERICS	These are the black pants, black shirt, and white Roman collar usually worn by priests on a daily basis. Clerics are the more modern "uniform" of a priest, which help Catholics and others identify him.
CASSOCK	A cassock, the traditional garb of a priest, is an ankle-length black robe that is buttoned down the front and which may be worn with or without a sash. The color is usually black for priests, purple for a bishop, and scarlet for a cardinal. The Pope wears a white cassock.
SURPLICE	From the Latin, *superpellicium,* which means, "over the furs," this shorter form of the alb was used by clergy, beginning in the 11th century, outside of Eucharistic worship and by choristers during the Divine Office. A priest wears a surplice over his cassock when he preaches, joins a procession, acts as a Eucharistic Minister, or for Baptisms and funerals.
HUMERAL VEIL	From the Latin word *humerus* or "shoulder," the white humeral veil is a wide oblong cloth used by the priest when carrying the Blessed Sacrament in procession, during Benediction, in carrying the Host to the repository on Holy Thursday, and in returning it on Good Friday. Worn like a shawl with ends that cover the hands, it is fastened across the chest with clasps. In processions of the Blessed Sacrament and at Benediction with a monstrance, only the hands are placed under the humeral veil, otherwise it covers the entire sacred vessel containing the Host. A deacon also wears it around his shoulders whenever he holds a sacred vessel.
COPE	The cope is a long mantle open in front that is held together with a clasp at the breast. It may be worn over an alb or surplice for solemn processions, benedictions, funerals, and weddings, and out-doors in wet weather.
SKULL CAP	Also called a zucchetto, it is worn by some clergy; cardinals wear scarlet, bishops use purple, and the Pope wears a white skull cap.

The following are accessory items for bishops:

PALLIUM	This is a narrow circular band of white wool, ornamented with six dark crosses with two hanging strips, one in front and one behind. It is worn around the neck by archbishops, who receive it from the Pope.
MITRE	From the Latin *mitra*, meaning "headband" or "turban," this item emerged by the 11th century as the distinctive headdress of bishops, though some abbots and others are allowed to wear them. Its origin is from a Roman simple cap. Eastern Orthodox bishops wear a crown-styled mitre. The skull cap is worn under the mitre.
CROSIER	The term crosier, derived from the Middle Latin word *crocia*, is the common name used for the pastoral staff of bishops. It is sometimes spelled crozier.

We Go to Mass
Linens Used During Mass

The linens used during the Holy Sacrifice of the Mass are: the corporal, purificator, pall, and finger towel. These linens, excepting the finger towel, are called the "holy cloths." All are made of white linen. The burse and chalice veil are also used during Mass.

CORPORAL

Taken from the Latin *corpus* or "body," the corporal is a piece of fine linen folded into nine sections with a small cross stitched in the center of the side nearest the celebrant. It is folded in three from both sides, and may be kept in a burse when not in use. The corporal is the most important of the holy cloths, for the priest spreads it on the altar and places the Host and the chalice on it after the Consecration. A corporal is also placed beneath any vessel containing the Blessed Sacrament; for example, on the "floor" of the tabernacle and beneath the monstrance at Benediction. Because of its close contact with the Blessed Sacrament, the corporal may not be handled by laymen without special permission. The priest first purifies the corporal before others wash it.

PURIFICATOR

From the Latin *purificare*, meaning "to make clean," the purificator is an oblong piece of linen, folded thrice, and placed over the chalice. It is used to to cleanse the chalice before the wine is poured; further, the priest wipes the chalice, his fingers, and his lips with the purificator after receiving the Precious Blood of Christ. Laymen must not handle purificators until a priest has washed them.

PALL

The pall is a stiff, square piece of starched linen, or cardboard covered with linen, which is used to cover the chalice at Mass to protect it from contamination. The upper side may be ornamented; the lower side must be plain. The term pall is from the Latin *pallium*, which means "cover" or "mantle." The use of the pall is optional.

FINGER TOWEL

There is no special significance placed on the finger towel; the priest uses it to dry his fingers after washing them before the Consecration.

BURSE

A burse is a purse or open-ended envelope about 12 inches square, which holds the corporal for Mass. The material of the burse should match the vestments.

CHALICE VEIL

The chalice veil is a square piece of silk used to cover the chalice and paten. It is usually made of the same color and design as the priest's vestments, though it may always be white.

We Go to Mass
Liturgical Colors

During Mass, various colors are used in the altar cloths and vestments. The color of these cloths and vestments varies according to the season of the Church calendar and the event being celebrated. The liturgical colors include: white, red, purple, rose, green, and black.

WHITE	White is the color for vestments worn during the Christmas and Easter seasons. White is also worn on all feasts of our Lord (except His Cross and Passion), for Our Lady, the angels, on the feasts of confessors, and for all saints who were not martyrs. White may also be worn during Masses of the dead, when black is not used. White is a color of purity, joy, and holiness. Since the time of Pius V (1566–72) white has also been the ordinary color of papal garments.
RED	Red vestments are worn during the vigil and feast of Pentecost, on the feast of the Precious Blood, during Masses for the Cross, on the feasts of Apostles and martyrs, and during feasts remembering the Passion of our Lord, such as Palm Sunday and Good Friday. Red is the color proper to cardinals and is used by the Pope when he sings a requiem Mass.
PURPLE	During Sundays of Advent and Lent, and also sometimes on the feast of All Souls, purple vestments are worn. Purple is the color for penance, conversion, and expiation.
ROSE	Rose vestments are worn only twice a year: th esecond sunday during Advent (Gaudete), and the fourth Sunday during Lent (Laetare). The rose vestment marks the halfway point of each penitential season.
GREEN	The season of Ordinary Time in the Church calls for green vestments. Ordinary Time is any time outside other seasons. Green is a symbol of hope and growth.
BLACK	Black vestments are worn during the Mass of the Presanctified on Good Friday, to celebrate All Souls Day, and at funerals. Black may also be worn during Masses for the dead, though white vestments are often worn instead to express the joy felt for the souls who have gone to be united with God.
GOLD	Vestments made of gold cloth are permitted in place of white, red, and green.
BLUE	This is a liturgical color prescribed in some dioceses of Spain for the feast of the Immaculate Conception.